LYNN QUITMAN TROYKA
EMILY R. GORDON
CY STROM

Simon & Schuster Workbook *for* Writers

THIRD CANADIAN EDITION

Prentice
Hall

TORONTO

ISBN 0-13-067587-3

Vice President, Editorial Director: Michael Young
Editor-in-Chief: David Stover
Marketing Manager: Sharon Loeb
Developmental Editor: Matthew Christian
Production Editor: Avivah Wargon
Copy Editor: Cy Strom
Proofreader: Imogen Brian
Production Coordinator: Peggy Brown
Page Layout: B.J. Weckerle
Creative Director: Mary Opper
Cover Design: Lisa LaPointe
Cover Image: Vincent Van Gogh (1853–1890), "The Sower," Rijksmuseum Kroller-Muller, Otterio, Netherlands/A.K.G., Superstock

Original edition published by Prentice-Hall Inc., a division of Pearson Education, Upper Saddle River, New Jersey.
Copyright © 1999, 1996, 1993, 1990, 1987 by Lynn Quitman Troyka.
This edition is authorized for sale in Canada only.

2 3 4 5   06 05 04 03

Printed and bound in Canada.

Contents

*Please note: There are no *Workbook* exercises that correspond to Chapters 32–36 of the *Simon & Schuster Handbook for Writers*, Third Canadian Edition.

Preface

The *Simon & Schuster Workbook for Writers*, Third Canadian Edition, continues the tradition, established by the first two editions, of serving dual purposes. It is designed foremost as a supplement of exercises and writing activities that parallel its parent, the *Simon & Schuster Handbook for Writers*, Third Canadian Edition. Also, it is designed as a self-contained textbook with concise explanations of key concepts followed by copious opportunities for practice. To those ends, this *Workbook* offers:

- Complete coverage of all basic topics: grammar, punctuation, mechanics, the writing process, and critical thinking. Technical terms are defined and explained simply and directly.

- Matching section heads and section numbers for easy cross-reference to the *Simon & Schuster Handbook for Writers*, Third Canadian Edition.

- Many pages on English as a second language, with special emphasis on count and noncount nouns, articles, verbals, prepositions, word order, and modal auxiliary verbs.

- Attention to using quotations and writing paraphrases and summaries—topics not usually included in workbooks on writing.

- Charts and checklists throughout to summarize and highlight key information. Photographs and occasional writing prompts are included to stimulate visual as well as linguistic thinking.

- Exercise sequencing that leads to independent work: moving from simpler tasks, such as identifying sentence elements; to guided writing, such as sentence combining; and on to original sentences, paragraphs, and essays.

- Exercise content in connected discourse to replicate more closely the activities of revising and editing real writing. The topics from across the curriculum are chosen for their engaging interest. New subject matter appears in many exercises to keep the material fresh and up-to-date.

Lynn Quitman Troyka
Emily R. Gordon
Cy Strom

1,2 and 3 Thinking About Purposes and Audiences; Planning and Shaping; Drafting and Revising

1: THINKING ABOUT PURPOSES AND AUDIENCES

Why write? In this age of cell phones, e-mail, the Internet, television, and film, why should you bother with writing? The answer has many parts.

Writing is a way of thinking and learning. Writing gives you opportunities to explore ideas and obtain information. By writing, you come to know subjects well and make them your own. When you write what you know, you are also teaching the reader.

Writing is a way of discovering. The act of writing allows you to make unexpected connections among ideas. As you write, thoughts develop and interconnect in new ways.

Writing creates reading. Writing creates a permanent record of your ideas for others to read and think about.

Writing ability is needed by educated people. College and university work demands that you write many different types of assignments. Most jobs require writing skills for preparing letters, memos, and reports. Throughout your life, your writing will reveal your ability to think clearly and use language to express ideas.

1a Understanding the elements of writing

Writing is a way of communicating a message to a reader for a purpose.

Let us look at the key words in this definition. **Communication** means that a message has a destination, a reader. The **message** of writing is its content. You need a thesis, a central idea that unites your writing. You also need enough content to support that thesis. Finally, the **reader** of your writing is your audience. **Purposes** for writing may reflect your own desires—or, more likely, may focus on your reader or your message.

1b Understanding purposes for writing

Students often think their purpose for writing is to complete a class assignment. However, purpose means more than that: It refers to what the writing seeks to achieve. Although writing to express yourself and writing to create a literary work are important, this workbook concentrates on the two purposes most frequently found in academic writing: to inform your reader and to persuade your reader.

Expressive writing is usually the private recording of your thoughts and feelings. A personal journal is an example of expressive writing.

Informative writing (also known as **expository writing**) seeks to give information and, when necessary, to explain it. Informative writing focuses on the subject being discussed. Informative writing includes reports of observations, ideas, scientific data, facts, and statistics. It can be found in textbooks, encyclopedias, technical and business reports, nonfiction books, newspapers, and magazines.

CHECKLIST FOR INFORMATIVE WRITING

1. Is its information clear?
2. Is its information complete and accurate?
3. Does it present facts, ideas, and observations that can be verified?
4. Is the writer's tone reasonable and free of distortions?

Persuasive writing (also known as **argumentative writing**) seeks to convince the reader about a matter of opinion. Persuasive writing focuses on the reader whom the writer wants to influence. Examples of persuasive writing include editorials, letters to the editor, reviews, sermons, business or research proposals, opinion essays in magazines, and books that argue a point of view.

CHECKLIST FOR PERSUASIVE WRITING

1. Does it present a point of view about which opinions vary?
2. Does it support its point of view with specifics?
3. Is its point of view based on sound reasoning and logic?
4. Are the points in the argument clear?
5. Does it evoke the intended reaction from the reader?

1c Understanding audiences for writing

Good writing is often judged by its ability to reach its intended audience. The more information you have about your audience's background, beliefs, and concerns, the better you can think about how to reach that audience.

In writing for your peers, as in a classroom "peer response group," be sure to understand what your instructor requires for both writers and readers. Approach the task with an upbeat, constructive attitude to make the most of the experience.

1c

CHECKLIST OF BASIC AUDIENCE CHARACTERISTICS

WHAT SETTING ARE THEY READING IN?

Academic setting?

Workplace setting?

Public setting?

WHO ARE THEY?

Age, gender

Ethnic backgrounds, political philosophies, religious beliefs

Roles (student, parent, voter, wage earner, property owner, other)

Interests, hobbies

WHAT DO THEY KNOW?

Level of education

Amount of general or specialized knowledge about the topic

Probable preconceptions brought to the material

GUIDELINES FOR PARTICIPATING IN PEER RESPONSE GROUPS

AS A RESPONDER

- Think of yourself in the role of a coach, not a judge.
- Consider your peers' writing as "works in progress."
- Briefly summarize a peer's writing as a check to determine that you understand what the writer intended.
- Start with positive comments.
- Be honest in your suggestions for improvements.
- Ground your responses in an understanding of the writing process, remembering that you are dealing with drafts, not finished products.
- Give concrete and specific responses.
- Follow your instructor's system for getting your comments into writing. If one member of your group is taking notes, speak clearly so the notes will be accurate.

AS A WRITER

- Adopt an attitude that encourages your peers to respond freely. Try to avoid defending your writing too aggressively.
- Remain open-minded when you hear responses.
- Ask for clarification if a comment is not clear to you. Ask for specifics.
- Remember that the writing is yours. You are its "owner." You decide what comments to use or not use.

1d Understanding the effect of tone

As an adult writing to an adult audience, you are expected to sound sensible and even-tempered. This stance is reflected in your tone—*what you say* and *how you say it.* Tone can be broadly described as **informal** or **formal.** Tone is informal in journals and freewriting. As you move from writing for the private you to writing for an audience, you are expected to move toward a more formal tone. This does not mean that you should use overblown language or put on airs that make you sound artificial (see 21e). Most audiences, including many readers of academic writing, expect a tone midway between informal and highly formal. Your tone should take into account the topic, purpose, and audience of your piece.

1e Using outside sources for writing

You are your first source for writing. For many college and university writing assignments you can draw on your own prior knowledge. For others, you will be expected to use outside sources, sources outside of what you already know. Guard against plagiarism, a major academic offence, by giving proper credit to the sources you use and using appropriate documentation (see Chapters 31 through 34 in the *Simon & Schuster Handbook*).

1f Knowing the tools that can help you as a writer

Before you begin tackling your writing assignments, you can benefit greatly from knowing what tools are widely available to help you.

1. **A computer for word processing:** A computer's word-processing software can prove a big help at various stages of the writing process (Chapter 2). If you don't own a computer, try to use one in your school's computer lab.

2. **Your personal bookshelf:** Your personal bookshelf needs to contain three essential volumes: a dictionary, a thesaurus, and a handbook for writers. A dictionary is indispensable. Most college and university bookstores offer a good variety of hardcover abridged or "college" dictionaries. Before choosing one, browse through it for definitions you want to learn or to understand more clearly. A portable paperback dictionary that you can carry with you can also be handy. Unabridged dictionaries list every word in English. The reference section of every library has one (usually on display) that everyone can consult.

Another valuable resource for writers is a thesaurus, which lists synonyms. The easiest to use are arranged alphabetically.

A handbook for writers, such as *The Simon & Schuster Handbook for Writers,* gives you detailed information about rules of grammar and punctuation, and other writing conventions. It also offers extensive advice about how to write successfully, whether for college or university, business, or the public.

3. **Your college or university library:** A college or university library, sometimes called a learning resources centre, is fully stocked with all manner of reference books, circulating books, resources for online access, and more. Spend some time getting to know what's available in your library. Then you can dive right in when the times comes.

    Concentrate most on your library's reference section. Today, many—but not all—reference books are available in print and online.

4. **Computer tools for writers:** Word-processing programs, such as Microsoft Word and WordPerfect, include aids for writers. These programs are built into your software. They offer some advantages, but they also have severe limitations. In no case are such tools substitutes for your own careful editing and proofreading. Software, after all, cannot "think" and make the reasonable distinctions that you can. Here is a list of some of these helpful applications:

    - Spell-check programs
    - Thesaurus programs
    - Grammar or style-check programs

2: PLANNING AND SHAPING

Experienced writers know that writing is a process, a series of activities that starts the moment they begin thinking about a subject and ends when they complete a final draft. Experienced writers also know that good writing is rewriting. Their drafts are filled with additions, cuts, rearrangements, and rewordings.

2a **Understanding the writing process**

For the sake of explanation, the different parts of the writing process are discussed separately in this chapter. In real life, you will find that the steps loop back and forth as each piece of writing develops.

AN OVERVIEW OF THE WRITING PROCESS

Planning calls for you to discover and compile ideas for your writing.

Shaping calls for you to organize your material.

Drafting calls for you to write your ideas in sentences and paragraphs.

AN OVERVIEW OF THE WRITING PROCESS *(continued)*

Revising calls for you to evaluate your draft and rewrite it by adding, deleting, changing, and rearranging.

Editing calls for you to check the correctness of your grammar, spelling, punctuation, and mechanics.

Proofreading calls for you to read your final copy to eliminate typing or handwriting errors.

2b Adjusting for each writing situation

As you think through and gather ideas (2d) for your topic, your task is to establish a focus, or a point of view, about the topic, and support for that focus. You also need to think about the purpose for your writing (1b) and the audience (1c).

2c Thinking through a topic for writing

Some assignments leave no room for making choices. You may be given very specific instructions, such as "Explain how plants produce oxygen." Your job with such assignments is to do exactly what is asked and not go off the topic.

Some instructors will ask you to write on whatever topic you wish. In such situations, you need to select a topic that is suitable for informative or persuasive writing in an academic situation, one that reflects your ability to think through ideas. You need to demonstrate that you can use specific, concrete details to support what you want to say. Be careful not to choose a topic that is too narrow, or you will not have enough to say.

When you choose or are assigned a topic that is very broad, you have to **narrow the subject.** To do this, you must think of different areas within the subject until you come to one that seems workable for an essay.

Any broad subject may contain hundreds of possible essay topics. Do not try to think of them all, but also do not jump on the first topic that occurs to you. Consider the purpose of the assignment, the audience, the word limit, the time available to you, and your own interests and knowledge. A suitably narrowed topic will enable you to move back and forth between general statements and specific details.

2d Gathering ideas for writing

Techniques for gathering ideas, sometimes called **prewriting strategies** or **invention techniques,** can help you while you are narrowing your topic. For example, they help you to discover how much you know about a topic before you decide whether or not to write on it. Experienced writers use many techniques for gathering ideas; we will discuss the most common ones in this chapter.

2e Keeping an idea book and writing in a journal

Many writers carry an **idea book**—a small notebook—with them at all times so that they can jot down ideas that spring to mind.

A **journal,** like an idea book, is a record of your ideas, but it is built from daily writing sessions. In your journal you can write about your opinions, beliefs, family, friends, or anything else you wish. The content and tone can be as personal and informal as you wish. Nevertheless, a journal is not a diary for merely listing things done during the day. It is a book for you to fill with what you want to think about.

Keeping a journal can help you in three ways. First, writing every day makes it easier for you to write. Second, a journal encourages close observation and thinking. Third, a journal is an excellent source of ideas when you need to write in response to an assignment.

2f Freewriting

Freewriting is writing down whatever comes into your mind without stopping to worry about whether the idea is good or the spelling is correct. You do nothing to interrupt the flow. Do not go back to review. Do not cross out. Some days your freewriting might seem mindless, but other days it can reveal interesting ideas. Freewriting works best if you set a goal, such as writing for ten minutes or until one page is filled. Sometimes you may decide to do focused freewriting—writing on a set topic—in preparation for an essay.

2g Brainstorming

In **brainstorming,** you make a list of all the ideas you can think of associated with a topic. The ideas can be listed as words, phrases, or complete sentences. List making, like freewriting, produces its best results when you let your mind work freely, producing many ideas before analyzing them.

Brainstorming is done in two steps. First make your list. Then go back and try to find patterns in the list and ways to group the ideas into categories. Set aside any items that do not fit into groups. The groups with the most items are likely to reflect the ideas that you can write about most successfully.

"Talking it over" with someone whose opinions you trust or in a peer response group is another technique that may help you discover and refine ideas. Ways of approaching a point of discussion include debating, questioning, analyzing (5d, 5e), synthesizing (5f), and evaluating.

2h Asking the journalist's questions

Another commonly used method for generating ideas is the journalist's questions: *Who? What? When? Why? Where?* and *How?* Asking such questions forces you to approach a topic from several different points of view.

2i Mapping

Mapping is much like brainstorming, but it is more visual. When you map, begin by writing your subject in a circle in the middle of a sheet of unlined paper. Next draw a line out from the centre and name a major division of your subject. Circle it, and from that circle move out to further subdivisions. Keep associating to further ideas and to details related to them. When you finish with one major division of your subject, go back to the centre and start again with another major division. As you go along, add anything that occurs to you for any section of the map. Continue the process until you run out of ideas.

2j Using incubation

When you allow your ideas to **incubate,** you give them time to grow and develop. Incubation works especially well when you need to solve a problem in your writing (for example, if material is too thin and needs expansion, if material covers too much and needs pruning, or if connections among your ideas are not clear for your reader). Time is a key element for successful incubation. You need time to think, to allow your mind to wander, and then to come back and focus on the writing.

One helpful strategy is to turn your attention to something entirely different from your writing problem. After a while, guide your mind back to the problem you want to solve. Another strategy is to allow your mind to relax and wander, without concentrating on anything special. Later, return to the problem you are trying to solve. At this point you might see solutions that did not occur to you before.

2k Shaping ideas

To shape the ideas that you have gathered (2d), you need to group them (see 2l) and sequence them (see 2m).

An essay has three basic parts: an introduction, a body, and a conclusion. The body consists of a number of paragraphs. The introduction and conclusion are usually one paragraph each. Chapter 4 discusses and illustrates various types of paragraphs.

2n

2l Grouping ideas by levels of generality

Effective writing includes both general statements and specific details. In both informative and persuasive writing, general statements must be developed with facts, reasons, examples, and illustrations.

To group ideas, review the material you accumulated while gathering ideas. Look for general ideas. Next group under them related, but less general ideas. If you find that your notes contain only general ideas, or only very specific details, return to gathering techniques to supply what you need.

2m Sequencing ideas for writing

Shaping ideas for writing also means placing them into a logical structure. You need to decide what should come first, second, and so on. Within the essay, and within individual body paragraphs, you can order ideas in various ways. The most common organizational strategies are generalization to specifics, climactic order (from least to most important), chronological order (from beginning to end), and spatial order (following a pattern in space, such as top to bottom).

2n Shaping writing by drafting a thesis statement

A **thesis statement** is the main idea of an essay. Because it prepares your reader for what you will discuss, the thesis statement must accurately reflect the content of the essay.

BASIC REQUIREMENTS FOR A THESIS STATEMENT

1. It states the essay's **subject**—the topic that you are discussing.
2. It reflects the essay's **purpose**—either to give your readers information or to persuade your readers to agree with you.
3. It includes a **focus**—your assertion that conveys your point of view.
4. It uses **specific language**—vague words are avoided.
5. It *may* briefly state the major subdivisions of the essay's topic.

Many instructors also require that the thesis statement appear as a single sentence at the end of the introductory paragraph.

In most writing situations you cannot be certain that a thesis statement accurately reflects what you say in the essay until you have written one or more drafts. To start shaping your essay, however, you can use a preliminary thesis statement. Even if it is too broad, it can guide you as you write. When the essay is completed, be sure to revise so that your final thesis statement accurately reflects the content of your essay.

Here are some thesis statements written for 500- to 700-word essays. The first two are for essays with an informative purpose, and the last two are for essays with a persuasive purpose.

TOPIC	nutrition
NO	Nutrition is important. [too broad]
YES	Nutrition has again become a concern for social agencies and governments.
TOPIC	radio
NO	Everyone listens to the radio. [too broad]
YES	The variety of radio programming ensures there is a program for every taste.
TOPIC	drunk driving
NO	Drunk driving is dangerous. [too broad]
YES	Unless drunk drivers are taken off our roads, they will continue to kill and injure thousands of people each year.
TOPIC	adoption
NO	Sometimes, adopted children have problems. [too broad]
YES	Adopted children should be able to find out about their birth-parents for psychological, medical, and moral reasons.

2o Using collaborative writing

Working in a group can stimulate people to think of ideas and to support each other during the writing process. Many professions require people to serve on committees, to reach general agreement on how to proceed, and to contribute equally to a written report. Discussing ideas often inspires greater creativity and shared confidence. The essence of **collaborative writing** is "Two (or more) heads are better than one."

GUIDELINES FOR COLLABORATIVE WRITING

GETTING UNDERWAY

1. Get to know each other's names. If you exchange phone numbers, you can be in touch outside of class.

2. Participate in the group process. Set a tone that encourages everyone to join in.

3. Facilitate the collaboration. As a group, assign work to be done between meetings. Distribute the responsibilities fairly. Decide whether to choose one discussion leader or to rotate leadership.

GUIDELINES FOR COLLABORATIVE WRITING *(continued)*

PLANNING THE WRITING

4. After discussing the project, brainstorm (see 2g) or use other techniques to think of ideas (see 2d through 2j).

5. As a group, choose the ideas that seem best. Incubate (see 2j), if time permits, and discuss the choices again.

6. As a group, divide the project into parts and distribute assignments fairly.

7. Take notes on your work so that you can be ready to report to the group.

8. As a group, sketch an overview (if you choose to outline, see 2p) of the paper to get a preliminary idea of how best to use the material contributed by individuals.

DRAFTING THE WRITING

9. Draft a first paragraph or two to set the direction for the rest of the paper. Each group member can draft a version, but agree on one version before getting too far into the rest of the draft.

10. Work on the rest of the paper. Decide whether each member of the group should write a complete draft or a different part. Use photocopies to share work.

REVISING THE WRITING

11. Read over the drafts. Check that everything useful has been incorporated.

12. Use the Revision Checklists in section 3c to decide on revisions. Work as a group, or assign sections to subgroups. Use photocopies to share work.

13. Agree on a final version. Assign someone to prepare it in final form and make photocopies.

EDITING THE WRITING

14. As a group, review photocopies of the final version. Do not leave the last stages to a subgroup. Draw on everyone's knowledge.

15. Use the Editing Checklist in section 3d to make sure that the final version has no errors. If necessary, retype. A sloppy final version reflects negatively on the entire group.

2p Knowing how to outline

Many writers find outlining to be a useful planning strategy. An **outline** helps pull together the results of gathering and ordering ideas and preparing a thesis statement. It also provides a visual guide and checklist. Some instructors require outlines because they want you to practise the discipline of thinking through the arrangement and organization of your writing.

An **informal outline** does not have to follow all the formal conventions of outlining. It simply *lists* the main ideas of an essay—the major subdivisions of the thesis statement—and the subordinate ideas and details.

A **formal outline** follows strict conventions concerning content and format. The material must be displayed so that relationships among ideas are clear and so that the content is orderly. A formal outline can be a **topic outline** or a **sentence outline:** Each item in a topic outline is a word or phrase, whereas each item in a sentence outline is a complete sentence.

Here are the conventions to follow in a formal outline.

1. **Introductory and concluding paragraphs.** The introductory and concluding paragraphs are not part of an outline.

2. **Thesis statement.** The thesis statement comes immediately before the outline itself.

3. **Numbers, letters, and indentations.** All parts of a formal outline are systematically indented. Capitalized roman numerals (I, II, III) signal major divisions of the topic. Indented capital letters (A, B) signal the next, more specific level of information. Further indented arabic numbers (1, 2, 3) show the third, even more specific level of information, and so on.

4. **More than one entry at each level.** At all points on an outline there is no I without a II, no A without a B, and so on. If a heading has only one subdivision, you need either to eliminate that subdivision or expand the material so that you have at least two subdivisions.

5. **Overlap.** Headings do not overlap. What is covered in A must be quite different from what is covered in B. All items in a subdivision are at the same level of generality. A main idea cannot be paired with a supporting detail.

6. **Parallelism.** All entries are grammatically parallel. For example, all items might start with *-ing* forms of verbs or all might be adjectives or nouns (see 18h).

7. **Capitalization and punctuation.** Capitalize only the first word of each heading. In a sentence outline, end each sentence with a period. Do not put periods at the end of items in a topic outline.

Here is a formal topic outline of an essay on living alone.

THESIS STATEMENT
Chances are high that adult men and women will have to know how to live alone, briefly or longer, at some time in their lives.

I. Living alone because of circumstances
   A. Grown children moving to other cities
      1. Going away to school
      2. Taking jobs
   B. Married people not being married forever
      1. A large percentage of marriages ending in divorce
      2. Eight out of ten married women becoming widowed, usually late in life

II. Taking care of practical matters
    A. Opening a chequing account
        1. Comparing bank services
        2. Comparing advantages of different kinds of chequing accounts
    B. Making major purchases
        1. Buying a computer
        2. Buying a car

III. Establishing new friendships
    A. Students getting used to going to classes without old friends
        1. Being able to concentrate better
        2. Being able to meet new friends
    B. Single adults going to the beach or parties

IV. Dealing with feelings of loneliness
    A. Understanding the feeling
    B. Avoiding depression
        1. Not overeating
        2. Not overspending
        3. Not getting into unwanted situations
            a. Taking the wrong job
            b. Going into the wrong relationship
    C. Keeping busy

3: DRAFTING AND REVISING

Drafting is getting ideas onto paper in rough sentences and paragraphs. Revision is taking a draft from its first to its final version by evaluating, adding, cutting, moving material, editing, and proofreading.

3a Getting started

If you have trouble getting started when the time arrives for drafting, you are not alone. Even professional writers sometimes have trouble getting started. Here are some time-proven methods experienced writers use to get started when they are blocked.

1. Don't stare at a blank page. Fill up the paper. Write words, scribble, or draw while you think about your topic. The movement of filling the paper while thinking can stimulate your mind to turn to actual drafting.

2. Picture yourself writing. Imagine yourself in the place where you usually write, with the materials you need, busy at work.

3. Picture an image or a scene. Start writing by describing what you see or hear.

4. Write your material in a letter to a friend. Doing this gives you a chance to relax. The letter can serve as a rough draft.

5. Write your material as if you were someone else. You can be a friend writing to you, an instructor writing to a class, a person in history writing

to you or to someone else. Once you take on a role, you may feel less inhibited about writing.

6. Start in the middle. If you do not know what to write in your introduction, start with a body paragraph.

7. Use "focused freewriting" (2f).

8. Change your method of writing. If you usually use a computer, try writing by hand.

3b Knowing how to draft

First drafts are not meant to be perfect; they are meant to give you something to revise. The direction of drafting is forward: **keep pressing ahead.** Do not stop to check spelling or grammar. If you are not sure a word or sentence is correct, circle it or put an X in the margin so that you can return to that spot later.

No single method of drafting an essay works for everyone. Following are a pair of methods you might try—or you might prefer to use another method that you have developed yourself.

1. Put aside all your notes from planning and shaping. Write a "discovery draft." As you write, be open to discovering ideas and making connections that spring to mind during the physical act of writing. When you finish a discovery draft, you can decide to use it either as a first draft or as part of your notes when you make a structured first draft.

2. Keep your notes from planning and shaping in front of you and use them as you write. Write a structured first draft, working through all your material. If you are working on a long essay, you may want to draft in chunks, a few paragraphs at each sitting.

3c Knowing how to revise

To revise your essay, you must first evaluate it. Then you make improvements and in turn evaluate them in the context of the surrounding material. This process continues until you are satisfied that the essay is in final draft.

When you revise, you need to pay special attention to your essay's title and thesis statement. Both of these features can help you stay on track, and they tell your reader what to expect.

The title of an essay plays an important organizing role. A good title can set you on your course and tell your readers what to expect. A title always stands alone. The opening of an essay should never refer to the essay's title as if it were part of a preceding sentence. For example, after the title "Knowing How to Live Alone," a writer should not begin the essay with the words, "This is very important." The title sets the stage, but it is not the first sentence of the essay.

The **thesis statement** expresses the central idea that controls and limits what the essay will cover. A thesis statement contains the **topic,** narrowed appropriately; the **focus,** which presents what you are saying about the topic; and the **purpose.** If

---

STEPS FOR REVISING

1. Shift mentally from suspending judgment (during idea gathering and drafting) to making judgments.
2. Read your draft critically to evaluate it. Be guided by the questions on the Revision Checklist on the following page.
3. Decide whether to write an entirely new draft or to revise the one you have.
4. Be systematic. You need to pay attention to many different elements of a draft, from overall organization to choice of words. Most writers work better when they concentrate on specific elements during separate rounds of revision.

MAJOR ACTIVITIES DURING REVISION

Add. Insert needed words, sentences, and paragraphs. If your additions require new content, return to idea-gathering techniques (see 2d through 2j).

Cut. Get rid of whatever goes off the topic or repeats what has already been said.

Replace. As needed, substitute new words, sentences, and paragraphs for what you have cut.

Move material around. Change the sequence of paragraphs if the material is not presented in a logical order (see 2m). Move sentences within paragraphs, or to other paragraphs, if arrangements seem illogical (see 4d and 4e).

---

your thesis statement does not match what you say in your essay, you need to revise either the thesis statement or the essay—sometimes both (see 2n).

A revision checklist can help you focus your attention as you evaluate your writing. Use a checklist provided by your instructor or compile your own based on the Revision Checklists on the following page.

REVISION CHECKLIST: THE WHOLE ESSAY AND PARAGRAPHS

The answer to each question should be "yes." If it is not, you need to revise. The reference numbers in parentheses tell you what chapter or section of the *Simon & Schuster Handbook* to consult.

1. Is your essay topic suitable and sufficiently narrow (2c)?
2. Does your thesis statement communicate your topic and focus (2n) and your purpose (1b)?
3. Does your essay reflect awareness of your audience (1c)?
4. Is your tone appropriate (1d)?
5. Is your essay logically organized (2m) and are your paragraphs logically arranged (4e)?
6. Have you cut material that goes off the topic?
7. Is your reasoning sound (5h–5j) and do you avoid logical fallacies (5k)?
8. Does your introductory paragraph prepare readers for what follows (4g)?
9. Does each body paragraph express its main idea in a topic sentence as needed (4b)? Are the main ideas clearly related to the thesis statement, and have you covered all that your thesis statement "promises" (2n)?
10. Are your body paragraphs sufficiently developed with concrete support for their main idea (4c)?
11. Have you used transitions effectively (4d-1, 4d-5)?
12. Do your paragraphs maintain coherence (4d)?
13. Does your conclusion provide a sense of completion (4g)?
14. Does your title reflect the content of the essay (3c-2)?

REVISION CHECKLIST: SENTENCES AND WORDS

The answer to each question should be "yes." If it is not, you need to revise. The reference numbers in parentheses tell you what chapter or section of the *Simon & Schuster Handbook* to consult.

1. Have you eliminated sentence fragments (13)?
2. Have you eliminated comma splices and run-together sentences (14)?
3. Have you eliminated confusing shifts (15a)?
4. Have you eliminated misplaced and dangling modifiers (15b and 15c)?
5. Have you eliminated mixed and incomplete sentences (15d and 15e)?
6. Are your sentences concise (16)?
7. Do your sentences show clear relationships among ideas (17)?
8. Do you use parallelism to help your sentences deliver their meaning gracefully, and do you avoid faulty parallelism (18)?

REVISION CHECKLIST: SENTENCES AND WORDS *(continued)*

9. Does your writing reflect variety and emphasis (19)?
10. Have you used exact words (20b)?
11. Is your usage correct (Usage Glossary)?
12. Do your words reflect an appropriate level of formality (21a-1)?
13. Do you avoid sexist language (21b), slang and colloquial language (21a-3), slanted language (21a-4), clichés (21d), and artificial language (21e)?

3d Knowing how to edit

When you **edit,** you check the correctness of your writing. You pay attention to grammar, spelling, and punctuation, and to the correct use of capitals, numbers, italics, and abbreviations. You are ready to edit once you have a final draft that contains suitable content, organization, development, and sentence structure. Once you have edited your work, you are ready to transcribe it into a final copy.

As you edit, be systematic. Use a checklist supplied by your instructor or one you compile from the following Editing Checklist.

EDITING CHECKLIST

The answer to each question should be "yes." If it is not, you need to edit. The reference numbers in parentheses tell you what chapter of the *Simon & Schuster Handbook* to consult.

1. Is your grammar correct (7 to 15)?
2. Is your spelling correct, and are your hyphens correct (22)?
3. Have you correctly used commas (24)?
4. Have you correctly used all other punctuation (25 through 29)?
5. Have you correctly used capital letters, italics, abbreviations, and numbers (30)?

3e Knowing how to proofread

When you **proofread,** you check a final version carefully before handing it in. You need to make sure your work is an accurate and clean transcription of your final draft. Proofreading involves a careful, line-by-line reading of an essay. You should proofread with a ruler so that you can focus on one line at a time. Remember that no matter how hard you have worked on other parts of the writing process, if your final copy is inaccurate or messy, you will not be taken seriously.

Name_____ Date _____

Adapting to Your Audience and Purpose

Look at this picture of an earthquake. Describe the scene as part of your response to each of the four different audiences described below. Use your own paper.

1. You have just seen a news report of a serious earthquake in South America. Some people are still trapped in the wreckage, while thousands are in need of shelter, food, and medical help. You work for a charity that offers rapid response volunteers in situations like this. Prepare a statement to be read out on local TV and radio that explains the services your organization offers and why people should donate money for an immediate relief mission to the area.

2. You recently moved to Victoria, British Columbia. Your grandmother is concerned about earthquake activity in the Pacific Rim and is worried about you. She doesn't know how you can live in a place where disaster might strike at any time. Write back explaining your attitude to this risk. Reassure her that, in the event of any tremors, you would know what to do.

3. While on a Study Abroad program recently, you were caught up in an earthquake that totalled the school building yet, miraculously, cost no lives. Write a short piece for your school's newspaper in Canada detailing this experience.

4. A minor earthquake has destroyed your apartment building and an adjacent strip mall, yet all the surrounding buildings are unscathed. You discover that cheap materials were used in the construction of both the apartment building and the mall. Write a letter to the builders in which you hold them responsible for this disaster. Make a clear link between their negligence and the collapse of the buildings.

EXERCISE 2-2
(2d–j)

Using Idea-Gathering Techniques

Select four topics from this list, and prepare to write by narrowing each one. Use a different idea-gathering technique for each: freewriting, brainstorming, the journalist's questions, and mapping. Use your own paper, but record your narrowed topic on the line next to each subject you use.

1. talent_____

2. someone I can count on _____

3. travelling alone _____

4. fitness_____

5. graduation _____

6. restaurants _____

7. the beach_____

8. my grandparents _____

9. a personal loss _____

10. choosing a computer _____

EXERCISE 2-3
(2l–m)

Grouping and Ordering Ideas

Select two of the topics you explored in Exercise 2-2. For each, group ideas in clusters of related material and then order the clusters. Remember that not every item in an idea-generating exercise has to appear in the final essay. Feel free to omit items that do not fit your pattern. If there are gaps, return to idea-gathering techniques to get more material. Your end products will be informal outlines. Use your own paper.

2-4

Name_____ Date _____

Writing Thesis Statements

A: Most of the following thesis statements are unacceptable because they are too broad or too narrow. Label each thesis *acceptable* or *unacceptable*. Then revise each unacceptable thesis to make it suitable for an essay of about 500 words.

EXAMPLE: The United States is a nice place to visit.

> *Its nearness to Canada, its cultural variety, and the lack of a language barrier make the United States an attractive choice for a family vacation.*

1. Planned budget cuts will do terrible damage to the university.

   _____

2. Many students do not study as much as they should.

   _____

3. My parents blame today's violence on movies, but I blame it on society.

   _____

4. I saw an interesting hockey game last week.

   _____

5. I fell in love when I was seventeen.

   _____

6. In interviews a job applicant should not beat around the bush.

   _____

7. Government job training programs have given me useful skills.

   _____

8. Remodelling an older home involves three major steps.

   _____

9. In May I visited Turkey.

   _____

10. The Norman Conquest occurred in 1066.

   _____

B: Write thesis statements for the four topics you narrowed in Exercise 2-2 and for six original topics. Be sure that each topic is suitably narrow for an essay of about 500 words and that the thesis statement shows a purpose and a point of view.

EXERCISES

EXAMPLE: Topic: *how shopping has been changed by the development of closed malls*

Thesis Statement: *The development of closed malls has led to a revolution in the way Canadians shop: We can shop easily at night and in rough weather, we see a greater variety of goods than in any single store, and we are encouraged to think of shopping as fun rather than as a chore.*

1. Topic _____

   Thesis Statement _____

2. Topic _____

   Thesis Statement _____

3. Topic _____

   Thesis Statement _____

4. Topic _____

   Thesis Statement _____

5. Topic _____

   Thesis Statement _____

6. Topic _____

   Thesis Statement _____

7. Topic _____

   Thesis Statement _____

8. Topic _____

   Thesis Statement _____

9. Topic _____

   Thesis Statement _____

10. Topic _____

   Thesis Statement _____

Name_____ Date _____

Planning a Formal Outline

The following topic outline contains twelve errors in form and logic. Revise the outline, using the guidelines listed in 2p. Draw a single line through each error and write your revision next to it.

Thesis Statement: Leaving a roommate for a single apartment can have definite draw-backs.

I. Unsatisfactory Furnishings
  A. Appliances
    1. Major
      a. Stove
      b. Refrigerator
    2. Minor
      a. Microwave
      b. Blender
      c. Toaster
      d. Mixer
    3. Washer
  B. Furniture
    1. Futon
    2. Living room
      a. Sofa
      b. Chairs
      c. Tables
    3. Kitchen
      a. Table
      b. Chairs
  C. Equipment
    1. For entertainment
      a. VCR
    2. Exercise
II. Not enough money to pay the bills
  A. Rent
  B. Utilities
    1. Gas
    2. Electricity
    3. Phone
  C. Food
    1. Groceries
  D. Entertainment

III. Inadequate companionship
   A. Loneliness is a frequent problem.
   B. Occasional fear
   C. Friendly neighbours

Making a Formal Outline

Convert one of the informal outlines you developed in Exercise 2-3 into a formal outline. Write a sentence outline or a topic outline, but be sure not to mix the two types. Begin by placing the thesis statement you developed in Exercise 2-4B at the top of your page. Use the list of conventions in 2p for guidance and as a checklist when you are done. Use your own paper.

Revising, Editing, and Proofreading Essays

A: Here is a middle draft of a short essay. It has already been revised, but it has not yet been edited. Edit the essay, using the Editing Checklist in 3d. If you like, you may also make additional revisions. When you are done, submit a carefully proofread copy of the completed essay to your instructor.

A Brief History of Utensils

Forks, knives, and spoons seam so natural to most of us that its hard to imagine eaten diner with out them. Yet many people, such as the chinese, use chopsticks instead, and other's use their hands to eat.

Knives are the oldest western utensils. The first ones were made of stone 1.5 million years ago. It was originally use to cut up dead animals after a hunt. The same knife were used to: butcher game slice cooked food, and kill enemies. Even later in History, nobles was the only ones who could afford separate knives for different uses. People use all-purpose knives, pointed like todays steak knives. The round-tipped dinner knife is a modern invention. It became popular in 17th cen. France because hostesses want to stop guests from picking they're teeth with the points of there dinner knives.

The spoon is also an anceint tool. Wooden spoons twenty thousand years old have been found in Asia; spoons of stone, wood, ivory, and even gold have been found in Egyptian tombs. Spoons scoop up foods that were to thick to sip from a bowl.

The fork is a newcomer. Forks did not become widely accepted until the eighteenth century; when the French nobility adopted the fork as a status symbol, and eating with ones hands became un-fashionable. At about the same time, individual place settings became the

Name_____ Date _____

rule to. Previous, even rich people had shared plates and glasses at meals, but know the rich demanded individual plates, glasses, forks, spoons, and knives. Today in North America, a full set of utensils is considered a necesity. We forget that as recently as the american revolution some people still considered anyone who use a fork to be a fussy showoff.

B: Here is the first draft of an essay. It needs a great deal of work, as most first drafts do. Revise the essay, using the Revision Checklist in 3c. Then edit your work, using the Editing Checklist in 3d. Finally, submit a carefully proofread copy of the completed essay.

A Canoe Trip

Last year I had an adventure of the sort that many people never experience in their lives, even though you may call it a typical Canadian experience, or at least a part of Canadian folklore. I went on a solo canoe trip to Northern Ontarios Temagami region. In this essay I will tell you my thoughts about going on a solo canoe trip and the benefits it had for both body and spirit.

I've been a pretty good canoeist since I was young. Nevertheless, when I told my friends of my intention to do solo trip, they replied that "Isn't that a dangerous thing your planning to do?" Admittedly, a solo trip may be dangerous. But many other sports and activites — including rock climbing, which has become hugely popular, is dangerous as well. A solo canoe trip need no be a cause for concern. As long as the canoeist is more experienced and takes the proper precautions. It is essential for you to be in good phsyical condition, of course, it is essential to wear at all times a life jacket in the canoe, and to come prepared with extra food and warm clothing. To have learned and able to apply techniques of woodcraft, etc. Having met all these conditions, the final preparation was to inform my friends and local folks of my route and the expected day of my return.

I choose a route that I knew I could do, a solo trip is no time to show foolish bravado. Then off I went. For six days I was alone beneath the vast sky, paddling hard against the waves and winds of Temagami. All the while, my senses were hieghtened, for my safety was in own hands. My eyes, ears, and nose were alert to smells, signs of wild animals, and changes in the weather. I listened to the wind roaring at night. One day I sat out a really awesome storm in my tent, perched on the shore of a tiny island. Late that afternoon, I watched with mounting excitement as a strong west wind gradually drove off the storm clouds and freed me from the storm, I could continue my travels. Every night I crawled into my tent exhausted but pleased with what I had accomplished.

On the last day, I rode the high waves of Ferguson Bay to my final destination, pitching up on the sandy shore with a breath of relief. As I mentioned earlier, a solo canoe trip has benefits fro the body, because it gives you exercise in the outdoors. Spiritually, I felt the deep, meditative calm of being alone with myself and my thoughts. I was reminded how small and vulnerable one single person is faced with the might of nature. At the same time, I had the satisfaction of depending only on myself and overcoming the challenges that confront me.

4 Writing Paragraphs

4a Understanding paragraphs

A paragraph is a group of sentences that work together to develop a unit of thought. Paragraphing permits you to subdivide material into manageable parts and, at the same time, to arrange those parts into a unified whole that effectively communicates its message.

To signal a new paragraph, you indent the first line five spaces in a typewritten paper and 2.5 cm (one inch) in a handwritten paper.

A paragraph's purpose determines its structure. In college and university, the most common purposes for writing are *to inform* and *to persuade* (as discussed in 1b). Some paragraphs in informative and in persuasive essays serve special roles: they introduce, conclude, or provide transitions (see 4g). Most paragraphs, however, are topical paragraphs, also called body paragraphs or developmental paragraphs. They consist of a statement of a main idea and specific, logical support for that main idea.

4b Writing unified paragraphs

A paragraph is unified when all its sentences relate to the main idea. Unity is lost if a paragraph contains sentences unrelated to the main idea.

The sentence that contains the main idea of a paragraph is called the topic sentence. The topic sentence focuses and controls what can be written in the paragraph. Some paragraphs use two sentences to present a main idea. In such cases, the first is the topic sentence and the second is the limiting or clarifying sentence which narrows the focus of the paragraph.

Topic sentence at the beginning of a paragraph: Most informative and persuasive paragraphs have the topic sentence placed first so that a reader knows immediately what to expect. Placing the topic sentence first also helps to ensure that the entire paragraph will be unified.

> Many first-jobbers suffer from the "semester syndrome." Students can usually count on being "promoted" at least twice a year—into the next semester. "Promotions" come regularly and at fixed intervals in school. At work, it's a different story. Promotions don't necessarily occur with any regularity, and sometimes they

1   don't occur at all. This point may seem like a very obvious one, but the fact that students are used to rapid advancement can make their transitions to work harder. Since as students they become so conditioned to advancement at a fixed rate, many first-jobbers become impatient when they are required to remain in one job or at one task without a promotion for longer than a "semester." They begin to feel they're not moving anywhere, and as a result many leave their first jobs much too soon.

—The staff of *Catalyst, Making the Most of Your First Job*

Topic sentence at the end of a paragraph: Some information and persuasive paragraphs present the supporting details before the main idea. The topic sentence, therefore, comes at the end of the paragraph. This technique is particularly effective for building suspense, but it should be used sparingly. In the following paragraph, notice how concrete details build up to the main idea.

2   I read Dreiser's *Jennie Gerhardt* and *Sister Carrie* and they revived in me a vivid sense of my mother's suffering: I was overwhelmed. I grew silent, wondering about the life around me. It would have been impossible for me to have told anyone what I derived from these novels, for it was nothing less than a sense of life itself. All my life had shaped me for the realism, the naturalism of the modern novel, and I could not read enough of them.

—RICHARD WRIGHT, "The Library Card," from *Black Boy*

Topic sentence implied: Some paragraphs make a unified statement without the use of a topic sentence. Writers must construct such paragraphs carefully, so that a reader can easily see the main idea. Paragraphs with implied topic sentences are rare in academic writing.

4c ## Supporting the main idea of a paragraph

A topic sentence is usually a generalization. A topical paragraph is developed by the sentences that support the topic sentence, offering specific, concrete details. Without development, a paragraph fails to make its point or capture a reader's interest.

The key to successful development of topical paragraphs is detail. Details bring generalizations to life by providing concrete, specific illustrations. A paragraph developed with good detail often has RENNS—an acronym that stands for *r*easons, *e*xamples, *n*umbers, *n*ames, and appeals to the five *s*enses. Use RENNS as a memory device to help you check the development of your paragraphs, but do not feel that every paragraph must have a complete menu of RENNS to be well developed. Here is a paragraph with two of the five types of RENNS.

3   However, the first ride I got took me on the way to New York rather than Washington. It was a big Standard Oil truck, heading for Wellsville. We drove out into the wild, bright country, the late November country, full of the light of Indian summer. The red barns glared in the harvested fields, and the woods were bare, but all the world was full of color and the blue sky swam with fleets of white clouds. The truck devoured the road with high-singing tires, and I rode throned in the lofty, rocking cab, listening to the driver telling me stories about all the people who lived in places we passed, and what went on in the houses we saw.

—THOMAS MERTON, *The Seven Storey Mountain*

This paragraph offers concrete, specific illustrations which describe Merton's first ride on the way to New York. It has *n*ames such as Standard Oil truck (not the general term *truck*), Wellsville, November country, and red barns (not the general term *buildings*). It appeals to the *s*enses by including many references to light and specific colours, as well as to the rocking motion of the cab and the sound of the tires.

4d Writing coherent paragraphs

A paragraph is coherent when its sentences are related to each other, not only in content but also in grammatical structures and choice of words. The techniques of coherence are transitional expressions, pronouns, repetition of key words, and parallel structures. Though they are discussed separately in this section for the sake of clear example, techniques of coherence usually work in unison.

Transitional expressions—words and phrases that signal connections among ideas—can help you achieve coherence in your writing.

COMMON TRANSITIONAL EXPRESSIONS AND THE RELATIONSHIPS THEY SIGNAL

RELATIONSHIP	EXPRESSIONS
Addition	also, in addition, too, moreover, and, besides, further, furthermore, equally important, next, then, finally
Example	for example, for instance, thus, as an illustration, namely, specifically
Contrast	but, yet, however, on the other hand, nevertheless, nonetheless, conversely, in contrast, on the contrary, still, at the same time, although
Comparison	similarly, likewise, in like manner, in the same way, in comparison
Concession	of course, to be sure, certainly, naturally, granted
Result	therefore, thus, consequently, so, accordingly, due to this
Summary	as a result, hence, in short, in brief, in summary, in conclusion, finally, on the whole
Time sequence	first, firstly, second, secondly, third, fourth, next, then, finally, afterwards, before, soon, later, during, meanwhile, subsequently, immediately, at length, eventually, in the future, currently
Place	in the front, in the foreground, in the back, in the background, at the side, adjacent, nearby, in the distance, here, there

Notice how transitional expressions (shown in boldface) help to make the following paragraph coherent.

4

The role of stress in the development of schizophrenic symptoms is particularly hard to study **since** what is stressful for one person may not be stressful for another. **Nonetheless,** two conclusions can be drawn. **First,** the biological predisposition to become mentally disorganized lowers a schizophrenic's resistance to stress in general, although some people who are so predisposed can tolerate more stress than others. **Second,** the issue of becoming independent from one's family of origin appears to pose special difficulties for individuals predisposed to schizophrenia. This is not surprising in view of the fact that mental, emotional, and social competence are requirements of successful completion of this task. The predisposed individuals may be impaired in each of these areas.

—Kayla F. Bernheim and Richard R. J. Lewine, *Schizophrenia*

When you use **pronouns** that clearly refer to nouns and other pronouns, you help your reader move from one sentence to the next. Notice how the pronouns (shown in boldface) help make the following paragraph coherent.

5

The men and women who perform the daring and often dangerous action that is part of almost every television and motion-picture story today are special people. **They** are professional stunt men and women. **They** know precisely what **they** are doing and how to do it. **Most** are extraordinary athletes with the grace and timing of dancers. **They** plan ahead what **they** must do. And **they** have no intention of getting hurt, although sometimes **they** do.

—Gloria D. Miklowitz, *Movie Stunts and the People Who Do Them*

You can achieve coherence by repeating **key words** in a paragraph. Notice how the careful repetition of the words *demand, difficulty, game(s), fun,* and *rules* (shown in boldface) help make this paragraph coherent.

6

We **demand difficulty** even in our **games.** We **demand** it because without **difficulty** there can be no **game.** A **game** is a way of making something hard for the **fun** of it. The **rules** of the **game** are an arbitrary imposition of **difficulty.** When the spoilsport ruins the **fun,** he always does so by refusing to play by the **rules.** It is easier to win at chess if you are free, at your pleasure, to change the wholly arbitrary **rules,** but the **fun** is in winning within the **rules.** No **difficulty,** no **fun.**

—John Ciardi, "Is Everybody Happy?"

Parallel structures (see Chapter 18) can help you achieve coherence. Using the same form of phrase or clause several times sets up a rhythm which gives unity to the paragraph. Notice how the parallel structures (shown in boldface) make this paragraph coherent.

7

This is our hope. **This is** the faith with which I return to the South. **With this faith we will be able to** hew out of the mountain of despair a stone of hope. **With this faith we will be able to** transform the jangling discords of our nation into a beautiful symphony of brotherhood. **With this faith we will be able to work together, to pray together, to struggle together, to go to jail together, to stand up for freedom together,** knowing that we will be free one day.

—Martin Luther King, "I Have a Dream"

4e Arranging a paragraph

Here are some of the most common ways to organize paragraphs.

From general to specific: An arrangement of sentences from the general to the specific is the most common organization for a paragraph. Such paragraphs often begin with a topic sentence and end with specific details.

8

Gifts from parents to children always carry the most meaningful messages. The way parents think about presents goes one step beyond the objects themselves—the ties, dolls, sleds, record players, kerchiefs, bicycles and model airplanes that wait by the Christmas tree. The gifts are, in effect, one way of telling boys and girls, "We love you even though you have been a bad boy all month" or, "We love having a daughter" or, "We treat all our children alike" or, "It is all right for girls to have some toys made for boys" or, "This alarm clock will help you get started in the morning all by yourself." Throughout all the centuries since the invention of a Santa Claus figure who represented a special recognition of children's behaviour, good and bad, presents have given parents a way of telling children about their love and hopes and expectations for them.

—Margaret Mead and Rhoda Metraux, *A Way of Seeing*

From specific to general: A less common arrangement moves from the specific to the general. The paragraph ends with a topic sentence and begins with the details that support the topic sentence.

9

They live up alongside the hills, in hollow after hollow. They live in eastern Kentucky and eastern Tennessee and in the western part of North Carolina and the western part of Virginia and in just about the whole state of West Virginia. They live close to the land; they farm it and some of them go down into it to extract its coal. Their ancestors, a century or two ago, fought their way westward from the Atlantic seaboard, came up on the mountains, penetrated the valleys, and moved stubbornly up the creeks for room, for privacy, for a view, for a domain of sorts. **They are Appalachian people, mountain people, hill people. They are white yeomen, or miners, or hollow folk, or subsistence farmers.**

—Robert Coles, "A Domain (of Sorts)"

From least to most important: A sentence arrangement that moves from the least to the most important is known as a **climactic sequence.** This arrangement holds the reader's interest because the best part comes at the end.

10

Joseph Glidden's invention, barbed wire, soon caught on—though not with everyone. Indians called it "devil's rope." Ranchers often cut it down so their cattle could graze freely. Most farmers, however, liked barbed wire. It kept cattle away from their crops. Cattle could break through most wire fences. With barbed wire, they quickly got the point. Eventually, ranchers started using barbed wire. With it, they separated the best cattle from the others to produce better breeds. Barbed wire helped railroads keep cattle off the tracks. As a result, the railroads expanded into new territory. **Glidden probably didn't realize it at the time, but the few hours he spent twisting wires would help speed the taming of the West.**

—*Small Inventions That Make a Big Difference,*
National Geographic Society

According to location: A paragraph that describes the relative position of objects to one another, often from a central point of reference, uses spatial **sequence.** The topic sentence usually gives the reader the location that serves as the orientation for all other places mentioned.

11   The bay in front of the dock was framed by the shores of the mainland, which curved together from both sides to meet in a point. At that vertex another island, rocky and tall, rose from the water. It looked uninhabited; and although a few cabins were scattered along the mainland, between and behind them was unbroken forest. It was my first sight of natural wilderness. Behind our tent too, and several other tents here and housed in their midst, was the forest. Over everything, as pervasive as sunshine, was the fragrance of balsam firs. It was aromatic and sweet and I closed my eyes and breathed deeply to draw in more of it.

—Sally Carrighar, *Home to the Wilderness*

According to time: A paragraph arranged according to time uses a **chronological sequence.**

12   About 30 years ago, a prince in India found a rare white tiger cub whose mother had been killed. The prince decided to raise the cub, which he named Mohan. When Mohan grew up, he fathered some cubs that were white. One of his cubs, Mohini, was sent to the National Zoo in Washington, D.C. Mohini was used to breed more white tigers for other zoos in the United States.

—"Who-o-o Knows?" *Ranger Rick*

4f Using rhetorical strategies in paragraphs

If you know a variety of **rhetorical strategies**, or rhetorical patterns, for paragraph development, you have more choices when you are seeking ways to help your paragraphs deliver their meanings most effectively. Although, for the purpose of illustration, the strategies shown here are discussed in isolation, in essay writing these often overlap. Be sure to use the rhetorical strategy that communicates your meaning most effectively.

Narration: Narrative writing tells about what is happening or what happened. Narration is usually written in chronological sequence.

13   During the 1870s, the business world was not yet ready for the typewriter. Inventor C. Latham Sholes and his daughter Lillian faced two major objections as they demonstrated Sholes's writing machine. "Too expensive and too slow," the businessmen protested. The response discouraged the inventor, but he didn't give up. At his home in Milwaukee, Wisconsin, he designed improvements for his machine. He also invented touch-typing, a system that enables a person to type fast without looking at the keys. Touch-typing was faster than handwriting. It could save both time and money. That caused businessmen's interest to perk up. By 1900, in offices all over the United States, the *clickety-clack* of typewriters was replacing the scratching of pens.

—*Small Inventions That Make a Big Difference,*
National Geographic Society

Description: Descriptive writing appeals to a reader's senses—sight, sound, smell, taste, and touch—creating a sensual impression of a person, place, or object.

> The forest was quiet except for the shrill cries of faraway toucans. Then many leaves began to rustle nearby. Seconds later crickets and cockroaches were hopping and crawling frantically in my direction. *What could be causing these creatures to run for their lives?* I wondered. Then I saw them: Tens of thousands of *army ants* were marching toward their fleeing prey—and me! The swarm of ants looked like a huge moving triangle, with the ants at the head of the swarm forming the widest part. And this part was as long as a school bus.
>
> —DOUG WECHSLER, "I Met the Rambo Ants"

14

Process: A process describes a sequence of actions by which something is done or made. It is usually developed in chronological order. If it is to be effective, a process must include all steps. The amount of detail included depends on whether you want to teach the reader how to do something or you merely want to offer a general overview of the process.

> To keep the big teams as nearly even as possible in the level of performance, a system called the draft has been devised. This is the way it works. Names of top college players who are graduating and want to turn pro are listed. Team representatives meet for a few days, usually in New York, to select the players they wish from this list. The team that placed last in the standings that year, gets first choice. The team next lowest in the standings gets the next choice, and so on. Naturally the representative will select the player the team needs the most. If one team gets a player that another team wants, that other team may trade an established team member or members for the draft choice. Naturally, a lot of wheeling and dealing goes on at this time.
>
> —BOB AND MARGUITA MCGONAGLE, *Careers in Sports*

15

Example: A paragraph developed by example uses one or more illustrations to provide evidence in support of the main idea.

> Getting right down to the gory details, ever since the earliest days of movie making, stars have been gushing, oozing, trickling, or dripping blood, as the case may be, on screen. Victims in silent movies "bled" chocolate syrup, which looked just like the real McCoy on the kind of black-and-white film used then. If a cowboy in a Western was to get shot, just before the scene was filmed a little chocolate syrup would be poured into the palm of his hand. Then, when the cameras started rolling and the cowboy got "blasted," he merely slapped his hand to his chest and what audiences saw was the bloody aftermath.
>
> —JANE O'CONNOR and KATY HALL, *Magic in the Movies*

16

Definition: A paragraph of definition explains the meaning of a word or concept. Because it is more thorough than the definition offered by a dictionary, such a paragraph is called an **extended definition.**

An extended definition may contain any of several elements, but it rarely includes all of them: (1) a dictionary definition, (2) a negative definition—what the term is *not*, (3) a comparison and contrast of definitions used by other people, (4) an explanation of how this term differs from terms with which it is often confused, and (5) an explanation of how the term originated. If the subject is a human quality, the definition may include (6) a discussion of how a person develops the quality and how the quality shows up in the individual's personality.

17   Now, consider for a moment just exactly what it is that you are about to be handed. It is a huge, irregular mass of ice cream, faintly domed at the top from the metal scoop, which has first produced it and then insecurely balanced it on the uneven top edge of a hollow inverted cone made out of the most brittle and fragile of materials. Clumps of ice cream hang over the side, very loosely attached to the main body. There is always much more ice cream than the cone could hold, even if the ice cream were tamped down into the cone, which of course it isn't. And the essence of ice cream is that it melts. It doesn't just stay there teetering in this irregular, top-heavy mass; it also melts. And it melts *fast*. And it doesn't just melt— it melts into a sticky fluid that *cannot* be wiped off. The only thing one person could hand to another that might possibly be more dangerous is a live hand grenade from which the pin had been pulled five seconds earlier. And of course if anybody offered you that, you could say, "Oh. Uh, well—no thanks."

—L. RUST HILLS, *How to Do Things Right*

Analysis and classification: **Analysis** divides things up, and **classification** puts things together. A paragraph developed by analysis, also known as **division,** divides one subject into its component parts. Paragraphs written in this pattern usually start by identifying the subject and then explain that subject's distinct parts. For example, a football team can be divided into its offensive and defensive teams, which can be divided further into the various positions on each.

A paragraph developed by classification discusses the ways that separate groups relate to one another. The separate groups must be *from the same class*; that is, they must have some underlying characteristic in common. For example, different types of sports—football, Rugby, and soccer—can be classified *together* according to their handling of the ball, their playing fields, the placement of their goals, and the like.

18   **There are three kinds of book owners.** The first has all the standard sets and best sellers—unread, untouched. (This deluded individual owns wood-pulp and ink, not books.) The **second** has a great many books—a few of them read through, most of them dipped into, but all of them as clean and shiny as the day they were bought. (This person would probably like to make books his own, but is restrained by a false respect for their physical appearance.) The **third** has a few books or many—every one of them dog-eared and dilapidated, shaken and loosened by continual use, marked and scribbled in from front to back. (This man owns books.)

—MORTIMER J. ADLER, "How to Mark a Book"

Comparison and contrast: **Comparison** deals with similarities, and **contrast** deals with differences between two objects or ideas. Paragraphs using comparison and contrast can be structured in two ways. A **point-by-point structure** allows you to move back and forth between the two items being compared. A **block structure** allows you to discuss one item completely before discussing the other.

POINT-BY-POINT STRUCTURE
Student body: college A, college B
Curriculum: college A, college B
Location: college A, college B

BLOCK STRUCTURE
College A: student body, curriculum, location
College B: student body, curriculum, location
Here is a paragraph structured point-by-point for comparison and contrast.

19
Some people say the business about the jolly fat person is a myth, that all of us chubbies are neurotic, sick, sad people. I disagree. Fat people may not be chortling all day long, but they're a hell of a lot *nicer* than the wizened and shriveled. Thin people turn surly, mean, and hard at a young age because they never learn the value of a hot-fudge sundae for easing tension. Thin people don't like gooey soft things because they themselves are neither gooey nor soft. They are crunchy and dull, like carrots. They go straight to the heart of the matter while fat people let things stay all blurry and hazy and vague, the ways things actually are. Thin people want to face the truth. Fat people know there is no truth. One of my thin friends is always staring at complex, unsolvable problems and saying, "The key thing is. . . ." Fat people never say that. They know there isn't any such thing as the key thing about anything.

—SUZANNE BRITT JORDAN, "That Lean and Hungry Look"

Here is a paragraph structured block style for comparison and contrast.

20
Many people think that gorillas are fierce and dangerous beasts. Stories have been told about gorillas attacking people. Movies have been made about gorillas kidnapping women. These stories and movies are exciting, but they are not true. In real life, gorillas are gentle and rather shy. They rarely fight among themselves. They almost never fight with other animals. They like to lead a quiet life—eating, sleeping, and raising their young.

—SUSAN MEYERS, *The Truth about Gorillas*

Analogy: Analogy is a type of comparison. By comparing objects or ideas from different classes, an analogy explains the unfamiliar in terms of the familiar. For example, the fight to find a cure for a disease might be compared to a war. Often a paragraph developed with analogy starts with a simile or metaphor (see 21c).

21
If clothing is a language, it must have a vocabulary and a grammar like other languages. Of course, as with human speech, there is not a single language of dress, but many: some (like Dutch and German) closely related and others (like Basque) almost unique. And within every language of clothes there are many different dialects and accents, some almost unintelligible to members of the mainstream culture. Moreover, as with speech, each individual has his own stock of words and employs personal variations of tone and meaning.

—ALISON LURIE, *The Language of Clothes*

Cause-and-effect analysis: Cause-and-effect analysis involves examining the origin or outcome of something that happened or might happen. Causes are what lead up to an event; effects are what result.

22
When a person is weightless, the slightest exertion causes motion. For example, if you pushed yourself away from a chair, you would continue to move away from it. There would be nothing to stop the motion. You would float in space. Should you let go of your book, it would hang in space. Push it ever so slightly, and the book would move in a straight line. Splash water, and it would form into round drops moving in all directions.

—FRANKLYN M. BRANLEY, *Mysteries of Outer Space*

4g Writing introductory, transitional, and concluding paragraphs

Introductory paragraphs, concluding paragraphs, and transitional paragraphs have special roles in an essay. **Introductions** prepare a reader for the topical paragraphs that follow, **conclusions** bring the topical paragraphs to a close for a reader, and **transitional paragraphs** help the reader move through complex material. Generally, special paragraphs are shorter than topical paragraphs.

Introductory paragraphs: In informative and persuasive writing, an introductory paragraph prepares readers for what lies ahead. For this reason, your introduction must relate clearly to the rest of your essay. If it points in one direction and your essay goes off in another, your reader will be confused—and may even stop reading.

In college and university writing, many instructors want an introductory paragraph to include a statement of the essay's thesis—its central idea. Although professional writers do not always use thesis statements in their introductory paragraphs, they can help student writers who need to practise clear essay organization. Here is an example of an introductory paragraph ending with a thesis statement.

> Basketball is a team game. Individual stars are helpful, but in the end, the team that plays together is the team that wins. No one player can hog the ball; no one player should do all the shooting. Every player, every coach and every fan knows that. But once in a while, a team needs a super effort by an individual. **In the National Basketball Association playoff game between Boston and Syracuse, Boston's Bob Cousy made one of the most spectacular one-man shows ever seen.**

23

—HOWARD LISS, *True Sports Stories*

An introductory paragraph often includes an **introductory device** to lead into the thesis and to stimulate reader interest. To be effective, an introductory device must relate clearly to the essay's thesis and to the material in the topical paragraphs.

INTRODUCTORY PARAGRAPHS

STRATEGIES TO USE

- Providing relevant background information
- Relating a brief, interesting story or anecdote
- Giving a pertinent statistic or statistics
- Asking a provocative question or questions
- Using an appropriate quotation
- Making an analogy
- Defining a key term
- Identifying the situation

➔

INTRODUCTORY PARAGRAPHS *(continued)*

STRATEGIES TO AVOID

- Obvious statements that refer to what the essay is about or will accomplish, such as "I am going to discuss the causes of falling oil prices"
- Apologies, such as "I am not sure this is right, but this is my opinion"
- Overworked expressions, such as "Haste really does make waste, as I recently discovered" or "Love is grand"

Transitional paragraphs: A transitional paragraph usually consists of one or two sentences that help the reader move from one major point to another in long essays. Here is a transitional paragraph that moves the reader between a series of details and an explanation of their possible source.

24   Now that we've sampled some of the false "facts" that clutter our storehouse of knowledge, perhaps you'd like to consider some of the possible reasons why we seem so susceptible to misinformation.

—WILLIAM P. GOTTLIEB, *Science Facts You Won't Believe*

Concluding paragraphs: In informative and persuasive writing, a conclusion brings discussion to a logical and graceful end. Too abrupt an ending leaves your reader suddenly cut off, and a conclusion that is merely tacked onto an essay does not give the reader a sense of completion. In contrast, an ending that flows gracefully and sensibly from what has come before it reinforces your ideas and increases the impact of your essay.

The concluding paragraph that follows summarized Cousy's "show."

25   In that game Bob Cousy scored a total of 50 points. He made 25 of them in regulation time, and 25 more in the four overtime periods. And he made 30 out of 32 foul shots. Even more important, he had scored his points at the right time. Four times he scored in the final seconds to keep the game going. Then he helped his team pull away. Basketball may be a team game, but most teams would not be sorry to have an individual like Bob Cousy.

—HOWARD LISS, *True Sports Stories*

CONCLUDING PARAGRAPHS

STRATEGIES TO USE

- Using any device appropriate for introductory paragraphs—but avoid using the same one in both the introduction and conclusion
- Summarizing the main points of the essay—but avoid a summary if the essay is less than three pages long
- Asking for awareness, action, or a similar resolution from readers
- Looking ahead to the future

STRATEGIES TO AVOID

- Introducing new ideas or facts that belong in the body of the essay
- Rewording your introduction
- Announcing what you have done, as in "In this paper, I have explained the drop in oil prices"
- Making absolute claims, as in "I have proved that oil prices do not affect gasoline prices"
- Apologizing, as in "Even though I am not an expert, I feel my position is correct" or "I may not have convinced you, but there is good evidence for my position"

Identifying Sentences That Do Not Fit the Topic Sentence

Identify the topic sentence in each paragraph, and write its number in the first column. Then, identify any irrelevant sentences (ones that do not fit the topic sentence), and write their numbers in the second column.

	Topic Sentence	Irrelevant Sentences

EXAMPLE [1]The flute is a very old instrument.[2]It existed as long ago as 3500 B.C. [3]My brother plays the flute. [4]Archaeologists digging in the cities of ancient Sumeria and Egypt have found well-preserved flutes. [5]When these flutes were tested, they sounded much like modern flutes. [6]However, they look different. [7]My brother's flute is silver. [8]Ancient flutes were played vertically, and they were 45 centimetres long but only a centimetre wide.

Topic Sentence: *1*   Irrelevant Sentences: *3, 7*

1. [1]Many people associate the clarinet with jazz or the Big Bands of the forties. [2]However, the clarinet has been around since ancient times. [3]The clarinet can be hard to play. [4]The first clarinet appeared in Egypt before 2700 B.C. [5]The double clarinet appeared about eight hundred years later. [6]The first modern Westerner to compose for the clarinet was a sixteenth century German, Johann Christoph Denner. [7]He improved the clarinet by making it of wood, using a single rather than a double reed, and increasing its length from 30 centimetres to 60 centimetres.

Name_____ Date _____

2. [1]The lute is the ancestor of many modern stringed instruments. [2]There is even a mural, dating from 2500 B.C., that shows a Babylonian shepherd playing a lute. [3]The guitar, the ukulele, and the sitar are descendants of the lute. [4]The sitar became popular in the West after the Beatles' George Harrison studied with Indian musician Ravi Shankar. [5]The violin, fiddle, and cello also are descended from the lute. [6]The bows used to play these instruments are an eighth-century Islamic addition to the tradition of stringed instruments.

_____   _____

3. [1]The trumpet is another instrument with a long history. [2]The first trumpets were made of bamboo cane or eucalyptus branches. [3]The eucalyptus tree is found in Australia and is the chief food source for koalas. [4]The first metal trumpets, made of silver, were found in the tomb of King Tutankhamen of Egypt, who died about 1350 B.C. [5]The Greek trumpets of the fifth century B.C. were made of carved ivory. [6]Like us, the Romans had both straight and J-shaped trumpets. [7]The Romans are often depicted in paintings as enjoying music.

_____   _____

4. [1]The first bagpipes were very unusual instruments. [2]They were made from the complete hide of a sheep or goat. [3]The chanter, a pipe with finger holes, was set in a wooden plug placed in the animal's neck. [4]The drones, the pipes that produced the bagpipe's sound, were set in wooden plugs placed in the forelegs. [5]Then as now, a blowpipe was used to fill the bag with air. [6]The player pressed the bag under one arm, forcing air out the drones, and fingered the chanter, making the bagpipe's famous sound. [7]The bagpipe originally came from Asia.

_____   _____

EXERCISES

5. [1]Many people assume the piano is an improved version of some older keyboard instrument, such as the harpsichord. [2]Actually, the harpsichord, the clavichord, and the piano are widely different. [3]In a harpsichord, the strings are plucked. [4]This plucking enables the instrument to sustain a note. [5]In the clavichord, the strings are struck by blades of metal. [6]Once a blade moves off a string, the note stops. [7]The first clavichord dates back to about 1385. [8]In the piano, the strings are struck by small hammers that rebound immediately. [9]The piano did not become popular until the eighteenth century.

_____   _____

| EXERCISE **4-2** |
| (4d) |

Identifying Transitions

Underline all the transitional words and expressions in these paragraphs. Then list the transitions on the lines provided.

1. Canada may be the "true north," but it also extends well to the south. Point Pelee, Canada's southernmost point, is further south than the northern tip of California. Similarly, Montreal is on the same parallel as the southern French city Bordeaux, and Toronto is on a line with Florence in Italy.

    _____

2. Most people think the boomerang is found only in Australia; however, this is not so. People use curved hunting sticks in four other parts of the world: Indonesia, eastern Africa, the Indian subcontinent, and the southwestern United States. In the United States, the Hopi, Acoma, and Zuni Indians use such sticks to hunt small animals. Few boomerangs are designed to return to their owners, but the Australian aborigines have perfected a kind that does return. In fact, the word "boomerang" comes from the aborigines' name for such a hunting stick.

    _____

3. Unlike most other circuses, Quebec's *Cirque du Soleil* has no animal acts. Nor does it boast of the size or number of its rings. In fact, all its acts take place in one ring—and sometimes the acts intentionally spill over into the audience, who sit right up close to the action. Since its beginnings in the 1980s, this unique circus has emphasized breathtaking acrobatics in addition to anarchic clowning that verges on theatre of the absurd. Finally, the theatrical staging and powerful music establish an unforgettable, magical mood.

    _____

Name_____ Date _____

4. Everyone knows the story of Cinderella. She was treated as a servant by her stepmother and stepsisters, helped by a fairy godmother, and finally rescued by a prince who identified her because her small foot fit the glass slipper that his "mystery woman" had left behind at the ball. Were glass slippers fashionable centuries ago, or did some-one make a mistake? Someone certainly made a mistake. In 1697, Charles Perrault translated Cinderella from Old French into modern French. Unfortunately, he mis-translated *vair* as *verre*, meaning "glass." Actually, *vair* means "white squirrel fur." So, Cinderella's shoes were much more comfortable than we had been told.

5. Dr. Joseph Guillotin did not invent the guillotine, although it was named after him. The guillotine had been in use throughout Europe since at least the early fourteenth century. In most places, the guillotine was reserved for executing nobility. During the French Revolution, Dr. Guillotin suggested to the French National Assembly that the machine become the country's official form of capital punishment. He wanted it to be used on criminals regardless of their social class. The Assembly agreed. The first victim of the French guillotine was a highwayman in 1792. Within a year, the heads of the nobility began to fall in the infamous Reign of Terror.

Identifying Devices That Provide Coherence

> EXERCISE **4-3**
> (4d)

Read this paragraph carefully, and then answer the questions that follow.

[1]Have you ever wondered how the painted lines in the road are made straight? [2]No one painting freehand could consistently keep lines straight, so machines are used. [3]Before a small road or street is painted, a highway crew marks it at 6-metre intervals, following an engineer's plan. [4]Then a gasoline-powered machine, about the size of a large lawnmower, is pushed along by one person. [5]The operator follows the marks on the road, while air pressure forces out a stream of paint or hot plastic. [6]Hot plastic lasts from eighteen months to three years; paint lasts from three to six months. [7]Of course, this machine is too slow for use on highways. [8]Instead, four-person crews use a large truck equipped with a pointer that can be used to fol-low the median strip, so there is no need to mark the road before painting. [9]The truck is faster than the one-person machine for other reasons as well: it has *two* adjustable sprayguns that paint lines at the required distances apart, and it moves at 8 kilometres an hour. [10]Crew members must have great skill. [11]In fact, they receive up to a year of training.

EXERCISES

1. Which words and phrases serve as transitional devices?

2. What key words are repeated (include all forms of the words)?

3. How does parallelism function in sentences 6 and 9?

4. What key words are later replaced by pronouns? List the nouns and the pronouns that substitute for them.

Organizing Sentences to Create a Coherent Paragraph

EXERCISE **4-4**
(4b–d)

Rearrange the sentences in each set to create a coherent paragraph. Write the letters of the sentences in their new order. Then write out the paragraph.

1. a. First, look at the source of the Web site and its author or authors.
   b. Always investigate sources carefully before citing them in a paper.
   c. Finally, read it through critically, and discover if the information is well supported with evidence.
   d. The kind of investigation is especially important for sources you locate on the World Wide Web.
   e. Next, evaluate the site for evidence of bias and see if its information is up-to-date.

2. a. Early humans imitated these "natural bridges" by chopping down tall tress and placing them across water.
   b. It was built of many logs tied together with rope.
   c. The first bridges were simply tress that had, by chance, fallen across streams.
   d. The bridge over the Euphrates River lasted for decades.
   e. The first genuine bridge was laid across the Euphrates River at Babylon about 700 B.C.

3. a. Sir Alexander Fleming discovered the penicillin mould, the first modern antibiotic, by accident in 1928.
   b. For the next 200 years, scientists sought a cure for infection.
   c. The Chinese used this soybean mould to treat skin infections.
   d. The first antibiotic was made from mouldy soybeans around 500 B.C.
   e. Soon after, other cultures began using mouldy bread and cobwebs to treat infected wounds.
   f. Strangely, they never looked into these folk remedies.

4. a. Two years later, Long's wife became the first woman to deliver a baby under anesthesia.
   b. Before the introduction of ether by Long, doctors had relied on crude methods of anesthesia.
   c. The use of ether in surgery started in 1842.
   d. In 1846 in Boston, the word "anesthesia," meaning "lack of feeling," was coined after the first use of ether in major surgery.

Name_____ Date _____

e. In that year, Dr. Crawford W. Long used ether to anesthetize a young man who was having a cyst removed from his neck.

f. These early methods included alcoholic intoxication, freezing the area of the operation, and having the patient inhale the fumes from burning narcotic plants.

Supporting the Topic Sentence

EXERCISE **4-5**
(4b–f)

For each topic sentence below, supply three to five relevant details. Then, using your own paper, write a unified and coherent paragraph using the topic sentence and your supporting details.

1. Topic Sentence: A foreign language credit should (should not) be required for high school graduation.
      Details:

2. Topic Sentence: Buying on credit can be disastrous.
      Details:

3. Topic Sentence: The _____ have contributed many things to
                                  (members of an ethnic group)
      Canadian culture.
      Details:

4. Topic Sentence: _____ is an exciting spectator sport.
      Details:

5. Topic Sentence: The laws regarding _____ should be changed.
       Details:

6. Topic Sentence: Choosing a college or university can be difficult.
       Details:

Organizing Details Within Paragraphs

Details in a paragraph are often organized in one of four patterns: chronological order (time), spatial order (location), general to specific, or climactic order (least important to most important). For each pattern, select a subject from the ones given, construct a topic sentence, and list three to five supporting details. Then, on your own paper, use the topic sentence and details to write a unified and coherent paragraph of at least four sentences. It may be possible to combine two closely related details in one sentence.

1. Chronological Order: the steps in applying to college or university; preparing for vacation; painting a room.
    Topic Sentence:
           Details:

2. Spatial Order: the view from the classroom window; the floor plan of the local video rental store; the layout of a basketball court.
    Topic Sentence:
           Details:

Name_____ Date _____

3. General to Specific: the advantages (disadvantages) of working while attending school full time; the mood on New Year's Eve; the reasons _____ is my favourite meal.
    Topic Sentence:
        Details:

4. Climactic Order: why I've chosen my career; how I control anger; how I would raise responsible children.
    Topic Sentence:
        Details:

Using Examples in Paragraphs

Write two paragraphs in which examples are used to support your topic sentence. In the first paragraph, use three to five short examples; in the second, use one extended example. First compose a topic sentence. Next, list the supporting example(s) you will use. After that, write your paragraphs, using your own paper.

    Select your topics from this list: the risks of walking alone at night; my favourite actor/actress; the advantages (disadvantages) of playing on a school team; how peer pressure can be hard to resist; professional athletes are overpaid (underpaid); the difficulty of adjusting to a new neighbourhood, school, or job.

1. MULTIPLE EXAMPLES

    Topic Sentence: _____

    Examples: a. _____

                    b. _____

                    c. _____

                    d. _____

                    e. _____

2. EXTENDED EXAMPLE

    Topic Sentence: _____

    Example: _____

Using Paragraph Development Strategies

Most paragraphs are developed through a combination of several of the strategies discussed in this chapter. Usually one strategy predominates, however. For each development strategy listed below, select a topic from the list; compose a topic sentence; list three to five details, examples, or other pieces of support; and then, using your own paper, write the paragraph.

1. NARRATIVE

    Topics: a time I surprised my friends; a success story; meeting someone special; recovering from a tragedy

    Topic Sentence: _____

    Examples: a. _____

                b. _____

                c. _____

                d. _____

                e. _____

2. DESCRIPTION

    Topics: a quiet corner in the library; a weekend evening at a local dance club; Silken Laumann or Mario Lemieux; an odd person in my neighbourhood

    Topic Sentence: _____

    Details: a. _____

                b. _____

                c. _____

                d. _____

                e. _____

Name_____ Date _____

3. PROCESS

    Topics: how to study for a test; how to plan a weekend at the cottage; how to select a pet; how to read a map

    Topic Sentence: _____

    Steps: a._____

                b._____

                c._____

                d._____

                e._____

4. DEFINITION

    Topics: my ideal job; a loyal friend; fear; science fiction

    Topic Sentence: _____

    Qualities: a._____

                b._____

                c._____

                d._____

                e._____

5. ANALYSIS AND CLASSIFICATION (pick one)

    Topics for Analysis: types of sports shoes; types of cars; types of fear; types of dreams

    Topic Sentence: _____

    Subgroups: a._____

                b._____

                c._____

                d._____

                e._____

    Topics for Classification: movies; desserts; suburbs; bosses

    Topic Sentence: _____

Individual
Components: a. _____

          b. _____

          c. _____

          d. _____

          e. _____

6. COMPARISON AND CONTRAST

Topics: my brother (sister) and I; being in the final year of high school and in the first year of college or university; team sports and individual competition; Jim Carrey's screen personality and that of another performer

Topic Sentence: _____

Points of Comparison
and Contrast: a. _____

          b. _____

          c. _____

          d. _____

          e. _____

7. ANALOGY

Topics: a possessive person and a spider in its web; starting a new job (attending a new school) and jumping into a cool pool; a lie and a forest fire; daydreaming and going for a walk

Topic Sentence: _____

Similarities: a. _____

          b. _____

          c. _____

          d. _____

          e. _____

8. CAUSE AND EFFECT

Topics: why I chose the school I am now attending; why I dropped an old friend; how a new baby affects a family

Topic Sentence: _____

Causes or
Effects: a. _____

        b. _____

Name_____ Date _____

c. _____

d. _____

e. _____

Revising Introductions and Conclusions

EXERCISE **4-9**
(4g)

Each of these introductions and conclusions is inadequate as part of a 500-word essay. Determine what is wrong with each. Then, using your own paper, revise each paragraph. Some may need to be completely rewritten.

1.
THE BUILDING OF THE CANADIAN PACIFIC RAILWAY

Introduction: The Canadian Pacific Railway was built to persuade British Columbia to enter Confederation, and for a century this railway symbolized Canadian unity. It also was known for political scandals, financial manipulations, and the backbreaking labour of thousands of European and Chinese immigrant workers, but this essay will not be able to treat these other things in enough detail.

Conclusion: In this paper I have tried to show how the Canadian Pacific Railway, the transcontinental railway completed in 1885, became an important Canadian symbol. By the way, it is not the same as the Canadian *National* Railway, which came into use in the 1920s.

2.
THE CAUSES OF VOLCANIC ERUPTIONS

Introduction: There are 850 active volcanoes in the world. More than 75 percent of them are located in the "Ring of Fire," an area that goes from the west coasts of North and South America to the east coast of Asia, all the way down to New Zealand. Twenty percent of these volcanoes are in Indonesia. Many are also in Japan, the Aleutian Islands (off Alaska), and Central America. Other big groups of volcanoes are in the Mediterranean Sea and Iceland. In contrast, there are only six volcanoes in Africa and three in Antarctica.

Conclusion: So this is why volcanoes erupt.

3.
SHOULD CAPITAL PUNISHMENT BE RESTORED?

Introduction: Yes, I agree with the question. Every year the rate of serious crime rises. Now is the time to get the murderers and rapists off the streets.

Conclusion: In this essay, I have proven beyond any doubt that the death penalty will discourage people from committing violent crimes, that it will save the taxpayers a lot of money, and that hardly anybody will be executed by accident.

4. **LET'S ABOLISH THE FEDERAL APPOINTMENT OF SUPREME COURT JUSTICES**

    Introduction: The constitutional provision that allows the federal government to appoint Supreme Court Justices should be amended.

    Conclusion: Fourth, the original BNA Act did not contemplate an activist role for Supreme Court justices in interpreting the Constitution in a quasi-legislative fashion. Since 1982, however, we have had the Charter of Rights and Freedoms. When the Court uses the Charter to decide a case, its members are often making new laws, not just interpreting existing law.

5.   **LEARNING A SECOND LANGUAGE**

    Introduction: In this essay I will discuss why it is important for English-speaking Canadians to speak and read more than one language. Knowing a second language helps people to explore another culture, keeps them in touch with their roots, and can make travelling much easier and more interesting. Therefore, all English-speaking Canadians should learn a second language.

    Conclusion: There are, then, three good reasons to learn a second language. First, knowing a language such as French or German enables a person to read some of the world's most important literature, philosophy, and science. Second, learning the language of our ancestors may help us to learn about our families and ourselves and may help us to preserve vanishing ways. Third, travel in Europe, Asia, South America, and even Quebec is easier when the traveller is able to speak to the people in their own language. Finally, once we have struggled to learn a new language we can understand how new-comers struggle to learn English. This can make us more patient and understanding, leading to better relations with our neighbours and co-workers.

EXERCISE 4-10
(4g)

Writing Introductions and Conclusions

Write introductory and concluding paragraphs for three of the topics listed here. Refer to the chapter for suggested strategies. Before writing, list your thesis statement and strategies on the lines below. Use a different strategy for each paragraph. Use your own paper.

TOPICS: selecting a sensible diet for life; violence in the stands at sports events; applying for a student loan; dealing with difficult neighbours; noise pollution; motorcycles; old movies; talking to your doctor; teenage marriage; computers in the classroom; science fiction monsters

ESSAY 1

Thesis Statement: _____

Strategy for Introduction:_____

Strategy for Conclusion:_____

ESSAY 2

Thesis Statement: _____

Strategy for Introduction:_____

Strategy for Conclusion:_____

ESSAY 3

Thesis Statement: _____

Strategy for Introduction:_____

Strategy for Conclusion:_____

5 *and* 6 Critical Thinking, Reading, and Writing; Writing Argument

5: CRITICAL THINKING, READING, AND WRITING

5a Understanding critical thinking

Although thinking comes naturally to you, awareness of *how* you think does not. Thinking about thinking is the key to thinking critically.

The word *critically* here has a neutral meaning. It does not mean taking a negative view or finding fault. Critical thinking is an attitude. If you face life with curiosity, you are a critical thinker. If you do not believe everything you read or hear, you are a critical thinker. If you enjoy contemplating the puzzle of conflicting theories and facts, you are a critical thinker.

5b Engaging in critical thinking

Critical thinking is a process that evolves from becoming fully aware of something to reflecting on it to reacting to it. The general process of critical thinking used in academic settings is described in the following chart.

STEPS IN THE CRITICAL THINKING PROCESS

1. **Summarize.** Get to know the literal meaning of the material. Restate to extract its main point.
2. **Analyze.** Break the whole into its component parts so you can see how they interrelate. Make inferences about unstated assumptions in the material. Evaluate it for underlying currents.
3. **Synthesize.** Connect what you have summarized and analyzed to what you know or are currently learning.
4. **Evaluate.** Judge the quality of the material on its own and as compared with related material.

5c Understanding the reading process

Purposes for reading vary. In college and university, most reading involves reading to learn new information, to appreciate literary works, or to review notes on classes or assignments. These types of reading involve rereading.

Your purpose in reading determines the speed at which you can expect to read. When you are hunting for a particular fact, you can skim the material until you come to what you want. When you read material about a subject you know well, you can move somewhat rapidly through most of it, slowing down when you come to new material. When you are unfamiliar with the subject, your brain needs time to absorb the new material, so you have to read slowly.

5d Engaging in the reading process

The full meaning of a passage develops on three levels: the literal, the inferential, and the evaluative. Most people stop reading at the literal level, but unless you move on to the next two steps you will not fully understand what you read.

1. Reading for literal meaning means understanding what is said. The literal level involves (a) the key facts, the central points in an argument, or the major details of plot and character, and (b) the minor details that fill out the picture.
2. Reading to make inferences means understanding what is implied (that is, indicated indirectly) but not stated. Often you have to infer information, or background, or the author's purpose.
3. Evaluative reading, necessary for critical thinking, occurs after you know an author's literal meaning and you have drawn as many inferences as possible from the material.

A major evaluative reading skill is differentiating fact from opinion. The difference between fact and opinion is sometimes quite obvious, but at other times telling fact from opinion can be tricky. Keep in mind that facts (numbers, statistics, dates, quotations) can be proven. Opinions, in contrast, reflect individual biases. Consider these examples:

OPINIONS	FACTS
The Greater Toronto Area is too crowded.	The Greater Toronto Area has the largest population of any urban area in Canada — over 4 million people.
Living in the Northwest Territories must be lonely.	The Northwest Territories have a population density of only 0.02 persons per square kilometre.
Quebec has the best autumn in the country.	Quebec's nickname is *la belle province*.

5e Engaging in critical reading

To read critically is to think about what you are reading while you are reading it. You can use some specific approaches, such as reading systematically and reading actively and closely.

To read systematically is to use a structured plan for delving into the material. First preview the material. Then read it carefully, seeking full meaning at all levels. Finally, review what you have read.

To read actively and closely is to annotate as you read. Annotation means writing notes in a book's margin or in a notebook, underlining or highlighting key passages, or using other codes that alert you to special material. Experiment to find what works best for you.

5f Distinguishing between summary and synthesis

A crucial distinction in critical thinking, critical reading, and writing resides in the differences between summary and synthesis. In the process of critical thinking, summary comes before synthesis.

To **summarize** is to condense the main message or central point of a passage. It is the gist of what the author is saying.

To **synthesize** is to connect what you are reading to what you already know or are currently learning. You cannot synthesize effectively until you have first summarized the material.

5g Writing a critical response

A critical response essay has two missions: to summarize a source's main idea and then to respond to the main idea with your reactions based on your synthesis. A well-written critical response accomplishes these two missions with grace and style.

5h Assessing evidence critically

The most important part of reasoning is evidence—facts, statistics, examples, and expert opinion. You will locate much of your evidence in secondary sources, which you should evaluate according to whether they are authoritative, reliable, well known, and current.

GUIDELINES FOR USING EVIDENCE EFFECTIVELY

1. **Evidence should be plentiful.** In general, the more evidence, the better. A survey that draws upon 100 people is more likely to be reliable than a survey involving only ten.
2. **Evidence should be representative.** Do not trust a statement if it is based on only some members of the group being discussed; it must be based on a truly *representative*, or typical, sample of the group.
3. **Evidence should be relevant.** Be sure the evidence you present truly supports your point and is not simply an interesting but irrelevant fact. For example, declining enrolment at a college *might* indicate poor teaching—but it also might indicate a general decline in the student population of the area, a reduction in available financial aid, higher admissions standards, or any number of other factors.
4. **Evidence should be accurate.** Evidence must come from reliable sources.
5. **Evidence should be qualified.** Avoid words such as *all, certainly, always,* or *never.* Conclusions are more reasonable if they are qualified with words such as *some, many, a few, probably, possibly, may, usually,* and *often.*

5i Assessing cause and effect critically

Cause and effect is a type of thinking that seeks the relationship between two or more pieces of evidence. You may seek either to understand the effects of a known cause or to determine the cause or causes of a known effect.

GUIDELINES FOR EVALUATING CAUSE AND EFFECT

1. **Clear relationship.** Causes and effects normally occur in chronological order: *First* a door slams; *then* a pie that is cooling on a shelf falls. However, a cause-and-effect relationship must be linked by more than chronological sequence. The fact that B happened after A does not prove that it was caused by A.
2. **A pattern of repetition.** To establish the relationship of A to B, there must be proof that every time A was present, B occurred.
3. **No oversimplification.** The basic pattern of cause and effect—single cause, single effect—rarely gives the full picture. Most complex social or political problems have *multiple causes*, not a single cause and a single effect.

cause 1
cause 2 ⟶ produce ⟶ effect B
cause 3

Similarly, one cause can produce *multiple effects*:

                                                             effect 1
cause A ⟶ produces ⟶ effect 2
                                                             effect 3

5j Assessing reasoning processes critically

Induction and **deduction** are reasoning processes. They are natural thought patterns that people use every day to think through ideas and to make decisions.

Induction is the process of arriving at general principles from particular facts or instances. Suppose you go to the supermarket and when you get home you notice that the eggs are smashed because the packer put a melon on top of them. The next week you come home from the market after the same person has bagged your groceries to find that a package of spaghetti has split open. The week after that the same packer puts a container of yogurt in upside down. It opens and you have to wash your groceries before you can put them away. You decide never to go on that person's line again because you want your groceries packed properly. You have arrived at this conclusion by means of induction.

Once you have become convinced that a certain grocery packer at your supermarket does a sloppy job, you will probably stay off that person's line—even if it is the shortest one. Your reasoning might go like this:

A. That grocery packer smashes groceries.
B. I can choose to get on that person's line or not.
C. If I choose to get on that person's line, my groceries will get smashed.

You reached this decision by means of deduction. Deduction moves from two or more general principles (A and B above) to a conclusion (C) about a specific instance.

A COMPARISON OF INDUCTIVE AND DEDUCTIVE REASONING		
	INDUCTION	**DEDUCTION**
Where the argument begins	with specific evidence	with a general claim
Type of conclusion	a general claim	a specific statement
Main use	to discover something new	to apply what is known

5k Recognizing and avoiding logical fallacies

Logical fallacies are flaws in reasoning that lead to illogical statements. They tend to occur most often when ideas are being argued. Most logical fallacies masquerade as reasonable statements, but they are in fact attempts to manipulate readers. Logical fallacies are known by labels that indicate how thinking has gone wrong. Some examples of logical fallacies are *hasty generalization, false analogy, begging the question, irrelevant argument, false cause, self-contradiction, red herring, argument to the person, guilt by association, jumping on the bandwagon, irrelevant authority, card-stacking, the either-or fallacy, appeal to ignorance,* and *ambiguity.*

6: WRITING ARGUMENT

When **writing argument** for your courses, you seek to convince a reader to agree with you concerning a topic open to debate. A written argument states and supports one position about the debatable topic. Support for that position depends on evidence, reasons, and examples chosen for their direct relation to the point being argued.

Written argument differs from everyday, informal arguing. Informal arguing often originates in anger and might involve bursts of temper or unpleasant emotional confrontations. An effective written argument, in contrast, sets forth its position calmly, respectfully, and logically.

6a Choosing a topic for a written argument

When you choose a topic for written argument, be sure that it is open to **debate.** Be careful not to confuse facts with matters of debate. A fact is the name of a university course or how many credits are required in a university curriculum. An essay becomes an argument when it takes a position concerning the fact or other pieces of information. For example, some people might think that postsecondary students should be free to choose whatever courses they want, while other people might think that certain courses should be required of all students.

A written argument could take one of these opposing positions and defend it. If you cannot decide what position to agree with because all sides of an issue have merit, do not get blocked. Instead, concentrate on the merits of one position, and present that position as effectively as you can.

6b Developing an assertion and a thesis statement for a written argument

An assertion is a statement that reflects a position about a debatable topic that can be supported by evidence, reasons, and examples (see 4c). The assertion acts as a preliminary form of your thesis statement. Although the wording of the assertion often does not find its way into the essay itself, the assertion serves as a focus for your thinking and your writing.

TOPIC	Buying on credit
ASSERTION	Buying on credit can be helpful.
ASSERTION	Buying on credit can be dangerous.

Next, based on your assertion, you compose a **thesis statement** (see 2n) to use in the essay. It states the *exact* position that you present and support in the essay.

THESIS STATEMENT	Buying on credit enables people to make necessary purchases without straining their budgets.
THESIS STATEMENT	Buying on credit causes people to go dangerously into debt.

To stimulate your thinking about the topic and your assertion about the topic, use the techniques for gathering ideas explained in 2e–k. Jot down your ideas as they develop. Many writers of arguments make a list of the points that come to mind. Use two columns to visually represent two contrasting points of view. Head the columns with labels that emphasize contrast: for example, *agree* and *disagree* or *for* and *against.*

6c Considering the audience for written argument

When a topic is emotionally charged, chances are high that any position being argued will elicit either strong agreement or strong disagreement in the reader. For example, topics such as abortion, capital punishment, and gun control arouse very strong emotions in many people.

The degree to which a reader might be friendly or hostile can influence what strategies you use to try to convince that reader. For example, when you anticipate that many readers will not agree with you, consider discussing common ground before presenting your position. Common ground in a debate over capital punishment might be that both sides agree that crime is a growing problem. Once both sides agree about the problem, there might be more tolerance for differences of opinion concerning whether capital punishment is a deterrent to crime.

6d Using the classical pattern for written argument

No one structure fits all written argument. However, for college and university courses, most written arguments include certain elements.

CHECKLIST FOR INFORMATIVE WRITING

1. **Introductory paragraph**: Sets the context for the position that is argued in the essay. (See 4g.)
2. **Thesis statement**: States the position being argued. In a short essay, it often appears at the end of the introductory paragraph. (See 2n.)
3. **Background information**: Gives the reader basic information needed for understanding the position being argued. This information can be part of the introductory paragraph or can appear in its own paragraph.
4. **Reasons or evidence**: Supports the position being argued. This material is the heart of the essay. The discussion of each reason or type of evidence usually consists of a general statement backed up with specific details or specific examples. Depending on the length of the essay, one or two paragraphs are devoted to each reason or type of evidence. The best order for presenting support depends on the impact you want to achieve. (See 4c.)
5. **Anticipation of opposing positions**: Mentions positions in opposition to the one being argued and responds to them briefly. This counter-argument can appear in its own paragraph, just before the conclusion or immediately after the introduction.
6. **Concluding paragraph**: Brings the essay to a logical end. It does not cut off the reader abruptly. (See 4g.)

6e Using the Toulmin model for argument

The Toulmin model for argument has recently gained popularity among teachers and students because it clarifies the major elements in an effective argument. The terms used in the Toulmin model may seem unfamiliar, but the concepts are ones you have encountered before.

ELEMENTS IN THE TOULMIN MODEL OF ARGUMENT

TOULMIN'S TERM	MOST FAMILIAR TERM
the claim	the main point
the support	data or other evidence
the warrant	underlying assumptions

6f Defining terms in written argument

When you **define terms,** you clarify the meaning of key words. Key terms are words that are central to your message. Key terms that are **open to interpretation** should be replaced with other, more specific terms.

NO	Buying on credit is bad.
YES	Buying on credit encourages people to buy things they do not need.
YES	Buying on credit makes it hard to see how much one is actually spending.

Some key terms might **vary with the context** of a discussion and should be explained. Abstract words such as *love, freedom,* and *democracy* have to be explained because they have different meanings in different situations.

Many students wonder whether they should use actual dictionary definitions in an essay. Looking up words in the dictionary to understand precise meanings is a very important activity for writers. Quoting a dictionary definition, however, is rarely wise. Using an **extended definition** is usually more effective. See the extended definition of an ice cream cone in 4f.

6g Reasoning effectively in written argument

The basis for a debatable position is often personal opinion or belief, and in such cases it is unrealistic to expect to change someone's mind with one written argument. Nevertheless, you still have an important goal: to convince your reader that your point of view has value. You can achieve this by combining three strategies:

1. **Be logical:** use solid evidence; analyze cause and effect carefully; and distinguish between fact and opinion.

6h

2. **Enlist the emotions of the reader:** appeal to the values and beliefs of the reader, usually by arousing the "better self" of the reader.

3. **Establish credibility:** show that you can be relied upon as a knowledge-able person with good sense by being accurate and not distorting facts.

6h **Establishing a reasonable tone in written argument**

To achieve a reasonable tone, **choose your words carefully.** Avoid exagger-ations and artificial language (see 21e). No matter how strongly you disagree with op-posing arguments, never insult the other side. Name-calling is impolite, shows poor self-control, and demonstrates poor judgment.

Distinguishing Fact from Opinion

EXERCISE 5-1
(5d)

Identify each passage as *fact* or *opinion*. Be prepared to explain your answers.

EXAMPLES Once people had little choice in what they ate.   fact

They would have preferred our food.   opinion

A. 1. The diet of prehistoric people
        was confined to what they could gather or catch.   _____
    2. Control of fire enabled people to cook their food.   _____
    3. Cooking undoubtedly improved the taste.   _____
    4. Gradually people learned to plant seeds and tame animals.   _____
    5. Planting and herding allowed people to settle in one place.   _____
    6. Some people must have longed for their former nomadic life.   _____
    7. Early civilizations sprang up in areas that could produce
        bountiful crops.   _____
    8. The fact that some could produce more than they needed
        freed others for nonagricultural chores.   _____
    9. Farming cannot have been very difficult if one person
        could produce so much food.   _____
   10. With such abundance I imagine many became wasteful.   _____
   11. People gradually learned to preserve food by curing, drying,
        and pickling.   _____
   12. My favourite pickle is the sweet gherkin.   _____
   13. Bacon is a form of cured meat still popular today.   _____
   14. Dried fruit does not taste as good as fresh fruit.   _____
   15. Some dehydration machines on today's market are great.   _____

B. 1. An international survey puts Canada in tenth place
        worldwide in the number of foreign tourists who visit.   _____
    2. Nine other countries are more interesting places to visit
        than Canada.   _____
    3. The fall in the value of the dollar may have encouraged
        more foreigners to visit Canada recently.   _____
    4. The Rocky Mountains attract crowds of tourists every year.   _____
    5. Banff, Alberta, is probably the most scenic spot in Canada.   _____
    6. Tourists from Japan can find salespeople in Banff who are
        able to serve them in their own language.   _____
    7. Banff National Park was Canada's first national park.   _____
    8. No other national park in Canada receives more visitors
        each year than Banff National Park.   _____

EXERCISES

Name_____ Date _____

9. With its galleries and museums, Ottawa is as worthwhile
   a place to visit as Montreal or Toronto.   _____

10. Métis architect Douglas Cardinal designed the Canadian
    Museum of Civilization in Hull, Quebec.   _____

11. Cardinal's masterpiece is superior to architect Moshe
    Safdie's National Gallery of Art in Ottawa.   _____

12. No other building in the National Capital Region has
    attracted as much controversy as Safdie's.   _____

13. The Peace Tower rises high above the Parliament Buildings.   _____

14. With the Peace Tower, the Parliament Buildings form the
    most beautiful architectural ensemble in Ottawa.   _____

7 Parts of Speech and Sentence Structures

PARTS OF SPEECH

Knowing grammar helps you understand how language works. Grammar describes the forms and structures of words. In this way, it offers an explanation of how language operates and how words make meaning to deliver their messages. Grammar also sets down the standards accepted by people who write and speak for educated audiences.

If you know the parts of speech, you have a basic vocabulary for identifying words, their various forms, and the sentence structures they build. The first part of this chapter explains each part of speech to help you identify words and their functions. Being able to do this is important because sometimes the same word can function as more than one part of speech. To identify a word's part of speech, you have to see how the word functions in a sentence.

We drew a **circle** on the ground. [*Circle* is an noun.]

Sometimes planes **circle** the airport before landing. [*Circle* is a verb.]

Running is good exercise. [*Running* is a noun.]

Running shoes can be very expensive. [*Running* is an adjective.]

7a Recognizing nouns

A **noun** names a person, place, thing, or idea.

Most nouns change form to show number: *week, ox* (singular); *weeks, oxen* (plural) (see 22c). Nouns also change form for the possessive case: *the mayor's decision* (see 27a). Nouns function as subjects (7k), objects (7l), and complements (7m): ***Marie** saw a **fly** in the **soup*** (subject, direct object, object of preposition); ***Marie** is a **vegetarian*** (subject, subject complement).

Articles often appear with nouns. The articles are *a, an*, and *the*, and they signal whether a noun is meant generally or specifically in a particular context.

Give me **a** pen. [General: any pen will do.]

Give me **the** pen on the desk. [Specific: only one pen will do.]

NOUNS		
PROPER	Names specific people, places, or things (first letter is always capitalized)	**John Lennon** **Paris** **Buick**
COMMON	Names general groups, places, people, things, or activities	**singer** **city** **car** **talking**
CONCRETE	Names things that can be seen, touched, heard, smelled, tasted	**landscape** **pizza** **thunder**
ABSTRACT	Names things *not* knowable through the five senses	**freedom** **shyness**
COLLECTIVE	Names groups	**family** **team** **committee**
NONCOUNT OR MASS	Names "uncountable" things	**water** **time**
COUNT	Names countable items	**lake** **minute**

7b Recognizing pronouns

A **pronoun** takes the place of a noun.

Peter is an engineer. [noun]

He is an engineer. [pronoun]

The word (or words) a pronoun replaces is called its **antecedent.**

Some pronouns change form to show **number:** *I, she, yourself* (singular); *we, they, themselves* (plural). Many pronouns change form to show **case:** *I, who* (subjective); *me, whom* (objective); *my, mine, whose* (possessive) (see Chapter 9).

PRONOUNS		
Personal *I, you, they, we, her, its, our,* and others	Refers to people or things	I saw **her** take **your** books to **them**
Relative *who, which, that, what, whomever,* and others	Introduces certain noun clauses and adjective clauses	**Whoever** took the book **that** I left must return it.
Interrogative *who, whose, what, which,* and others	Introduces a question	**Who** called?
Demonstrative *this, these, that, those*	Points out the antecedent	Is **this** a mistake?
Reflexive; Intensive *myself, yourself, herself, themselves,* and all *-self* or *-selves* words	Reflects back to the antecedent; intensifies the antecedent	They claim to support **themselves.** I **myself** doubt it.
Reciprocal *each other, one another*	Refers to individual parts of a plural antecedent	We respect **each other.**
Indefinite *all, anyone, each*	Refers to nonspecific persons or things	**Everyone** is welcome here.

7c Recognizing verbs

A **main verb** expresses an action, an occurrence, or a state of being.

I **leap**. [action]

Claws **grab**. [action]

The sky **becomes** cloudy. [occurrence]

He **seems** sad. [state of being]

A **linking verb** connects a subject with one or more words—called a **subject complement**—that rename it or describe it.

Georges Vanier **was** Governor General. [*Georges Vanier* = subject, *was* = linking verb, *Governor General* = subject complement]

Georges Vanier **was** popular. [*Georges Vanier* = subject, *was* = linking verb, *popular* = subject complement]

The most common linking verb is *be* (8e). Verbs describing the workings of the senses sometimes function as linking verbs: *feel, smell, taste, sound, look*, and so on. Other linking verbs include *appear, seem, become, remain*, and *grow*.

Auxiliary verbs, also known as **helping verbs**, are forms of *be, do, have*, and several other verbs that combine with main verbs to make verb phrases.

This season many new television series **have imitated** last year's hit shows. [*have* = auxiliary, *imitated* = main verb, *have imitated* = verb phrase]

Programs **are becoming** more and more alike. [*are* = auxiliary, *becoming* = main verb, *are becoming* = verb phrase]

Soon we **may** not **be able to tell** the programs apart. [*may be able* = auxiliary verb, *to tell* = main verb, *may be able to tell* = verb phrase]

7d Recognizing verbals

Verbals are made from verb parts but they cannot function as verbs, because they do not change form to show time (tense) changes. They function as nouns, adjectives, or adverbs.

VERBALS AND THEIR FUNCTIONS		
TYPE	**FUNCTION**	**EXAMPLE**
Infinitive *to* + simple form of verb	1. Noun: names an action, state, or condition	**To eat** now is inconvenient.
	2. Adjective or adverb: describes or modifies	Still, we have far **to go**.
Past participle *-ed* form of regular verb	Adjective: describes or modifies	**Boiled, filtered** water is usually safe to drink.
Present participle *-ing* form of verb	1. Noun (called a gerund) 2. Adjective: describes or modifies	**Running** water may not be safe.

7e Recognizing adjectives

An **adjective** modifies—that is, describes—a noun or a pronoun. Adjectives also modify word groups—clauses and phrases—that function as nouns.

He received a **low** grade on the first quiz. [*Low* modifies noun *grade*.]

His second grade was **higher**. [*Higher* modifies noun phrase *his second grade*.]

That he achieved a B average was **important**. [*Important* modifies noun clause *that he achieved a B average*.]

Descriptive adjectives such as *low* and *higher* show levels of "intensity," usually by changing form (*low, lower, lowest*). For more information about these changes, see Chapter 12.

Determiners are sometimes called **limiting adjectives**. Articles, one type of these limiting adjectives, are discussed in 7a. The chart that follows lists types of determiners.

DETERMINERS (LIMITING ADJECTIVES)

Articles
a, an, the

The students made **a** bargain.

Demonstrative
this, these, that, those

Those students rent **that** house.

Indefinite
any, each, other, some, few, and others

Few films today have complex plots.

Interrogative
what, which, whose

What answer did you give?

Numerical
one, first, two, second, and others

The **fifth** question was tricky.

Possessive
my, your, their, and others

My violin is older than **your** cello.

Relative
what, which, whose, whatever, whichever, whoever

We don't know **which** road to take.

7f Recognizing adverbs

An **adverb** modifies—that is, describes—a verb, an adjective, another adverb, or a clause.

In winter the ice on ponds may freeze **suddenly**. [*Suddenly* modifies verb *may freeze.*]

It is **very** tempting to go skating. [*Very* modifies adjective *tempting.*]

People die **quite** needlessly when they fall through the ice. [*Quite* modifies adverb *needlessly.*]

Always wait until the ice has thickened enough to hold your weight. [*Always* modifies entire clause.]

Most adverbs are easily recognized because they are formed by adding -*ly* to adjectives (*wisely, quickly, devotedly*). Yet some adjectives also end in -*ly* (*motherly, chilly*). Also, many adverbs do not end in -*ly* (*very, always, not, yesterday, well*). See Chapter 12 for an explanation of how confusion between adverbs and adjectives can be avoided.

Conjunctive adverbs are a group of adverbs that function (1) to modify the sentences to which they are attached, and (2) to help create logical connections in meaning between independent clauses.

CONJUNCTIVE ADVERBS AND THE RELATIONSHIPS THEY EXPRESS	
RELATIONSHIP	**WORDS**
Addition	*also, furthermore, moreover, besides*
Contrast	*however, still, nevertheless, conversely, nonetheless, instead, otherwise*
Comparison	*similarly, likewise*
Result or Summary	*therefore, thus, consequently, accordingly, hence, then*
Time	*next, then, meanwhile, finally, subsequently*
Emphasis	*indeed, certainly*

Construction has slowed traffic on the expressway; **therefore,** people are looking for other routes to work.

People have been complaining for weeks. **Finally,** one more lane has been opened during rush hour.

7g Recognizing prepositions

A **preposition** signals the beginning of a prepositional phrase. It is followed by a noun or pronoun (called the **object of the preposition**), and it indicates the relationship of that noun or pronoun to another word. The object of the preposition is never the subject of the sentence. Here is a list of prepositions.

about	before	despite
above	behind	down
across	below	during
after	beneath	except
against	beside	excepting
along	between	for
among	beyond	from
around	but	in
as	by	inside
at	concerning	into

like	past	underneath
near	regarding	unlike
next	round	until
of	since	up
off	through	upon
on	throughout	with
onto	till	within
out	to	without
outside	toward	
over	under	

Prepositional expressions are formed by combinations of single-word prepositions.

according to	due to	instead of
along with	except for	in the midst of
apart from	in addition to	on account of
as for	in back of	on top of
as regards	in case of	out of
as to	in front of	up to
because of	in lieu of	with reference to
by means of	in place of	with regard to
by reason of	in regard to	with respect to
by way of	in spite of	with the exception of

A **prepositional phrase** consists of a preposition (or prepositional expression), its object, and any modifying words. A prepositional phrase always starts with a preposition: *above their heads, in the pool, in front of the store.*

7h Recognizing conjunctions

A **conjunction** connects words, phrases, or clauses. **Coordinating conjunctions** join two or more grammatically equivalent structures.

COORDINATING CONJUNCTIONS

and	or	for
but	nor	so
		yet

And, but, yet, or, and *nor* can join like structures of any kind: two or more nouns, verbs, adjectives, adverbs, phrases, and all types of clauses.

Joe is majoring in Computer Technology **and** Engineering. [nouns]

He finds his course interesting **but** demanding. [adjectives]

In his spare time, he works on his car, **and** he helps care for his grandfather. [independent clauses]

For and *so* can connect only independent clauses.

> Joe helps his grandfather, **for** he does not want the man to move to a nursing home.

Correlative conjunctions function in pairs, joining equivalent grammatical constructions.

CORRELATIVE CONJUNCTIONS

both . . . and	neither . . . nor
either . . . or	not only . . . but (also)
whether . . . or	

> **Both** industrialized **and** agricultural nations are developing new strategies to protect the environment.

Subordinating conjunctions begin certain dependent clauses that function as modifiers.

SUBORDINATING CONJUNCTIONS

after	even though	though	where
although	if	unless	wherever
as	once	until	whether
because	since	when	while
before	so that	whenever	

> **Because** of the unpredictability of hurricanes, many lives are lost each year.
> People sometimes refuse to evacuate **although** they are warned in plenty of time.

 ## 7i Recognizing interjections

An **interjection** is a word or expression used to convey surprise or other strong emotions. An interjection can stand alone, usually punctuated with an exclamation point, or can be part of a sentence, usually set off with commas. Interjections occur only rarely in academic writing.

> **Oh** no!
> **Darn!** I lost my keys.
> **Well,** how much will it cost to fix my car?

SENTENCE STRUCTURES

 ## 7j Defining the sentence

The *sentence* can be defined in several ways. On its most basic level, a sentence starts with a capital letter and finishes with a period, question mark, or exclamation point. Sentences can be classified according to purpose. Most sentences are **declarative;** they make a statement.

> Pizza is fattening.

Some sentences are **interrogative;** they ask a question:

> How fattening is pizza?

Some sentences are **imperative;** they give a command:

> Give me a pizza!

Some sentences are **exclamatory;** they exclaim:

> What a large pizza!

Grammatically, a sentence contains at least one **independent clause,** that is, a group of words that can stand alone as an independent unit, in contrast to a **dependent clause,** which cannot stand alone. Sometimes a sentence is described as a "complete thought," but the concept of "complete" is too vague to be useful.

To begin your study of the sentence, consider its basic structure. A sentence consists of two parts: a subject and a predicate.

7k Recognizing subjects and predicates

The **simple subject** is the word or group of words that acts, is acted upon, or is described. In the sentence *The saxophonist played*, the simple subject is the one word *saxophonist*. The **complete subject** is the simple subject and all the words related to it.

> The **pianist** sang. [simple subject]
>
> **The new pianist** sang. [complete subject]

A subject can be **compound,** that is, can consist of two or more nouns or pronouns and their modifiers.

> **The audience** and **the club manager** applauded. [compound subject]

The **predicate** is the part of the sentence that says what the subject is doing or experiencing, or what is being done to the subject. The predicate usually comes after its subject, and it always contains a verb. The **simple predicate** contains only the verb. The **complete predicate** is the simple predicate and all the words related to it.

> The pianist **sang.** [simple predicate]
>
> The pianist **sang beautifully.** [complete predicate]

A predicate can be **compound,** that is, consisting of two or more verbs.

> The pianist **sang** and **swayed.** [compound predicate]

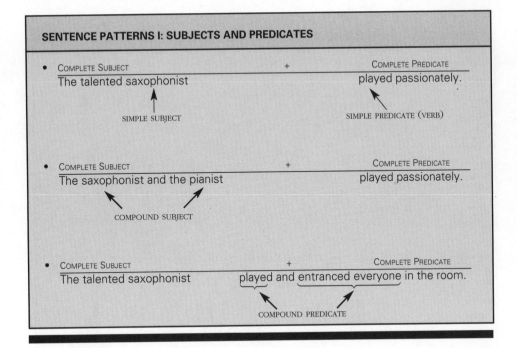

SENTENCE PATTERNS I: SUBJECTS AND PREDICATES

- COMPLETE SUBJECT + COMPLETE PREDICATE
  The talented saxophonist   played passionately.
  SIMPLE SUBJECT   SIMPLE PREDICATE (VERB)

- COMPLETE SUBJECT + COMPLETE PREDICATE
  The saxophonist and the pianist   played passionately.
  COMPOUND SUBJECT

- COMPLETE SUBJECT + COMPLETE PREDICATE
  The talented saxophonist   played and entranced everyone in the room.
  COMPOUND PREDICATE

---

71   Recognizing direct and indirect objects

1   Recognizing direct objects

A **direct object** occurs in the predicate of a sentence. It receives the action of a transitive verb (8f), completing its meaning.

Their agent called **the music critics.** [direct object]

To find the direct object, make up a *whom?* or *what?* question about the verb. (The agent negotiated what? *A contract.* The agent called whom? *The music critics.*) A direct object may be compounded:

They played **their hit** and **a new song.**

2   Recognizing indirect objects

An **indirect object** occurs in the predicate of a sentence. It answers a *to whom?, for whom?, to what?,* or *for what?* question about a verb.

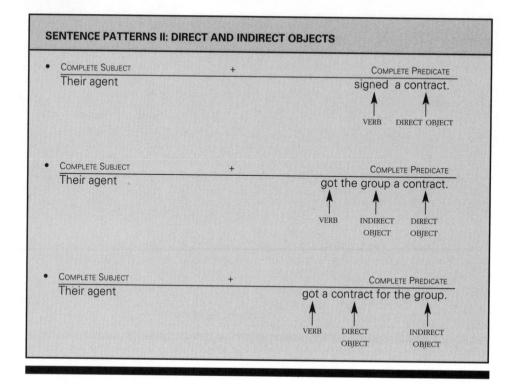

He tried to get **them** an album deal. [indirect object]

7m Recognizing complements, modifiers, and appositives

1 Recognizing complements

A **complement** occurs in the predicate of a sentence. It renames or describes the subject or object. A **subject complement** is a noun, pronoun, or adjective that follows a linking verb, such as *was* or *seems*, and renames or describes the subject.

The owner was **a jazz lover.** [noun as subject complement]

The owner was **generous.** [adjective as subject complement]

An **object complement** is a noun or adjective that immediately follows the direct object and either renames or describes it.

The group considered itself **lucky.** [adjective as object complement]

The owner called them **exceptional.** [adjective as object complement]

He began to consider himself **a patron of the arts.** [noun phrase as object complement]

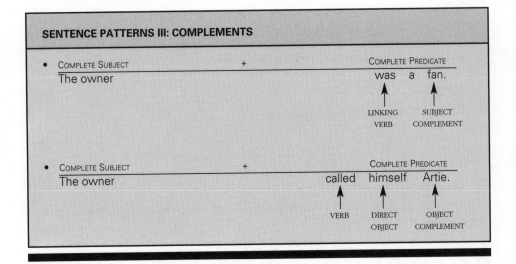

SENTENCE PATTERNS III: COMPLEMENTS

- COMPLETE SUBJECT + COMPLETE PREDICATE
  The owner / was a fan.
  LINKING VERB / SUBJECT COMPLEMENT

- COMPLETE SUBJECT + COMPLETE PREDICATE
  The owner / called himself Artie.
  VERB / DIRECT OBJECT / OBJECT COMPLEMENT

2 Recognizing modifiers

Modifiers are words or groups of words that describe other words. There are two basic kinds of modifiers: adjectives and adverbs.

Adjectives modify only nouns or words acting as nouns, such as pronouns, noun phrases, or noun clauses. They may appear in the subject or the predicate of a sentence.

> The **talented** saxophonist played a **mellow** tune. [Adjective *talented* modifies noun *saxophonist.*; adjective *mellow* modifies noun *tune.*]

Adverbs modify verbs, adjectives, other adverbs, or independent clauses. They may appear in the subject or the predicate of a sentence.

> The audience responded **warmly.** [Adverb *warmly* modifies verb *responded.*]

> They swayed **quite** excitedly in their seats. [Adverb *quite* modifies adverb *excitedly.*]

> **Enthusiastically,** they demanded more. [Adverb *enthusiastically* modifies independent clause.]

3 Recognizing appositives

An **appositive** is a word or group of words that renames the word or group of words preceding it. Generally, appositives are nouns used to rename other nouns, although adjectives and verbs are also sometimes renamed by appositives.

The group's manager, **Jon Franklin,** was ready to take the next step. [*Jon Franklin* renames the noun *manager.*]

He picked his targets: **the record companies and the television shows.** [*The record companies and the television shows* renames the noun *targets.*]

7n Recognizing phrases

A **phrase** is a group of words that lacks a subject or a predicate (7k). Phrases function as parts of speech. They cannot stand alone as sentences.

A **noun phrase** functions as a noun in a sentence.

Some political terms have unusual histories.

The seating plan in the French legislature during their Revolution gives us our names for political radicals, conservatives, and moderates.

A **verb phrase** functions as a verb in a sentence.

The members **were seated** in a semicircular room. The most radical members **were located** to the left of the chairperson's platform, the more conservative to the right.

A **prepositional phrase** functions as an adjective or adverb. It is formed by a preposition (7g) followed by a noun or pronoun.

This arrangement enabled members **with similar views** to talk **during meetings.** [*with similar views* modifies *members; during meetings* modifies *to talk.*]

An **absolute phrase,** which consists of a participle (7d, 8b) preceded by a subject, modifies the entire sentence to which it is attached. An absolute phrase cannot stand alone as a sentence because it lacks a true verb.

The moderates being in the centre, physical fights were avoided. [*Being* is the present participle of *to be; the moderates* acts as a subject.]

Verbal phrases use forms of verbs that do not express time (7d), so they cannot function as verbs in sentences. Instead, they function as nouns or modifiers. Verbal phrases are formed with infinitives, past participles, or present participles.

Infinitive phrases contain a verb's simple form preceded usually, but not always, by the word *to.* Infinitive phrases function as nouns, adjectives, or adverbs.

Politicians love **to debate every issue.** [infinitive phrase = noun as object of verb *love*]

Physically separating politicians works **to prevent debates from becoming fist fights.** [infinitive phrase = adverb modifying verb *works*]

Gerund phrases use the present participle—a verb's *-ing* form—as a noun.

Understanding the origin of certain terms helps us recognize the repetition of historical patterns. [gerund phrase = noun functioning as sentence subject]

(In the example above, notice *recognize the repetition of historical patterns* too. It is an infinitive phrase, but one that does not use *to.*)

Participial phrases function as adjectives. They are formed from a verb's present participle—its *-ing* form—or from its past participle—the *-ed* form of a regular verb.

Imitating the French plan, we now call radicals leftists, conservatives right-wingers, and moderates centrists. [present participle phrase = adjective modifying *we*]

These labels, **copied by many governments,** continue long after the revolution that gave them birth. [past participle phrase = adjective modifying *labels*]

Telling the difference between a gerund phrase and a present participle phrase can be tricky because both contain a verb form that ends in *-ing*. Remember that a gerund phrase functions *only* as a noun, and a participial phrase functions *only* as an adjective.

Seeing liver on the dinner menu, I decided to fast. [participial phrase as adjective describing *I*]

Seeing liver on the dinner menu made me want to fast. [gerund phrase as subject of sentence]

7o Recognizing clauses

A clause is a group of words that contains a subject and a predicate (7k). Clauses are divided into two categories: **independent clauses** (also known as **main clauses**) and **dependent clauses** (including **subordinate clauses** and **relative clauses**).

1 Recognizing independent clauses

An **independent clause** contains a subject and a predicate. It can stand alone as a sentence. However, it cannot begin with a subordinating conjunction (7h) or a relative pronoun (7b) because those words make a clause dependent (7o-2).

SENTENCE PATTERNS IV: INDEPENDENT CLAUSES

THE SENTENCE
INDEPENDENT CLAUSE

COMPLETE SUBJECT	+	COMPLETE PREDICATE
The saxophonist		played.

---

2   Recognizing dependent clauses

A **dependent clause** contains a subject and a predicate and usually starts with a word that makes the clause unable to stand alone as a sentence. A dependent clause must be joined to an independent clause.

Some dependent clauses start with **subordinating conjunctions** such as *although, because, when, until.* A subordinating conjunction indicates a relationship between the meaning in the dependent clause and the meaning in the independent clause. For a chart listing these relationships, see 17f.

Because clauses that start with subordinating conjunctions function as adverbs, they are called **adverb clauses** (or sometimes **subordinate clauses**).

They modify verbs, adjectives, other adverbs, and entire independent clauses. Adverb clauses may appear in different parts of sentences, but they always begin with a subordinating conjunction. They usually answer some question about the independent clause: *how? why? when?* or *under what conditions?*

Many Canadians wait to travel to Europe **until they can get low air fares.**

If a family has relatives in another country, an international vacation can be relatively inexpensive.

The number of Canadians visiting Eastern Europe has grown rapidly **since the Iron Curtain fell in 1989.**

✿ PUNCTUATION ALERT: When an adverb clause comes before an independent clause, separate the clauses with a comma. ✿

Since the Iron Curtain fell in 1989, the number of Canadians visiting Eastern Europe has grown rapidly.

Other dependent clauses act as adjectives. These **adjective clauses** (also called **relative clauses**) start with relative pronouns such as *who, which,* and *that* or relative adverbs such as *when* or *where.* Adjective clauses modify nouns, pronouns, and groups of words functioning as nouns.

The word starting an adjective clause refers to something specific—an antecedent—in the independent clause.

The concert hall, **which held 12 000 people,** was sold out in one day.

The tickets **that I bought** were the last ones in the balcony.

See 10f for a discussion of when to use *who, which,* or *that.* See 24e for a discussion of when to use commas with relative clauses.

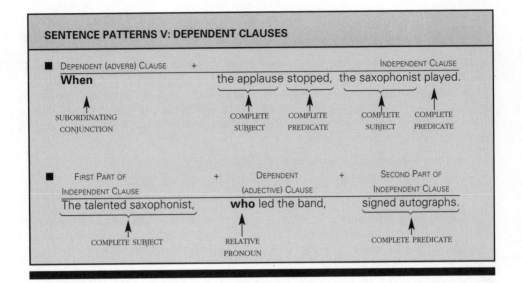

Noun clauses function as subjects, objects, or complements. Noun clauses begin with many of the same words as adjective clauses: *that, who, which* (in all their forms), as well as *when, where, whether, why,* or *how*. Noun clauses do not modify. They replace a noun or pronoun with a clause.

It depends on your generosity. [pronoun as subject]

Whether I can buy the camera depends on your generosity. [noun clause as subject]

Whoever wins the contest will appear in publicity photos. [noun clause as subject]

Because they start with similar words, it is easy to confuse noun clauses and adjective clauses. A noun clause *is* a subject, or complement; an adjective clause *modifies* a subject, object, or complement. The word at the start of an adjective clause has a specific antecedent elsewhere in the sentence; the word that starts a noun clause does not.

Elliptical clauses are grammatically incomplete in order to be brief and to the point. Usually the omission is limited to *that, which,* or *whom* in adjective clauses, the subject and verb in adverb clauses, or the second half of a comparison.

Lima is one of the places **[that] I want to visit this summer.** [relative pronoun omitted from adjective clause]

After [I visited] São Paolo, I decided to return to South America. [subject and verb omitted from adverb clause]

An apartment has less storage space **than a house [has].** [second half of comparison omitted]

7p

7p Recognizing sentence types

Sentences have four basic structures: simple, compound, complex, and compound-complex.

A **simple sentence** is composed of a single independent clause with no dependent clauses. It has one subject and one predicate. However, a simple sentence is not always short. The subject or predicate may be compound, and the sentence may contain modifying words or phrases.

The beagle is one of the world's most popular dogs.

It is a member of the hound family.

The bassett and the harrier are also hounds.

A **compound sentence** is composed of two or more independent clauses joined by a coordinating conjunction or a semicolon. There are seven coordinating conjunctions: *and, but, or, nor, for, so,* and *yet.* Compound sentences operate according to principles of coordination.

❖ PUNCTUATION ALERT: A comma is usually put before a coordinating conjunction that joins two independent clauses. ❖

The beagle is know for its large, velvety ears, **but** its hazel eyes are even more attractive.

The beagle is believed to be one of the oldest breeds of hounds, **and** it is still used to hunt.

A **complex sentence** is composed of one independent clause and one or more dependent clauses.

❖ PUNCTUATION ALERT: A comma is usually put after a dependent clause when it occurs before an independent clause. ❖

Because it has an erect, white-tipped tail, the beagle can be seen and followed even in high grass and bushes.

Although the beagle lost some of its popularity at the beginning of this century, it has become recognized as the ideal pet for anyone **who wants a medium-sized hound.**

A **compound-complex sentence** contains two or more independent clauses and one or more dependent clauses.

The beagle gets along well with other dogs **since it is a pack animal, and** it is patient with boisterous children **who might be too rough to allow near less sturdy pets.**

Although the beagle can be a delight, it is not an easy animal to keep **because it loves to wander off hunting and investigating,** so an owner needs to be alert.

Name_____ Date _____

Identifying Nouns

Underline all the nouns. Write them on the lines to the right

EXAMPLE   Many <u>people</u> have now seen, or at least heard about, "<u>e-books</u>." ___people___   ___"e-books"___

1. Some observers say that e-books will replace books printed on paper.   _____ _____
2. It is essential to distinguish between these digital books and the appliances used for reading them.   _____ _____
3. At its simplest, a digital book is an electronic version of a printed work.   _____ _____
4. It is created by scanning a PDF file.   _____ _____
5. The appliance that reads it is a device that resembles a small laptop.   _____ _____
6. Costing a few hundred dollars, these appliances feature screens but no keyboards.   _____ _____
7. They run for a long time on batteries and can store several books.   _____ _____
8. Some of these appliances are designed to work with your own library of downloaded digital books.   _____ _____
9. Without the appliance, you would be unable to read the books, which are encrypted and stored on your computer.   _____ _____
10. Other devices use modems to download works directly from electronic libraries over the same lines used by telephones and faxes.   _____ _____
11. Some companies are producing software that will enable digital books to be displayed on any personal computer.   _____ _____
12. Even so, digital books may never be as popular as their traditional counterparts.   _____ _____
13. Screens do not offer a pleasant environment for reading very long texts.   _____ _____
14. In addition, highlighting or annotating a digital book is awkward.   _____ _____
15. Certain types of books, however, are popular in electronic form.   _____ _____

16. They include dictionaries, encyclopedias, directories, commercial catalogues, and manuals. _____ _____

17. Readers of this type of book are generally looking for a small amount of specific information. _____ _____

18. When doing lengthy reading, however, people seem to prefer to print out on-screen text. _____ _____

19. They are using paper—a simple but effective viewing technology—as their preferred interface. _____ _____

Identifying Pronouns

Underline all the pronouns. Write them on the lines to the right. If a sentence contains no pronouns, write *none* on the line.

EXAMPLE Since the 1930s, scientists have been trying to get chimpanzees to communicate with <u>them</u>. ___*them*___ _____

1. In the 1940s, one couple raised a chimpanzee named Vickie in their home. _____ _____

2. They treated her as if she were a human child. _____ _____

3. They tried to teach Vickie to say English words by shaping her mouth as she made sounds. _____ _____

4. She learned to say only three words: *Mama, Papa,* and *cup.* _____ _____

5. Even that was amazing because chimpanzees do not have the right vocal structures to produce human sounds. _____ _____

6. Realizing this, scientists in the 1960s began teaching sign language to their chimpanzees. _____ _____

7. Chimpanzees have their own ways of communicating among themselves. _____ _____

8. One chimpanzee was taught over a hundred words in American Sign Language. _____ _____

9. She also formed her own original sentences. _____ _____

10. She would even hold simple conversations with anyone who knew sign language. _____ _____

11. Other chimpanzees were trained to ask for what they wanted by pressing a series of symbols on a computer keyboard. _____ _____

12. Chimpanzees are not the only animals whose trainers "talk" with them. _____ _____

EXERCISES

Name_____ Date _____

13. Gorillas, dolphins, and even parrots supposedly can _____ _____
    communicate with us.
14. Not everyone believes this is possible. _____ _____
15. Some say members of different species can have _____ _____
    only limited communication with one another.
16. What do you think about animal speech? _____ _____
17. Would you want to have conversations with your _____ _____
    pets?

EXERCISE 7-3
(7c)

Identifying Verbs

Underline all verbs, including complete verb phrases. Write them on the lines to the right.

EXAMPLE Everyone <u>desires</u> a happy life. ___*desires*___ _____

1. These tips can lead to such a life. _____ _____
2. Always recognize your good qualities. _____ _____
3. Everyone has positive traits, such as sympathy _____ _____
   or generosity.
4. You should think of these qualities often. _____ _____
5. Sometimes, another person may cause us _____ _____
   problems.
6. Discuss that problem with a friend or a loved one. _____ _____
7. You might also ask yourself several questions. _____ _____
8. Who is at fault, and why is that person at fault? _____ _____
9. Always take responsibility for your part of the _____ _____
   problem.
10. A solution to the problem may require a joint _____ _____
    effort.
11. What else might lead to a happy life? _____ _____
12. Tolerate other people's behaviours. _____ _____
13. Accept their differences. _____ _____
14. Also, do not dwell upon the past mistakes of _____ _____
    your own life.
15. Mistakes are part of a continuous learning _____ _____
    process.

16. Without mistakes, you might not learn the
    right way.

    _____ _____

17. Look back at all your successes, not your
    failures.

    _____ _____

18. Be available to assist others.

    _____ _____

19. They would do the same for you in most cases.

    _____ _____

20. Above all, always find time for relaxation, and
    enjoy everything around you.

    _____ _____

Identifying Forms of Verbs

EXERCISE 7-4
(7c–d)

Decide if each italicized word or phrase is a verb, an infinitive, a past participle, a present participle, or a gerund (a present participle used as a noun). Write your answers on the lines to the right.

EXAMPLE   Perfume *refers* to a fragrant fluid preparation with
an appealing scent.

_____verb_____

1. The word "perfume" *originates* from the Latin "per fumum,"
   which can be translated as "through smoke."

   _____

2. *Scenting* the body is a custom that dates back to the ancient
   Egyptians.

   _____

3. Once the Egyptians had learned how *to extract* the scent from
   flower petals, they then burned natural oils to scent temples,
   private homes, and royal palaces.

   _____

4. There *is* evidence that even Egyptian tombs were scented with
   fragrant ointments and oils.

   _____

5. The Egyptian discovery eventually *spread* to all parts of Europe.

   _____

6. An Arab physician discovered a way to produce a *distilled* fluid
   that could be used in the perfume-making process.

   _____

7. This process greatly *reduced* the cost of making the essential
   oils that went into perfume.

   _____

8. The first modern perfume to combine *scented* oils that were
   blended into alcohol was made in 1370.

   _____

9. Europeans *called* it "Hungary Water," since the perfume was
   created by order of Queen Elizabeth of Hungary.

   _____

10. Some records *suggest* that the perfume industry prospered
    in Renaissance Italy.

    _____

11. *To improve* the industry, Catherine de Medici's personal
    perfumer searched for a way to refine perfume in the
    sixteenth century.

    _____

Name_____ Date _____

12. During the 1500s, many *considered* France to be the perfume   _____
centre of Europe.
13. Louis XIV, who was dubbed the "perfume king," was   _____
responsible for the industry's *increasing* popularity.
14. Much later, fragrance makers in Paris, like Chanel, contributed   _____
their names to the *growing* industry.
15. France still *produces* some of the most expensive fragrances   _____
in the world.   _____
16. *To increase* the size of the market, manufacturers have extended   _____
the industry to men.
17. There *are* many different categories of perfume, including floral   _____
blends, which are the most popular.   _____
18. *Gaining* popularity is the spice-blends category, which consists   _____
of aromas like clove, cinnamon, and nutmeg.
19. Men's perfume *derives* from fragrances such as citrus, spice,   _____
and lavender.
20. Perfumes are also cleverly used *to hide* undesirable smells   _____
common to paints and cleaners.

| EXERCISE **7-5** |
| (7e) |

Identifying Adjectives

Underline all adjectives, except the articles *a, an*, and *the*. Write them on the lines to the right.

EXAMPLE   The abacus is a <u>useful</u> instrument.   *useful*   _____

1. It allows people to perform arithmetical   _____   _____
calculations.
2. The most familiar form of the abacus is the   _____   _____
Chinese *suan p'an*.
3. It is made of small beads that are strung on   _____   _____
parallel wires.
4. The wires are in a rectangular frame.   _____   _____
5. The first abacus was composed of a straight   _____   _____
row of shallow grooves in the sand, into which
pebbles were placed.
6. Later models used firm slate or boards, which   _____   _____
allowed the entire abacus to be moved.

7. On the portable abacus, pebbles are arranged in order along the parallel lines. _____   _____

8. The value of each pebble is determined by its exact position, not by its unique shape. _____   _____

9. The abacus works on the fundamental principle of place-value notation. _____   _____

10. With this ingenious system of notation, only a few beads are needed to represent large numbers. _____   _____

11. The beads are given numerical values when they are shifted in one direction. _____   _____

12. Calculations are made as each bead changes from its previous position. _____   _____

13. The bead's first value is erased after it has been moved to a new position. _____   _____

14. Moving the beads allows the counter to be reused for other calculations. _____   _____

15. The abacus is a memory aid for a person making mental calculations. _____   _____

16. The abacus is still widely used today among the Asian peoples, as well as in Russia. _____   _____

17. The Japanese culture uses the *soroban* form of the abacus. _____   _____

18. Russian society uses the *tschoty* form. _____   _____

19. At one time, people in Canada typically used calculating machines to perform their complex calculations. _____   _____

20. These machines performed physical calculations rather than the mental calculations that the abacus was used for. _____   _____

Name_____ Date _____

EXERCISE 7-6
(7f)

Identifying Adverbs

Underline all the adverbs and circle all the conjunctive adverbs. Remember that some phrases or clauses can function as adverbs. Write your answers on the lines to the right. If there are no adverbs, write *none* on the line.

EXAMPLE   Chimpanzees, <u>commonly</u> called chimps, belong to the ape family; (however) they form the single species, *Pan troglodytes*.

	Adverb	Conj. Adverb
	commonly	*however*

1. Chimps only inhabit the tropical rain forests of central Africa.

2. They are the most intelligent of all apes.

3. Chimps are also the most easily taught.

4. Typically, except for a white patch near its rump, the chimp's coat of fur is black; however, its face is mostly bareskinned and may be black, spotted, or pale.

5. Chimpanzee hands, feet, and ears have a more pinkish tone.

6. Chimps are extremely noisy; indeed, they will often shriek, scream, and slap the ground.

7. However, when humans enter their territory, the chimps usually quiet down.

8. While living in the forest, chimps do not just swing from branch to branch to get around.

9. They are also quite skilled in the ability to walk on the ground.

10. Generally, chimps walk on all fours; still, they do sometimes walk and run in an upright position, much like a human.

11. In fact, when standing erect, a chimp may be from 1.25 to 1.75 metres tall.

Identifying Prepositions and Their Objects

Underline all prepositions and circle their objects. Write them on the lines to the right.

	Prepositions	Objects
EXAMPLE The bicycle has been a form of (local transportation) for (years)	*of*	*local transportation*
	for	*years*

1. In China, there are over 300 million bicycles on the road.

2. The bicycle began to develop after the creation of a French model, the *célérifère*.

3. The *célérifère*, a type of foot-powered scooter, had a stationary front wheel, unlike those that followed.

4. Until the invention of a German baron solved the problem of the stationary front wheel, the *célérifère* could not be steered.

5. Karl von Drais developed the first steerable wheel for his new bicycle, called the *draisienne*.

6. Several years later, in a Scottish workshop, blacksmith Kirkpatrick MacMillan created the first bicycle with pedals.

7. The pedals were attached to the rear wheels and were controlled by means of cranks.

8. During the 1860s, the French *vélocipède*, which had pedals attached to the front wheels, was introduced.

9. In England in 1876, H. J. Lawson developed a bicycle made with a chain and sprocket that controlled the front wheel.

10. Just nine years later, J. K. Starley developed the "safety bicycle," which became the prototype for today's bicycle.

11. Instead of a larger front wheel, Starley's bicycle had wheels that were equal in size.

12. During the 1880s, pneumatic tires, rubber tires filled with compressed air, were introduced.

13. The two- and three-speed hub gears, along with the derailleur gear, were developed in the 1890s.

14. Later developments of the bicycle led to attempts to motorize it.

7-8

Name_____ Date _____

Identifying Conjunctions

Underline all coordinating and subordinating conjunctions. Write them in column 1. Then indicate the type of conjunction by writing CC or SC in column 2.

	1	**2**
EXAMPLE <u>Although</u> headaches are sometimes symptoms of disease, most headaches are only temporary.	*although*	*SC*
1. Usually, headaches occur apart from other symptoms, and they leave no aftereffects.	_____	_____
2. Headaches are often caused when tension puts a strain on the muscles of the head and neck.	_____	_____
3. Headaches are also possible if a person gets too little or too much sleep.	_____	_____
4. Being in a noisy room can also give a person a headache before she has a chance to leave.	_____	_____
5. The brain tissues themselves do not ache because the brain has no feeling.	_____	_____
6. The pain of a headache comes from the muscles of the head and face where feeling nerves are plentiful.	_____	_____
7. The cause of a particular headache may be a mystery, but there are only two basic causes of headaches.	_____	_____
8. The first kind is called a tension headache, for it is caused by strain on the face, neck, and scalp muscles whenever a person is under stress.	_____	_____
9. Vascular headaches, the second kind, occur when blood vessels in the head swell and press against nearby tissues.	_____	_____
10. Generally, headaches are nothing to worry about unless they occur more than three times a week.	_____	_____

Identifying the Parts of Speech: Review

Write the part of speech of each underlined word on the corresponding numbered line.

Chewing[1] gum was discovered[2] in the 1860s during[3] a search for rubber materials.[4] Gum is very much a North American product[5] and[6] it is rarely[7] found anywhere outside Canada and the United States. The recipe for[8] chewing gum received[9] its[10] first patent in 1869. The basic raw material used[11] for all gum is the natural gum known as chicle. Since[12] it is very expensive and hard to obtain, synthetic[13] materials and other natural gums are often used in place of[14] chicle. Bubble gum differs[15] from regular gum because it is made[16] with[17] rubber latex, a compound that provides[18] the gum with the strength to make a bubble. Sugarless gum is made[19] from[20] sugar alcohols,[21] such as xylitol and mannitol, not[22] from regular sugar. North American wholesale[23] factory sales of chewing gum have often[24] approximated one billion[25] dollars.

1._____   10._____   18._____

2._____   11._____   19._____

3._____   12._____   20._____

4._____   13._____   21._____

5._____   14._____   22._____

6._____   15._____   23._____

7._____   16._____   24._____

8._____   17._____   25._____

9._____

Name_____ Date _____

Identifying Subjects and Predicates

A: Draw a line in each of these sentences to separate the complete subject from the complete predicate.

EXAMPLE The ice in a skating rink / does not melt.

1. Warm air cannot melt the ice.
2. The temperature beneath the ice is kept very low.
3. This keeps the ice from melting even in the sun.
4. The ice at a figure-skating rink is 5 centimetres thick.
5. Ice hockey rinks have slightly thicker layers of ice.
6. The ice is on a concrete floor.
7. The concrete contains 2.5-centimetre pipes located no more than 5 centimetres apart.
8. An Olympic-sized rink has about 16 kilometres of piping.
9. A very cold liquid, like the antifreeze in cars, circulates through the pipes.
10. The liquid absorbs heat from the concrete.
11. Machinery keeps the liquid at $-3°$ to $-8°C$.
12. More and more people are enjoying an afternoon of skating at an ice rink.

B: Draw a single line under the simple subject and a double line under the verb. Be sure to underline the complete verb and all parts of compound subjects and verbs. Write them on the lines to the right.

	Subject	*Verb*
EXAMPLE Most <u>Canadians</u> <u>brush</u> their teeth daily.	*Canadians*	*brush*
1. The original toothbrushes were simply twigs with one soft, shredded end.	_____	_____
2. People rubbed these "chew sticks" against their teeth.	_____	_____
3. The first genuine toothbrushes originated in China 500 years ago.	_____	_____
4. The bristles came from hogs.	_____	_____
5. Hogs living in the cold regions of China grew stiff bristles.	_____	_____
6. During this time, few Europeans brushed their teeth regularly.	_____	_____
7. Horsehair toothbrushes and small sponges were used by some Europeans.	_____	_____

8. Many men and women picked their teeth clean after meals. _____ _____

9. The stems of feathers or special toothpicks were employed for this. _____ _____

10. Brass or silver toothpicks were safer than animal-hair toothbrushes. _____ _____

11. Germs developed on animal bristles, leading to frequent infections. _____ _____

12. There was no solution to this problem until the 1930s. _____ _____

13. The discovery of nylon led to a big change in the toothbrush industry and made tooth care easier. _____ _____

14. Nylon was tough and resisted the growth of germs. _____ _____

15. The first nylon-bristle brushes were sold in North America in 1938. _____ _____

16. Unfortunately, they were very hard on gums. _____ _____

17. Soft gum tissue scratched and bled easily. _____ _____

18. In the 1950s, a new, softer version of the nylon toothbrush was developed. _____ _____

19. It cost five times as much as the old, harder brushes. _____ _____

20. With this development, dental care improved. _____ _____

21. Dentists and oral surgeons have made some suggestions for dental health. _____ _____

22. Toothbrushes should be used regularly and should be replaced every few months. _____ _____

23. Bent bristles are useless in cleaning teeth and can cut gums. _____ _____

| EXERCISE **7-11** |
| (7I) |

Identifying Objects

Draw a single line under all direct objects and a double line under all indirect objects. Not all sentences have both. Write your answers on the lines to the right.

		Direct Object	*Indirect Object*
EXAMPLE	Indian guests at the first Massachusetts colony Thanksgiving gave the Pilgrims popcorn.	*popcorn*	*Pilgrims*

1. Parents in the American colonies served their children popcorn with cream and sugar for breakfast. _____ _____

7-12

Name_____ Date _____

2. Earlier, West Indians had sold Columbus necklaces _____ _____
   made of popcorn.
3. The Aztec Indians of Mexico wore strings of _____ _____
   popcorn in their religious ceremonies.
4. By the 1880s, people could buy their friends special _____ _____
   machines to pop corn.
5. People had to buy themselves popcorn in 25-pound _____ _____
   sacks.
6. Stores charged customers one dollar for such a _____ _____
   sack.
7. North Americans could buy electric poppers begin- _____ _____
   ning in 1907.
8. By the 1940s, most movie theatres sold their _____ _____
   customers popcorn.
9. Another popular food has a more recent origin. _____ _____
10. In Frankfurt, Germany, butchers sold people hot _____ _____
    dogs.
11. Immigrants sold New Yorkers the first American hot _____ _____
    dogs at Coney Island in 1871.
12. In 1904 they started giving customers buns to _____ _____
    protect their hands.
13. Before that, it was common to lend customers _____ _____
    gloves.
14. That must have cost the vendors a fortune. _____ _____

EXERCISE 7-12
(7m–1)

Identifying Complements

Decide if each italicized word is a subject complement or an object complement. Indicate your answer by writing *SC* or *OC* in column 1. Then indicate if it is a noun or an adjective by writing *N* or *Adj* in column 2.

	1	*2*
EXAMPLE Chocolate is *delicious*.	SC	Adj
1. Strawberries are not true *berries*.	_____	_____
2. They are an *offshoot* of the rose plant family.	_____	_____
3. Strawberries taste *sweet*.	_____	_____

4. Harpo Marx was not a *mute*. _____ _____
5. Many considered his silence *charming*. _____ _____
6. In fact, friends have called him *talkative*. _____ _____
7. Many people consider elephants *fearless*. _____ _____
8. However, mice can make them *frantic* with fright. _____ _____
9. Carrots are not a *remedy* for poor eyesight. _____ _____
10. This belief is a *myth*. _____ _____
11. Only for improving night vision are they *helpful*. _____ _____
12. India ink is not *Indian*. _____ _____
13. It is *Chinese*. _____ _____
14. Lions are *cats*, or felids. _____ _____
15. Many people mistakenly call them the *rulers* of the cat family. _____ _____
16. Yet the largest cat is the *tiger*. _____ _____
17. The Siberian tiger is the *king* of all felids. _____ _____
18. A rabbit is a *lagomorph*. _____ _____
19. It is not a *rodent*. _____ _____
20. Its distinguishing feature is its *digestive system*. _____ _____
21. People mistakenly consider pigs *dirty*. _____ _____
22. Yet pigs are very *clean* _____ _____
23. Often, their owners leave pig sties *unclean*. _____ _____

Identifying and Using Adjectives and Adverbs

EXERCISE **7-13**
(7m–2)

A: Decide if each italicized word is an adjective or an adverb. Write your identifications on the lines to the right.

EXAMPLE   Aspirin is the *most*[a] *frequently*[b] *used*[c] painkiller in the world.

a. *adverb* _____

b. *adverb* _____

c. *adjective* _____

1. It is *related*[d] to an *old*[e] folk-remedy made from the bark of the willow tree.

d. _____

e. _____

2. Aspirin was *originally*[f] made by a *French*[g] scientist.

f. _____

g. _____

Name_____ Date _____

3. However, the discoverer did not realize what a *truly*[h] *important*[i] medicine it was.

4. The formula was *ignored*[j] for *forty*[k] years.

5. In 1893, a *young*[l] *German*[m] chemist was looking for a cure for his father's arthritis.

6. *Luckily,*[n] he tried the *Frenchman's*[o] formula.

7. The mixture got rid of his father's pain *almost*[p] *completely*[q]

8. Chemists at the Bayer Company *quickly*[r] realized this was a *key*[s] discovery.

9. Bayer began producing aspirin in 1899, and it *soon*[t] became the most *prescribed*[u] drug in the world.

10. *Every*[v] year *new*[w] discoveries are made about aspirin's benefits.

h._____
i._____
j._____
k._____
l._____
m._____
n._____
o._____
p._____
q._____
r._____
s._____
t._____
u._____
v._____
w._____

B: Fill in the blanks in each sentence with adjectives or adverbs as needed. Write your answers in column 1, and in column 2 identify each as an adjective or an adverb.

	1	*2*
EXAMPLE I had a (an) _____ day with my sister.	terrific	adjective
1. We left very _____ this morning.	_____	_____
2. The highway was _____ , so we hit no traffic.	_____	_____
3. Since the sun was _____ shining we kept the sunroof open.	_____	_____
4. Her _____ car is fun to drive.	_____	_____
5. We arrived at the museum _____ earlier than we thought we would.	_____	_____

6. We _____ found a (an) _____ parking   _____   _____
   spot right near the main entrance.

7. _____ , since we were both so hungry,   _____   _____
   there was a (an) _____ cafe right next to
   the museum that was serving breakfast.

8. After strolling around the museum, we both   _____   _____
   knew what we _____ wanted to do next:
   visit the _____ museum gift shop.

9. We bought a (an) _____ vase for our   _____   _____
   mother's birthday next week; _____ , it
   was on sale.

10. _____ , we headed for home, because both   _____   _____
    of us were _____ exhausted from a great day
    out together.

Identifying Appositives

Appositives in these sentences have been italicized. On the lines to the right, write the words or phrases modified by the appositives.

EXAMPLE Foster Hewitt, *a young journalist*,   *Foster Hewitt*
             became an early sports broadcaster.

1. Hewitt made his first radio broadcast of a hockey game, a   _____
   minor-league contest, on March 22, 1923.

2. Some people say that this match, *an otherwise forgotten game*   _____
   between Kitchener and Toronto Parkdale, was the occasion of
   the world's first hockey broadcast.

3. At the rink, Hewitt spoke through a telephone, *itself a fairly re-*   _____
   cent invention.

4. His telephoned commentary was received by a radio transmit-   _____
   ter, *the means by which his words reached the radio audience.*

5. Later, Hewitt was given his own broadcasting studio, *a small*   _____
   glass booth at the rink, equipped with a radio set.

6. Hewitt also broadcast the first game played at Maple Leaf   _____
   Gardens, *home of Toronto's NHL team*, in 1931.

7. His broadcasts, *a Saturday night tradition for decades*, helped   _____
   create the legend of the great Maple Leaf teams of long ago.

8. Hewitt invented the famous shout *"He shoots, he scores!"*   _____

9. If he could have collected royalties on this phrase, *a favourite*   _____
   cry of generations of Canadian children, he would have become
   a very wealthy man.

Name_____ Date _____

10. Over the years, countless French-speakers listened in amuse-   _____
    ment to Hewitt's attempts to pronounce the names *Léo Boivin*
    and Yvan Cournoyer.

11. In the 1950s, *the "Age of Television,"* Hewitt began broadcasting   _____
    televised hockey games.

12. Hewitt's son *Bill* began to take over the television work in the   _____
    1960s.

13. Still, it was Foster Hewitt, *the veteran play-caller,* who was cho-   _____
    sen to announce the 1972 series between Canada and the Soviet
    Union.

14. Hewitt later said that this series, *the one featuring Paul*   _____
    Henderson's winning goal, was the highlight of his long career.

Identifying Phrases

A: Identify the italicized phrases, and write on the lines to the right *NP* for a noun phrase,
      VP for a verb phrase, *PP* for a prepositional phrase, and *AP* for an absolute phrase.

EXAMPLE   Many people live in fear *of going bald.*   *PP*

1. Going bald is *something one has little control over.*   _____

2. Some people *have tried* hair transplants or toupees.   _____

3. *A few people* just shave their heads completely.   _____

4. Most of us associate baldness *with men.*   _____

5. *Their hair loss usually occurring only at the top of their heads,*   _____
   women are less likely to appear dramatically bald.

6. *The most common form of balding* is "male pattern baldness."   _____

7. In this condition, hair *is lost* from the top and front of the scalp.   _____

8. *With people normally losing up to 125 hairs per day,* finding a few   _____
   hairs in our combs should be no cause for concern.

9. New hair *is developing* constantly.   _____

10. Usually, a new hair replaces *each lost hair.*   _____

11. However, *in male pattern baldness* no replacement hairs develop.   _____

12. Male pattern baldness was once considered to be inherited *from the*   _____
    mother's side of the family.

13. *Dermatologists not believing this any longer*, bald men cannot blame _____
   their mothers.

14. Instead, many factors *appear to be involved*. _____

B: Identify the italicized verbal phrases, and write on the lines to the right *inf* for an infinitive
   phrase, *part* for a participial phrase, and *ger* for a gerund phrase.

EXAMPLE   *Understanding alcohol's effects* on the body is important.   *ger*

1. *Believing myths about drinking*, many people do not have an   _____
   accurate idea of alcohol's impact.

2. Some people say they drink *to relax*.   _____

3. *Drinking large amounts of beer*, other people deny they have a   _____
   problem because "it's only beer."

4. *Having a cup of coffee*, some claim, will make them sober enough to   _____
   drive.

5. *Putting faith* is these myths can be dangerous.   _____

6. Alcohol works *to weaken* many parts of the body.   _____

7. Drinkable alcohol, *called ethanol*, is made up of very small particles.   _____

8. *Travelling throughout the body*, these particles can quickly enter   _____
   every organ.

9. *Burning in the throat* is the first sign of damage.   _____

10. *To slow down absorption of alcohol*, avoid carbonated drinks.   _____

11. *Speeding passage of alcohol into the small intestines*, carbonated   _____
   mixers may accelerate the impact of even small amounts of alcohol.

12. *Eating before or during drinking* can slow down absorption.   _____

13. Milk products are very likely *to have* such an effect.   _____

14. *Drinking alcohol* also results in a false sense of warmth, which can   _____
   be fatal to those who then fail to dress properly in cold weather.

Identifying Dependent Clauses

> EXERCISE **7-16**
> (7o–2)

Underline all dependent clauses. Write the first and last words of each dependent clause on
the lines to the right.

EXAMPLE   Most people are unaware <u>that the potato is
   originally from Peru</u>.   <u>that . . . Peru</u>

1. Spanish explorers who came to the New World seeking gold discovered   _____
   the potato.

2. Because it is such a nutritious food, the potato is now grown in at least   _____
   130 countries.

Name_____ Date _____

3. Half a kilo of potatoes, which is more than most people eat at one _____
   time, has only about 360 calories, about 110 per potato.
4. If a potato is eaten without butter, it is 99.9 percent fat free.   _____
5. Since a hectare of potatoes produces twice as much food as two _____
   hectares of grain, it is an efficient crop.
6. The average annual world crop is about 290 million tonnes, although _____
   about half is fed to farm animals.
7. The potato produces more nutritious food more quickly on less land _____
   under poorer conditions than any other major food crop does.
8. The potato can survive almost wherever humans can.   _____
9. The jungles, where humidity causes diseases deadly to the potato, _____
   are the only parts of the world where it cannot grow.
10. When gasoline still cost only pennies a gallon, automaker Henry Ford _____
    predicted that potatoes would be used to make fuel.
11. Researchers have discovered that one hectare of potatoes can _____
    produce more than 11 000 litres of fuel a year.
12. Currently, the former Soviet Union produces one-third of the world's _____
    potatoes, while Canada produces just 1 percent.

Using Subordination

EXERCISE 7-17
(7o–2)

Using the subordinating conjunction or relative pronoun given in parentheses, join each of
these pairs of sentences. You may sometimes need to omit a word, but no major rewordings
are required.

EXAMPLE   Eight different species of potatoes are grown.
          Most North Americans know only one kind of potato. (although)
          Although most North Americans know only one kind of potato, eight different
          species are grown.

1. Potatoes grown from seed may not inherit the parent plant's characteristics.
   Potatoes are usually grown from the eye of a planted piece of potato. (since)

   _____

2. Potato blossoms look like those of the poisonous nightshade plant.
   Centuries ago, Europeans were afraid to eat potatoes. (because)

   _____

3. Tomatoes, tobacco, and eggplant are all relatives of the potato.
   They do not look alike. (although)

   _____

4. The sweet potato is not related to the potato.
   Its Indian name, *batata,* was mistakenly taken to mean "potato" by its European "discoverers." (even though)

   _____

5. The potato skin is a good source of dietary fibre.
   Most people throw it away. (which)

   _____

6. About 25 percent of Canada's potato-farming land is located in Prince Edward Island.
   This island province has only 0.1 percent of Canada's total land area. (while)

   _____

7. Would you believe something?
   Twelve percent of the U.S. potato crop is made into potato chips. (that)

   _____

8. There are misinformed people.
   They believe the potato is only a poor person's food. (who)

   _____

9. They overlook something.
   Potatoes have nourished the people of Europe since the eighteenth century. (that)

   _____

10. Nutritious potatoes allowed the population to expand until 1845.
    Europe—especially Ireland—was almost destroyed by a disease that killed the potato crop. (when)

   _____

11. Potato chips were created in New England.
    A hotel chef became angry with a fussy customer. (because)

   _____

12. The customer sent back his french fries twice, saying they were not crisp enough.
    No one else had ever complained. (although)

   _____

Name_____ Date _____

13. The chef apparently had a bad temper.
    He decided to teach the man a lesson. (who)

    _____

14. He cut the potatoes paper-thin and fried them.
    They were too crispy to pick up with a fork. (until)

    _____

15. The customer tasted these potatoes.
    He was delighted. (once)

    _____

16. The chef never got his revenge, but he did get his own restaurant.
    These "chips" became very popular. (so that)

    _____

Identifying Different Types of Sentences

EXERCISE 7-18
(7p)

Underline all subjects once and all verbs twice. Then circle and label all coordinating conjunctions (*CC*), subordinating conjunctions (*SC*), relative pronouns (*RP*), and conjunctive adverbs (*CA*). Finally, on the lines to the right, label each sentence as *simple, compound, complex,* or *compound-complex.*

EXAMPLE Forgetting is the loss of information previously   compound
         stored in the memory, (and) ᶜᶜ all of us
         have experienced it.

1. Forgetting is not always permanent.   _____

2. Interference sometimes keeps us from remembering.   _____

3. When this happens, we may not be able to stop thinking about   _____
   something else even though we know it is wrong.

4. For example, we may not recall a friend's name, and we may even _____
   want to call her by someone else's name.

5. Other times, we try hard to remember, but our memories may not _____
   work at all.

6. The information seems lost until we receive a clue that helps us re- _____
   member.

7. Some scientists believe that memories may completely fade away, _____
and then we can never get them back.

8. Recent studies show that storing memory changes the brain tissue. _____

9. However, no one has shown that these changes can be erased, so _____
the "fading-away" theory of forgetting remains unproven.

10. Scientists who believe in the interference theory of forgetting iden- _____
tify different kinds of interference.

11. Sometimes learning new material is made difficult by conflicting old _____
material.

12. Confusion between the old material and the new makes it hard to _____
remember either one.

13. Coming upon similar material soon after learning something can also _____
interfere.

14. Scientists have shown this in experiments, but everyday experience _____
can convince us too.

15. Anyone trying to learn two similar languages, such as French and _____
Spanish, at the same time knows the feeling of confusion.

Writing Different Types of Sentences

EXERCISE **7-19**
(7p)

A: Combine these groups of simple sentences according to the directions in parentheses. It will be necessary to add coordinating conjunctions, subordinating conjunctions, or relative pronouns. Sometimes it will be necessary to drop or change a few words. Since most passages can be combined in several ways, take the time to draft a few alternatives and then select the version you like best. Try to use at least one elliptical clause in this exercise.

EXAMPLE   Sometimes people repress their memories. They cannot recall anything about an event. (compound)
Sometimes people repress memories, so they cannot recall anything about _____
an event. _____

1. Psychoanalysis helps people deal with these forgotten memories.
Psychoanalysis works at exploring them consciously. (compound)

_____

_____

2. Repression can make life difficult.
Repression is the burying in the unconscious of fearful experiences. (complex)

_____

_____

EXERCISES

Name_____ Date _____

3. People repress frightening thoughts and experiences.
   Then they try to go on living normally. (compound)

   _____

   _____

4. People repress experiences.
   They avoid having to relive them.
   They feel better for a time. (compound-complex)

   _____

   _____

5. Experiments show something.
   People forget bad experiences quickly.
   People forget good experiences less quickly. (complex)

   _____

   _____

6. Repression occurs in the mentally ill.
   It occurs also in mentally healthy people. (compound)

   _____

   _____

7. A certain kind of learning atmosphere leads to better memory.
   This kind of learning atmosphere is the kind where people can relax. (complex)

   _____

   _____

8. Any student knows this.
   So does any teacher. (compound)

   _____

   _____

9. People are often distracted in stressful situations.
   They simply do not see everything.
   Therefore, they cannot remember everything. (compound-complex)

   _____

   _____

10. This may explain something.
    Accident victims often do not recall details of their experiences. (complex)

    _____

    _____

11. Many people do not remember much from their childhoods.
    This does not mean that they are repressing bad memories. (compound)

    _____

    _____

12. They may have been too interested in some events to notice any others.
    These other events were happening at the same time.
    Maybe their childhoods were simply too boring to remember. (compound-complex)

    _____

    _____

B: Using independent and dependent clauses, expand each of these simple sentences,
     making a compound, then a complex, and finally a compound-complex sentence.

EXAMPLE   He is always late.

          (compound) *He is always late, and his brother is always early.*

          (complex) *He is always late because he oversleeps.*

          (compound-complex) *He is always late when there is a test, so the teacher is
          moving him to a later class.*

 1. Fast food is not cheap.

    (compound) _____

    (complex) _____

    (compound-complex) _____

    _____

 2. The movie theatre was crowded.

    (compound) _____

    (complex) _____

    (compound-complex) _____

    _____

Name_____ Date _____

3. Read contracts before you sign them.

    (compound) _____

    (complex) _____

    (compound-complex) _____

    _____

4. Ice cream is a popular dessert.

    (compound) _____

    (complex) _____

    (compound-complex) _____

    _____

5. Grocery stores should be open twenty-four hours a day.

    (compound) _____

    (complex) _____

    (compound-complex) _____

    _____

C: Write complete sentences by adding one or more independent clauses to each of these subordinate clauses.

EXAMPLE   if I have a chance
          If I have a chance, I'll learn to draw.

1. because she speaks Cantonese

    _____

2. whoever found my keys

    _____

3. before you rule on the motion from the floor

    _____

4. even though he had a valid ticket

    _____

5. where my cat has gone

_____

6. that she bought from a sidewalk vendor

_____

7. who has the floppy disk with my essay

_____

8. since she took an Internet tutorial

_____

9. whether this boa constrictor is the friendly one

_____

10. if the sky looks threatening

_____

8 Verbs

8a Understanding verbs

Verbs convey information about what is happening, what has happened, and what will happen. In English, a verb tells of an action (*move, juggle, race*), an occurrence (*become, change, happen*), or a state of being (*be, seem, feel, exist*).

North Americans **enjoy** sports. [action]

Football **becomes** more popular every year. [occurrence]

Soccer **is** a new favourite of many people. [state of being]

Verbs convey information through their person, number, tense, mood, and voice. Three types of verbs are **main verbs, linking verbs,** and **auxiliary verbs.**

VERB FORMS

8b Recognizing the forms of main verbs

Every main verb has five forms. The simple form is also known as the dictionary form or the base form. The simple form shows action (or occurrence or state of being) taking place in the present for *I, you, we,* and *they: I travel, they explore.*

The past-tense form indicates an action or occurrence or state of being completed in the past. The past tense of all regular verbs adds final *-ed* or *-d* to the simple form. Many verbs, however, are irregular. That is, their past-tense forms, and often their past participles as well, either change in spelling or use different words instead of adding *-ed* or *-d; ring, rang, rung; fly, flew, flown.* The principal parts of common irregular verbs are listed in 8d. Except for the past tense of *be* (8e), the past tense form of each verb is the same for all persons and numbers.

The past participle is the third form. In regular verbs, the past participle has the same form as the past tense. However, for many irregular verbs these forms differ and must be memorized (see 8d).

To function as a verb, a past participle must combine with an auxiliary verb (8e) in a **verb phrase.** Verb phrases formed with past participles make the **perfect** tenses (8i) and **passive** constructions (8n): *I have succeeded; they are shocked.* For a discussion of other uses of the past participle, see 7d.

The present participle adds *-ing* to the simple form. To function as a verb, a present participle combines with a subject and one or more auxiliary verbs. Otherwise, present participles function as adjectives.

The infinitive uses the simple form, usually but not always following *to*. The infinitive functions as a noun, adjective, or adverb, not a verb.

8c Using the *-s* form of verbs

Except for *be* and *have* (8e), all verbs in the present tense add an *-s* or *-es* ending to the simple form when the subject is third person singular: *Everybody likes candy.*

Be and *have*—irregular verbs—do not use their simple forms in the third person singular of the present tense. Instead, *be* uses *is* and *have* uses *has*:

Candy **is** fattening; it **has** a lot of calories.

8d Using regular and irregular verbs

A **regular verb** is one that forms its simple past and past participle by adding *-ed* or *-d* to the simple form. Most verbs in English are regular: *walk, walked, walked; bake, baked, baked.* Some regular verbs, however, require spelling changes at the end of the simple form: *deny, denied.* (See 22e.)

Some speakers omit the *-ed* sound in the past tense. If you are unused to hearing or pronouncing this sound, particularly before a word beginning with a *t* or *d*, you may forget to add it when you write the past tense or past participle. Nevertheless, written English requires the *-ed* ending.

About two hundred of the most common verbs in English are **irregular:** They do not add the *-ed* or *-d* to form the past tense or past participle. They form the past and past participle in different ways. Some irregular verbs change an internal vowel in the simple form to make the past tense and past participle: *ring, rang, rung.* Some change an internal vowel and add an ending other than *-ed* or *-d: rise, rose, risen.* Some use the simple form throughout: *cost, cost, cost.*

Unfortunately, a verb's simple form does not indicate whether the verb is irregular or regular. If you do not know the principal parts of a verb you are using, you need to find them in a college dictionary.

COMMON IRREGULAR VERBS

SIMPLE FORM	PAST TENSE	PAST PARTICIPLE
arise	arose	arisen
awake	awoke *or* awaked	awaked *or* awoken
be (is, am, are)	was, were	been
bear	bore	borne *or* born
beat	beat	beaten
become	became	become
begin	began	begun
bend	bent	bent
bet	bet	bet
bid (offer)	bid	bid
bid (command)	bade	bidden
bind	bound	bound
bite	bit	bitten *or* bit
blow	blew	blown
break	broke	broken
bring	brought	brought
build	built	built
burst	burst	burst
buy	bought	bought
cast	cast	cast
catch	caught	caught
choose	chose	chosen
cling	clung	clung
come	came	come
cost	cost	cost
creep	crept	crept
cut	cut	cut
deal	dealt	dealt
dig	dug	dug
dive	dived *or* dove	dived
do	did	done
draw	drew	drawn
drink	drank	drunk
drive	drove	driven
eat	ate	eaten
fall	fell	fallen
feed	fed	fed

COMMON IRREGULAR VERBS *(continued)*

SIMPLE FORM	PAST TENSE	PAST PARTICIPLE
feel	felt	felt
fight	fought	fought
find	found	found
flee	fled	fled
fling	flung	flung
fly	flew	flown
forbid	forbade *or* forbad	forbidden
forget	forgot	forgotten *or* forgot
forgive	forgave	forgiven
forsake	forsook	forsaken
freeze	froze	frozen
get	got	got *or* gotten
give	gave	given
go	went	gone
grow	grew	grown
hang (suspend)*	hung	hung
have	had	had
hear	heard	heard
hide	hid	hidden
hit	hit	hit
hurt	hurt	hurt
keep	kept	kept
know	knew	known
lay	laid	laid
lead	led	led
leave	left	left
lend	lent	lent
let	let	let
lie	lay	lain
light	lighted *or* lit	lighted *or* lit
lose	lost	lost
make	made	made
mean	meant	meant
pay	paid	paid
prove	proved	proved *or* proven

*When it means to execute by hanging, hang is a regular verb: "In wartime, armies routinely hanged deserters."

➔

COMMON IRREGULAR VERBS *(continued)*

SIMPLE FORM	PAST TENSE	PAST PARTICIPLE
put	put	put
quit	quit	quit
read	read	read
rid	rid	rid
ride	rode	ridden
ring	rang	rung
rise	rose	risen
run	ran	run
say	said	said
see	saw	seen
seek	sought	sought
send	sent	sent
set	set	set
shake	shook	shaken
shine (glow)*	shone	shone
shoot	shot	shot
show	showed	shown *or* showed
shrink	shrank	shrunk
sing	sang	sung
sink	sank *or* sunk	sunk
sit	sat	sat
slay	slew	slain
sleep	slept	slept
sling	slung	slung
speak	spoke	spoken
spend	spent	spent
spin	spun	spun
spring	sprang *or* sprung	sprung
stand	stood	stood
steal	stole	stolen
sting	stung	stung
stink	stank *or* stunk	stunk
stride	strode	stridden
strike	struck	struck
strive	strove	striven
swear	swore	sworn

*When it means to polish, shine is a regular verb: "We shined our shoes."

COMMON IRREGULAR VERBS *(continued)*

SIMPLE FORM	PAST TENSE	PAST PARTICIPLE
sweep	swept	swept
swim	swam	swum
swing	swung	swung
take	took	taken
teach	taught	taught
tear	tore	torn
tell	told	told
think	thought	thought
throw	threw	thrown
understand	understood	understood
wake	woke *or* waked	waked *or* woken
wear	wore	worn
wring	wrung	wrung
write	wrote	written

8e Using auxiliary verbs

The verbs *be, do,* and *have* function both as main verbs and as auxiliary (or helping) verbs. Auxiliary verbs combine with main verbs to make verb phrases. *Be*, the most common verb in English, is the most irregular as well.

THE FORMS OF *BE*

Simple Form	be
Past Tense	was, were
Past Participle	been
***-s* Form**	is
Present Participle	being

PERSON	PRESENT TENSE	PAST TENSE
I	am	was
you (singular)	are	were
he, she, it	is	was
we	are	were
you (plural)	are	were
they	are	were

Do and *have* are not as irregular as *be*.

THE FORMS OF *DO* AND *HAVE*

Simple Form	do	**Simple Form**	have
Past Tense	did	**Past Tense**	had
Past Participle	done	**Past Participle**	had
***-s* Form**	does	***-s* Form**	has
Present Participle	doing	**Present Participle**	having

When used as main verbs, forms of *be* are **linking verbs.** They join a subject to a **subject complement** (7m-l), a word or group of words that renames or describes the subject.

Water pollution **is** a danger to many communities. [*is* = linking verb, *water pollution* = subject, *a danger to many communities* = subject complement]

Underground streams **are** sources of well water. [*are* = linking verb, *underground streams* = subject, *sources of well water* = subject complement]

When used alone as main verbs, *have* is transitive and *do* can be transitive. Transitive verbs must be followed by a direct object (see 8f).

Combined with participles of main verbs, forms of *be* and *have* are **auxiliary verbs,** or **helping verbs,** that help the participles to show tense (8i, j) and mood (8l).

I **am waiting.** [auxiliary verb *am* + present participle *waiting* = present progressive tense]

The news **has been expected** for days. [auxiliary verb *has* + auxiliary verb *been* + past participle *expected* = present perfect tense in the passive voice]

The auxiliary verbs *will* and *shall* help to create two tenses: the future (*I shall try, you will pass*) and, with *have* and past participles of main verbs, the future perfect (*I shall have tried, you will have passed*). *Will* and *shall* never change form. Formal writing reserves *shall* for the first person (*I, we*) and *will* for all other persons (*you, he, she, it, they*).

The verbs *can, could, may, might, should, would, must,* and *ought to* are called **modal auxiliary verbs.** Modal auxiliary verbs have only one form; they do not change, no matter what constructions they appear in.

Modal auxiliaries add to the main verb a sense of needing, wanting, or having to do something, or a sense of possibility, permission, or ability.

The ant **can carry** many times its own weight. [ability]

Ants **may be observed** gathering around crumbs on the sidewalk. [possibility]

We **must sweep** up dropped food or we **might attract** ants in our homes. [necessity, possibility]

Always use the simple form of the verb after a modal auxiliary.

8f Using intransitive and transitive verbs

The difference between *I see clearly* and *I see a fire* is that the first sentence tells *how* the subject does something while the second points to *what* the subject does. In the first sentence, the verb is **intransitive**, while in the second it is transitive—the action of the verb carries over to whatever is named in the **direct object**. Many verbs in English can be both intransitive and transitive depending upon how they are used in particular sentences.

INTRANSITIVE (NO OBJECT)	TRANSITIVE (WITH AN OBJECT)
The trees **shook** in the wind.	The boys **shook** the apple tree.
The train **leaves** tonight.	The train **leaves** the station.

The verbs *lie* and *lay* are particularly confusing. *Lie* is intransitive (it cannot be followed by an object). *Lay* is transitive (it must be followed by an object). Some of their forms, however, are similar. Get to know these forms so that you can use them with ease.

	LIE	LAY
SIMPLE FORM	lie	lay
PAST TENSE	lay	laid
PAST PARTICIPLE	lain	laid
-s FORM	lies	lays
PRESENT PARTICIPLE	lying	laying

To *lie* means to place oneself down or to recline; to *lay* means to place something else down.

INTRANSITIVE	Oscar **lies** on the couch. Oscar **lay** on the couch. [*on the couch* = modifier]
TRANSITIVE	Oscar **lays** bricks for a living. Oscar **laid** bricks for a living. [*bricks* = direct object]

VERB TENSE

8g Understanding verb tense

The tense of a verb indicates *when* the action, occurrence, or state of being it expresses takes place. Verbs are the only words that change form to express time.

English verb tenses are divided into two general groups: simple and perfect.

The three **simple tenses** divide time into present, past, and future. The **present** tense describes what is happening, what is true at the moment, and what is always true. It uses the simple form (8b) and the *-s* form (8c).

I **study** Italian at the university.

Joe **studies** hard all the time.

The **past tense** tells a completed action or a condition that has ended. It uses the past tense form (8b, 8d).

We **joined** the Italian conversation group.

We **hoped** to practise speaking.

The **future tense** indicates action not yet taken. This tense uses the auxiliary verbs *will* or *shall* and the simple form (8b).

We **shall see** an Italian movie at the next meeting.

The second group of tenses are the **perfect tenses.** They also divide time into present, past, and future (8i).

All six tenses also have **progressive forms,** made from the *-ing* form and the verb *to be* (8j).

8h Using the simple present tense

The **simple present tense** describes what is happening or what is true at the moment, and what is generally or consistently true. It can express a future occurrence with verbs like *start, stop, begin, end, arrive,* and *depart.* The present tense is also used to describe or discuss action in a work of literature.

8i Forming and using the perfect tenses

The perfect tenses usually describe actions or occurrences that have already been completed or that will be completed before another point in time.

The **present perfect tense** shows that an action begun in the past continues into the present, or that an action completed in the past affects the present.

Betty **has applied** for a summer job.

We **have** always **tried** to do our best.

The **past perfect tense** indicates that an action was completed before another one took place.

The blizzard **had trapped** the climbers before they could get down the mountain.

The **future perfect tense** indicates that an action will be complete before some specified or predictable time.

The space craft **will have sent** back pictures of the outer planets before it flies out of the solar system.

8j Forming and using progressive forms

Progressive forms use the present participle along with the various forms of *be* and other auxiliary verbs. They show that an action or condition is ongoing.

The **present progressive** indicates something taking place at the time it is written or spoken about.

Rents **are rising.**

The **past progressive** shows the continuing nature of a past action.

The fire **was spreading** rapidly when the firefighters arrived.

The **future progressive** shows that a future action will continue for some time.

After vacation, **we shall be returning** to our study of verb tenses.

The **present perfect progressive** describes something that began in the past and is likely to continue in the future.

The kitchen tap **has been dripping** for weeks.

The **past perfect progressive** describes an ongoing condition in the past that has been ended by something stated in the sentence.

The stereo **had been playing** well until the movers dropped it.

The **future perfect progressive** describes an action or condition continuing until some specific future time.

On November 11, **we shall have been going** together for two years.

SUMMARY OF TENSES INCLUDING PROGRESSIVE FORMS

SIMPLE TENSE

	REGULAR VERB	IRREGULAR VERB	PROGRESSIVE FORM
Present	I talk	I eat	I am talking, I am eating
Past	I talked	I ate	I was talking, I was eating
Future	I will talk	I will eat	I will be talking, I will be eating

PERFECT TENSE

	REGULAR VERB	IRREGULAR VERB	PROGRESSIVE FORM
Present	I have talked	I have eaten	I have been talking, I have been eating
Past Perfect	I had talked	I had eaten	I had been talking, I had been eating
Future Perfect	I will have talked	I will have eaten	I will have been talking, I will have been eating

---

8k Using accurate tense sequence

Sentences often have more than one verb, and these verbs often refer to actions taking place at different times. Showing the right time relationships—that is, using

8k

accurate tense sequences—is necessary to avoid confusion. The tense of the verb in an independent clause determines the possibilities for verb tense in that sentence's dependent clauses.

SUMMARY OF SEQUENCE OF TENSES

WHEN INDEPENDENT-CLAUSE VERB IS IN THE SIMPLE PRESENT TENSE, FOR THE DEPENDENT-CLAUSE VERB:

Use the present tense to show same-time action.

> The director **says** that the movie **is** a tribute to factory workers.
> I **avoid** shellfish because I **am** allergic to it.

Use the past tense to show earlier action.

> I **am** sure that I **deposited** the cheque.

Use the present perfect tense to show a period of time extending from some point in the past to the present.

> They **claim** that they **have visited** the planet Venus.

Use the future tense for action to come.

> The book **is** open because I **will be reading** it later.

WHEN INDEPENDENT-CLAUSE IS IN THE PAST TENSE, FOR THE DEPENDENT-CLAUSE VERB:

Use the past tense to show earlier action.

> I **ate** dinner before you **offered** to take me out for pizza.

Use the past perfect tense to emphasize earlier action.

> The sprinter **knew** she **had broken** the record.

Use the present tense to state a general truth.

> Christopher Columbus **discovered** that the world **is** round.

WHEN INDEPENDENT-CLAUSE VERB IS IN THE PRESENT PERFECT OR PAST PERFECT TENSE, FOR THE DEPENDENT-CLAUSE VERB:

Use the past tense.

> The milk **has become** sour since I **bought** it last week.
> The price of sugar **had** already **declined** when artificial sweeteners first **appeared**.

WHEN INDEPENDENT-CLAUSE VERB IS IN THE FUTURE TENSE, FOR THE DEPENDENT-CLAUSE VERB:

Use the present tense to show action happening at the same time.

> You **will be** rich if you **win** the prize.

Use the past tense to show earlier action.

> You **will** surely **win** the prize if you **remembered** to mail the entry form.

> **SUMMARY OF SEQUENCE OF TENSES** *(continued)*
>
> **Use the present perfect tense to show future action earlier than the action of the independent-clause verb.**
>
> The river **will flood** again next year unless we **have built** a better dam by then.
>
> WHEN THE INDEPENDENT-CLAUSE VERB IS IN THE FUTURE PERFECT TENSE, FOR THE DEPENDENT-CLAUSE VERB:
>
> **Use either the present tense or the present perfect tense.**
>
> Dr. Chang **will have delivered** 5000 babies by the time she **retires.**
>
> Dr. Chang **will have delivered** 5000 babies by the time she **has retired.**

MOOD

8l Understanding mood

The **mood** of a verb conveys a writer's attitude toward a statement. The most common mood in English is the **indicative mood.** It is used for statements about real things, or highly likely ones, and for questions about fact: *The car started; how much does that jacket cost?* Most statements are in the indicative mood.

The **imperative mood,** which always uses the simple form of the verb, expresses commands and direct requests. The subject is often omitted in an imperative sentence. It is assumed to be *you: Sit down! Please do not smoke in here.*

The **subjunctive mood** expresses conditions including wishes, recommendations, indirect requests, and speculations (see 8m). The subjunctive mood in English is rare. Therefore, its forms are less familiar than those of the indicative mood and the imperative mood.

8m Using correct subjunctive forms

The **present subjunctive** of all verbs except *be* uses the simple form of the verb for all persons and numbers. The present subjunctive of *be* is *be* for all persons and numbers.

It is important that the vandals **be** [not *are*] found

I am demanding that he **pay** [not *pays*] his bill.

The past subjunctive uses the same form as the past indicative. The past subjunctive of *be* for all persons and numbers is the same as the past plural indicative, *were.*

He wishes he **were** [not *was*] richer.

Although the subjunctive is not as common as it once was, it is still used in four situations:

1. Use the subjunctive in *if* clauses and some *unless* clauses for speculations or conditions contrary to fact.

   Unless a meltdown **were** [not *was*] to take place, the risks from a nuclear power plant are small.

2. Use the subjunctive for judgments introduced by *as if* or *as though*.

   The runner looks as though he **were** [not *was*] about to collapse.

3. Use the subjunctive in *that* clauses for wishes, indirect requests, recommendations, and demands.

   I wish that this building **were** [not *was*] air-conditioned.

   Her mechanic recommended that she **look** [not *looked*] for a new car.

4. Use the subjunctive in certain standard expressions.

   Please let me be.   Come what may. ...

   Be that as it may. ...   Far be it from me. ...

Modal auxiliary verbs like *would, could, might,* and *should* can convey speculations and conditions contrary to fact and are often used with the subjunctive:

If my father **were** [not *was*] here, he would gladly cook the fish.

When the independent clause expresses a conditional statement with a modal auxiliary, be sure to use the appropriate subjunctive form, not another modal auxiliary, in the dependent clause.

NO	If I **would have** studied for the final, I **might have** improved my grade.
YES	If I had studied for the final, I **might have** improved my grade.

VOICE

8n Understanding voice

The **voice** of a verb indicates whether a subject does or receives the action named by the verb. English has two voices: active and passive.

In the **active voice,** the subject performs the action.

Roaches **infest** most cities.

In the **passive voice,** the subject is acted upon, and the person or thing doing the action often appears as the object of the preposition *by.*

Roaches **are considered** a nuisance by many people.

The passive voice uses verb phrases. A past participle indicates the action, and a form of *be* specifies person, number, and tense: *is seen, were seen, have been seen.*

80 Writing in the active voice, not the passive voice, except to convey special types of emphasis

The active voice emphasizes the doer of the action, so active constructions have a more direct and dramatic effect. Active constructions also use fewer words than passive constructions. Therefore, use the active voice wherever you can. Most sentences in the passive voice can easily be converted to the active voice.

PASSIVE   Bicycling tours **are often taken by young travellers.**

ACTIVE   **Young travellers often take** bicycling tours.

However, the passive voice is useful in two special situations.

1. You should use the passive voice when the doer of the action is unknown or unimportant.

    The painting **was stolen** some time after midnight. [Who stole the painting is unknown.]

2. You can also use the passive voice to focus attention on the action rather than the doer of the action. For example, in a passage about important contributions to the history of biology, you might want to emphasize a doer by using the active voice.

    William Harvey **studied** the human circulatory system.

    However, in a passage summarizing what scientists know about circulation, you might want to emphasize what was done.

    The human circulatory system **was studied** by William Harvey.

Writing Present-Tense Verbs

Fill in the blanks with the third person singular, present tense of the verbs in parentheses.

EXAMPLE Every driver (to hope) _hopes_ to avoid an accident.

1. However, sometimes a cautious driver (to rush) _____ to cross railroad tracks but doesn't make it.
2. Even if the driver (to tie) _____ in the race with the train, he or she loses.
3. A standard diesel locomotive (to weigh) _____ 135 tonnes.
4. The train engineer (to need) _____ nearly 2 kilometres to stop a train that is going 100 km/h.
5. Often, a driver (to attempt) _____ to go around lowered gates at the crossing.
6. A person who (to fail) _____ to obey warning signs, gates, and signals is in great danger.
7. Similarly, a driver who (to start) _____ across the tracks before the gates have been lifted puts all the people in the car in danger.
8. The safety gate (to open) _____ only when both directions of the train's path are clear.
9. If a driver (to wait) _____ for only one train to pass, he or she may not realize that another train may be coming from the opposite direction.
10. Another dangerous situation (to occur) _____ when slick pavement and excessive speeds cause a driver to skid onto the tracks.
11. A police officer (to report) _____ that many train-related accidents are caused by drivers whose abilities have been impaired by alcohol or drugs.
12. Adverse weather (to affect) _____ driving conditions as well.
13. A safety bulletin (to recommend) _____ that drivers watch carefully for the yellow or black "RR" signs.
14. Such a sign (to warn) _____ drivers to slow down for an oncoming train.
15. A nearby sign (to post) _____ the appropriate speed limit, which should always be observed near a railroad crossing.
16. Because of traffic laws, a school bus (to stop) _____ completely at railroad crossings—even when the gates are not lowered.
17. The law (to require)_____ the same safety procedure for trucks carrying combustible or hazardous materials.
18. When behind a vehicle of this sort, a driver (to know) _____ not to follow too closely or to become impatient.
19. When a driver (to hear) _____ a bell suddenly activate while passing over the tracks, he or she should not panic.
20. The device (to allow) _____ enough time for the driver to cross the tracks before the train arrives.
21. The gate (to remain) _____ raised until the car gets over to the other side.

22. If a driver (to brake) _____ and reverses, he or she may be blocked by a car in the rear.

23. A train (to cause) _____ an accident only when drivers are careless or impatient.

24. A driver (to face) _____ severe penalties for not obeying the warning gates and lights.

25. If a driver (to practise) _____ safety and caution, others will follow, making railroad crossings safer for all other drivers.

Writing Past-Tense Verbs

> **EXERCISE 8-2**
> **(8d–1)**

Fill in the blanks with the past-tense forms of the verbs in parentheses.

EXAMPLE Have you ever (to wonder) _wondered_ why people fly kites?

1. Malayans (to start) _____ to use kites for ceremonial purposes at least 3000 years ago.

2. In ancient hieroglyphics Egyptians (to record) _____ legends about kites.

3. Yet kites probably (to develop) _____ first in China.

4. In the Han Dynasty, the emperor (to use) _____ kites to intimidate invaders.

5. He (to insert) _____ bamboo pipes into the kites.

6. When flown above the invaders' camp, the kites (to issue) _____ moaning sounds that (to startle) _____ the men below.

7. Because the night was dark, the men (to perceive) _____ nothing in the sky above them.

8. It is not surprising that they (to jerk) _____ up their tents and immediately (to head) _____ for home.

9. More recently, Benjamin Franklin (to employ) _____ a kite for his experiments with electricity.

10. An Englishman, George Pocock, (to pull) _____ a carriage and passengers with two 2.4-metre kites.

11. The Wright brothers (to experiment) _____ with kites even after their success with the airplane.

12. And you (to imagine) _____ that people flew kites just for fun!

Writing Irregular Past-Tense Verbs

> **EXERCISE 8-3**
> **(8d–2)**

Fill in the blanks with the correct past-tense forms of the irregular verbs in parentheses.

EXAMPLE The first correspondents (to write) _wrote_ on clay, parchment, or papyrus.

Name_____ Date _____

1. Once couriers (to run) _____ from one person to another with memorized messages.
2. What we consider the postal system (to arise) _____ from such beginnings.
3. Augustus Caesar (to build) _____ roads to accommodate his messengers.
4. When the Roman Empire (to fall) _____ , it (to bring) _____ an end to the Roman postal system.
5. However, by the thirteenth century the China of Kublai Khan (to have) _____ a system of messengers and horses.
6. At about the same time, the Aztecs (to find) _____ a method to disperse packages of fish among their villages.
7. During the 1400s England's Edward IV (to set) _____ up post houses for carrying both official and private mail.
8. Henry VIII (to make) _____ Sir Brian Tuke the first Master of the Posts.
9. In 1683 Charles II (to begin) _____ the London Penny Post.
10. It (to cost) _____ just one cent to mail a letter anywhere in London.
11. In 1639 the colony of Massachusetts (to give) _____ Richard Fairbanks the right to handle mail arriving by ship.
12. The Second Continental Congress (to choose) _____ Benjamin Franklin as the first American postmaster general in 1775.
13. Twenty years earlier, as deputy postmaster general for the British colonies, Franklin had opened the first official post office in what later (to become) _____ Canada.
14. He (to oversee) _____ the establishment of the Halifax post office, which linked the Nova Scotia colony to the American colonies and to England.
15. The British conquest of New France (to mean) _____ that after the peace treaty of 1763, Franklin was given the responsibility of opening post offices in Quebec City, Montreal, and Trois-Rivières.
16. As Canada (to grow) _____ , so did its postal service, which was made a government priority after Confederation.
17. For many years, Canadians could boast that their postal service (to lead) _____ the world in efficiency and willingness to adopt the new technologies of rail and air transport.

EXERCISE 8-4
(8e)

Conjugating be

The verb *be* has many irregular forms. Fill in the chart with all of its forms. Then check yourself by looking at the chart in 8e.

	Person	Present Tense	Past Tense
Singular	First	_____	_____
	Second	_____	_____
	Third	_____	_____
Plural	First	_____	_____
	Second	_____	_____
	Third	_____	_____

Present Participle _____   Past Participle _____

Using the Verb be

> **EXERCISE 8-5**
> **(8e)**

Fill in the blanks with appropriate forms of the verb *be*.

For some people a garden _____ a hobby. For others it _____ a necessity. In either case, _____ a gardener is hard work.

The first thing you must do each spring _____ prepare the garden plot with spade, plow, or rototiller. Your muscles _____ sure to ache after a day of turning the soil. Planting and mulching _____ next. I _____ always excited to see new plants coming up. You will _____ too. However, weeds _____ apt to grow faster than the seeds you planted.

Unless your idea of an aerobic workout _____ thirty minutes with a hoe, you should _____ enthusiastic about mulch. Mulch can _____ straw mounded around plants or plastic sheets covering the ground between rows. If you _____ using plastic, _____ sure you have the kind that can breathe. Otherwise, there will _____ inadequate mois-ture for your plants.

A garden _____ guaranteed to cultivate your patience while you _____ cultivating it. It cannot _____ rushed. If you hope _____ a successful gardener, you must _____ willing to work at it.

Name_____ Date _____

Using Helping Verbs

Fill in the blank with helping verbs from this list. Some sentences have several possible answers, but be sure to use each helping verb at least once.

are	do	is	was
be	does	may	were
can	has	seem	will
could	have	should	would

EXAMPLE   In order for a child to develop into a helpful member of society, the family unit _should_ act as a mini-society.

1. Children who volunteer time, first in the home and then in society, _____ destined to develop qualities like self-sacrifice and a strong commitment to the community.
2. The year 2001 _____ declared the International Year of Volunteers, a project supported by the federal government.
3. Volunteerism _____ be defined as the willingness to go beyond self-interest.
4. People who volunteer in their communities _____ contribute freely toward the common good.
5. Without doubt, volunteering _____ require giving more than spare change: it requires energy, time, and commitment.
6. Children raised in homes with limits on their behaviour _____ to learn that they are not the centre of attention.
7. A family _____ act as a mini-society by demanding of the child what society eventually will.
8. Society _____ eventually expect an honest, responsible, and respectful individual to develop.
9. Society _____ most benefit from a member who is willing to share, to help others, and to encourage the growth of the community
10. The family _____ responsible for instilling in a child these important values at an early age.
11. Parents _____ begin teaching a child about volunteerism as early as the age of three by assigning routine household chores.
12. At first, children _____ merely be expected to pick up after themselves and keep their rooms in order.

13. A few years later, the child _____ be responsible for chores that involve the home, such as mopping and vacuuming the floor or helping with the dishes.

14. It has been found that children who participated in family chores _____ taught that family is not only about fun; it is also about cooperation.

15. Giving children money for doing chores _____ be an obstacle in the learning process because money teaches them that they should expect something in return for their efforts.

16. A child can _____ taught the three R's of good citizenship at an early age: respect, responsibility, and resourcefulness.

17. Volunteering _____ become an important part of family values in Canada, both for parents and children.

18. In fact, over 7.5 million Canadians _____ participated actively in community service every year for the past few years, making each community a better place.

Identifying Transitive, Intransitive, and Linking Verbs

EXERCISE **8-7**
(8f)

Identify each italicized verb by writing *transitive, intransitive,* or *linking* on the lines at right.

EXAMPLE   The platypus of Australia *is* an unusual animal.   _____*linking*_____

1. Europeans first *saw* the platypus in 1796.   _____
2. The platypus *is* nocturnal.   _____
3. Usually it *stays* out of sight.   _____
4. The Europeans *could* hardly *believe* their eyes.   _____
5. The platypus *has* a bizarre appearance.   _____
6. Its bill *resembles* that of a duck.   _____
7. However, the bill *is* really a soft snout.   _____
8. With the bill the platypus *probes* in the mud for food.   _____
9. The platypus *has* a tail and fur like a beaver.   _____
10. With its webbed feet it *swims* well.   _____
11. Nevertheless, the feet *have* claws for digging in the river banks.   _____
12. The platypus *is* a mammal.   _____
13. Yet is *lays* eggs.   _____
14. After hatching, the young *nurse*.   _____
15. No wonder one scientist *named* the platypus paradoxus.   _____
16. It *is* indeed a paradox.   _____

Name_____ Date _____

Writing Sentences with Transitive and Intransitive Verbs

Write two sentences for each of the following verbs, one in which it is transitive and one in which it is intransitive.

EXAMPLE   swim
         The champion swims quickly.
         The champion swims the distance in record time.

1. operate

   intransitive:_____

   transitive: _____

2. multiply

   intransitive:_____

   transitive: _____

3. meet

   intransitive:_____

   transitive: _____

4. lift

   intransitive:_____

   transitive: _____

5. evaporate

   intransitive:_____

   transitive: _____

8-9

Distinguishing the Forms of
lie/lay, sit/set, and rise/raise

A: The forms of *lie* and *lay, sit* and *set*, and *rise* and *raise* are easily confused. Fill in their forms below. Then check yourself by looking at the chart in 8f.

	-s Form	Past Tense	Past Participle	Present Participle
lie				
lay				
sit				
set				
rise				
raise				

B: Fill in the blanks with the verb in parentheses that best suits the meaning of each sentence.

EXAMPLE   The morning sun (raised, rose) _rose_ over the Prairie landscape.

1. Dawn revealed a small number of grain elevators (setting, sitting) _____ by the railway line.

2. The railway, which (laid, lay) _____ across the Prairie, stretched eastward to Lake Superior, where the city of Thunder Bay (lays, lies) _____.

3. In Thunder Bay, more grain elevators (raised, rose) _____ their profiles against the dawn sky.

4. The wheat (laying, lying) _____ in the Prairie elevators was newly harvested.

5. In Thunder Bay, however, much of the wheat had (laid, lain) _____ in the elevators for days.

6. Some wheat already (sat, set) _____ in the holds of oceangoing ships, ready for export.

7. The first grain elevators (raised, rose) _____ above the Prairie landscape soon after the first rail lines were (laid, lain) _____.

8. Farmers' cooperatives often (raised, rose) _____ the funds to erect the wooden, box-like structures.

9. Huge concrete grain elevators, like those in Thunder Bay, were usually (sat, set) _____ up by private companies.

10. The grain elevator got its name from the conveyor belt used to (raise, rise) _____ buckets of grain up into the storage compartment.

8-10

Using the Perfect and Progressive Tenses

EXERCISE **8-10**
(8i–j)

Fill in the blanks with the verb forms described in parentheses. Be prepared to discuss why each verb is appropriate in its sentence.

EXAMPLE   The aftereffects of kisses (to cause: present perfect) *have caused* researchers to recommend a daily dose of this sign of affection.

1. German physicians and psychologists (to discover: present perfect) _____ that a kiss can improve a person's health.

2. Spouses who (to kiss: present perfect progressive) _____ their partner each day before work since the beginning of their marriage tend to live healthier, happier, and longer lives than those who don't.

3. Researchers (to begin: present progressive) _____ to understand why.

4. One researcher, Dr. Arthur Sazbo, (to study: present perfect progressive) _____ those who kiss and those who don't.

5. He (to find: present perfect) _____ that those who kiss their spouses in the morning miss fewer workdays because of illness than do those who don't.

6. Furthermore, it turns out that those who kisses (to get: past perfect progressive) _____ into fewer automobile accidents while on the way to work than those who didn't.

7. It also seems that spouses who start the day with a kiss (to earn: present progressive) _____ 30 percent more than those who do not.

8. Dr. Sazbo (to say: past perfect) _____ that the difference is that spouses who kiss start their day with a more positive attitude, one which allows them to get through their day more easily.

9. In fact, kissing is linked to living longer; on average, those who kiss (to live: present progressive) _____ five years longer than those who don't.

10. Why is it that kisses (to have: present perfect progressive) _____ such huge effects on people?

11. Dr. Sazbo (to suggest: present perfect) _____ that since a kiss is a form of approval, those who don't experience one in the morning do not have the same positive feelings and confidence as those who do kiss.

12. With this report, new superstitions (to start: present progressive) _____ to develop already.

13. Perhaps, people all along (to know: present perfect) _____ that a morning kiss is the right way to start the day.

14. But they could not (to understand: present perfect) _____ why this is true until very recently.

15. Certainly, the physicians and psychologists who (to study: present perfect progressive) _____ kisses strongly recommend them for a boost in spirit, health, and happiness.

Identifying Active and Passive Verbs

> **EXERCISE 8-11**
> **(8n)**

Underline the entire main verb in each sentence, and then identify it as *active* or *passive* on the lines to the right.

EXAMPLE   The Louvre _contains_ some of the world's most famous art work.   _active_

1. The Louvre in Paris was not built as an art museum.   _____

2. The original Louvre was constructed in the twelfth century as a fortress.   _____

3. Francis I erected the present building as a residence.   _____

4. A gallery connecting it with the Tuileries Palace was started by Henry IV and completed by Louis XIV.   _____

5. A second gallery, begun by Napoleon, would have enclosed a great square.   _____

6. However, it was not finished until after his abdication.   _____

7. Revolutionaries overthrew the Bastille on July 14, 1789.   _____

8. Just four years later the art collection of the Louvre was opened to the public.   _____

9. The collection can be traced back to Francis I.   _____

10. Francis, an ardent collector, invited Leonardo da Vinci to France in 1515.   _____

11. Leonardo brought the *Mona Lisa* with him from Italy.   _____

12. Nevertheless, the royal art collection may have been expanded more by ministers than by kings.   _____

13. Cardinals Richelieu and Mazarin can take credit for many important acquisitions.   _____

14. Today the Louvre has a new entrance.   _____

15. The entrance, a glass pyramid in the courtyard, was designed by I. M. Pei.   _____

16. Pei's name can be added to a distinguished list of Louvre architects.   _____

Name_____ Date _____

EXERCISE 8-12
(8o)

Revising for the Active Voice

A: Change each of the passive sentences you identified in Exercise 8-11 into the active voice. You may need to add words to act as subjects of your new sentences. Use your own paper.

B: On the lines at the right, identify each sentence as *active* or *passive*. Then rewrite each passive sentence into the active voice. However, if you think a sentence is better left passive, write your reason on the line instead.

EXAMPLE   Today's country of Zimbabwe was named after important ruins.
　　　　　　Patriots named today's country of
　　　　　　Zimbabwe after important ruins.　　　　　　　___passive___

1. The ruins were not known by people outside Africa until 1868.　_____

2. The largest of the ruins, Great Zimbabwe, has two main structures.　_____

3. The building on the hill was constructed primarily for defence.　_____

4. Its stones are fitted together without mortar.　_____

5. A lower, elliptical building is encircled by a nine-metre wall.　_____

6. An inner wall forms a passage to a sacred enclosure.　_____

7. Majestic soapstone sculptures were discovered there.　_____

8. The enclosure contains towers twelve metres high.　_____

9. Ancestors of the Shona-speaking people maintained　_____
Great Zimbabwe as a trade centre from the 12th through
the 15th centuries.

10. Tools for working with gold have been found in the ruins.　_____

11. The Shona traded gold and ivory with Arab merchants.　_____

9 Case of Nouns and Pronouns

9a **Understanding case**

The **case** (form) of a noun or pronoun shows how that word relates to other words in a sentence. For example, *we, us,* and *our* are three different cases of the first-person-plural pronoun:

As **we** walked through the park, a crowd gathered around **us** to see **our** pet alligator.

English has three cases: **subjective, objective,** and **possessive.** Nouns use one form for the subjective and objective cases and have a separate possessive form, made with the apostrophe. Many pronouns, however, have three distinct forms for the three cases. **Personal pronouns,** the most common type of pronouns, have a full range of forms (cases) that show changes in **person** (first, second, and third person) and **number** (singular and plural). (For an explanation of *person*, see 11a).

CASES OF PERSONAL PRONOUNS					
	SUBJECTIVE		**OBJECTIVE**		**POSSESSIVE**
	Singular/Plural		**Singular/Plural**		**Singular/Plural**
First person	I	we	me	us	my/mine	our/ours
Second person	you	you	you	you	your/yours	your/yours
Third person	he she it	they	him her it	them	his her/hers its	their/theirs

The plural of *you* is simply *you.* Avoid the nonstandard plural *yous,*
A pronoun in the **subjective case** functions as a subject of a sentence or clause.

We needed an apartment. [*We* is the subject.]

130

A pronoun in the **objective case** functions as a direct object or an indirect object.

A friend called **us** one night. [*Us* is the direct object.]

He told **us** a secret. [*Us* is the indirect object.]

He had a surprise for **us.** [*Us* is the object of a preposition.]

A pronoun in the **possessive case**, or possessive pronoun, indicates possession or ownership.

♣ PUNCTUATION ALERT: Do not use an apostrophe in a possessive pronoun. ♣

He said that **his** neighbour was moving next month.

We called the neighbour and agreed to sublet **her** apartment.

Its windows look out over a park.

9b Using the same cases for pronouns in compound constructions as in single constructions

A compound construction contains more than one subject or object (see 7k, 7l). This compounding has no effect on the choice of a pronoun case.

He and I saw the eclipse of the sun. [compound subject]

The beauty of the eclipse astounded both **him** and **me.** [compound object]

If you are unsure which case to use, try this "drop test." Temporarily *drop all of the compound element except the pronoun in question*, and then you will be able to tell which pronoun case is needed. Here is how the method works for compound subjects.

EXAMPLE **Janet and (me, I)** read that the moon has one-eightieth the mass of the earth.

STEP **1** Drop *Janet and.*

STEP **2** Which reads correctly: "**Me** read that the moon has one-eightieth the mass of the earth" or "**I** read that the moon has one-eightieth the mass of the earth"?

STEP **3** Answer: Janet and **I** read that the moon has one-eightieth the mass of the earth.

The same test works for compound objects:

EXAMPLE The instructor told **Janet and (I, me)** that the moon has one-fiftieth the volume of the earth.

STEP **1** Drop *Janet and.*

STEP **2** Which reads correctly: "The instructor told **I** that the moon has one-fiftieth the volume of the earth" or "The instructor told **me** that the moon has one-fiftieth the volume of the earth"?

STEP **3** Answer: The instructor told Janet and **me** that the moon has one-fiftieth the volume of the earth.

When pronouns in a **prepositional phrase** (7n) occur in compound constructions (*The book was about* **him** *and* **me**), the pronouns often appear in the wrong case. You may hear people say "with he and I" or "between you and I," but this usage is incorrect. A prepositional phrase always includes an object, so any pronouns that follow words such as *with, to, from, for, after*, or *between* must be in the objective case. See 7g for a complete list of prepositions.

NO	The reward will be divided **between you and I.** [*I* is in the subjective case and cannot follow a preposition.]
YES	The reward will be divided **between you and me.** [*Me* is in the objective case, so it is correct.]

9c Matching noun and pronoun cases in appositives

When one or more pronouns occur in an **appositive** (7m-3)—a word or group of words that renames the noun or noun phrase next to it—the pronoun takes the same case as the noun replaced.

NO	**Us** working women lead productive lives. [*Working women* is the subject, so *us*, an objective pronoun, is incorrect.]
YES	**We** working women lead productive lives. [*We* is a subjective pronoun: correct.]
NO	Someone ought to give working mothers, **she** and **I,** better job opportunities. [*Working mothers* is the object, so *she* and *I*, subjective pronouns, are incorrect.]
YES	Someone ought to give working mothers, **her** and **me,** better job opportunities. [*Her* and *me* are objective pronouns: correct.]

9d Avoiding the objective case after linking verbs

A **linking verb** connects the subject to a word that renames it. Such a renaming word is called a **complement.** Because a pronoun coming after a linking verb renames the subject, that pronoun must be in the subjective case.

Is Lee at home? This is **he.** [*He* renames *this*, the subject, so the subjective case is required.]

Who is there? It is **I.** [*I* renames *it*, the subject, so the subjective case is required.]

The winner of the speed skating event was **she.** [*She* renames *the winner*, the subject, so the subjective case is required.]

In speech and informal writing the objective case is often used in these situations, but academic writing is more formal and requires the subjective case.

9e Using *who, whoever, whom,* and *whomever*

Who and *whoever*, which function as both **relative** and **interrogative pronouns** (7b), change forms in the different cases. Within each case, however, they remain the same for all persons and for singular and plural.

CASES OF RELATIVE AND INTERROGATIVE PRONOUNS		
SUBJECTIVE	**OBJECTIVE**	**POSSESSIVE**
who	whom	whose
whoever	whomever	—

To determine whether *who, whom, whoever,* or *whomever* is correct in a dependent clause (7o-2), temporarily drop everything in the sentence up to the pronoun in question, and make substitutions—remembering that *he, she, they, who,* and *whoever* are subjects, and *him, her, them, whom,* and *whomever* are objects.

STEP 1   I asked (**who, whom**) attended the World Series.

STEP 2   Omit *I asked.*

STEP 3   Test what other pronoun would make a sensible sentence: "**He** attended the World Series" or " **Him** attended the World Series."

STEP 4   Answer: "**He** attended the World Series."

STEP 5   Therefore, because *he* is subjective, *who,* which is also subjective, is correct: "I asked **who** attended the World Series."

The subjective case is called for even when expressions such as *I think* and *he says* come between the subject and the verb. Ignore these expressions when determining the correct pronoun.

He is the pitcher **who** [I think] will be elected Most Valuable Player.

This process also works for the objective case (*whom*), as well as for *whoever* and *whomever.*

At the beginning of questions, use *who* if the question is about the subject and *whom* if the question is about the object. If you are unsure, reword the question as a statement.

Who repaired the radio? ["*I* repaired the radio" uses the subjective pronoun *I,* so *who* is correct.]

Jacques admires **whom**? ["Jacques admires *him*" uses the objective pronoun *him,* so *whom* is correct.]

To **whom** does Jacques speak about becoming an electrician? ["Jacques speaks to *me* about becoming an electrician" uses the objective pronoun *me,* so *whom* is correct.]

In speech and formal writing, *who* is often used for both subjects and objects (*Who does Jacques ask?*), but such practice is nonstandard and should be avoided in academic writing.

9f Using the pronoun case after *than* or *as*

When a pronoun follows *than* or *as*, the pronoun case carries essential information about what is being said. For example, the following two sentences convey two very different messages, simply because of the choice between the words *me* and *I* after *than*.

1. My sister photographs landscapes more **than me.**
2. My sister photographs landscapes more **than I.**

Sentence 1 means "My sister photographs landscapes more *than she photographs me.*" On the other hand, sentence 2 means "My sister photographs landscapes more *than I photograph landscapes.*" To make sure that any sentence of comparison is clear, either include all the words in the second half or mentally fill in the words to check whether you have chosen the correct pronoun case.

9g Using pronouns with infinitives

Objective pronouns occur as both subjects and objects of infinitives (7d).

His nephew wanted *him* **to challenge** *me* to a raft race. [*Him* is the subject of the infinitive *to challenge*; *me* is the object of the infinitive; both are in the objective case.]

9h Using pronouns with *-ing* words

A **gerund** is the *-ing* form of a verb that functions as a noun: ***Singing in the shower*** *is a common pastime.* When a noun or pronoun precedes a gerund, the possessive case is called for.

Igor's singing annoyed the neighbours.

His singing annoyed the neighbours.

In contrast, the **present participle** is the *-ing* form that functions as an adjective. It does not take the possessive case.

Igor, **singing in the shower,** annoyed the neighbours.

9i Using *-self* pronouns

Reflexive pronouns reflect back on the subject or object.

The diver prepared **herself** for the finals.

She had to force **herself** to relax.

Reflexive pronouns should not be used as substitutes for subjects or objects.

The diver and **I** [not *myself*] wished the sportscasters would go away.

They bothered her and **me** [not *myself*] for interviews.

Intensive pronouns provide emphasis.

The diver felt that competing **itself** was stressful enough without giving interviews.

The sportscasters acted as though they **themselves** were the only reason for the event.

Avoid the following nonstandard forms of reflexive and intensive pronouns in academic writing: *hisself*, nonstandard for *himself; theirself, theirselves, themself,* and *themselfs,* nonstandard for *themselves.*

Knowing the Personal Pronouns

The personal pronouns change form to show whether they are being used as subjects, objects, or possessives and to match the person and number of their antecedents. Fill in this chart with the appropriate forms of the personal pronouns. Then check yourself by looking at the chart at the beginning of this chapter.

	Person	*Subjective Case*	*Objective Case*	*Possessive Case*
Singular	First	_____	_____	_____
	Second	_____	_____	_____
	Third	_____	_____	_____
Plural	First	_____	_____	_____
	Second	_____	_____	_____
	Third	_____	_____	_____

Identifying Pronoun Case

Underline the personal pronouns. Then on the lines to the right indicate their cases.

EXAMPLE <u>I</u> recently read an article about
<u>my</u> least favourite animal.   *subjective*   *possessive*

1. Just thinking about cockroaches makes   _____   _____
   me uncomfortable.
2. How do they affect you?   _____   _____
3. The author of the article says that the cockroach   _____   _____
   is his enemy.
4. He is a pest-control specialist.   _____   _____
5. According to him, cockroaches have been around   _____   _____
   since before the dinosaurs.
6. Roaches have lasted this long because their   _____   _____
   bodies are perfect for what they do.
7. They can eat almost anything and can survive   _____   _____
   on very little.
8. A dozen of them can live for a week on the glue   _____   _____
   of one postage stamp.

Name_____ Date _____

9. One variety can live for a month without food as
   long as it has water.   _____ _____

10. They reproduce very quickly, 100 000 offspring
    a year from a single pair.   _____ _____

11. A scientist who has spent ten years studying
    roaches says each one has its own personality.   _____ _____

12. She learned this by studying their nighttime
    behaviour.   _____ _____

13. Research shows that they learn from experience
    and change their behaviour to escape danger.   _____ _____

14. No place is free from them—even submarines.   _____ _____

15. One roach destroyed a $975,000 computer by
    getting inside it and eating its wires.   _____ _____

16. Roaches can also harm us because they may
    carry dangerous bacteria.   _____ _____

17. Our best defence against roaches may be new
    chemicals that stop them from reproducing.   _____ _____

18. In the meantime, we may have to continue sharing _____ _____
    our planet with them.

Using Personal Pronouns

EXERCISE **9-3**
(9a)

Select the correct pronoun from the choices in parentheses. Write your answers on the
lines to the right.

EXAMPLE My family and (I, me) visited Ottawa last spring.   _____*I*_____

1. Other tourists and (we, us) were delighted by what (we, us) saw.   _____

2. (It, Its) is a beautiful city.   _____

3. By the end of the week, each of (us, ours) had a favourite place.   _____

4. My little brother was impressed by what (he, his) saw at the
   Royal Canadian Mint.   _____

5. (He, Him) and (I, me) took a tour of the Mint.   _____
                                                      _____

6. We could not believe (our, ours) eyes when we saw people actually   _____
   making money.

7. As (he, him) and (I, me) watched people minting coins,
my brother said it was a great job because the people could
keep some money for (them, themselves). _____

8. I told (he, him) that he was kidding (him, himself) if he really
believed that. _____

9. Employees have security people watching (them, themselves)
and the money (it, itself) is counted and recounted to prevent theft. _____

10. I wondered if (them, their) working around money all day might
make money less exciting to these people after a while. _____

11. Still, it was fascinating for (we, us) to watch all that money
being coined. _____

12. The Parliament Buildings were (me, my) favourite place. _____

13. Near the Parliament Buildings stands a statue of John A. Macdonald _____
(hisself, himself), looking out over the capital.

14. Standing near that statue made my sister and (I, me) feel very calm, _____
as if Macdonald were watching out for (us, ourselves).

15. My sister said that the most exciting place for (she, her) was the _____
Canadian Museum of Civilization, in Hull.

16. This is probably because of (her, hers) desire to be an anthropologist. _____

17. If (you, yous) go to Ottawa, make a trip to Hull to visit the _____
Museum of Civilization even if (you, your) are not planning to be an
anthropologist or archaeologist.

18. Children will especially enjoy the chance the Museum gives _____
(they, them) to see old films of Native ceremonies and practices.

19. While there, they can also see for (theirselfs, themselves) _____
towering totem poles.

20. Now that I have told you about my family's favourite places _____
in the National Capital Region, will you tell me about (your, yours)?

Identifying and Using Personal Pronouns as Appositives and Complements

EXERCISE **9-4**
(9c, d)

A: Underline all personal pronouns used as appositives or complements. Then draw an
arrow connecting each to its antecedent. Be prepared to explain why each pronoun takes
the case it does.

EXAMPLE   The winner is I.

1. The partners, he and she, have been together for years.

2. A legend in his own time is he.

3. The judges selected the best cheesecake, ours.

Name_____ Date _____

4. The first ones in the group to marry were they.

5. The letter finally reached the addressee, me, six years later.

B: Select the correct pronoun for formal situations from the choices in parentheses. Write your answers on the lines to the right.

EXAMPLE The smartest couple, you and (I, me) _____,   _____I_____
         will be on the cover of the yearbook.

1. If anyone deserves a medal, it is (she, her) _____ .   _____
2. Our travel agent has booked a vacation tour for us,   _____
   just you and (I, me) _____ .
3. The recipient of the donated heart was (he, him) _____ .   _____
4. I saw the thieves, (he, him) _____ and his brother.   _____
5. Altos, (I, me) _____ for one, don't get to sing any of the   _____
   great opera roles.

> **EXERCISE 9-5**
> **(9e)**

Using who *and* whom

Select the correct relative or interrogative pronoun (*who, whom, whoever,* or *whomever*) from the choices in parentheses. Write your answers on the lines to the right.

EXAMPLE The number of children (who, whom) are in a   *who*
         family may affect the intelligence of all the children.   _____

1. Researchers (who, whom) studied over 350 000 men in the 1940s
   found that IQ fell as family size increased.   _____
2. Children (who, whom) were born into a family later tended to have
   lower IQs.   _____
3. Recent research supports the theory that (whoever, whomever) is
   born first has an advantage.   _____
4. Children (who, whom) researchers checked for IQ and school
   performance did better if they were the oldest in small families.   _____
5. (Whoever, Whomever) was an only child, however, scored like a
   younger child.   _____

6. (Who, Whom) can be sure why these trends occur? _____

7. It may be that younger children receive less mental stimulation _____
because their brothers and sisters (who, whom) teach them
are immature.

8. Only children, (who, whom) are usually considered lucky, may miss _____
out because they never have a chance to grow by teaching their own
younger brothers and sisters.

9. Perhaps parents' attention, no matter to (who, whom) it is given, is _____
limited, so there is simply more of it per child in smaller families.

10. Of course, there are highly intelligent and successful people _____
(who, whom) are born into large families.

11. Teachers and parents of young children should be careful about _____
(who, whom) they make judgments.

12. We cannot use these studies to predict the future of (whoever, _____
whomever) we please, because in the end success depends on a
lot more than birth order and family size.

13. Few successful people (who, whom) have been asked the secret of _____
their success talk about birth order.

14. Often, successful people give credit to their drive to achieve _____
something and to the people (who, whom) supported them.

15. For example, listen to the speeches at any awards ceremony and you _____
will hear people thanking the parents, teachers, and friends without
(who, whom) they could not have succeeded.

16. (Who, Whom) would you thank if you were giving such a speech? _____

Choosing Pronoun Cases Carefully

Select the correct pronoun from the choices in parentheses. Write your answers on the
lines to the right.

EXAMPLE   The National Film Board has trained Canadian   *them*
filmmakers and funded (they, them) since 1939.

1. After he had proved (him, himself) as an innovative filmmaker in _____
England, Scottish-born John Grierson was invited to come to
Canada in 1938.

2. Canadian authorities wanted (he, him) to give advice on a _____
government-run film agency.

3. (His, Him) studying the question led Grierson to recommend _____
setting up the National Film Board.

4. Grierson became the first commissioner of the new agency, known _____
as the NFB; no other commissioner has been as influential as
(he, him).

EXERCISES

Name_____ Date _____

5. It was (he, him) who invented the term documentary and who   _____
   inspired the NFB to become a world leader in documentary
   filmmaking.

6. A highly creative man, Grierson hired many other talented people   _____
   and inspired (they, them) to do some of their best work.

7. During the Second World War, the NFB played an important role   _____
   through (it, its) informing and encouraging soldiers and civilians.

8. The NFB also publicized the aims and efforts of the Allies to U.S.   _____
   audiences before the United States (it, itself) entered the war in
   late 1941.

9. By 1945, the agency was fighting with the government to keep   _____
   the independence that allowed (it, itself) to explore social problems
   and advocate workers' rights.

10. That year, Grierson resigned his position; many people believe   _____
    (he, him) to have been forced out.

11. The NFB renewed (it, itself) in the 1950s, when directors such as   _____
    Norman McLaren began to win awards for innovative work in
    animation.

12. In the 1970s, under Kathleen Shannon, the NFB's Studio D   _____
    produced films by women, dealing with women's work and
    (their, they) position in society.

13. By the 1990s, however, much of the NFB's funding had been cut,   _____
    Studio D was closed down, and filmmakers were questioning the
    NFB's importance to their profession and (them, themselves).

10 Pronoun Reference

The meaning of a pronoun comes from its **antecedent,** the noun or pronoun to which the pronoun refers. In order for your writing to communicate its message clearly, each pronoun must relate directly to an antecedent. You can accomplish this by following a few simple rules.

10a Making a pronoun refer clearly to a single antecedent

To be understood, a pronoun must refer to a specific single (or compound) antecedent.

> Frederick Banting first studied arts at university, and although **he** did poorly, **his** application to medical school was accepted.

Often the same pronoun fits more than one possible antecedent. This situation can be confusing.

> Many people hardly distinguish Frederick Banting from the co-discoverer of insulin, Charles Best. **He** was several years older, and was **his** teacher as well as a scientific colleague. **He** came from a farming family, whereas **his** colleague's father was a medical doctor. **He** won the Nobel Prize for the discovery along with project director J.J.R. Macleod and shared the prize money with **him**, for **he** believed that **he** had been unjustly denied recognition.

A writer can clarify such a passage by replacing some pronouns with nouns so that each remaining pronoun clearly refers to a single antecedent.

> Many people hardly distinguish Frederick Banting from the co-discoverer of insulin, Charles Best. **Banting** was several years older, and was **Best's** teacher as well as a scientific colleague. **Banting** came from a farming family, whereas **his** colleague's father was a medical doctor. **Banting** won the Nobel Prize for the discovery along with project director J.J.R. Macleod and shared the prize money with **Best**, for **Banting** believed that **Best** had been unjustly denied recognition.

Using *said* and *told* with pronouns that appear to refer to more than one person is especially likely to create confusion. Use quotation marks and slightly reword the sentence to make the meaning clearer.

NO	Her aunt told her she was returning to school.
YES	Her aunt told her, "You are returning to school."
YES	Her aunt told her, "I am returning to school."

10b Placing pronouns close to their antecedents for clarity

If too much material comes between a pronoun and its antecedent, unclear pronoun reference results. Readers lose track of the meaning of a passage if they have to trace too far back to find the antecedent of a pronoun.

NO	**Crowfoot**, the Blackfoot chief who had settled on a reserve with his people in 1881, refused to let them join Louis Riel's second revolt, the 1885 North-West Rebellion — but not because of contentment with life on the reserve or satisfaction with the Canadian government, and certainly not because of timidity. **He** did not join the revolt because it could not possibly succeed. In fact, **he** was a legendary war chief who once killed a grizzly bear with only a spear. [Although *he* can refer only to *Crowfoot,* too much material comes between the first pronoun and its antecedent.]
YES	**Crowfoot**, the Blackfoot chief who had settled on a reserve with his people in 1881, refused to let them join Louis Riel's second revolt, the 1885 North-West Rebellion — but not because of contentment with life on the reserve or satisfaction with the Canadian government, and certainly not because of timidity. **Crowfoot** did not join the revolt because it could not possibly succeed. In fact, **he** was a legendary war chief who once killed a grizzly bear with only a spear.

10c Making a pronoun refer to a definite antecedent

A noun in its possessive form (*the car's exhaust*) cannot also serve as the subject (*The car stalled*) or object (*I sold the car*) of its sentence. Thus a pronoun cannot refer to a noun in its possessive form.

NO	**Galen's** formula for cold cream has not changed much since **he** invented it 1700 years ago. [*He* cannot refer to the possessive *Galen's.*]
YES	**Galen's** formula for cold cream has not changed much since **the Roman physician** invented it 1700 years ago.

An adjective serves as a modifier, not as a subject or object. Thus a pronoun cannot refer to an adjective.

NO	Janet works at the **cosmetics** counter. **They** are inexpensive. [*They* cannot refer to the adjective *cosmetics.*]
YES	Janet works at the cosmetics counter. **The products** are inexpensive.
NO	**Pink** lipstick is always popular. It is Janet's favourite colour.
YES	**Pink** lipstick is always popular. Janet's favourite colour is **pink.**

Pronouns such as *it, that, this*, and *which* are particularly prone to unclear reference. As you write and revise, check carefully to see that each of these pronouns refers to only one antecedent that can be determined easily by your readers. When necessary, replace the confusing pronoun with a noun.

NO   Annie Taylor, a 43-year-old widow, was the first person to go over Niagara Falls in a barrel. **This** was fantastic. [What does *this* refer to? Her age? Her being a widow? A female being the first person to go over the Falls?]

YES   Annie Taylor, a 43-year-old widow, was the first person to go over Niagara Falls in a barrel. **That anyone would want to do this** was fantastic.

NO   After going over the Falls, Taylor admitted she could not swim. **It** was very dangerous. [What does *it* refer to?]

YES   After going over the Falls, Taylor admitted she could not swim. **Her stunt** was very dangerous.

In speech, such statements as *it said in the papers* and *at the United Nations they say* are common. Such expressions are inexact, however, and should be avoided.

The newspapers report [not *It said in the newspapers*] that many United Nations officials receive high salaries.

A United Nations spokesperson says [not *At the United Nations they say*] that the high salaries are rewards for doing difficult jobs well.

A piece of writing has to stand on its own, so when you are referring to a title, be sure to repeat or reword whatever part of the title you want to use. Do not use a pronoun in the first sentence of an essay to refer to the essay's title.

TITLE   *Airport Security Must Be Strict*

NO   Yes, I agree with this.

YES   Because of the dangerous state of world affairs, airport security must be strict.

10d Not overusing *it*

It has three different uses in English.

1. *It* is a personal pronoun: *Rachel decided which VCR she wants, but she doesn't have enough money to buy **it** yet.*
2. *It* is an expletive, a word that postpones the subject: ***It** is lucky that the price of VCRs is falling.*
3. *It* is part of idiomatic expressions of weather, time, or distance: ***It** is raining.*

All of these uses are acceptable, but combining them in the same sentence can create confusion.

NO	**It** was fortunate that I tried the new restaurant on the day that **it** opened an outdoor cafe section, because **it** was a sunny day.
YES	I was fortunate to try the new restaurant on the day that the outdoor cafe section opened, because **it** was a sunny day.

10e Using *you* only for direct address

You is used frequently in speech and informal writing to refer to general groups of people (*You can never tell what fashions will be popular*). In academic writing, however, *you* is acceptable only if the writer is directly addressing the reader. For example, *you* is used in this workbook because we, the authors, are directly addressing you, our reader. Similarly, your instructor might write on one of your essays: "Your introduction makes me want to read on."

You should not be used in academic writing to refer to people in general, however.

NO	At many libraries, **you** can check books out for two weeks. [Does this mean that libraries have a special circulation period just for the reader?]
YES	At many libraries, **borrowers** can check books out for two weeks.

10f Using *who, which*, and *that* correctly

Who refers to people or to animals with names or special talents.

The Pied Piper, **who** led all the plague-carrying rats out of Hamlin, Germany, on July 22, 1376, was a real man.

The movie *Willard* featured a rat named Ben, **who** was the hero's friend.

Which and *that* refer to animals, things, and sometimes anonymous or collective groups of people. The choice between *which* and *that* depends on whether the clause introduced by the pronoun is restrictive (essential) or nonrestrictive (nonessential). Use *that* with restrictive clauses and *which* with nonrestrictive clauses. Use *who* for people in both kinds of clauses.

♣ COMMA CAUTION: Set off nonrestrictive clauses with commas. For a fuller explanation, see 24e. ♣

Rats, **which** often carry disease-bearing fleas, are health problems.

Garbage, **which** rats love, must be cleaned up before the rats can be driven out.

Rats **that** have been inbred for generations are the ideal lab animals.

All traits **that** might interfere with experiments have been eliminated.

Lab workers **that** handle rats every day probably are not repelled by them.

10-1

Using Pronouns to Refer to a Single Nearby Antecedent

Underline the pronouns in these passages. Then, if the antecedents are clear and close enough to their pronouns, copy the sentences onto the lines. If the antecedents are unclear or too far away, use the lines to revise the sentences.

EXAMPLE   Henry C. Wallace and <u>his</u> son Henry A. Wallace held the same cabinet post. <u>He</u> was the Secretary of Agriculture under U.S. presidents Harding and Coolidge, and <u>he</u> was Secretary of Agriculture under Franklin Roosevelt.

> *Henry C. Wallace and his son Henry A. Wallace held the same cabinet post. The elder Henry C. Wallace was the Secretary of Agriculture under U.S. Presidents Harding and Coolidge, and the younger Henry A. Wallace was the Secretary of Agriculture under Franklin Roosevelt.*

1. Unlike most recent Canadian prime ministers, three out of the first five Canadian prime ministers were born in Scotland or England. Most of them were born in Canada.

   _____

2. The first Canadian-born prime minister, Sir John Abbott, held office in 1891 and 1892; the last British-born prime minister was John Turner. He led the government for a few weeks in 1984.

   _____

   _____

3. For religious reasons, Zachary Taylor refused to take the presidential oath of office on a Sunday, so David Rice Atchison (president of the Senate) was president for a day. He spent the day appointing his temporary cabinet.

   _____

   _____

4. Calvin Coolidge was sworn into office by his own father.

   _____

5. An American Indian, Charles Curtis, became vice-president when Herbert Hoover was elected president in 1928. He was one-half Kaw.

   _____

   _____

Name_____ Date _____

6. William DeVance King, vice-president under Franklin Pierce, was in Cuba during the election and had to be sworn in by an act of Congress, never bothering to return to Washington. A month later, never having carried out any official duties, he died.

   _____

   _____

7. The Republicans got their elephant and the Democrats got their donkey as symbols from political cartoonist Thomas Nast.

   _____

   _____

8. Like their British counterparts, Conservatives in Canada are nicknamed "Tories," but unlike theirs, Liberals in Canada are called "Grits," not "Whigs."

   _____

   _____

9. The first woman presidential candidate was Victoria Woodhull. Years before Geraldine Ferraro ran for vice-president, she was on the Equal Rights Party ticket—in 1872.

   _____

   _____

10. The first woman to lead a major party in the Canadian House of Commons was Audrey McLaughlin, and the second was Kim Campbell. She became the first woman prime minister.

    _____

    _____

11. As a child, president-to-be Andrew Johnson was sold as an indentured servant to a tailor. He was supposed to work for seven years, but he ran away.

    _____

    _____

Using Pronouns to Refer to Definite Antecedents

Revise these vague passages so that all pronouns have definite antecedents. Be alert for implied antecedents and the misuse of *it, they*, and *you*.

EXAMPLE   Ordinary people could soon be living and working aboard space stations. They are unusual but quite safe.

> *Ordinary people could soon be living and working aboard space stations. The stations are unusual but quite safe.*

1. A California company called the Space Island Group is planning to recycle one of the shortest-lived components of the space shuttle. It is ingenious.

   _____

   _____

2. Engineers at SIG plan to construct dozens of wheel-shaped space stations using empty shuttle fuel tanks. They are eminently suited to the task.

   _____

   _____

3. A shuttle's fuel tanks are huge. Each one is 8.5 metres in diameter and nearly 50 metres long—approximately the size of a jumbo jet. It jettisons them just before it reaches orbit, leaving them to burn up and crash into the ocean.

   _____

   _____

4. Over a hundred of these tanks, known as ETs, have been used and destroyed since the first shuttle launch in 1981. So you can see how much hardware has gone to waste.

   _____

   _____

5. Using ETs to form manned space stations—and developing passenger shuttles to take people to them—was originally NASA's idea. At first, they were enthusiastic about this possbility.

   _____

   _____

6. However, it would have taken too long for NASA to develop and test passenger shuttles, so it was dropped.

   _____

   _____

Name_____ Date _____

7. SIG's plan is to build the passenger shuttles and lease them to commercial airlines. They believe that this is the fastest way to get ordinary people into space.

_____

_____

8. The space stations will also be leased—at a rate of US $10 to $20 per cubic foot per day—to anyone wishing to run a business in space. You simply take the shuttle, transfer to the space station, and set up your office.

_____

_____

9. While the space stations have a projected life of 30 years, they claim that tenants would fully pay for them within 2 to 3 years. This means that the passenger shuttle program could actually operate at a profit.

_____

_____

EXERCISE 10-3 (10e)

Revising to Eliminate Misuse of you

Revise this paragraph to eliminate the inappropriate use of *you*. Begin by changing "You have to be careful" to "Everyone has to be careful." Then change further uses of *you* to suitable nouns or pronouns. It may be necessary to change some verbs in order to have them agree with new subjects.

You have to be careful when buying on credit. Otherwise, you may wind up so heavily in debt that it will take years to straighten out your life. Credit cards are easy for you to get if you are working, and many finance companies are eager to give you instalment loans at high interest rates. Once you are hooked, you may find yourself taking out loans to pay your loans. When this happens, you are doomed to being forever in debt.

There are, of course, times when using credit makes sense. If you have the money (or will have it when the bill comes), a credit card can enable you to shop without carrying cash. You may also want to keep a few gasoline credit cards with you in case your car breaks down on the road. Using credit will allow you to deal with other emergencies (tuition, a broken water heater) when you lack the cash. You can also use credit to take advantage of sales. However, you need to recognize the difference between a sale item you need and one you want. If you cannot do this, you may find yourself dealing with collection agents, car repossessors, or even bankruptcy lawyers.

11 Agreement

SUBJECT–VERB AGREEMENT

11a Understanding subject-verb agreement

Subject-verb agreement occurs at least once per sentence. To function correctly, subjects and verbs must match in number (singular or plural) and in person (first, second, or third).

The human **brain weighs** about 1.5 kilograms. [*brain* = singular subject in the third person; *weighs* = singular verb in the third person]

Human **brains weigh** about 1.5 kilograms. [*brains* = plural subject in the third person; *weigh* = plural verb in the third person]

A QUICK REVIEW OF PERSON FOR AGREEMENT

The **first person** is the speaker or writer. *I* (singular) and *we* (plural) are the only subjects that occur in the first person.

SINGULAR   *I* see a field of fireflies.

PLURAL   *We* see a field of fireflies.

The **second person** is the person spoken or written to. *You* (both singular and plural) is the only subject that occurs in the second person.

SINGULAR   *You* see a shower of sparks.

PLURAL   *You* see a shower of sparks.

The **third person** is the person or thing being spoken or written of. Most rules for subject-verb agreement involve the third person. A subject in the third person can vary widely—for example, *student* and *students* (singular and plural people), *table* and *tables* (singular and plural things), and *it* and *they* (singular and plural pronouns).

SINGULAR   The **scientist sees** a cloud of cosmic dust.

　　　　　　　She (he, it) sees a cloud of cosmic dust.

PLURAL   The **scientists see** a cloud of cosmic dust.

　　　　　　　They see a cloud of cosmic dust.

11b Using the final -*s* or -*es* either for plural subjects or for singular verbs

Subject-verb agreement often involves one letter: *s.* The key is the difference between the -*s* added to subjects and the -*s* added to verbs.

Plural subjects are usually formed by adding -*s* or -*es* to singular nouns. **Singular verbs** in the present tense of the third person are formed by adding -*s* or -*es* to the simple form—with the exceptions of *be (is)* and *have (has)*.

Visualizing how the -*s* works in agreement can help you remember when it is needed. The -*s* (or -*es* when required) can take only one path at a time, either the top or the bottom, as in this diagram.

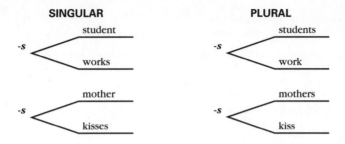

Even though the final -*s* does not appear in some subjects, the principle of the memory device holds. This final -*s* does not appear in the following situations: in subjects that are plural without an -*s* (such as *people, children*); in plural personal pronouns (*we, you, they*); in the plural demonstrative pronouns (*these, those*); and in certain indefinite pronouns when they are used as plurals (*few, some, more, many, most, all*).

A **person** on a diet often **misses** sweets.

People enjoy candy or cake after meals.

They learn to substitute fruit for pasty.

❖ USAGE ALERT: Do not add -*s* to the third-person singular main verb after a modal auxiliary verb (a helping verb such as *can, might, must, would*—see 8e). ❖

11c For agreement, ignoring words between a subject and verb

Words that separate the subject from the verb can cause confusion about what the verb should agree with. To locate the subject of the sentence, ignore prepositional phrases or phrases that start with *including, together with, along with, accompanied by, in addition to, except*, or *as well as.*

The best **workers** in the bookkeeping department **have** received raises.

The top-selling sales **representative,** along with her husband, **is going** to visit Banff as a bonus.

11d Using verbs with subjects connected with *and*

When two or more subjects are joined by *and*, they function as a group; therefore, they need a plural verb.

Club soda and iced tea are popular summer drinks.

My friend and I prefer cold milk.

However, if the word *each* or *every* precedes subjects joined by *and*, use a singular verb.

Each cat and dog in the animal shelter **deserves** a home.

When *each* or *every* follows subjects joined by *and*, however, it does not affect the basic rule: use a plural verb for subjects joined by *and:*

The SPCA and the Humane Society each **need** our support.

The one exception to the *and* rule occurs when the parts combine to form a single thing or person.

Beans and rice is a popular vegetarian dish.

My husband and business partner keeps our tax records.

11e Making the verb agree with the subject closest to it

When you join subjects with *or* or *nor* or correlative conjunctions, *either . . . or, neither . . . nor, not only . . . but (also)* , make the verb agree with the subject closest to it. Unlike *and*, these conjunctions do not create plurals. For the purpose of agreement, ignore everything before the final subject.

~~Neither Benny Goodman nor~~ **Louis Armstrong** is heard on the radio often.

~~Either the Andrews Sisters or~~ **Frank Sinatra was** my mother's favourite singer.

11f Using verbs in inverted word order

In questions, the verb comes before the subject. Be sure to look ahead to check that the subject and verb agree.

Is jazz popular?

Expletive constructions postpone the subject by using *there* or *here* plus a form of the verb *be*. Check ahead in such sentences to identify the subject, and make the form of *be* agree with the subject.

There were many **bands** that played swing in the forties.

There is still a dedicated **audience** for this music.

Introductory *it* plus a form of the verb *be* can be an expletive construction as well, but one that always takes a singular verb.

It is young musicians who strive to capture the sound of the Big Bands.

11g Using verbs with indefinite pronouns

Indefinite pronouns do not refer to any particular person, thing, or idea. They take their meanings from context. Indefinite pronouns are usually singular, and therefore they take singular verbs. Here is a list of singular indefinite pronouns:

each	everyone	no one
every	everybody	nobody
one	everything	nothing
either	anyone	someone
neither	anybody	somebody
another	anything	something

Everybody talks about the weather but **no one does** a thing about it.

No matter was **someone forecasts, something** different **seems** to happen.

Two indefinite pronouns, *both* and *many*, are always plural and require a plural verb.

Both of them **accept** the decision.

A few indefinite pronouns—*none, some, more, most, any*, and *all*—may be either singular or plural, depending on the meaning of the sentence.

All of the weather forecasts we hear **are** based on probabilities.

We hate bad weather, but **some is** inevitable.

11h Using verbs in context for collective nouns

A **collective noun** names a group of people or things: *family, group, audience, class, number, committee, team*. When the group acts as one unit, use a singular verb. When the members of the group act individually, use a plural verb.

The **jury is** hearing evidence. [*Jury* refers to a single unit, so the verb is singular.]

The **jury disagrees** on a verdict. [The jury members take separate action, so the verb is plural.]

11i Making a linking verb agree with the subject—not the subject complement

Even when the **subject complement** (7m-1) that follows a linking verb (7c) differs in number (singular and plural) from the subject, the verb must agree with the subject.

The best **part** of the week **is** Saturday and Sunday.

but

Saturday and Sunday are the best part of the week.

11j Using verbs that agree with the antecedents of *who, which*, and *that*

Who, which, and *that* have the same form in singular and plural, so you must find their antecedents (10a) before you can decide whether the verb is singular or plural.

The **tenants who move** into this apartment will need to paint it. [*Who* refers to *tenants*, so the verb *move* is plural.]

The **tenant who moves** into this apartment will need to paint it. [*Who* refers to *tenant*, so the verb *moves* is singular.]

Be especially careful to identify the antecedent of *who, which*, or *that* when you see *one of the* or *the only one of the* in a sentence.

George Boyd is one of the **tenants who want** to hire a new janitor. [*Who* refers to *tenants*, so *want* is plural.]

George Boyd is the only **one** of the tenants **who wants** to hire a new janitor. [*Who* refers to *one*, so *wants* is singular.]

11k Using verbs with amounts, fields of study, and other special nouns

Subjects that refer to times, sums of money, distance, or measurement are considered singular and take singular verbs.

Seventy-five cents is the toll over the bridge.

One and six-tenths kilometres makes a mile.

Many words that end in *-s* or *-ics* are singular in meaning despite their plural appearance. These include *news, ethics, economics, mathematics, physics, politics, sports, statistics* (as a course of study).

Mathematics is necessary for many daily tasks.

Athletics demands total commitment.

In contrast, other words are plural even though they refer to one thing. These include *jeans, pants, scissors, clippers, tweezers, eyeglasses, thanks, riches.*

The **scissors are** on the desk.

Using singular verbs for titles of written works, companies, and words as terms

Arm and Hammer is a popular brand of baking soda.

Cats, the musical, **is** based on a book of poems by T. S. Eliot.

PRONOUN–ANTECEDENT AGREEMENT

 Understanding pronoun-antecedent agreement

The form of most pronouns depends on what their **antecedents** are (10a), so the connection between a pronoun and its antecedent must be clear. These connections are reflected by agreement in number (singular or plural), person (first, second, or third) and gender (male or female).

Singular pronouns must refer to singular antecedents, and plural pronouns must refer to plural antecedents.

The **ocean** has **its** own plant and animal life.

The **oceans** have **their** own plant and animal life.

First-person pronouns must refer to first-person antecedents, second-person pronouns to second-person antecedents, and third-person pronouns to third-person antecedents.

Beginning **drivers** have to watch **their** [third person: not *your*] instructors for directions.

 Using pronouns with antecedents connected with *and*

Two or more antecedents joined by *and* require a plural pronoun, even if each antecedent by itself is singular.

Dalhousie University and UBC are centres of ocean exploration because of **their** coastal locations.

When *each* or *every* precedes singular nouns joined by *and*, use a singular pronoun.

Each scuba diver and sailor hopes to locate a sunken treasure for **herself** or **himself**.

Also when the singular nouns joined by *and* refer to the same person or thing, use a singular pronoun.

Our **captain and diving instructor** warned us to stay near **her.**

11o Making the pronoun agree with the nearest antecedent

Antecedents joined by the conjunctions *or* or *nor*, or correlative conjunctions (such as *either . . . or, neither . . . nor*), often mix masculine and feminine or singular and plural nouns. To find the needed pronoun, ignore everything before the final antecedent.

~~Either the seals or~~ the porpoise will do **its** act.

~~Either the porpoise or~~ the **seals** will do **their** act.

~~Neither Bob nor~~ **Jane** likes to share **her** training methods.

~~Neither Jane nor~~ **Bob** likes to share **his** training methods.

11p Using pronouns with indefinite-pronoun antecedents

Indefinite pronouns (see 11g for a list) are usually singular. When they are, the pronouns that refer to them should also be singular.

Everyone should know **his or her** Social Insurance number.

No one can be expected to know **his or her** driver's licence number.

11q Avoiding sexist pronoun use

In the past, the masculine pronoun was used to refer to indefinite pronouns as well as to nouns and pronouns that name general categories to which any person might belong: *Everyone should admit his mistakes.* Today people are more conscious that *he, his, him,* and *himself* exclude women. Many writers try to avoid using masculine pronouns to refer to the entire population.

WAYS TO AVOID USING ONLY THE MASCULINE PRONOUN TO REFER TO MALES AND FEMALES TOGETHER

Solution 1   Use a pair of pronouns—but try to avoid a pair more than once in a sentence or in many sentences in a row.

Everyone hopes that **he or she** will win the scholarship.

A successful doctor knows that **he or she** has to work long hours.

Solution 2   Revise into the plural.

Many people hope that **they** will win the scholarship.

Successful doctors know that **they** have to work long hours.

Solution 3   Recast the sentence.

Everyone hopes to win the scholarship.

Successful doctors should expect to work long hours.

Some indefinite pronouns can be either singular or plural, depending on the meaning of the sentence. When the indefinite pronoun is plural, then the pronouns that refer back to it should be plural.

Many students do not realize they have a talent for mathematics. **Some** have learned this attitude from **their** parents.

11r Using pronouns with collective-noun antecedents

A **collective noun** names a group of people or things: *family, group, audience, class, number, committee, team,* and the like. When the group acts as one unit, use a singular pronoun to refer to it. When the members of the group act individually, use a plural pronoun.

The **committee** has elected **its** new chairperson. [The *committee* is acting as one unit, so the pronoun is singular.]

The **committee** expressed **their** opinions about the election campaign. [The *committee* is acting as individuals, so the pronoun is plural.]

Making Subjects and Verbs Agree

A: Fill in the blanks on the right with the present-tense forms of the verbs in parentheses. Be sure each verb agrees in person and number with the subject of the sentence. (11b)

EXAMPLE   The Cuna Indians (to produce) an unusual kind of art.   _produce_

1. Cuna Indians (to occupy) the San Blas Islands off the coast of Panama.   _____

2. The outside world (to associate) them with distinctive women's clothing.   _____

3. Cuna women (to wear) blouses containing two panels of appliquéd cloth.   _____

4. The Cuna word *mola* (to refer) to either a blouse or one of its panels.   _____

5. The Cuna (to work) their molas in reverse appliqué.   _____

6. Traditional appliqué (to consist) of turning under edges of a piece of fabric and sewing it onto a larger piece.   _____

7. Molas (to use) a different technique.   _____

8. A Cuna woman (to baste) together several layers of cloth of different colours.   _____

9. She then (to cut) through all but the bottom layer.   _____

10. When turned under, the upper layers (to reveal) contrasting colours.   _____

B: Fill in the blanks on the right with the appropriate present-tense forms of the verbs in parentheses. (11c-e)

EXAMPLE   Most resources of the earth (to be) not renewable.   _are_

1. Neither coffee grounds nor an apple core (to need) to be thrown out.   _____

2. Food waste, along with grass clippings, (to make) good compost.   _____

3. Many items from your garbage (to be) recyclable.   _____

4. Aluminum cans, plastic jugs, and glass bottles (to deserve) a second life.   _____

5. One of the most tedious jobs (to seem) to be sorting garbage.   _____

6. Yet rewards from such work (to be) immeasurable.   _____

7. Every recycled bottle and can (to mean) a saving of resources.   _____

8. Not only an adult but also a child (to be) capable of helping the environment.   _____

9. Learning what to recycle, as well as being willing to do it, (to become) necessary.   _____

10. You and I each (to be) expected to do our part.   _____

C: Circle the subjects and underline the verbs. If the verb does not agree with the subject, cross it out and write the correct form on the line to the right. If the verb does agree, write *correct* on the line. (11f, i)

Name_____ Date _____

EXAMPLE (Kyoto) the historical capital of Japan, a~~X~~ really   _____*is*_____
many cities in one.

1. Has Ken and Sara ever visited Japan?   _____
2. There is several places they should see.   _____
3. It is cities like Kyoto that transmit Japanese culture.   _____
4. Japanese history seems alive here.   _____
5. There is more than two thousand temples in Kyoto.   _____
6. In the city are also castles and luxurious residences.   _____
7. There is peaceful Zen gardens.   _____
8. Japanese art and architecture reveals the history of the empire.   _____
9. Yet there is also a very modern city.   _____
10. From all over the world comes visitors to Kyoto.   _____

D: Fill in the blanks on the right with the present-tense forms of the verbs in parentheses. (11g, h)

EXAMPLE Most of Chicago's visitors (to be) impressed by   _____*are*_____
its architecture.

1. The Chicago School (to be) a group of architects at the turn of the century.   _____
2. Some (to be) known throughout the world.   _____
3. Not everyone in the group (to be) considered a genius.   _____
4. Yet all (to have) contributed to the appearance of the city.   _____
5. A number of buildings (to be) considered architectural landmarks.   _____
6. Many (to share) certain features like Chicago windows.   _____
7. One of the most famous styles (to be) Frank Lloyd Wright's Prairie House.   _____
8. A tour group visiting Chicago today (to be) sure to enjoy a drive down _____
the Magnificent Mile.
9. A family often (to prefer) a walking tour.   _____
10. Few (to be) exempt from the charms of a constantly building city.   _____

E: Circle the antecedent of each italicized *who, which*, or *that*. Then fill in the blanks on the right with the appropriate present-tense forms of the verbs in parentheses. (11j)

EXAMPLE   The *Book of Kells* is one of many manuscripts *that* (to belong)   ___belong___
to Trinity College, Dublin.

1. Its source is a mystery *that* (to continue) to baffle scholars. _____

2. Anyone *who* (to see) it marvels at its brilliant illumination. _____

3. The book, *which* (to be) considered a masterpiece, contains full-page _____
illustrations of the Gospels.

4. No one *who* (to study) the book can fail to be impressed by it. _____

5. The paintings, *which* (to be) done in minute details, retain their _____
vivid colours.

6. There is also decoration *that* (to appear) to have no relationship to _____
the text.

7. Some of the pictures, *which* (to stem) from unknown origins, seem _____
strange for a religious book.

8. One does not expect birds *that* (to wear) ecclesiastical garb. _____

9. Nor does one expect the humour *that* (to pervade) some of the _____
illustrations.

10. The text, *which* (to be) written in beautiful script, combines _____
two translations.

F: Fill in the blanks on the right with the appropriate present-tense forms of the verbs in parentheses. (11k,l)

EXAMPLE   Two and a half centimetres (to equal) approximately one inch.   ___equals___

1. Ten dollars (to seem) like a lot of money to see just one movie. _____

2. The news (to be) available 24 hours a day on some radio and _____
television stations.

3. *Bonnie and Clyde* (to show) moviegoers the violent rise and fall of a _____
Depression-era gang.

4. Forty thousand kilometres (to be) the circumference of the earth at _____
the equator.

5. When there are children in a home, scissors (to belong) in a safe place. _____

6. Four hundred and fifty-four grams (to make) one pound. _____

7. Faber & Faber (to remain) known for both hiring T. S. Eliot as an _____
editor and publishing his work.

8. Physics (to deal) with the basic principles governing our universe. _____

9. Eyeglasses (to get) lost easily because once we take them off we _____
cannot see well enough to look for them.

10. Dun and Bradstreet (to rate) businesses so people can see if a _____
company is a safe investment.

Name_____ Date _____

G: Fill in the blanks on the right with the appropriate present-tense forms of the verbs in parentheses. (11a-l)

EXAMPLE Everyone (to dream) during sleep.   _____*dreams*_____

1. No one (to know) why we (to dream).   _____
2. Dreams (to occur) during a special kind of sleep, known as REM.   _____
3. REM (to stand) for Rapid Eye Movement.   _____
4. A total of about two hours a night (to get) spent in this dream state. _____
5. There (to be) many theories about why people dream and what the   _____
    rapid movement of our eyeballs (to mean).
6. Some (to suggest) that REM sleep occurs when the brain rids itself _____
    of unnecessary images.
7. According to this theory, dreams (to represent) random signals.   _____
8. Others (to believe) that dreaming helps the brain establish patterns _____
    for thinking.
9. Human newborns, they say, (to spend) about half their sleep time   _____
    dreaming.
10. The babies, who (to receive) huge amounts of new information every _____
    day, many be developing plans for processing what they see and hear.
11. In contrast, the elderly (to devote) only 15 percent of their sleep _____
    time to dreaming.
12. Why we dream and what dreams mean (to form) a big mystery.   _____
13. Psychologists (to think) dreams help people deal with emotional issues. _____
14. The population often (to lack) the time necessary to cope with   _____
    complicated emotional situations.
15. For example, people in the middle of divorce often (to have) long, _____
    detailed dreams.
16. In contrast, people with peaceful lives generally (to claim) their _____
    dreams are dull.
17. Sigmund Freud said that dreams (to protect) us from painful truths. _____
18. There (to exist) a radical new theory which (to propose) that dreams _____
    do something entirely different.
19. While awake, people (to learn) about the environment, but in dreams _____
    the flow of new information about the world is cut off.
20. Each dream (to combine) new information with information already   _____
    in the brain, and new ways of dealing with the world (to be) rehearsed.

Making Pronouns and Antecedents Agree

Select a personal pronoun that agrees with the subject of each of these sentences. Write your answers on the lines to the right. Some items have more than one correct answer.

EXAMPLE   The group has _____ meeting here.   _____*its*_____

1. Anyone can get _____ name in the news.   _____
2. None of the cheques were cashed; _____ finally expired.   _____
3. The chef cut _____ on the thumb while peeling carrots.   _____
4. A person should insure _____ valuables.   _____
5. The family has _____ eye on a new house.   _____
6. The codebreakers shared _____ secrets.   _____
7. Everybody has _____ own dreams and goals.   _____
8. One can be happy only if _____ has respect for _____ . _____
9. Children never realize how loud _____ can be.   _____
10. The graduating class wore _____ rings proudly.   _____
11. My mother and her sister took _____ vacation together.   _____
12. Either Mike or John wears a patch over _____ eye.   _____
13. All are welcome; _____ just need to call for directions to the party. _____
14. Neither documentaries nor the news is given enough money
    by _____ network.   _____
15. Wawa and Petawawa get _____ names from the Algonquin
    language.   _____
16. Either John Turner or Charles Tupper had _____ term as
    prime minister end after only two months.   _____
17. Cars cost more than _____ owners expect them to.   _____
18. Venus and Mars have _____ orbits nearer to Earth than to any
    other planets.   _____
19. The band starts _____ tour tomorrow night.   _____
20. Any of the candidates could win; _____ are very much alike. _____

Revising Sentences for Agreement

Revise each of these passages so that all pronouns agree with their antecedents in person, number, and gender. You may also have to change verbs or other words. Some sentences can be revised in more than one way. Take the time to try several, and select the version you like best.

EXERCISES

Name_____ Date _____

EXAMPLE   The human population creates most environmental problems because they have minimum requirements for food and space.

The human population creates most environmental problems because it has minimum requirements for food and space.

1. The number of people that needs to be absorbed into Canada each month is 48 000. They are made up of 33 000 births and 15 000 immigrants.

   _____

2. All need to have basic services. He needs food, clothing, and shelter.

   _____

3. A higher birth rate and a greater survival rate are modern trends. Together, it makes the world population double in 35 years.

   _____

4. Either disease or war may be the result, some people say. They will be ways of reducing the population.

   _____

5. There are theories about how many people the earth can support, but it varies from 500 000 000 (less than 10 percent of the current population) to 15 billion (between two and three times the current population).

   _____

6. Anyone in a world of 15 billion people would not have many luxuries in their lives.

   _____

7. Life in the poorest tropical countries is horrible. They are often very short and miserable.

   _____

8. The food supply in these countries is already too small, but rapidly growing populations means they will become even less adequate.

   _____

9. Nobody can be sure of the outcome if we do not make some changes. They can be sure, however, that more people will go hungry.

   _____

10. Neither the dependence on only a few grain crops nor the beef-eating habit is likely to last much into the future. They are too wasteful of food resources.

_____

11. China and India have a combined population of over two billion. Those are about one-third of the world's people.

_____

12. To make room for more towns, some tropical countries are cutting down its rain forests.

_____

13. Third World governments must take steps to use the forest wisely, or they will disappear.

_____

12 Using Adjectives and Adverbs

12a Distinguishing between adjectives and adverbs

Both **adjectives** and **adverbs** are **modifiers**—words or groups of words that describe other words. Because adjectives and adverbs function similarly in sentences, distinguishing between them is sometimes difficult.

ADJECTIVE   The **quick** messenger delivered the payroll.

ADVERB   The messenger **quickly** delivered the payroll.

The key to distinguishing between adjectives and adverbs is that they modify different types of words or groups of words.

SUMMARY OF DIFFERENCES BETWEEN ADJECTIVES AND ADVERBS

WHAT ADJECTIVES MODIFY	EXAMPLE
nouns	The **busy** *lawyer* rested.
pronouns	*She* felt **triumphant**.

WHAT ADVERBS MODIFY	EXAMPLE
verbs	The lawyer *spoke* **quickly**.
adverbs	The lawyer spoke **very** *quickly*.
adjectives	The lawyer was **extremely** *busy*.
independent clauses	**Therefore**, *the lawyer rested*.

Adjectives and adverbs are sometimes confused because of the *-ly* ending. In many cases, an adverb is formed by adding *-ly* to an adjective: *soft, softly; grand, grandly; beautiful, beautifully*. However, even though many adverbs end in *-ly*, some do not: *well, very, worse*. Also some words that end in *-ly* are adjectives: *lively, friendly*. The *-ly* ending, therefore, is not a foolproof way to identify adverbs.

To determine whether an adjective or an adverb is called for, see how the word functions in its sentence. If a noun or pronoun is being modified, use an adjective. If a verb, adjective, or other adverb is being modified, use an adverb.

12b Using adverbs—not adjectives—to modify verbs, adjectives, and other adverbs

Only adverbs modify verbs, adjectives, and other adverbs. You should avoid using adjectives as adverbs.

NO   It snowed **heavy** last night. [Adjective *heavy* cannot modify verb *snowed*.]

YES   It snowed **heavily** last night. [Adverb *heavily* modifies the verb *snowed*.]

Good–well: The words *good* and *well* can be confusing. As an adjective, *good* can modify nouns or noun substitutes.

The **good** news spread. [Adjective *good* modifies noun *news*.]

The reopened factory would be **good** for the town. [Adjective *good* modifies noun phrase *the reopened factory*.]

Good cannot modify verbs. Only *well*, an adverb, can modify verbs.

NO   The project started off **good.** [Adjective *good* cannot modify verb *started off*.]

YES   The project started off **well.** [Adverb *well* modifies verb *started off*.]

YES   The **good** project started off **well.**

One exception exists: *well* is used as an adjective to describe conditions of health.

I don't feel **well.**

The patient is **well.**

Only adverbs modify adjectives and other adverbs.

NO   This is a **true fattening** dessert. [Adjective *true* cannot modify adjective *fattening*.]

YES   This is a **truly fattening** dessert. [Adverb *truly* modifies adjective *fattening*.]

12c Not using double negatives

A **double negative** is a statement that contains two negative modifiers. Negative modifiers include *no, never, not, none, nothing, hardly, scarcely,* and *barely.* They should not occur in the same sentence.

NO   Some people do **not** have **no** pity for the needy.

YES   Some people do **not** have any pity for the needy.

NO   They **never** donate **no** food.

YES   They **never** donate food.

NO   She could **not hardly** pay the rent.

YES   She could **hardly** pay the rent.

12d Using adjectives—not adverbs—as complements after linking verbs

Linking verbs indicate a state of being or a condition. They serve to connect the subject to a word that renames or describes it. If the subject is being described after a linking verb, an adjective is needed. If, however, the verb is being described, an adverb is needed.

> The bee was **angry.** [Adjective *angry* describes the subject *bee* after linking verb *was.*]
>
> The bee attacked **angrily.** [Adverb *angrily* describes the action verb *attacked.*]

Bad–badly: The words *bad* (adjective) and *badly* (adverb) are often misused with linking verbs, especially verbs related to the senses, such as *feel.* Only the adjectives *bad* or *good* are correct when a verb is operating as a linking verb.

FOR DESCRIBING A FEELING	The coach felt **bad.** [not *badly*]
FOR DESCRIBING A SMELL	The locker room smelled **bad.** [not *badly*]
FOR DESCRIBING A SOUND	The half-time band sounded **good.** [not *well*]

12e Using correct comparative and superlative forms of adjectives and adverbs

By using special forms of adjectives and adverbs, you can make comparisons. Most adjectives and adverbs show degrees of comparison by means of *-er* and *-est* endings or by being combined with the words *more* and *most.* (Adjectives and adverbs show diminishing or negative comparison by combining with the words *less* and *least: less jumpy, least jumpy; less surely, least surely.*)

FORMS OF COMPARISON FOR REGULAR ADJECTIVES AND ADVERBS	
FORM	**FUNCTION**
Positive	Used when nothing is being compared
Comparative	Used when only two things are being compared—with *-er* endings or *more* (or *less*)
Superlative	Used when three or more things are being compared—with *-est* ending or *most* (or *least*)

Positive	Comparative	Superlative
green	greener	greenest
happy	happier	happiest
selfish	less selfish	least selfish
beautiful	more beautiful	most beautiful

Her tree is **green.**

Her tree is **greener** than his tree.

Her tree is the **greenest** one on the block.

The choice of whether to use *-er/-est* or *more/most, less/least* depends largely on the number of syllables in the adjective or adverb. With **one-syllable words,** the *-er/est* endings are most common: *large, larger, largest* (adjective); *far, farther, farthest* (adverb). With **words of three or more syllables,** *more/most* are used: *energetic, more energetic, most energetic.* With **adverbs of two or more syllables,** *more/most* are used: *easily, more easily, most easily.* With **adjectives of two syllables,** practice varies. Often you will form comparatives and superlatives intuitively, based on what you have heard or read for a particular adjective. If neither form sounds natural for a given adjective, consult your dictionary for the recommended form.

Be careful not to use a **double comparative** or **double superlative.** The words *more* or *most* cannot be used if the *-er* or *-est* ending has been used.

Some comparative and superlative forms are irregular. Learn this short list.

IRREGULAR COMPARATIVES AND SUPERLATIVES

POSITIVE (1)	COMPARATIVE (2)	SUPERLATIVE (3+)
good (adjective)	better	best
well (adjective and adverb)	better	best
bad (adjective)	worse	worst
badly (adverb)	worse	worst
many	more	most
much	more	most
some	more	most
little	less	least

12f Avoiding too many nouns as modifiers

Sometimes nouns can modify other nouns: *bird watching, fishing pole, fire drill.* These terms create no problems, but when nouns pile up in a list of modifiers, it can be difficult to know which nouns are being modified and which nouns are doing the modifying.

NO	I misplaced my **electric garage door opener rebate coupon.**
YES	I misplaced **the coupon needed to get a rebate on the electric opener for my garage door.**

EXERCISES

Name_____ Date _____

Identifying Adjectives and Adverbs

On the lines to the right, identify each of the italicized words as an adjective or adverb. (Following common usage, the titles of books also appear in italics; however, these are nouns, never adjectives or adverbs.)

EXAMPLE   Rohinton Mistry won the Governor General's Award   _____*adjective*_____
            for his *first* novel.

1. Agatha Christie is famous for her *mystery* novels.   _____
2. She *also* wrote romantic novels, under a pen name.   _____
3. Joseph Conrad was a *highly* respected English writer.   _____
4. His *native* language was Polish.   _____
5. He *always* had trouble speaking but not writing English.   _____
6. *Gone with the Wind* was Margaret Mitchell's *only* book.   _____
7. Upon Sinclair wrote *The Jungle* hoping to improve conditions in the *Chicago* stockyards.   _____
8. In *his* book he called for large social and economic reforms.   _____
9. Sinclair's work led *directly* to regulations governing food purity.   _____
10. Each year, Canadian publishers introduce about 10 000 *different* books in both French and English.   _____
11. The *typical* Canadian book author earns less than $10 000 a year from writing.   _____
12. The federal government is a *major* supporter of Canadian publishing.   _____
13. In 1979, *4479* writers belonged to writers' unions in Canada, according to a federal study.   _____
14. Only *recently* have women authors been widely accepted.   _____
15. Many nineteenth-century English female authors became *widely* popular writing under men's names.   _____
16. George Eliot was *really* Mary Anne Evans, while Charlotte Brontë wrote as Currer Bell and her sister Emily Brontë wrote as Ellis Bell.   _____
17. *Other* famous writers have also used pen names.   _____
18. George Orwell was *actually* the pen name of Englishman Eric Arthur Blair.   _____

19. Popular *romance* novelist Barbara Cartland also publishes under
the name Barbara Hamilton McCorquodale.   _____

20. Even Agatha Christie *sometimes* chose a pseudonym: _____
Mary Westmacott.

Distinguishing Adjectives from Adverbs

From the choices in parentheses, select the correct modifier for each sentence. Write your
answers on the lines to the right.

EXAMPLE   Aspirin can cause a (severe, severely) upset stomach   *severely*
in some people.

1. Pain sufferers (annual, annually) spend milions of dollars on aspirin.   _____
2. Over 200 kinds of headache medicines containing aspirin are   _____
(available, availably).
3. Many of us feel taking aspirin can make us (good, well).   _____
4. However, aspirin has many (serious, seriously) side effects.   _____
5. Aspirin (common, commonly) causes bleeding in the stomach.   _____
6. This can make us feel (bad, badly).   _____
7. Bleeding occurs when an undissolved aspirin tablet lies on the   _____
(delicate, delicately) stomach wall.
8. For most of us, the amount of blood lost is not   _____
(dangerous, dangerously).
9. However, some (slow, slowly) dissolving tablets can cause prolonged   _____
bleeding, leading to great discomfort.
10. (High, Highly) quality aspirin dissolves more quickly and is less likely _____
to cause a problem.
11. Aspirin has a (lengthy, lengthily) history.   _____
12. Our (ancient, anciently) ancestors chewed the leaves and bark of   _____
the willow tree.
13. They contain a substance (chemical, chemically) related to aspirin.   _____
14. Aspirin itself was introduced as a painkiller and fever reducer more   _____
(recent, recently).
15. Coming on the market in 1899, it (quick, quickly) became the best-   _____
selling nonprescription drug in the world.
16. The tablet form so (popular, popularly) today was introduced by   _____
Bayer in 1915.
17. Taking an aspirin a day has (late, lately) been claimed to be good   _____
for the heart.
18. Some research shows that men who take aspirin (regular, regularly)   _____
after a heart attack are less likely to have another attack.

Name_____ Date _____

19. No one knows why this is so, but some healthy people have been   _____
    (quick, quickly) to start taking aspirin daily.

20. Doctors advise us to think (careful, carefully) before we do this   _____
    because there is no evidence that aspirin prevents first heart attacks.

Using Comparatives and Superlatives

A: Fill in the comparative and superlative forms of the adjectives and adverbs listed on the left.

	Comparative	*Superlative*
EXAMPLE tall	*taller*	*tallest*
1. *bad*	_____	_____
2. *badly*	_____	_____
3. *forgiving*	_____	_____
4. *free*	_____	_____
5. *good*	_____	_____
6. *gracefully*	_____	_____
7. *handsome*	_____	_____
8. *hot*	_____	_____
9. *little*	_____	_____
10. *loudly*	_____	_____
11. *many*	_____	_____
12. *much*	_____	_____
13. *powerfully*	_____	_____
14. *pretty*	_____	_____
15. *quickly*	_____	_____
16. *some*	_____	_____
17. *sweetly*	_____	_____
18. *sympathetically*	_____	_____
19. *talented*	_____	_____
20. *well*	_____	_____

B: Use the adjectives and adverbs above in sets of sentences that show how the three forms are related to changes in meaning. Use your own paper.

EXAMPLE   I am tall. (positive)

I am taller than my sister. (comparative)

I am the tallest person in my family. (superlative)

Writing with Adjectives and Adverbs

EXERCISE **12-4**
(12)

Write a paragraph describing someone, something, or someplace wonderful. Some suggestions: your favourite restaurant, your favourite movie star, an exciting amusement park, your most treasured possession.

Be sure to have a topic sentence (4b). Develop your idea with four to six sentences, each containing strong and appropriate adjectives and adverbs. Try not to use so many modifiers in any one sentence that the main idea gets lost. Use your own paper.

Sentence Fragments

A sentence **fragment** is part of a sentence punctuated as though it were a complete sentence. You can avoid writing sentence fragments if you recognize the difference between a fragment and a complete sentence.

13a Testing for sentence completeness

If you write sentence fragments frequently, you need a system to check that your sentences are complete. Here is a test to use if you suspect that you have written a sentence fragment.

TEST FOR SENTENCE COMPLETENESS

1. **Is the word group a dependent clause?** If yes, there is a sentence fragment.
2. **Is there a verb?** If not, there is a sentence fragment.
3. **Is there a subject?** If not, there is a sentence fragment.

QUESTION 1: Is the word group a dependent clause?

If the answer is yes, you are looking at a sentence fragment. Dependent clauses are clauses that contain subordinating words as explained in 7o-2. To be part of a complete sentence, a dependent clause must be joined to an independent clause.

One type of subordinating word is a **subordinating conjunction.** Some of the most frequently used are *after, although, because, if, when, where,* and *until.*

FRAGMENT	**If** I see him.
REVISED	**If** I seem, I'll give him your message.
FRAGMENT	**Where** the park is.
REVISED	The city will build a hospital **where** the park is.

❖ USAGE ALERT: When a dependent clause starting with a subordinating conjunction comes before an independent clause, a comma usually separates the clauses. ❖

Another type of subordinating word is a **relative pronoun.** The most common relative pronouns are *who, which,* and *that.*

FRAGMENT	The class **that** we wanted.
REVISED	The class **that** we wanted was full.
FRAGMENT	The students **who** registered early.
REVISED	The students **who** registered early got the classes they wanted.

Questions are an exception—they can begin with words such as *when, where, who,* and *which* without being sentence fragments.

When is the meeting?

Who is your favourite author?

QUESTION 2: Is there a verb?

If there is no verb, you are looking at a sentence fragment.

FRAGMENT	Yesterday the math lab hiring tutors.
REVISED	Yesterday the math lab **was** hiring tutors.
FRAGMENT	Today the math lab hiring tutors.
REVISED	Today the math lab **is** hiring tutors.
FRAGMENT	Chosen for their math ability.
REVISED	The tutors **are** chosen for their math ability.
REVISED	Chosen for their math ability, the tutors also **work** well with other students.
FRAGMENT	Each tutor to work with eight students.
REVISED	Each tutor **works** with eight students.
REVISED	Each tutor **is assigned** to work with eight students.

QUESTION 3: Is there a subject?

If there is no subject, you are looking at a sentence fragment. To find a subject, ask a "who?" or "what?" question about the verb.

FRAGMENT	Worked in the library. [Who worked? Unknown]
REVISED	**The students** worked in the library.

Every sentence must have its own subject. A sentence fragment without a subject often results when the missing subject is the same as the subject in the previous sentence.

NO	In September, the new dormitories were opened. **Were occupied immediately.**
YES	In September, the new dormitories were opened. **They were occupied immediately.**

Imperative statements—commands and some requests—are an exception. Imperative statements imply the word *you* as the subject.

Sit down! = (You) sit down!

13b Revising dependent clauses punctuated as sentences

To correct a dependent clause punctuated as a sentence (see the discussion of Question 1 in 13a), you can do one of two things: (1) You can join the dependent clause to an independent clause that comes directly before or after. (2) You can drop the subordinating conjunction or relative pronoun. Whichever strategy you use, if necessary, add words to create an independent clause.

FRAGMENT	Students often change their majors. **When they start taking courses.**
REVISED	Students often change their majors when they start taking courses. [joined into one sentence]
REVISED	Students often change their majors. They start taking courses and realize they are unhappy. [subordinating conjunction dropped to create an independent clause]
FRAGMENT	The chemistry major is looking for a lab partner. **Who is dependable.**
REVISED	The chemistry major is looking for a lab partner who is dependable. [joined into one sentence]

13c Revising phrases punctuated as sentences

To correct a phrase punctuated as a sentence (see the discussions of Questions 2 and 3 in 13a), either you can rewrite it as an independent clause by adding the missing subject or verb, or you can join it to an independent clause that comes directly before or after.

A phrase containing a verbal (a gerund, an infinitive, a past participle, or a present participle) but no verb is not a sentence.

FRAGMENT	The college administration voted last week. **To offer a new program in nursing.**
REVISED	The college administration voted last week to offer a new program in nursing. [joined into one sentence]
REVISED	The college adminstration voted last week. The members decided to offer a new program in nursing. [rewritten]
FRAGMENT	**Speaking to the students.** The dean explained the new program.
REVISED	Speaking to the students, the dean explained the new program. [joined into one sentence]
REVISED	The dean spoke to the students. She explained the new program. [rewritten]

FRAGMENT	**Seated in the auditorium.** The students listened carefully.
REVISED	Seated in the auditorium, the students listened carefully. [joined in one sentence]
REVISED	The students were seated in the auditorium. They listened carefully. [rewritten]

A **prepositional phrase** contains a preposition (for a complete list see 7g), its object, and any modifiers.

FRAGMENT	She planned to take Biology 102. **During summer session.**
REVISED	She planned to take Biology 102 during summer session. [joined into one sentence]
REVISED	She planned to take Biology 102. It was offered in summer session. [rewritten]

An **appositive** is a word or word group that renames a noun or group of words functioning as a noun.

FRAGMENT	Many students liked the biology professor. **A teacher of great skill and patience.**
REVISED	Many students liked the biology professor, a teacher of great skill and patience. [joined into one sentence]
REVISED	Many students liked the biology professor. She was a teacher of great skill and patience. [rewritten]

Compound predicates contain two or more verbs, plus their objects and modifiers, if any. To be part of a complete sentence, a predicate must have a subject. If the second half of a compound predicate is punctuated as a sentence, it is a sentence fragment.

FRAGMENT	The professor was always available for conferences. **And answered students' questions clearly.**
REVISED	The professor was always available for conferences and answered students' questions clearly. [joined into one sentence]
REVISED	The professor was always available for conferences. And she always answered students' questions clearly. [rewritten]

13d Revising sentence fragments in lists and examples

Sentence fragment problems sometimes come up when people write lists and examples. Unless a list or example is formatted as a column in point form, it must be part of a complete sentence.

You can connect a list fragment by attaching it to the preceding independent clause with a colon or a dash. You can correct an example by attaching it to an independent clause (the punctuation you use—typically, a semicolon, a dash, or a comma—will depend on the meaning) or by rewriting it as a complete sentence. (Chapters 24, 25, 26, and 29 discuss the uses of these punctuation marks.).

FRAGMENT	You have a choice of desserts. **Carrot cake, butter tarts, apple pie, or peppermint ice cream.** [The list cannot stand on its own as a sentence.]
REVISED	You have a choice of desserts: carrot cake, butter tarts, apple pie, or peppermint ice cream. [joined into one sentence with a colon]
REVISED	You have a choice of desserts—carrot cake, butter tarts, apple pie, or peppermint ice cream. [joined into one sentence with a dash]
FRAGMENT	There are several good places to go for brunch. **For example, the Bluenose Inn and Peggy's Retreat.** [Examples cannot stand on their own as a sentence.]
REVISED	There are several good places to go for brunch—for example, the Bluenose Inn and Peggy's Retreat. [joined into one sentence with a dash]
REVISED	There are several good places to go for brunch. For example, there are the Bluenose Inn and Peggy's Retreat. [rewritten with the addition of a main verb]

13e Recognizing intentional fragments

Professional writers sometimes intentionally use fragments for emphasis and effect. The ability to judge the difference between an acceptable and unacceptable sentence fragment comes from much exposure to reading the work of skilled writers. Many instructors do not accept sentence fragments in student writing.

13-1

Revising Fragments

A: Explain what is wrong with each fragment and then rewrite it as a complete sentence.

EXAMPLE   graduating in June

> *There is no subject and "graduating" is not a conjugated verb.*
> *I am graduating in June.*

1. beside the rice cooker

   _____

   _____

2. tutors his roommate in Russian

   _____

   _____

3. whoever breaks the piñata

   _____

   _____

4. considered the best in her class

   _____

   _____

5. and plans to study Swahili

   _____

   _____

6. my least favourite course this term

   _____

   _____

7. studying constantly

   _____

   _____

8. when Ahmed entered the university

   _____

   _____

Name_____ Date _____

9. where you can locate ten dialogues by Plato

_____

_____

10. Kofi hoping for understanding

_____

_____

B: Write two corrected versions of each fragment. Be sure to use the fragment differently in each and identify how you have used it (as illustrated in the parentheses below).

EXAMPLE   eating an orange

> *Eating an orange can be messy. (subject)*
> *Eating an orange, he swallowed a pit. (adjective)*

1. when Natasha arrived on campus

_____

_____

2. looks for affordable child care

_____

_____

3. who borrowed my vacuum cleaner

_____

_____

4. to use HTML or another markup language

_____

_____

5. buried under last week's laundry

_____

_____

6. trying to get a visa

_____

_____

7. historians and anthropologists

_____

_____

8. the instructor who helped me the most

_____

_____

9. in the computer lab

_____

_____

10. a man shaking hands with his enemy

_____

_____

Revising Fragments Within Passages

EXERCISE **13-2**
(13c)

There is one fragment in each passage below. Find it and correct it in whatever way you feel is most appropriate.

EXAMPLE   Clothing often indicates a person's social standing. This has been the case for centuries. Although some clothing certainly was inspired by the need for protection from the elements. Even today, style, material, and colour all act as social labels.

Clothing often indicates a person's social standing. This has been the case for centuries, although some clothing certainly was inspired by the need for protection from the elements. Even today, style, material, and colour all act as social labels.

1. The oldest shoe ever found was a sandal. Which dated from 2000 B.C. It was found in an Egyptian tomb. Sandals were the usual footwear in tropical areas.

_____

_____

EXERCISES

Name_____ Date _____

2. Archaeologists are interested in the clothing of our ancestors. They have discovered hundreds of sandal designs. Each usually representative of a particular culture at a particular time. However, other types of shoes were also worn.

_____

_____

3. The oldest nonsandal shoe found has been a leather wrap-around. Shaped like a moccasin. Rawhide lacing could be pulled tight to keep the shoe snugly on the foot. This shoe came from Babylonia.

_____

_____

4. Upper-class Greek women favoured a similar shoe. The preferred colours were red and white. Roman women also wore red and white closed shoes. And green or yellow ones for special occasions.

_____

_____

5. Lower-ranking Roman women wore undyed open sandals. Senators wore brown shoes. With tied black leather straps wound around the lower leg. Consuls, who were high-ranking officials, wore white shoes.

_____

_____

6. Boots were first used by soldiers. The Assyrians created a calf-high laced leather boot. The sole was reinforced with metal. Enabling the Assyrians to walk and fight in relative comfort.

_____

_____

7. Greek and Roman soldiers resisted wearing Assyrian-style boots. They preferred sandals with hobnail soles. To provide better grip and extended wear. They did wear boots for long journeys.

_____

_____

8. Horse-riding cultures adopted boots quickly. They appreciated the boot's sturdiness. And the ability of the boot heel to help their foot stay in the stirrup. Boots became standard combat gear.

_____

_____

9. The heeled boot was the ancestor of modern high-heeled shoes. The original high heels were worn by men in sixteenth-century France. Women's shoe fashions at the time were less dramatic. Because women's feet were covered by floor-length dresses.

_____

_____

10. During this time, the overcrowded cities were filthy. The streets were filled with human and animal waste. The elevation provided by high heels and thick soles kept men out of the muck. And enabled them to stay a bit cleaner.

_____

_____

11. The clogs of Northern Europe served a similar purpose. Worn over good leather shoes in the winter. These wooden shoes protected the wearer from snow and mud. They could also be worn alone in warm weather.

_____

_____

12. King Louis XIV of France was short. During his seventy-two-year reign, the longest in the history of Europe. France was a centre of culture and refinement. France was also at its peak of military power.

_____

_____

13. Louis hated being short. To compensate, he wore high-heeled boots. He was imitated by his courtiers. The males as well as the females.

_____

_____

14. Louis's response was to wear even higher heels. His people tried to keep up with him. Once the competition was over. The men returned to their regular height.

_____

_____

EXERCISES

Name_____ Date _____

15. The female members of Louis's court kept their high heels. Thus beginning the pattern we have today. With rare exceptions, such as in the mid-1970s, men have been expected to keep their feet on the ground. Women still have the choice to wear or not wear high heels.

_____

_____

16. Athletic shoes earned the name "sneakers" because of their rubber bottoms. Which enabled wearers to walk silently, to "sneak" around. The invention of the sneaker depended upon another invention. Charles Goodyear mixed rubber with sulphur to make it more useful.

_____

_____

17. Before this important discovery in the 1860s. Using rubber was impractical because it became sticky when warm and brittle when cold. People immediately realized the value of Goodyear's discovery. Rubber-soled shoes became popular.

_____

_____

18. The first athletic shoes appeared shortly after this. Rubber soles on canvas tops, called Keds. The name came from a blend of *ped*, the root form of the Latin word for "foot," and "kid." The brand is still around.

_____

_____

19. The kirst Keds were not very stylish by modern standards. The soles were black. The canvas was brown. In imitation of men's leather shoes.

_____

_____

20. Flat soles were standard on sneakers until 1972. In that year, new shoes with a number of startling changes were introduced. Featuring lightweight nylon tops, waffle soles for traction, a wedged heel, and a cushioned mid-sole to reduce impact shock. These shoes began to drive the old ones off the market.

_____

_____

Revising Fragments Within Paragraphs

Circle the number of any fragments. Then correct each fragment by connecting it to the main clause or by adding words to complete it. Use your own paper.

A.   [1]Paul Bertoia, an immigrant from near Udine in Friuli, the northeast of Italy. [2]Arrived alone in Toronto after World War I. [3]In search of work and relatives, he went on to Edmonton. [4]There he stayed in a boardinghouse/inn. [5]Known to its residents as the Roma Hotel. [6]One floor was occupied completely by Friulan sojourners. [7]And the next floor by Trevisans from a neighbouring region of Italy. [8]Each floor had its own cooking, dialect, card games, and camaraderie. [9]Even though the inn was named for Italy's capital and the native Edmontonians considered everyone in the building an Italian migrant. [10]When Mr Bertoia boarded with kinfolk in Drumheller. [11]He associated chiefly with people from his home town near Udine. [12]And later, when he came to Toronto, became involved in benevolent organizations like the Fratellanza. [13]Which took in members. [14]From all over the Italian peninsula. [15]His ethnic reference group changed according to his setting.

—Robert F. Harney, "Boarding and Belonging"

B.   [1]The striped barber pole is a symbol left over from the times. [2]When barbers doubled as surgeons. [3]As early as the fifth century. [4]Roman barbers pulled teeth, treated wounds. [5]And bled patients. [6]Records show that in 1461 the barbers of London were the only people practising surgery. [7]In the city. [8]However, under Henry VIII, less than a hundred years later. [9]Parliament passed a law limiting barbers to minor operations. [10]Such as blood letting and pulling teeth. [11]While surgeons were prohibited from "barbery and shaving." [12]The London barbers and surgeons were considered one group until 1745. [13]In France and Germany, barbers acted as surgeons. [14]Until even more recent times.

[15]Barbers usually bled their patients. [16]To "cure" a variety of ailments. [17]Because few people could read in those days. [18]Pictures were commonly used as shop signs. [19]The sign of the barber was a pole painted with red and white spirals. [20]From which was suspended a brass basin. [21]The red represented the blood of the patient. [22]The white the bandage. [23]And the basin the bowl used to catch the blood. [24]In Canada, the bowl is often omitted. [25]But it is still common on British barber poles. [26]Some American barbers added a blue stripe. [27]Probably to make the colours match the American flag.

14 Comma Splices and Run-Together Sentences

A **comma splice,** also known as a **comma fault,** occurs when a single comma joins independent clauses. A comma is correct between two independent clauses only when it is followed by a coordinating conjunction (see 7h).

> COMMA SPLICE   The car skidded, it hit a mailbox.

A **run-together sentence,** also known as a **run-on sentence** or a **fused sentence,** occurs when two independent clauses are not separated by punctuation nor joined by a comma with a coordinating conjunction.

> RUN-TOGETHER SENTENCE   The car skidded it hit a mailbox.

Comma splices and run-together sentences are two versions of the same problem: incorrect joining of two independent clauses. If you tend to write comma splices and run-together sentences, it may be because you don't recognize them.

HOW TO FIND AND CORRECT COMMA SPLICES AND RUN-TOGETHER SENTENCES

FINDING COMMA SPLICES AND RUN-TOGETHER SENTENCES

1. Look for a pronoun starting the second independent clause.
   NO Alexander Graham Bell was a productive inventor, **he** held many patents.
2. Look for a conjunctive adverb or other transitional expression starting the second independent clause.
   NO Canadians celebrate Bell as one of their own, **however,** he was born in Scotland and lived many years in the United States.
3. Look for a second independent clause that explains or gives an example of information in the first clause.
   NO Bell was the genius behind many inventions, the telephone is the best known.

FIXING COMMA SPLICES AND RUN-TOGETHER SENTENCES

1. Use a period or a semicolon between clauses.
2. Use a comma and a coordinating conjunction between clauses.
3. Use a semicolon and a conjunctive adverb between clauses.

14a Recognizing comma splices and run-together sentences

To recognize comma splices and run-together sentences, you need to be able to recognize an **independent clause.** As explained in 7o-1, an independent clause contains a subject and a predicate. An independent clause can stand alone as a sentence because it is a complete grammatical unit. A sentence may contain two or more independent clauses only if they are joined properly (with a comma and coordinating conjunction *or* with a semicolon).

14b Using a period or semicolon to correct comma splices and run-together sentences

A **period** can separate the independent clauses in a comma splice or run-together sentence. A **semicolon** can separate independent clauses that are closely related in meaning (see 25a).

COMMA SPLICE	In the 1880s, Sir Francis Galton showed that fingerprints are unique for each person, he was an English anthropologist.
CORRECTED	In the 1880s, Sir Francis Galton showed that fingerprints are unique for each person. He was an English anthropologist.
RUN-TOGETHER SENTENCE	Mark Twain used fingerprints to solve murders in *Life on the Mississippi* and *Pudd'nhead Wilson* these were popular books.
CORRECTED	Mark Twain used fingerprints to solve murders in *Life on the Mississippi* and *Pudd'nhead Wilson*; these were popular books.

14c Using coordinating conjunctions to correct comma splices and run-together sentences

When ideas in independent clauses are closely related, you might decide to connect them with a coordinating conjunction that fits the meaning of the material (see 7h). Two independent clauses joined by a coordinating conjunction and a comma form a compound sentence, also known as a coordinate sentence.

❖ PUNCTUATION ALERT: Use a comma before a coordinating conjunction that links independent clauses. ❖

COMMA SPLICE	In 1901, England began fingerprinting criminals, their prints were kept on file with the police.
CORRECTED	In 1901, England began fingerprinting criminals, **and** their prints were kept on file with the police.

RUN-TOGETHER SENTENCE	Edward Richard Henry, of London's Metropolitan Police, invented a system of classifying fingerprints the modern police forces use a version of this original system.
CORRECTED	Edward Richard Henry, of London's Metropolitan Police, invented a system of classifying fingerprints, **and** the modern police forces use a version of this original system.

14d Revising an independent clause into a dependent clause to correct a comma splice or run-together sentence

You can revise a comma splice or run-together sentence by changing one of two independent clauses into a dependent clause. This method is suitable when one idea can be logically subordinated to the other. Sentences composed of one independent clause and one or more dependent clauses are called complex sentences. Inserting an appropriate subordinating conjunction (see 7h) in front of the subject and verb is one way to create a dependent clause.

❖ PUNCTUATION ALERT: Do not put a period after a dependent clause that is not attached to an independent clause, or you will create a sentence fragment (see Chapter 13). ❖

COMMA SPLICE	Giving blood is nearly painless, many people are reluctant to undergo the procedure.
CORRECTED	Giving blood is nearly painless, **although many people are reluctant to undergo the procedure.**
RUN-TOGETHER SENTENCE	Transfusion centres test donated blood it is given to patients in transfusions.
CORRECTED	Transfusion centres test donated blood **before it is given to patients in transfusions.**

A relative pronoun can also be used to correct a comma splice or run-together sentence by creating a dependent clause.

COMMA SPLICE	People want to donate blood, they are screened with a questionnaire and a blood test.
CORRECTED	People **who want to donate blood** are screened with a questionnaire and a blood test. [restrictive dependent clause]

14e Using a semicolon or a period before a conjunctive adverb or other transitional expression between independent clauses

Conjunctive adverbs and other transitional expressions link ideas between sentences. Remember, however, that these words are *not* coordinating conjunctions, so they cannot work with commas to join independent clauses. Conjunctive adverbs and other transitional expressions require that the previous sentence or clause end in a period or semicolon.

Conjunctive adverbs include such words as *however, therefore, also, next, then, thus, furthermore,* and *nevertheless* (see 7f for a fuller list).

COMMA SPLICE	Many people object to being fingerprinted, **nevertheless,** fingerprinting remains a requirement for certain jobs.
CORRECTED	Many people object to being fingerprinted. **Nevertheless,** fingerprinting remains a requirement for certain jobs.

Transitional words include *for example, for instance, in addition, in fact, of course,* and *on the other hand* (see 4d for a fuller list).

RUN-TOGETHER SENTENCE	Not everyone disapproves of fingerprinting **in fact,** some parents have their children fingerprinted as a safety measure.
CORRECTED	Not everyone disapproves of fingerprinting. **In fact,** some parents have their children fingerprinted as a safety measure.

A conjunctive adverb or other transitional expression can appear in various locations within an independent clause. In contrast, a coordinating conjunction can appear only between the dependent clauses it joins.

Many people object to being fingerprinted. Fingerprinting, **nevertheless,** remains a requirement for certain jobs.

Many people object to being fingerprinted. Fingerprinting remains, **nevertheless,** a requirement for certain jobs.

Many people object to being fingerprinted. Fingerprinting remains a requirement for certain jobs, **nevertheless.**

Many people object to being fingerprinted, **but** fingerprinting remains a requirement for certain jobs.

Name_____ Date _____

Revising Comma Splices and Run-Together Sentences

EXERCISE 14-1
(14a–e)

A: Correct each comma splice or run-together sentence in any of the ways shown in this chapter.

EXAMPLE   Many people think of the Middle Ages they think of knights in shining armour.

> *When many people think of the Middle Ages, they think of knights in shining armour.*

1. The term *chivalry* comes from *chevalier* meaning "knight" and is related to *cheval* meaning "horse," thus a knight is an armed horseman.

   _____

   _____

2. Chivalry was more than a code by which a knight lived it became a distinct culture.

   _____

   _____

3. In the Middle Ages birth specified class only knighthood and the church offered social mobility.

   _____

   _____

4. Knighthood was a privilege, not a right, it had to be earned.

   _____

   _____

5. Every knight could confer the rank on another he considered worthy he took responsibility for the one so honoured.

   _____

   _____

6. A knight was expected to have his own horse and armour unless he owned land, he had to earn his horse's keep by serving another.

_____

_____

7. Many knights pledged fealty to one noble some became mercenaries, hiring themselves as free lances to whoever needed them.

_____

_____

B: Correct each comma splice or run-together sentence in the way indicated.

EXAMPLE   Most knights belonged to the landed gentry, they desired knighthood because of its status.
(Make into two separate sentences.)

Most knights belonged to the landed gentry. They desired knighthood because of its status.

1. Even princes considered knighthood an honour it made them part of a universal fraternity.
(Add a semicolon.)

_____

_____

2. The honour was conferred by tapping the knight on the shoulders with the flat of a sword, after three taps the knight was given a belt and spurs to signify his new rank.
(Make into two separate sentences.)

_____

_____

3. For his part, the knight vowed to uphold the code of chivalry, the code established certain rules of behaviour.
(Turn one part into a dependent clause.)

_____

_____

Name_____ Date _____

4. The knight promised loyalty to his faith and to his feudal lord he pledged to die willingly for either should death be necessary.
   (Add a semicolon and a conjunctive adverb.)

   _____

   _____

5. He was expected to fight to uphold his ideals he was also expected to show mercy.
   (Turn one part into a dependent clause.)

   _____

   _____

6. Knighthood is still granted in England it is given for outstanding achievement.
   (Add a semicolon.)

   _____

   _____

7. Today recipients include both men and women their achievements are often related to statesmanship or the arts.
   (Add a comma and a coordinating conjunction.)

   _____

   _____

C: Correct each comma splice or run-together sentence in four ways: (1) make each into two separate sentences by inserting a period; (2) add a semicolon; (3) add a coordinating conjunction to create a compound sentence—you will also need to add a comma unless the clauses are very short; (4) add a subordinating conjunction or relative pronoun—you may need to drop a word—to create a complex sentence.

EXAMPLE   The didgeridoo is an unusual musical instrument, it was developed by Australian Aborigines.

   1. *instrument. It was developed . . .*

   2. *instrument; it was developed . . .*

   3. *instrument, for it was developed . . .*

   4. *The didgeridoo, which was developed by Australian Aborigines, is an unusual instrument.*

1. To make a didgeridoo, Aborigines choose a long eucalyptus branch, they bury it in the ground.

   _____

   _____

   _____

   _____

2. Termites eat out the middle of the branch, the Aborigines then dig it up.

   _____

   _____

   _____

   _____

3. They carve the instrument they decorate it with pigments.

   _____

   _____

   _____

   _____

4. They play it by blowing into one end it makes a mournful sound.

   _____

   _____

   _____

   _____

5. The pitch is low, the sound carries well.

   _____

   _____

   _____

   _____

Name_____ Date _____

Revising Comma Splices and
Run-Together Sentences Within Passages

Find the comma splice or run-together sentence in each passage. Correct each in any way shown in this chapter. You may need to change punctuation or wording, but try to keep the meaning of the original passage.

EXAMPLE   Some of the most beautiful temples in the world are those of Angkor. Angkor is a Cambodian region it served as the capital of the ancient Khmer empire between the 9th and 15th centuries. The empire once extended into what are today Vietnam, Laos, and Thailand.

Some of the most beautiful temples in the world are those of Angkor. Angkor is a Cambodian region that served as the capital of the ancient Khmer empire between the 9th and 15th centuries. The empire once extended into what are today Vietnam, Laos, and Thailand.

1. The king Jayavarman II introduced into the empire an Indian royal cult. The cult held that the king was related spiritually to one of the Hindu gods, consequently, the king was thought to fill on earth the role the gods had in the universe.

   _____

   _____

2. Each king was expected to build a stone temple. The temple, or _wat_, was dedicated to a god, usually Shiva or Vishnu, when the king died, the temple became a monument to him as well.

   _____

   _____

3. Over the centuries the kings erected more than seventy temples within 200 km^2. They added towers and gates they created canals and reservoirs for an irrigation system.

   _____

   _____

4. The irrigation system made it possible for farmers to produce several rice crops a year. Such abundant harvests supported a highly evolved culture, the irrigation system and the rice production were what we would call labour-intensive.

_____

_____

5. The greatest of the temples is Angkor Wat, it was built by Suryavarman II in the 12th century. Like the other temples, it represents Mount Meru, the home of the Hindu gods. The towers represent Mount Meru's peaks while the walls represent the mountains beyond.

_____

_____

6. The gallery walls are covered with bas-reliefs they depict historical events. They show the king at his court, and they show him engaging in activities that brought glory to his empire.

_____

_____

7. The walls also portray divine images. There are sculptures of *apsarases*, they are attractive women thought to inhabit heaven. There are mythical scenes on the walls as well.

_____

_____

8. One scene shows the Hindu myth of the churning of the Sea of Milk. On one side of the god Vishnu are demons who tug on the end of a long serpent, on the other are heavenly beings who tug on the other end. All the tugging churns the water.

_____

_____

9. Vishnu is the god to whom Angkor Wat is dedicated. In Hindu myth he oversees the churning of the waters, that churning is ultimately a source of immortality.

_____

_____

10. Another temple is the Bayon, it was built by Jayavarman VII around A.D. 1200 Jayavarman VII was the last of the great kings of Angkor. He built the Bayon in the exact centre of the city.

_____

_____

Name_____ Date _____

11. The Bayon resembles a step pyramid. It has steep stairs that lead to terraces near the top around its base are many galleries. Its towers are carved with faces that look out in all directions.

_____

_____

12. Jayavarman VII was a Buddhist, the representations on Bayon are different from those on earlier temples. Some scholars think they depict a Buddhist deity with whom the king felt closely aligned.

_____

_____

13. To build each temple required thousands of labourers they worked for years. After cutting the stone in far-off quarries, they had to transport it by canal or cart. Some stone may have been brought in on elephants.

_____

_____

14. Once cut, the stones had to be carved and fitted together into lasting edifices, thus, in addition to requiring laborers, each project needed artisans, architects, and engineers. Each temple was a massive project.

_____

_____

15. Angkor was conquered by the Thais in the 1400s, it was almost completely abandoned. The local inhabitants did continue to use the temples for worship, however, and a few late Khmer kings tried to restore the city.

_____

_____

16. The Western world did not learn about Angkor until the nineteenth century, a French explorer published an account of the site. French archaeologists and conservators later worked in the area and restored some of the temples. More recent archaeologists have come from India.

_____

_____

17. Today the Angkor Conservancy has removed many of the temple statues. Some of the statues need repair, all of them need protection from thieves. Unfortunately, traffic in Angkor art has become big business among people with no scruples. There is even a booming business in Angkor fakes.

_____

_____

18. Theft is just one of the problems Angkor faces today, political upheaval has taken its toll. Although Angkor mostly escaped Cambodia's civil war, some war damage has occurred.

_____

_____

19. More damage has been done by nature, however, trees choke some of the archways, vines strangle the statues, and monsoons undermine the basic structures.

_____

_____

20. Today many Cambodians do what they can to maintain the temples of Angkor. They clean stones or sweep courtyards or pull weeds. No one pays them, they do it for themselves and their heritage.

_____

_____

15 Awkward Sentences

A sentence can seem correct at first glance but still have flaws that keep it from delivering a sensible message. Sentences may be sending unclear messages because of shifts in person and number, in subject and voice, in tense and mood, and between direct and indirect discourse; misplaced modifiers; dangling modifiers; mixed structures; or incomplete structures.

PROOFREADING TO FIND SENTENCE FLAWS

- Finish your revision in enough time so you can put it aside and go back to it with fresh eyes that can spot flaws more easily.
- Work backwards, from your last sentence to your first, so that you can see each sentence as a separate unit free of a context that might lure you to overlook flaws.
- Ask an experienced reader to check your writing for sentence flaws. If you make an error discussed in this chapter, you likely make that error repeatedly. Once you become aware of it, you will have made a major step toward eliminating that type of error.
- Proofread an extra time exclusively for any error that you tend to make more than any other.

15a Avoiding unnecessary shifts

Unless the meaning or grammatical structure of a sentence requires it, do not shift person and number, subject and voice, and tense and mood. Also, do not shift from indirect to direct discourse within a sentence without using punctuation and grammar to make the changes clear.

1 | Staying consistent in person and number

Person in English includes the **first person** (*I, we*), who is the speaker; the **second person** (*you*), who is the person spoken to; and the **third person** (*he, she, it, they*), who is the person or thing being spoken about. Do not shift person within a sentence or a longer passage unless the meaning calls for a shift.

NO   **We** need to select a college with care. **Your** future success may depend upon **your** choice. [*We* shifts to *your.*]

YES   **We** need to select a college with care. **Our** future success may depend upon **our** choice.

Number refers to one (singular) and more than one (plural). Do not start to write in one number and then shift suddenly to the other.

NO   A college **freshman** has to make many adjustments. **They** have to work harder and become more responsible. [The singular *freshman* shifts to the plural *they.*]

YES   College **freshmen** have to make many adjustments. **They** have to work harder and become more responsible.

A common source of confusion in person and number is a shift to the second-person *you* from the first-person *I* or a third-person noun such as *persons*, or *people*. You can avoid this error if you remember to reserve *you* for sentences that directly address the reader (10e), and to use third-person pronouns for general statements.

NO   The French **president** serves for seven years. **You** can accomplish much in such a long term. [*President*, third person, shifts to *you*, second person.]

YES   The French **president** serves for seven years. **He** can accomplish much in such a long term.

NO   **I** would be afraid to give someone such power for so long a time. **You** might decide **you** disliked his policies. [*I*, first person, shifts to *you*, second person.]

YES   **I** would be afraid to give someone such power for so long a time. **I** might decide **I** disliked his policies.

2 | Staying consistent in subject and voice

The **subject** of a sentence is the word or group of words that acts, is acted upon or is described: *The **bell** rings.* The **voice** of a sentence is either active (*The bell rings*) or passive (*The bell **is rung***). Whenever possible, use the active voice.

NO   The chemistry **student lit** a match too near the supplies, and some pure **oxygen was ignited.** [The subject shifts from *student* to *oxygen*, and the voice shifts from active to passive.]

15a

YES	The chemistry **student lit** a match too near the supplies, and **he ignited** some pure oxygen.
NO	When **people heard** the explosion, **the hall was filled.**
YES	When **people heard** the explosion, **they filled** the halls.
YES	**People,** hearing the explosion, **filled** the halls.

3   Staying consistent in tense and mood

Tense refers to the ability of verbs to show time. Tense changes are required when time movement is described: *I expect the concert will start late.* If tense changes are illogical, the message becomes unclear.

NO	Traffic accidents **kill** thousands of people as they **drove** on Canadian highways each year. [The tense shifts from the present *kill* to the past *drove.*]
YES	Traffic accidents **kill** thousands of people as they **drive** on Canadian highways each year.
NO	India **loses** few people in traffic accidents. Unfortunately, ten thousand people a year **died** of cobra bites. [The shift occurs between sentences. The present tense *loses* shifts to the past tense *died.*]
YES	India **loses** few people in traffic accidents. Unfortunately, ten thousand people a year **die** of cobra bites.

Mood refers to whether a sentence is a statement or question (**indicative mood**), a command or request (**imperative mood**), or a conditional or other-than-real statement (**subjunctive mood**). Shifts among moods blur your message. The most common shift is between the imperative and indicative moods.

NO	Better home security is available to all of us. First, **install** deadbolt locks on all doors. Next, **you can install** inexpensive window locks. [The verb shifts from the imperative *install* to the indicative *you can install.*]
YES	Better home security is available to all of us. First, **install** deadbolt locks on all doors. Next, **install** inexpensive window locks.
YES	Better home security is available to all of us. First **you can install** deadbolt locks on all doors. Next, **you can install** inexpensive window locks.

4   Avoiding unmarked shifts between indirect and direct discourse

Indirect discourse *reports* speech or conversation; it is not enclosed in quotation marks. **Direct discourse** *repeats* speech or conversation exactly and encloses the spoken words in quotation marks. Sentences that mix indirect and direct discourse without quotation marks and other markers confuse readers.

NO	The admissions officer said I could get into the hairdressing program, but do you really want to apply? [The first clause is indirect discourse; the second shifts to unmarked direct discourse.]
YES	The admissions officer said I could get into the hairdressing program, but asked whether I really wanted to apply. [indirect discourse]
YES	The admissions officer said I could get into the hairdressing program, but asked, "Do you really want to apply?" [This revision uses direct and indirect discourse correctly.]

15b Avoiding misplaced modifiers

A **misplaced modifier** is a description incorrectly positioned within a sentence, resulting in distorted meaning. Always check to see that your modifiers are placed as close as possible to what they describe. The various kinds of misplaced modifiers are discussed below.

An **ambiguous placement** means that a modifier can refer to two or more words in a sentence. Little limiting words (such as *only, just, almost, even, hardly, nearly, exactly, merely, scarcely, simply*) can change meaning according to where they are placed. Consider how the placement of *only* changes the meaning of this sentence: *Scientists say that space exploration is important.*

Only scientists say that space exploration is important.

Scientists **only** say that space exploration is important.

Scientists say **only** that space exploration is important.

Scientists say that **only** space exploration is important.

Squinting modifiers also cause ambiguity. A squinting modifier appears to describe both what precedes and what follows it.

NO	The dock that was constructed **partially** was destroyed by the storm. [What was partial—the construction or the destruction?]
YES	The dock that was **partially** constructed was destroyed by the storm.
YES	The **partially** constructed dock was destroyed by the storm.
YES	The dock that was constructed was **partially** destroyed by the storm.

Wrong placement means that the modifiers are far from the words they logically modify.

NO	The British Parliament passed a law forbidding Scots to wear kilts **in 1746.** [This sentence says kilts could not be worn only in 1746.]
YES	**In 1746,** the British Parliament passed a law forbidding Scots to wear kilts.
NO	This was an attempt, **of which the kilt was a symbol,** to destroy Scottish nationalism. [This sentence says the kilt represented the destruction of Scottish nationalism.]
YES	This was an attempt to destroy Scottish nationalism, **of which the kilt was a symbol**.

An **interrupting placement** is an interruption that seriously breaks the flow of the message. A **split infinitive** is a particularly confusing kind of awkward placement. An infinitive is a verb form that starts with *to: to buy, to sell.*

NO   The herb sweet basil was thought **to,** in medieval Europe, **have** strange effects on people who ate it.

YES   In medieval Europe, the herb sweet basil was thought **to have** strange effects on people who ate it.

Generally, avoid interruptions between subject and verb, between parts of a verb phrase, and between verb and object.

15c Avoiding dangling modifiers

A **dangling modifier** modifies what is implied but not actually stated in a sentence. Dangling modifiers can be hard for a writer to spot because the writer's brain tends to supply the missing information, but the reader cannot supply it, and confusion results.

NO   **Learning about bamboo, the plant's versatility** amazed me. [This sentence says the plant's versatility is learning.]

You can correct a dangling modifier by revising the sentence so that the intended subject is expressed.

YES   **Learning about bamboo, I** was amazed by the plant's versatility.

YES   **I learned about bamboo** and was amazed by its versatility.

NO   **When measured, a Japanese scientist** recorded 1.25 metres of growth in one bamboo plant in twenty-four hours. [The scientist was not measured.]

YES   **When he measured the growth of one bamboo plant, a Japanese scientist** recorded 1.25 metres of growth in twenty-four hours.

15d Avoiding mixed sentences

A **mixed sentence** has two or more parts that do not make sense together. In a **mixed construction,** a sentence starts out taking one grammatical form and then changes, confusing the meaning.

NO   When the North-West Mounted Police included Sam Steele and Charles Constantine became folk heroes. [The opening dependent clause is fused with the independent clause that follows.]

YES   The North-West Mounted Police included Sam Steele and Charles Constantine, who became folk heroes. [*When* had been dropped, making the first clause independent; and *who* has been added, making the second clause dependent and logically related to the first.]

NO   To writers, such as Pierre Berton, romanticized their adventures. [A prepositional phrase, such as *to writers,* cannot be the subject of a sentence.]

YES	Writers, such as Pierre Berton, romanticized their adventures. [Dropping the preposition *to* clears up the problem.]
YES	To writers, such as Pierre Berton, their adventures were romantic. [Inserting a logical subject, *their adventures*, clears up the problem; and independent clause is now preceded by a modifying prepositional phrase.]

In **faulty predication**, sometimes called **illogical predication**, the subject and predicate do not make sense together.

NO	The **job** of the Mounties **kept** order in the North.
YES	**Mounties kept** order in the North.
YES	The **job** of the Mounties **was to keep** order in the North.

Faulty predication is the problem in several common, informal constructions: *is when, is where,* and *reason is because.* Avoid these constructions in academic writing.

NO	In dangerous territory **is where** the Mounties worked.
YES	The Mounties worked in dangerous territory.
NO	**One reason** the Mounties were so popular **was because** they had a dashing image.
YES	**One reason** the Mounties were so popular **was that** they had a dashing image.
YES	The Mounties were so popular **because** they had a dashing image.

15e Avoiding incomplete sentences

An **incomplete sentence** is missing words, phrases, or clauses necessary for grammatical correctness or sensible meaning. Do not confuse an incomplete sentence with an elliptical construction. An **elliptical construction** deliberately leaves out words that have already appeared in the sentence: *I have my book and Joan's [book].* The chief rule for an elliptical comparison is that the words left out must be *exactly* the same as the words that do appear in the sentence.

NO	When migrating, most **birds travel** 40 to 50 kilometres per hour, but **the goose** 95 kilometres per hour. [The word *travel* cannot take the place of *travels,* needed in the second clause.]
YES	When migrating, most **birds travel** 40 to 50 kilometres per hour, but the **goose travels** 95 kilometres per hour.
NO	Flying **in fog** and **water,** many migrating birds perish.
YES	Flying **in fog** and **over water,** many migrating birds perish.

In writing a comparison, be sure to include all words needed to make clear the relationship between the items or ideas being compared.

NO	Young people learn languages faster. [*Faster* indicates a comparison, but none is stated.]
YES	Young people learn languages faster than adults do.

NO   Some employers value bilingual employees more than people who speak only English. [not clear: Who values whom?]

YES   Some employers value bilingual employees more than they value people who speak only English.

NO   A French speaker's enjoyment of Paris is greater than a nonspeaker. [*Enjoyment* is compared with a *nonspeaker*; a thing cannot be compared logically with a person.]

YES   A French speaker's enjoyment of Paris is greater than a nonspeaker's.

NO   Unfortunately, foreign languages have such a reputation for difficulty. [In academic writing, comparisons begun with *such, so,* and *too* must be completed.]

YES   Unfortunately, foreign languages have such a reputation for difficulty that many students are afraid to try to learn one.

Small words—articles, pronouns, conjunctions, and prepositions—that are needed to make sentences complete sometimes drop out. If you tend accidentally to omit words, proofread your work an extra time solely to find them.

NO   Naturalists say squirrel can hide as much twenty bushels food dozens of spots, but it rarely remembers where most of food is hidden.

YES   Naturalists say **a** squirrel can hide as much **as** twenty bushels **of** food **in** dozens of spots, but it rarely remembers where most of **its** food is hidden.

Revising to Eliminate Shifts

A: Revise this paragraph to eliminate shifts in person and number. The first sentence should become "The next time you watch a western movie, notice whether it contains any sign language." Use your own paper.

     The next time I watch a western movie, notice whether it contains any sign language. Some people consider sign language the first universal language. Although few people use them today, it is a Native North American language with a lengthy history. You can find some tribal differences, but basic root signs are clear to everyone who studies it.

     Sign language differs from the signage used by hearing-impaired people. For instance, he indicates the forehead to mean *think* while a Sioux pointed to the heart. You also use extensive facial expression in speaking to someone with a hearing loss while Native North Americans maintained a stoic countenance. She believed the signs could speak for itself. Ideally you made the signs in round, sweeping motions. They tried to make conversation beautiful.

B: Revise this paragraph to eliminate shifts in verb tense. The first sentence should read "No one knows why sailors *wear* bell-bottom pants." Use your own paper.

     No one knows why sailors wore bell-bottom pants. However, three theories were popular. First, bell-bottoms will fit over boots and keep sea spray and rain from getting in. Second, bell-bottoms could be rolled up over the knees, so they stayed dry when a sailor must wade ashore and stayed clean when he scrubbed the ship's deck. Third, because bell-bottoms are loose, they will be easy to take off in the water if a sailor fell overboard. In their training course, sailors were taught another advantage to bell-bottoms. By taking them off and tying the legs at the ends, a sailor who has fallen into the ocean can change his bell-bottom pants into a life preserver.

C: Identify the shift in each passage by writing its code on the line to the right: *1* for a shift in person or number, *2* in subject or voice, *3* in tense, *4* in mood, or *5* in discourse (confusing direct and indirect quotation). Then revise each sentence to eliminate the shift.

EXAMPLE When people speak of a fisherman knit sweater, you mean one from the Aran Isles.   <u>   1   </u>

     When people speak of a fisherman knit sweater, they mean one from the Aran Isles.

1. The Aran Isles are situated off the coast of Ireland. Galway is not far from the Isles.

                <u>   </u>

2. An Islander has a difficult life. They must make their living by fishing in a treacherous sea.

                <u>   </u>

Name_____ Date _____

3. They use a simple boat called a *curragh* for fishing. It is also used to ferry their market animals to barges.

_____

_____

4. Island houses stood out against the empty landscape. Their walls provide scant protection from a hostile environment.

_____

_____

5. In 1898 John Millington Synge first visited the Aran Isles. They are used as the setting for *Riders to the Sea* and other of his works.

_____

_____

6. Whether people see the Synge play or Ralph Vaughan Williams's operatic version of *Riders to the Sea*, you will feel the harshness of Aran life.

_____

_____

7. The mother Maurya has lost her husband and several sons. They are all drowned at sea.

_____

_____

8. When the body of another son is washed onto the shore, his sister identifies it from the pattern knitted into his sweater.

_____

_____

9. Each Aran knitter develops her own combination of patterns. The patterns not only produce a beautiful sweater, but they will have a very practical purpose.

_____

_____

10. The oiled wool protected the fishermen from the sea spray while the intricate patterns offer symbolic protection as well as identification when necessary.

_____

_____

11. When you knit your first Aran Isle sweater, you should learn what the stitches mean. Don't choose a pattern just because it is easy.

_____

_____

12. A cable stitch represents a fisherman's rope; winding cliff paths are depicted by the zigzag stitch.

_____

_____

13. Bobbles symbolize men in a curragh while the basket stitch represented a fisherman's creel and the hope that it will come home full.

_____

_____

14. The tree of life signifies strong sons and family unity. It was also a fertility symbol.

_____

_____

15. When someone asks you did you knit your Aran Isle yourself, you can proudly say that you did and you also chose the patterns.

_____

_____

Eliminating Misplaced and Dangling Modifiers

EXERCISE **15-2**
(15b–c)

A: Underline each misplaced modifier. Then revise the sentence, placing the modifier where it belongs.

EXAMPLE   Inexperienced people are afraid to paint their own homes <u>often</u>.

> _Inexperienced people are often afraid to paint their own homes._

1. To paint one's house frequently one must do it oneself.

_____

2. All homeowners almost try to paint at one time or another.

_____

3. They try to usually begin on a bedroom.

_____

4. They think no one will see it if they botch the job by doing so.

_____

Name_____ Date _____

5. Most people can learn to paint in no time.

_____

6. The uncoordinated should only not try it.

_____

7. People have a distinct advantage that have strong arm muscles.

_____

8. Prospective painters can always exercise lacking strength.

_____

9. Novices need to carefully purchase all supplies, such as brushes, rollers, and drop cloths.

_____

10. They must bring home paint chips exactly to match the shade desired.

_____

11. It takes as much time nearly to prepare to paint as it does to do the actual job.

_____

12. Painters are in for a surprise who think they are done with the last paint stroke.

_____

13. Painters need to immediately clean their own brushes and put away all equipment.

_____

14. They can be proud of their accomplishment in the long run.

_____

15. Then can they enjoy only the results of their labour.

_____

16. Painting one's own home can, when all is said and done, be extremely satisfying.

_____

B: Revise each sentence to eliminate dangling modifiers. You may have to add or change a few words. If a sentence is acceptable as written, write *correct* on the line.

EXAMPLE Advising a group of young women in his neighbourhood, many discussions focusing on love problems were led by Samuel Richardson.

Advising a group of young women in his neighbourhood, Samuel Richardson led many discussions focusing on love problems.

1. Playing the role of a caring and wise father, the girls were told by Richardson how to handle various situations.

_____

_____

2. To help the girls, letters to their suitors were sometimes written for them by Richardson.

_____

_____

3. After writing a number of successful letters, the idea of writing a book of model letters occurred to Richardson.

_____

_____

4. To prepare the book, it included letters written as if from adults to sons, daughters, nieces, and nephews.

_____

_____

5. When ready to send advice, a letter was copied out by a parent, and just the names changed.

_____

_____

6. Bought by many, Richardson, was a successful author.

_____

_____

7. While working on one letter, enough ideas for a whole book occurred to Richardson.

_____

_____

8. By writing a series of letters between a girl and her faraway parents, young readers would be entertained and instructed.

_____

_____

Name_____ Date _____

9. Upon finishing *Pamela*, or *Virtue Rewarded* in 1740, a new form of literature had been invented by Richardson.

_____

_____

10. After years of development, we call this form the novel.

_____

_____

11. Being a nasty person, Horace Walpole's only novel wasn't very attractive either.

_____

_____

12. Imitated by others for over 200 years, his *The Castle of Otranto* was the first gothic novel.

_____

_____

13. Although badly written, Walpole invented the themes, atmosphere, mood, and plots that have filled gothic novels ever since.

_____

_____

14. Featuring gloomy castles filled with dark secrets, people are entertained by gothic movies too.

_____

_____

C: Underline all misplaced and dangling modifiers in this paragraph. Then revise the paragraph to eliminate them. You can change or add words and otherwise revise to make the material sensible.

[1]The art of carving or engraving marine articles, sailors developed scrimshaw while sailing on long voyages. [2]Practised primarily by whalermen, sperm whale teeth were the most popular articles. [3]Baleen was another popular choice which was also called whalebone. [4]A sailor needed something to occupy his time with whaling voyages taking several years. [5]Imagination or available material only limited scrimshaw. [6]All kinds of objects were produced by the scrimshander, canes, corset busks, cribbage boards. [7]From whaling scenes to mermaids the sailor used everything to decorate his work. [8]A sailor doing scrimshaw often drew his own ship. [9]The most frequently depicted ship, the *Charles W. Morgan*, is, at present, a museum ship at Mystic Seaport. [10]It is possible to easily see it on a visit to Connecticut.

Eliminating Mixed Constructions, Faulty Predication, and Incomplete Sentences

A: Revise these mixed sentences to eliminate faulty predication and mixed constructions. It may be necessary to change, add, or omit words.

EXAMPLE   Easter is when Russians traditionally exchanged eggs.

On Easter Russians traditionally exchanged eggs.

1. When one thinks of Carl Fabergé created Easter eggs for the tsars.

   _____

2. Because Fabergé was a talented goldsmith was the reason he was able to make exquisite objects.

   _____

3. Working for the court of Imperial Russia was able to combine craftsmanship and ingenuity.

   _____

4. The object of Fabergé pleased his clients by creating unique works of art.

   _____

5. When he included gems in his creations but they did not overshadow his workmanship.

   _____

6. In adapting enamelling techniques achieved a level seldom matched by other artisans.

   _____

7. With buyers in Europe expanded his clientele beyond the Russian royal family.

   _____

8. Because he had no money worries meant few restrictions on imagination.

   _____

9. Although Fabergé created other examples of the jeweller's art, but it is the Imperial Easter eggs for which he is most remembered.

   _____

10. In the most famous eggs contained surprises inside—a hen, a ship, a coach.

    _____

11. When one egg opened to reveal a model of a palace.

    _____

Name_____ Date _____

12. Because the most ambitious creation represented an egg surrounded by parts of a cathedral.

_____

13. An artist is when one practises an imaginative art.

_____

14. One reason Fabergé is so admired is because he was a true artist.

_____

B: Revise these incomplete sentences to supply any carelessly omitted words or to complete compound constructions and comparisons clearly. Write *correct* if the sentence has no errors.

EXAMPLE   Cuneiform was system of writing with wedgelike marks.

  Cuneiform was a system of writing with wedgelike marks.

1. The use of cuneiform began and spread throughout ancient Sumer.

_____

2. This picture language of the Sumerians is thought to be older than the Egyptians.

_____

3. Like hieroglyphics, early cuneiform used easily recognizable pictures represent objects.

_____

4. When scribes began using a wedge-shaped stylus, greater changes occurred.

_____

5. The new marks were different.

_____

6. They had become so stylized.

_____

7. Early Sumerian tablets recorded practical things such lists of grain in storage.

_____

8. Some tablets were put clay envelopes that were themselves inscribed.

_____

9. Gradually ordinary people used cuneiform as much as official scribes.

_____

10. _The Epic of Gilgamesh_, written in Akkadian cuneiform, is older than any epic.

_____

11. The Code of Hammurabi recorded in cuneiform a more comprehensive set of laws.

_____

12. No one could decipher cuneiform script until someone discovered the Record of Darius.

_____

13. Because it was written in three languages, it served the same purpose.

_____

14. Today we understand cuneiform as much, if not more than, we understand hieroglyphics.

_____

C: Revise these paragraphs, changing, adding or deleting words a you see best, in order to eliminate mixed and incomplete sentences. Circle the number of the one sentence that contains no errors.

[1]Although wild rice may be the caviar of grains is not really rice. [2]It is, however, truly wild. [3]One reason is because it needs marshy places in order to thrive. [4]By planting it in prepared paddies can produce abundant crops. [5]Nevertheless, most wild rice grows naturally along rivers and lake shores northern U.S. states and Canada. [6]In certain areas only Native People are allowed harvest the rice. [7]Connoisseurs think wild rice tastes better than any grain. [8]It is surely the most expensive. [9]Some hostesses serve it with Cornish hens exclusively, but the creative cook, with many dishes. [10]Try it in quiche or pancakes; your guests will be so pleased.

16 Conciseness

Conciseness refers to writing that is direct and to the point. In concise writing, every word contributes to the clear presentation of the author's message.

16a Eliminating wordy sentence structures

1 Revising unnecessary expletive constructions

An **expletive** postpones the subject by putting *it* or *there* plus a form of the verb *be* before the subject. If you remove the expletive and revise slightly, you place the subject in a position of greater impact—the beginning of the sentence.

NO	It is fun to taste foods from other cultures.
YES	Tasting foods from other cultures is fun.
NO	There is a new Greek restaurant opening in town.
YES	A new Greek restaurant is opening in town.

2 Revising unnecessary passive constructions

For most writing, the active voice (see 8n, o) adds liveliness as well as conciseness. When a passive construction (see 8n, o) names the doer of an action, it does so in a phrase starting with *by*. To change a passive sentence into an active sentence, make the noun or pronoun in the *by* phrase the subject of the sentence.

| NO | The cafeteria was boycotted by students to protest high prices. |
| YES | Students boycotted the cafeteria to protest high prices. |

You can also revise a sentence from passive to active by finding a new verb. In this technique you keep the same subject but change the verb voice.

| PASSIVE | Buzz Hargrove **was elected** leader of the Canadian Auto Workers. |
| ACTIVE | Buzz Hargrove **won** the leadership of the Canadian Auto Workers. |

3 | Combining sentences, and reducing clauses and phrases

Often when you revise, you can combine sentences or reduce a clause to a phrase or a phrase to a single word, making your writing more concise and your original idea clearer.

Combining sentences: Look carefully at sets of sentences in your draft. You may be able to reduce the information in an entire sentence to a group of words that you can include in another sentence.

TWO SENTENCES	In 1985, Mel Fisher found *Nuestra Senora de Atocha* 60 kilometres west of Key West, Florida. The *atocha* was a Spanish treasure ship.
COMBINED SENTENCES	In 1985, Mel Fisher found the Spanish treasure ship *Nuestra Senora de Atocha* 60 kilometres west of Key West, Florida.
TWO SENTENCES	The *Atocha* was heading for Spain in 1622 when it sank in a hurricane. It was loaded with gold and silver.
COMBINED SENTENCES	The *Atocha* was heading for Spain in 1622 when it sank in a hurricane, along with its load of gold and silver.

Shortening clauses: You can often reduce adjective clauses (see 7o-2) to phrases, sometimes just by dropping the relative pronoun and its verb.

Earlier, Fisher had found the *Santa Margarita*, **which was the *Atocha's* sister ship.**

Earlier, Fisher had found the *Santa Margarita*, **the *Atocha's* sister ship.**

Sometimes you can reduce the clause to a single word.

Fisher's find will make **people who invested in his company** rich.

Fisher's find will make **investors** rich.

Creating elliptical constructions (7o-2) is another way to reduce clauses, but be sure to omit only strongly implied words.

While they were searching for the *Atocha*, Fisher's son and daughter-in-law drowned.

While searching for the *Atocha*, Fisher's son and daughter-in-law drowned.

Shortening phrases: You may be able to shorten phrases or reduce them to single words.

In 1966, Fisher had begun to search for **the fleet that the *Atocha* was leading.**

In 1966, Fisher had begun to search for **the *Atocha* fleet.**

In twenty years, Fisher found more than a hundred **ships that had been wrecked.**

In twenty years, Fisher found more than a hundred **shipwrecks.**

4   **Using strong verbs and avoiding nouns formed from verbs**

Your writing will have more impact when you choose strong verbs—verbs that directly convey action—instead of forms of *be* or *have*. Using strong verbs also reduces the number of words in your sentences.

NO	The city council **has a plan** to build a new stadium.
YES	The city council **plans** to build a new stadium
NO	Being home to a professional baseball team **is a way to promote** civic pride.
YES	Being home to a professional baseball team **promotes** civic pride.

When you look for weak verbs to revise, look too for **nominals**—nouns created from verbs, often by adding suffixes such as *-ance, -ment,* or *-tion.* For clear, concise writing, turn nominals back into verbs.

NO	The company **was involved in the importation** of catchers' mitts.
YES	The company **imported** catchers' mitts.

5   **Using pronouns for conciseness**

Replacing nouns with pronouns can reduce wordiness. When changing nouns to pronouns, be sure that each pronoun's antecedent is unambiguous (see 10a–10c) and that each pronoun agrees with its antecedents (see 11m–11p).

16b   Eliminating unneeded words

Imprecise and showy language creates wordiness. See 21e for advice on recognizing and avoiding showy (pretentious) language. When a writer tries to write very formally or tries to reach an assigned word limit, **padding** usually results. Sentences are loaded down with **deadwood**—empty words and phrases that add nothing but confusion.

PADDED	The lifeguards, who watch out for the safety of beachgoers, closed the beach near the water when a shark was sighted and seen.
CONCISE	The lifeguards closed the beach when a shark was sighted.
PADDED	After two hours, a fishing boat full of fishermen reported seeing the shark leave the local area of the shore, so the beach was declared reopened to the public.
CONCISE	Two hours later, a fishing boat reported seeing the shark leave the area, so the beach was reopened.

On the next page is a chart showing a few of the most common empty phrases. Before you use one of these, be sure it adds to the meaning of your passage. For a more complete list, refer to the *Simon & Schuster Handbook for Writers,* Chapter 16.

GUIDE FOR ELIMINATING EMPTY WORDS AND PHRASES

EMPTY WORD OR PHRASE	WORDY EXAMPLE	REVISION
as a matter of fact	**As a matter of fact,** statistics show that many marriages end in divorce.	Statistics show that many marriages end in divorce.
because of the fact that	**Because of the fact that** a special exhibit is scheduled, the museum will be open until ten o'clock.	Because of a special exhibit, the museum will be open until ten o'clock.
in fact	**In fact,** the physicist published her results yesterday.	The physicist published her results yesterday.
in view of the fact that	**In view of the fact that** the rainfall was so heavy, we may have flooding.	Because the rainfall was so heavy, we may have flooding.
seems	It **seems** that the union called a strike over health benefits.	The union called a strike over health benefits.
tendency	The team had a **tendency** to lose home games.	The team often lost home games.

16c Revising redundancies

Intentional repetition can create a powerful effect, but unplanned repetition of words or ideas (known as **redundancy**) can make an essay boring.

NO The school is building a new **parking** lot to provide more **parking space.**

YES The school is building a new **lot** to provide more **parking space.**

NO The model was **slender in shape** and **tall in height.**

YES The model was **slender** and **tall.**

Name_____ Date _____

Eliminating Wordy Sentence Structures

Revise these sentences to eliminate wordy sentence structures. You may need to delete expletives, change passive sentences to the active voice, reduce clauses to phrases or phrases to words, and/or replace weak, heavily modified verbs with strong direct verbs.

EXAMPLE   It is Art Deco that became an international style in the 1920s and 1930s.

> *Art Deco became an international style in the 1920s and 1930s.*

1. Art Deco took its name from an exposition that was held in Paris in 1925.

   _____

2. Art Deco may be defined as a style that used shapes that were bold and streamlined and that experimented with new materials.

   _____

3. In the 1920s Art Deco was influenced by public fascination with technology and the future.

   _____

4. In addition to architecture, which it dominated, the style could be found in designs for glassware, appliances, furniture, and even advertising art.

   _____

5. The Marine Building in Vancouver and the Chrysler Building in New York are exemplifications of the dynamic style of Art Deco.

   _____

6. After the crash of the stock market in 1929, Art Deco became less extravagant in its expression of modern ideas and themes.

   _____

7. There was a restraint and austerity in the Art Deco of the Great Depression.

   _____

8. Builders of architecture made use of rounded corners, glass blocks, and porthole windows.

   _____

9. They had a liking for roofs that were flat.

_____

10. Buildings that had plain exteriors often were decorated with lavish care inside and had furniture to match.

_____

Eliminating Unneeded Words

Revise these sentences to eliminate unneeded words and phrases.

EXAMPLE   It seems that many cultures considered the first of May the official beginning of summer.

Many cultures considered the first of May the official beginning of summer.

1. As a matter of fact, the Romans gave sacrifices to the goddess Maia on the first day of the month named for her.

_____

2. It seemed that the Celts also celebrated May Day as the midpoint of their year.

_____

3. One of the most important of the May Day celebrations that exist is the Maypole.

_____

4. In a very real sense, the Maypole represented rebirth.

_____

5. In Germany a Maypole tree was often stripped of all but the top branches for the purpose of representing new life.

_____

6. In the case of Sweden, floral wreaths were suspended from a crossbar on the pole.

_____

7. The English had a different type of tradition.

_____

8. Holding streamers attached to the top of the Maypole, villagers danced around it in an enthusiastic manner.

_____

Name_____ Date _____

9. In view of the fact that May Day had pagan beginnings, the Puritans disapproved of it.

_____

10. Thus it was suppressed by Oliver Cromwell after the overthrow of Charles I.

_____

Eliminating Redundancies

Revise these passages to eliminate unnecessary repetition of words and redundant ideas. Retain helpful repetition.

EXAMPLE   Stamps are small in size, and it takes many in number to make a good collection.

Stamps are small, and it takes many to make a good collection.

1. Many new collectors express astonished amazement at the number of stamps to be collected.

_____

2. They get excited about each and every new stamp they acquire.

_____

3. They hope to make their collections totally complete.

_____

4. Soon it becomes perfectly clear that a complete collection is impossible.

_____

5. Then they may take the pragmatic approach and be practical.

_____

6. They limit their collections by confining them to one country, continent, or decade.

_____

7. At that point in time, their collections will again provide great satisfaction.

_____

8. It is a consensus of opinion that collecting stamps can be educational.

_____

9. It can teach about past history or the geography of the earth.

_____

10. Nevertheless, a new collector should not become discouraged by overstepping possibility and trying to collect too much.

_____

Revising for Conciseness

EXERCISE **16-4**
(16a–c)

Revise these paragraphs to eliminate wordiness, pointless repetitions, and redundancies. Combine sentences as necessary.

A: The deadly bubonic plague was a disease that killed one-third of Europe's population of people. It was in the fourteenth century. This Asian disease came from Asia. It began this way. To begin with, there was a group of merchants from Genoa. They were attacked by infected bandits while they were at a Crimean trading outpost. They became infected. Diseased corpses were thrown over the outpost walls by the bandits, and this was a factor in the merchants catching the plague. Many of the merchants got the disease. They had a tendency to die from the disease. Those who were survivors of the disease went home. The plague was brought back with them. The first European city to have an outbreak was Constantinople in Europe. This happened in 1334. The disease had symptoms of a horrible nature. The disease then spread to the rest of Europe.

B.   Auguste Escoffier was the most famous chef at the turn of the century between 1880 and World War I. In a very real sense, he was the leader of the culinary world of his day. Until that point in time, the best chefs were found in private homes. With Escoffier came an era of fine dining at restaurants to which the nobility and wealthy flocked in order to eat well. After Escoffier joined César Ritz, the luxury hotel owner, they worked as a team together to attract such patrons as the Prince of Wales. Ritz had a tendency to make each and every guest feel personally welcome. It was Escoffier who added the crowning touch by preparing dishes made especially for guests. He created dishes for the prince and for celebrities such as those well known in the entertainment world. He concocted a soup which was called _consommé favori de Sarah Bernhardt_ for the actress of the same name. There was an opera singer for whom he created _poularde Adelina Patti_. As a matter of fact, another singer was fortunate to have more than one dish named for her. When Nellie Melba, an Australian singer, sang in _Lohengrin_, Escoffier served pêches melba, a combination of poached peaches and vanilla ice cream. To commemorate the swans of _Lohengrin_, he served the dessert in a swan that was made of ice. Melba toast was created by Escoffier during one of the periods when Melba was trying to diet. Today, despite the fact that many people have not heard of Nellie Melba, they are familiar with melba toast. As a young army chef, Escoffier had to prepare horse meat and even rat meat for the purpose of feeding the troops. It is obvious that he left those days far behind him when he became the most renowned chef of his day.

17 Coordination and Subordination

Coordination and subordination help your writing gracefully communicate relationships between ideas. **Coordination** of sentences gives equal weight to your ideas, and **subordination** emphasizes one idea over others.

COORDINATION

17a Understanding coordination

A **coordinate** (or **compound**) **sentence** consists of independent clauses (7o-1) joined by a semicolon or a coordinating conjunction (*and, but, for, nor, or, so,* or *yet*).

❖ PUNCTUATION ALERT: You will never be wrong if you put a comma before a coordinating conjunction that joins two independent clauses. ❖

PATTERNS FOR COORDINATE (COMPOUND) SENTENCES		
	, and	
	, but	
	, for	
independent clause	, nor	independent clause
	, or	
	, so	
	, yet	
	;	

Each coordinating conjunction has a specific meaning that establishes the relationship between the ideas in a coordinate sentence.

COORDINATING CONJUNCTIONS AND THE RELATIONSHIPS THEY EXPRESS	
RELATIONSHIPS	**WORDS**
addition	*and*
contrast	*but, yet*
result or effect	*so*
reason or choice	*for*
choice	*or*
negative choice	*nor*

Tuition was increasing, **and** the price of the meal plan was going up even more.
Her schedule was tight, **but** she knew he needed to get a job.

17b Using coordinate sentences to show relationships

Coordinate sentences communicate that the ideas in each independent clause carry equal weight. At the same time, they explain the relationships among those ideas more effectively than a group of separate sentences would.

UNCLEAR RELATIONSHIPS — We planned a picnic. It rained. We had brought a lot of food. We had to make other arrangements. The food would spoil. We went to the ballfield in the park to use the dugout. It was full of water. We all went home.

CLEAR RELATIONSHIPS — We planned a picnic, **but** it rained. We had brought a lot of food, **so** we had to make other arrangements, **or** the food would spoil. We went to the ballfield in the park to use the dugout, **but** it was full of water, **so** we all went home.

17c Using coordinate sentences for effect

Coordination can be used to pile up details for dramatic effect. Consider this passage, in which coordinate sentences present an unfolding of events.

Scott woke up before the alarm went off. He was hungry, but he skipped breakfast. He raced to the showroom, **and** then he had to stand in the cold for fifteen minutes waiting for the place to open. Finally, the manager arrived, **but** before he could put the key in the lock, Scott blurted out, "I got this card; it says my car has arrived."

17d Avoiding the misuse of coordination

Coordination is illogical when ideas in the joined independent clauses are not related and when ideas do not unfold in a purposeful sequence. Avoid illogically coordinated sentences.

NO   Bicycles are becoming a popular means of transportation, **and** they are dangerous on city streets. [Each independent clause is true, but the ideas are not related.]

YES   Bicycles are becoming a popular means of transportation, **yet** the crowded conditions on city streets can make riding them dangerous.

Like all good techniques, coordination can be used too often. Overused coordination can result from writing down whatever comes into your head and not revising later. Avoid overusing coordination.

NO   Hawaii is famous for its coral, **and** some of it is very shiny and hard, **so** it can last indefinitely. Some Hawaiian coral is black, **and** some is gold or pink, **and** Hawaii has $10 million a year in coral sales, **but** worldwide sales are $500 million a year.

YES   Hawaii is famous for its coral. Some of it is very shiny and hard enough to last indefinitely. Hawaiian coral comes in black, gold, and pink. Although Hawaii has $10 million a year in coral sales, worldwide sales are $500 million a year.

NO   Laughter seems to help healing, **so** many doctors are prescribing humour for their patients, **and** some hospitals are doing the same. Comedians have donated their time to several California hospitals, **and** the nurses in one large hospital in Texas have been trained to tell each patient a joke a day.

YES   Laughter seems to help healing. Many doctors and hospitals are prescribing humour for their patients. Comedians have donated their time to several California hospitals, and the nurses in one large hospital in Texas have been trained to tell each patient a joke a day.

SUBORDINATION

17e Understanding subordination

A sentence that uses subordination contains at least two clauses: (1) an **independent clause** (7o-1), which can stand on its own as a sentence, and (2) a **dependent clause** (7o-2), which cannot stand alone. Subordination joins related but separate items so that one is featured—the one in the independent clause.

Two types of dependent clauses are adverb clauses and adjective clauses. **Adverb clauses** are dependent clauses that start with **subordinating conjunctions,** words such as *after, before, until, when, so that,* and *although.*

❖ PUNCTUATION ALERT: (1) When a dependent clause that starts with a subordinating conjunction occurs before the independent clause, separate the clauses with a comma. (2) When such a clause follows the independent clause, separate the clauses with a comma *unless* the dependent clause is essential to the meaning of the independent clause (24e). ❖

> **While tuition had increased,** the price of the meal plan had gone up even more.

> **Although her schedule was tight,** she knew she needed to get a job.

Adjective clauses are dependent clauses that start with **relative pronouns** (such as *who, which,* and *that*); relative adverbs (such as *where*); or a preposition before a "relative" word (such as ***to*** *whom,* ***above*** *which*).

❖ PUNCTUATION ALERT: When an adjective clause is nonrestrictive—that is, when the clause is not essential to the meaning of the sentence—separate it from the independent clause with commas. ❖

> Tuition, **which was high,** increased again.

> The student, **who was already on a tight schedule,** needed to get a job.

17f Choosing the subordinating conjunction appropriate to your meaning

Each subordinating conjunction expresses a different relationship between the major and minor ideas in the subordinate sentences.

SUBORDINATING CONJUNCTIONS AND THE RELATIONSHIPS THEY EXPRESS	
RELATIONSHIPS	**WORDS**
time	*after, before, once, since, until, when, whenever, while*
reason or cause	*as, because*
purpose or result	*in order that, so that*
condition	*if, even if, provided that, unless*
contrast	*although, even though, though, whereas*
location	*where, wherever*
choice	*rather than, than, whether*

Notice how a change in the subordinating conjunction can change your meaning.

> **After** you have been checked in, you cannot leave the security area without a pass. [time limit]

17h

Because you have been checked in, you cannot leave the security area without a pass. [reason]

Unless you have been checked in, you cannot leave the security area without a pass. [condition]

Although you have been checked in, you cannot leave the security area without a pass. [concession]

17g Using subordination to show relationships

Subordination directs your reader's attention to the idea in the independent clause, while using the ideas in the dependent clause to provide context and support. Subordination communicates relationships among ideas more effectively than a group of separate sentences does.

UNCLEAR RELATIONSHIPS   I waited at the bus station. I thought I saw Marcia. She was my baby-sitter fifteen years ago. I was gathering the courage to approach her. She boarded a bus and was gone.

CLEAR RELATIONSHIPS   As I waited at the bus station, I thought I saw Marcia, who was my baby-sitter fifteen years ago. While I was gathering the courage to approach her, she boarded a bus and was gone.

17h Avoiding the misuse of subordination

Subordination is illogical when the subordinating conjunction does not make clear the relationship between the independent and dependent clauses. Avoid illogical subordination.

NO   Before some provinces made wearing seat belts mandatory, the number of fatal automobile accidents fell. [illogical: The fatality rate fell as a result of, not prior to, the seat belt laws.]

YES   After some provinces made wearing seat belts mandatory, the number of fatal automobile accidents fell.

NO   Because he was deaf when he wrote them, Beethoven's final symphonies were masterpieces. [illogical: It was not Beethoven's deafness that led to his writing symphonic masterpieces.]

YES   Although Beethoven was deaf when he wrote his final symphonies, they are musical masterpieces.

Like all good writing techniques, subordination can be overused. Overusing subordination means crowding together too many images or ideas, so that readers become confused and lose track of the message. Avoid overusing subordination.

NO   As a result of water pollution, many shellfish beds, which once supported many families that had lived in the areas for generations, are being closed, which is causing hardships for these families.

YES   As a result of water pollution, many shellfish beds are being closed. This is causing hardships for the many families that have supported themselves for generations by harvesting these waters.

NO   A new technique for eye surgery, which is supposed to correct nearsightedness, which previously could be corrected only by glasses, has been developed, although many doctors do not approve of it because it can create unstable eyesight.

YES   A new technique for eye surgery, which is supposed to correct near-sightedness, has been developed. Previously, nearsightedness could be corrected only by glasses. Because the new technique can create unstable eyesight, however, many doctors do not approve of it.

17i Balancing subordination and coordination

Coordination and subordination are not always used in separate sentences. **Compound-complex sentences** combine coordination with subordination to make sentences that flow.

> Since only a few people are supposed to have this mathematical mind, part of what makes us so passive in the face of our difficulties in learning mathematics is that we suspect all the while we may not be one of "them," and we spend our time waiting to find out when our nonmathematical minds will be exposed.
>
> —SHEILA TOBIAS, *Overcoming Math Anxiety*

17-1

EXERCISE **17-1**
(17a–d)

Combining Sentences and Coordination

Combine these sentences using coordination. For the first five sentences, use the coordinating conjunction given; for the rest, use whatever coordinating conjunction you feel is most appropriate. It may be necessary to add or change a few words, but major rewriting is not needed.

EXAMPLE Television and multimedia have captured the world's attention. Newspapers are still influential and profitable. (But)

> *Television and multimedia have captured the world's attention, but newspapers are still influential and profitable.*

1. Many Canadians made their fortunes as newspaper owners. Others bought newspapers after making their mark in other fields. (and)

_____

2. Reformer George Brown wanted to promote his political ideals. He founded the *Globe* in 1844. (so)

_____

3. K. C. Irving of New Brunswick founded a huge industrial empire based on oil refining, transportation, and pulp and paper. Later he added local newspapers to his holdings. (;)

_____

4. Conrad Black likes to tell how he started his newspaper empire with a small loan. His wealthy family already had major business investments in other fields. (but)

_____

5. We should not forget other Canadian newspaper tycoons such as the Thomsons and the Beaverbrooks. We should also not ignore lesser-known mavericks like Margaret "Ma" Murray, owner of the *Bridge River-Lillooet News*. (nor)

_____

6. The Trudeau government was concerned that newspaper ownership was becoming concentrated in too few hands. In 1980 it set up a royal commission to study the problem.

_____

7. Tom Kent was named head of the commission. He had been a newspaper editor and adviser to prime ministers.

     _____

8. Kent recommended that the government limit the size of newspaper empires. Soon Canadians would all be reading the same opinions written by employees of a small number of wealthy men.

     _____

9. Little was done about the Kent Commission recommendations. The newspaper empires continued to grow.

     _____

10. Kent did not know that his report would be ignored by the Trudeau government. Also, he could not have guessed that by the 1990s, Conrad Black would own the majority of Canada's daily newspapers.

     _____

11. Defenders of big newspaper chains say that size is a good thing. Only wealthy owners can afford the staff and resources to produce the best newspapers.

     _____

12. Some people also look back with nostalgia to the legendary days of the strong-willed newspaper boss. They argue that we can find their counterparts today only among opinionated media tycoons.

     _____

Combining Sentences with Subordination

EXERCISE **17-2**
(17e–h)

Combine these sentences using subordination. For the first five sentences, use the subordinating conjunction or relative pronoun given; for the rest, use whatever subordinating conjunction or relative pronoun you feel is most appropriate. Some items have more than one correct answer, but most make sense only one way, so decide carefully which sentence comes first and where to place the subordinating conjunction or relative pronoun. It may sometimes be necessary to add or change a few words, but major rewriting is not needed.

EXAMPLE   Many businesses around the world started using fragrances. Researchers found that fragrances have a stimulating effect on people. (after)

Many businesses around the world started using fragrances after researchers found that fragrances have a stimulating effect on people.

EXERCISES

Name_____ Date _____

1. A company in Toronto was one of the first ones to install a fragrancing unit in its office ventilation system. It was installed to control employee behaviour. (in order to)

   _____

2. The company was careful about which fragrances it introduced into the workplace. Some fragrances rev people up, and some calm them down. (because)

   _____

3. The scents were designed by Toronto-based Aromasphere, Inc. The company created a time-release mechanism to send the scents directly into the work area. (which)

   _____

4. Bodywise Ltd. in Great Britain received a patent for a fragrance. It began to market its scent, which contains androstenone, an ingredient of male sweat. (once)

   _____

5. The scent was adopted by a U.S. debt-collection agency. Another agency in Australia reported that chronic debtors who received scented letters were 17 percent more likely to pay than were those who received unscented letters. (after)

   _____

6. Researchers have recently discovered how much odour can influence behaviour. Smell is still the least understood of the five senses.

   _____

7. Aromasphere's employees have been asked to keep logs of their moods. They do this in the workplace.

   _____

8. Researchers have raised many concerns about trying to change human behaviour. They feel that this kind of tampering may lead to too much control over employees.

   _____

9. Smells can have an effect on people. They may be completely unaware of what is happening.

   _____

10. Employees are forewarned, however, that they will be exposed to mood-altering fragrances. Such employees may protest against the introduction of the scents in the workplace.

_____

11. Even psychiatric wards emit a scent. It makes the patients calm.

_____

12. International Flavors and Fragrances of New York is the world's largest manufacturer of artificial flavours and aromas. It has developed many of the scents commonly used today.

_____

13. It has even created a bagel scent. Bagels lose their aroma when they are kept in plexiglass.

_____

14. There wasn't a true commercial interest in these products. Researchers began to understand the anatomy of smell.

_____

15. It turns out that olfactory signals travel to the limbic region of the brain. The region regulates hormones of the autonomic nervous sytem.

_____

Expanding Sentences with Coordination and Subordination

EXERCISE **17-3**
(17a–h)

Add to each sentence below in two ways. First add an independent clause, using a coordinating conjunction. Then add a dependent clause beginning with either a subordinating conjunction or a relative pronoun.

EXAMPLE   Travelling by balloon is exciting.

> _Travelling by balloon is exciting, and I hope to do it again soon._
> _Travelling by balloon is exciting because the wind is unpredictable._

1. Public transportation in the city is inadequate.

_____

_____

2. Teaching a nervous partner to dance can be frustrating.

_____

_____

Name_____ Date _____

3. The park looked especially beautiful at sunset.

   _____

   _____

4. Never buy a stereo without listening to it first.

   _____

   _____

5. Exercise can be fun.

   _____

   _____

6. Mexican food is tasty.

   _____

   _____

7. Watching a tape at home with friends is better than going to the movies.

   _____

   _____

8. The cost of food keeps going up.

   _____

   _____

9. A small car may be difficult to handle in rough weather.

   _____

   _____

10. Keeping a pet in an apartment requires compromises.

   _____

   _____

Using Coordination and Subordination in a Paragraph

These paragraphs are full of choppy sentences. Revise them using coordinating and subordinating conjunctions so that the sentences are smoother and more fully explain the relationships between ideas. Many correct versions are possible. Take the time to try several, and select the version you like best.

Senet is a game. It was played by ancient Egyptians. It was very popular. Egyptians began putting senet boards into tombs as early as 3100 B.C. Tomb objects were intended for use in the afterlife. They give us a good idea of daily life.

Many senet boards and playing pieces have been found in tombs. The hot, dry air of the tombs preserved them all. Tomb paintings frequently show people playing the game. Hieroglyphic texts describe it. Numerous descriptions of the game survive. Egyptologists think it was a national pastime.

Senet was a game for two people. They played it on a board marked with thirty squares. Each player had several playing pieces. They probably each had seven. The number did not matter as long as it was the same for both. Opponents moved by throwing flat sticks. The sticks were an early form of dice. Sometimes they threw pairs of lamb knuckles instead. Players sat across from each other. They moved their pieces in a backward S line. The squares represented houses. They moved through the houses.

By the New Kingdom the game began to take on religious overtones. The thirty squares were given individual names. They were seen as stages on the journey of the soul through the netherworld. New Kingdom tomb paintings showed the deceased playing senet with an unseen opponent. The object was to win eternal life. The living still played the game. They played it in anticipation of the supernatural match to come.

18 Parallelism

18a Understanding parallelism

Parallelism is related to the concept of parallel lines in geometry. In writing, parallelism calls for the use of equivalent grammatical forms to express equivalent ideas. Parallel forms match words with words in the same form, phrases with similar phrases, or clauses with other clauses composed of the same verb forms and word orders.

Parallelism helps you communicate that two or more items in a group are equally important and makes your writing more graceful. For this reason, it is a good idea to avoid the error of faulty **parallelism**—using nonequivalent grammatical patterns.

PARALLEL WORDS	A triathlon includes **running, swimming** and **cycling.** [The -*ings* are parallel in form and equal in importance.]
PARALLEL PHRASES	Training requires **an intense exercise program** and **a carefully regulated diet.** [The phrases are parallel in structure and equal in importance.]
PARALLEL CLAUSES	Most people prefer to watch the triathlon rather than participate **because the triathlon is so difficult** and **because their couches are so comfortable.** [The clauses starting with *because* are parallel in structure and equal in importance.]

18b Using words in parallel form

Words in lists or other parallel structures must occur in the same grammatical form. Be sure to use such matching forms for parallel items.

NO	The warm-up includes **stretches, sit-ups,** and **sprinting.**
YES	The warm-up includes **stretches, sit-ups,** and **sprints.**
YES	The warm-up includes **stretching, doing sit-ups,** and **sprinting.**

NO	The strikers had tried **pleading, threats,** and **shouting.**
YES	The strikers had tried **pleading, threatening,** and **shouting.**
YES	The strikers had tried **pleas, threats,** and **shouts.**

18c Using phrases and clauses in parallel forms

Phrases and clauses in parallel structures must occur in the same grammatical form. Be sure to use such matching forms for parallel items.

NO   The kitchen crew **scraped the grill, the salt shakers were refilled, and were taking out the trash.**

YES   The kitchen crew **scraped the grill, refilled the salt shakers,** and **took out the trash.**

18d Using parallel structures with coordinating and correlative conjunctions and with *than* and *as*

Whenever you join words, phrases, or clauses with coordinating conjunctions or correlative conjunctions (7h), be sure they occur in parallel form.

Happiness is good health **and** a bad memory

—INGRID BERGMAN

We are the carriers of health and disease—**either** *the divine health of courage and nobility* **or** *the demonic disease of hate and anxiety.*

—JOSHUA LOTH LIEBMAN

Simple pleasures can be **as** *satisfying* **as**, if not *more satisfying* **than**, rare luxuries.

18e Repeating function words in parallel elements

To strengthen the effect of parallelism, repeat words that begin parallel phrases or clauses. Such words include prepositions (7g), articles (*a, an, the*), and the *to* of an infinitive (7d).

To *find* a fault is easy; **to** *do* better may be difficult.

—PLUTARCH

Use parallel clauses beginning with *and who, and whom,* or *and which* when they follow clauses beginning with *who, whom* or *which.*

I have in my own life a precious friend, a woman of 65 **who has** lived very hard, **who is** wise, **who listens** well, **who has** been where I am and can help me understand it; **and who represents** not only an ultimate ideal mother to me but also the person I'd like to be when I grow up.

—JUDITH VIORST, "Friends, Good Friends—and Such Good Friends"

18f Using parallel, balanced structures for impact

Parallel structures characterized by balance serve to emphasize the meaning that sentences deliver. Balanced, parallel structures can be words, phrases, clauses, or sentences.

Deliberate, rhythmic repetition of parallel, balanced word forms and word groups reinforces the impact of a message. (For information about misused repetition, see 16c.) Consider the impact of this famous passage:

> **Go back to** Mississippi, **go back to** Alabama, **go back to** South Carolina, **go back to** Georgia, **go back to** Louisiana, **go back to** the slums and ghettos of our northern cities, knowing that somehow this situation can and will be changed.
>
> —MARTIN LUTHER KING, JR., "I Have a Dream"

King's structures reinforce the power of his message. An ordinary sentence would have been less effective: "Return to your homes in Mississippi, Alabama, South Carolina, Georgia, Louisiana, or the cities, and know that the situation will be changed."

A **balanced sentence** has two parallel structures, usually sentences, with contrasting content. A balanced sentence is a coordinate sentence (see 17a), characterized by opposition in the meaning of the two structures, sometimes with one cast in the negative: *Mosquitos do not bite, they stab.*

18g Using parallel sentences for impact in longer passages

Parallel sentences in longer passages provide coherence (4d). The carefully controlled repetition of words and word forms creates a pattern that enables readers to follow ideas more easily.

18h Using parallelism in outlines and lists

Items in formal outlines and lists should be in parallel structure. Without parallelism, the information may not be clear to the reader and may not communicate the relative importance of the items. (For information about developing outlines, see 2p).

Outline not in parallel form

TYPES OF FIRE EXTINGUISHERS

    I. The Class A Type
        A. Contains water or water-chemical solution
        B. For fighting wood, paper, or cloth fires

II. Class B

    A. Foam, dry chemicals, or carbon dioxide "snow"

    B. Use against grease or flammable-liquid fires

III. Class C

    A. Containing dry chemicals

    B. Electrical fires

Outline in parallel form

TYPES OF FIRE EXTINGUISHERS

  I. Class A

    A. **Contains** water or water-chemical solution,

    B. **Fights** wood, paper, or cloth fires

 II. Class B

    A. **Contains** foam, dry chemicals, or carbon dioxide "snow"

    B. **Fights** grease or flammable-liquid fires

III. Class C

    A. **Contains** dry chemicals,

    B. **Fights** electrical fires

List not in parallel form

HOW TO ESCAPE A FIRE

1. Feel the door for heat, and don't open it if it is hot.
2. You should open the door slowly.
3. Smoke?
4. If there is smoke, close the door and leave by another door or window.
5. If there is no other exit—try crawling under the smoke.
6. Be sure to use the stairs; the elevator should be avoided.
7. The fire department.
8. Re-enter the building? No!

List in parallel form

HOW TO ESCAPE A FIRE

1. **Feel** the door for heat; **do** not **open** it if it is hot.
2. **Open** the door slowly.
3. **Check** the hall for smoke.
4. **If there is** smoke, **close** the door and **leave** by another door or window.
5. **If there is** no other exit, **crawl** under the smoke.
6. **Use** stairs, never an elevator.
7. **Call** the fire department.
8. **Do** not **re-enter** the building.

Name_____ Date _____

Identifying Parallel Elements

Underline parallel words, phrases, and clauses.

EXAMPLE   Many ancient writers <u>in Greece</u> and <u>in Rome</u> wrote about underwater ships.

1. They hoped these ships would be used for exploration and travel.

2. Leonardo Da Vinci felt that humanity would be destroyed by a great flood because of its proud and evil ways.

3. Therefore, just as earlier he had made plans for a helicopter, he made plans for an underwater ship.

4. However, the first working submarine was designed by a British mathematician and built by a Dutch inventor.

5. It was designed in 1578, built in 1620, and successfully tested from 1620 to 1624.

6. This submarine was equipped with oars, so it could be used either on the surface or below the surface.

7. King James I of England actually boarded the submarine and took a short ride.

8. James's praise soon made submarines the talk of the town and the focus of scientific investigation.

9. A much later model featured goatskin bags attached to holes in the bottom of the ship. When the vessel was to submerge, the bags would fill with water and pull the ship downward; when the vessel was to rise, a twisting rod would force water from the bags, and the lightened ship would surface.

10. David Bushnell, a student at Yale during the American Revolution, designed and built a war-submarine, the *Turtle*.

11. It was intended to sneak up on British warships and attach explosives to their hulls.

12. Despite successful launching and steering, the *Turtle* failed on its only mission when the pilot was unable to attach the explosives to the British target ship.

13. The first successful wartime submarines were developed by the South in the American Civil War: small, four-person ships called "Davids" and a full-sized submarine called the "Hunley."

14. New submarines were designed throughout the nineteenth century, but providing dependable power and steering to navigate remained problems for years.

15. The development of the gasoline engine and the invention of the periscope solved these problems before the beginning of World War I.

18-2

Writing Parallel Elements

Fill in the blanks with words, phrases, or clauses, as appropriate.

EXAMPLE Writing a paper involves _researching, outlining,_ and _presenting accurate information_.

1. She rides her bicycle ten kilometres a day because she loves _____ , but hates _____ .

2. _____ a broken cell phone is much more difficult than _____ a new one.

3. After work tonight, I'd like to pick up my favourite movie, _____ , and _____ .

4. Libraries must be _____ and _____ .

5. When I misplaced my new sunglasses, I checked for them _____ and _____ .

6. We took the children to a park _____ , _____ , and _____ .

7. In my spare time, I listen to music that is _____ and _____ .

8. My professor is always on the move: constantly _____ , and _____ .

9. The player who is the most _____ and _____ will receive the award.

10. The best place to buy concert tickets at a reduced rate is located at _____ and _____ .

11. A successful attorney is _____ and _____ .

12. For the recital, Sarah wants to _____ and _____ .

13. After it began to _____ and _____ he shut the windows so that the rain wouldn't get inside the house.

14. I'll call my sister either _____ or _____ .

15. The students _____ and _____ until the professor granted them a larger curve on the exam.

19 Variety and Emphasis

19a Understanding variety and emphasis

Your writing style has **variety** when your sentence lengths and patterns vary. Your writing style has **emphasis** when your sentences are constructed to reflect the relative importance of your ideas. Variety and emphasis are closely related. They represent the joining of form and meaning.

19b Varying sentence length

If you vary your sentence length, you signal distinctions among your ideas so that your readers can understand the focus of your material. Also you avoid the monotony created by an unvarying rhythm.

Strings of too many short sentences rarely establish relationships and levels of importance among ideas. Such strings suggest that the writer has not thought through the material and decided what to emphasize.

NO   Ants are much like human beings. It is embarrassing. They farm fungi. They raise aphids as livestock. They launch armies into wars. They use chemical sprays to alarm and confuse enemies. They capture slaves.

YES   Ants are so much like human beings as to be an embarrassment. They farm fungi, raise aphids as livestock, launch armies into wars, use chemical sprays to alarm and confuse enemies, capture slaves.

—LEWIS THOMAS, "On Societies as Organisms"

Too often, compound sentences are only short sentences strung together with *and* or *but*, without consideration of the relationships among the ideas. Consider this passage, which babbles along.

NO   Sodium is an element and some people think that it is the same as salt, but sodium is just one element in salt, and it also contains chlorine.

YES   Sodium is an element. Some people think it is the same as salt; however, sodium is just one element in salt. In fact, salt also contains chlorine.

As can be seen in the passage below, you can emphasize one idea among many others by expressing it in a sentence noticeably different in length or structure from the sentences surrounding it.

> Mistakes are not believed to be part of the normal behavior of a good machine. **If things go wrong, it must be a personal, human error, the result of fingering, tampering, a button getting stuck, someone hitting the wrong key.** The computer, at its normal best, is infallible. I wonder whether this can be true.
>
> —LEWIS THOMAS, "To Err is Human"

 ## Using an occasional question, mild command, or exclamation

To vary your sentence structure and to emphasize material, you can call on four basic sentence types. The most typical English sentence is **declarative:** it makes a statement—it declares something. A sentence that asks a question is called **interrogative.** Occasional questions help you involve your reader. A sentence that issues a mild or strong command is called **imperative.** Occasional mild commands are particularly helpful for gently urging your reader to think along with you. A sentence that makes an exclamation is called **exclamatory.**

Consider the following examples from *Change!* by Isaac Asimov.

QUESTION   The colonization of space may introduce some unexpected changes into human society. **For instance, what effect will it have on the way we keep time?** Our present system of time keeping is a complicated mess that depends on accidents of astronomy and on 5,000 years of primitive habit.

MILD COMMAND   **Consider the bacteria.** These are tiny living things made up of single cells far smaller than the cells in plants and animals.

EXCLAMATION   **The amazing thing about the netting of the coelacanth was that till then zoologists had been convinced the fish had been extinct for 60 million years!** Finding a living dinosaur would not have been more surprising.

19d Choosing the subject of a sentence according to your intended emphasis

Because the subject of a sentence establishes the focus for that sentence, choose a subject that corresponds to the emphasis you want to communicate. The following sentences, each of which is correct grammatically, contain the same information. Consider, however, how changes of the subject (and its verb) influence meaning and impact.

Our **poll shows** that most voters prefer Jones. [emphasis on the poll]

Most **voters prefer** Jones, according to our poll. [emphasis on the voters]

Jones is preferred by most voters, according to our poll. [emphasis on Jones]

19e Adding modifiers to basic sentences for variety and emphasis

Sometimes you may want a very short sentence for its dramatic effect, but you usually need to modify simple subjects and verbs. The technique you use will depend on the focus of your sentence.

BASIC SENTENCE	Traffic stopped.
ADJECTIVE (7E, 12)	**Rush-hour** traffic stopped.
ADVERB (7F, 12)	Traffic stopped **suddenly.**
PREPOSITIONAL PHRASE (7N)	**In the middle of rush hour,** traffic stopped **on the bridge.**
PARTICIPIAL PHRASE (7N)	**Blocked by an overturned tractor-trailer,** traffic stopped, **delaying hundreds of travellers.**
ABSOLUTE PHRASE (7N)	**The accident blocking all lanes,** traffic stopped.
ADVERB CLAUSE (7o-2)	**Because all lanes were blocked,** traffic stopped **until the trailer could be removed.**
ADJECTIVE CLAUSE (7o-2)	Traffic, **which was already slow,** stopped.

You can also position modifiers in a sentence according to the emphasis that you want to achieve. Be sure, however, to avoid misplaced modifiers (15b).

19f Inverting standard word order

Standard word order in the English sentence places the subject before the verb: *The mayor walked* into the room. Because this pattern is so common, it is set in people's minds. Any variation from the pattern creates emphasis. Inverted word order places the verb before the subject. *Into the room walked the mayor.* Used too often, inverted word order can be distracting, but used sparingly, it can be very effective.

19g Repeating important words or ideas to achieve emphasis

Repeating carefully chosen words can help you to emphasize your meaning, but choose for repetition only those words that contain a main idea or that use rhythm to focus attention on a main idea.

> Our approach to multiculturalism encourages the devaluation of that which it claims to wish to protect and promote. **Culture** becomes an object for display rather than the heart and soul of the individuals formed by it. **Culture,** manipulated into social and political usefulness, becomes folklore—as René Lévesque said—lightened and simplified, stripped of the weight of the past. None of the **cultures** that make up our "mosaic" seems to have produced history worthy of exploration or philosophy worthy of consideration.
>
> —Neil Bissoondath, "The Simplification of Culture"

Name_____ Date _____

Varying Sentence Beginnings by Varying Subjects

<table>
<tr><td>EXERCISE **19-1**
(19d)</td></tr>
</table>

Revise each sentence so that it begins with the word or words given.

EXAMPLE A look at our history shows that North Americans have enjoyed following the latest fads.

North Americans: *North Americans have enjoyed following the latest fads*
throughout our history.

1. Parents usually think the dances their teenagers like are strange.

   The dances: _____

2. In the early 1900s, fifteen women were fired by the management of the magazine where they worked.

   In the early 1900s, the management: _____

3. They had offended management by dancing the Turkey Trot during their lunch hour.

   Their offence: _____

4. Other popular dances of the period included the Grizzly Bear, the Kangaroo Dip, and the Bunny Hug.

   The Grizzly Bear: _____

5. Alvin "Shipwreck" Kelly invented flagpole sitting.

   Flagpole sitting: _____

6. No one knows the source of his nickname.

   The source: _____

7. Pie plates from the Frisbee Baking Company were the first Frisbees.

   The first Frisbees: _____

8. A Harvard student began a goldfish swallowing fad in 1939.

   The goldfish swallowing fad: _____

9. Reporters saw him swallow a live three-inch fish.

   He: _____

10. Australians invented the Hula Hoop for use in gym classes.

    The Hula Hoop: _____

Expanding Sentences with Modifiers

A: Expand these simple sentences in the ways stated in parentheses.

EXAMPLE   The moon was shining.

(prepositional phrase) *The moon was shining through the trees.*

1.   The sofa is wearing out.

(adjective) _____

(adverb clause) _____

(participial phrase) _____

2.   My father swam daily.

(adverb) _____

(adjective clause) _____

(absolute phrase) _____

3.   The performance was splendid.

(prepositional phrase) _____

(adjective) _____

(adverb clause) _____

4.   The snow fell silently.

(participial phrase) _____

(adverb) _____

(adjective clause) _____

5.   Lewis finished writing the concerto.

(absolute phrase) _____

(prepositional phrase) _____

(adjective) _____

Name_____ Date _____

B: Add the several elements given to each of the following sentences.

EXAMPLE   The astronaut was welcomed home.
            (adjective modifying *astronaut*; adverb modifying was *welcomed*; prepositional
            phrase modifying *home*)

            *The brave astronaut was warmly welcomed home from space.*_____

1. The celebration included a parade.
    (adjectives modifying *celebration* and *parade*; prepositional phrase modifying *parade*)

    _____

2. The crowd was dressed in shorts and shirts.
    (absolute phrase; adjective modifying *shirts*)

    _____

3. The major stopped traffic.
    (adjective clause modifying *major*, adverb clause)

    _____

4. The astronaut rode in a car.
    (adjectives modifying *astronaut* and *car*, adverb modifying *rode*)

    _____

5. Youngsters tried to get autographs.
    (adverb clause; adjective clause modifying *youngsters*)

    _____

6. The major gave a speech.
    (absolute phrase; two adjectives modifying *speech*)

    _____

7. Everyone cheered.
    (two adverb clauses)

    _____

8. The celebration ended.
    (prepositional phrase modifying *ended*)

    _____

9. Everyone headed home.
    (participial phrase modifying *everyone*)

    _____

10. The street cleaners came out.
    (prepositional phrase modifying *came out*; adverb clause)

    _____

Revising to Emphasize the Main Idea

Using sentence combining, revise each passage into one or two sentences that emphasize its main idea. To do this, select the most effective subject for the sentence, stay in the active voice whenever possible, use a variety of sentence types (simple, compound, complex, compound-complex) and modifiers, and change clauses into phrases where practical.

EXAMPLE Retail chains are closing outlets. Firms are laying off many employees. There is a changed relationship between some workers and their bosses.

> *Because retail chains are closing outlets and firms are laying off many employees, there is a changed relationship between some workers and their bosses.*

1. There is a new emphasis on teamwork. There is a new emphasis on trust in the workplace. Managers hope that the shift in attitude will benefit their businesses.

_____

_____

2. Companies are trying to make a difference. They are experimenting with group talks among employees. These groups discuss issues dealing with workers as individuals and as team members.

_____

_____

3. The talks are very helpful for managers. The workers involved are those who are still with the company. They have survived the massive cutbacks and need a boost in morale.

_____

_____

4. These experimental groups also break down barriers in the workplace. These barriers tend to separate one department from another. This separation takes away any feelings of teamwork and cooperation.

_____

_____

5. Teamwork is critical for companies that want to regain competitiveness. These groups strive to remove obstacles that prevent communication and respect among workers. Teamwork is a necessary step in the right direction.

_____

_____

20 Understanding the Meaning of Words

20a Using dictionaries

Good dictionaries show how language has been used and is currently being used. Such dictionaries give not only a word's meaning, but also much additional important information.

An individual dictionary entry usually includes the following information: spelling; word division into syllables (syllabication); pronunciation; parts of speech; grammatical forms (plurals, parts of verbs including irregular forms, etc.); word origin; meanings; related words (nouns, adjectives); synonyms; words used in sample sentences; usage labels; and idioms that include the word.

The spelling is given first, with the word usually divided into syllables by centred dots. The pronunciation follows. Here you will sometimes see unusual symbols, such as /ə/, the **schwa** or "uh" sound. These symbols are explained in a pronunciation key, usually located in the dictionary's introduction or at the bottom of each page. The part of speech comes next. It is usually abbreviated, such as *n* for *noun* or *vt* for *transitive verb*. The dictionary also gives the principal parts of each word (for regular verbs, the *-ed* form for past tense and past participle, the *-ing* form for the present participle). The word's history (known as the etymology) usually follows. The word's meanings come next. If a word can be used as more than one part of speech, the meanings are grouped according to the parts of speech. Usage labels give additional important information, indicating which words are *slang, poetic,* or *dialect*.

Dictionaries come in several varieties. **Unabridged** ("unshortened") dictionaries have the most in-depth, accurate, complete, and scholarly entries of the various kinds of dictionaries. They give many examples of a word's current uses and changes in meanings over time. They also include infrequently used words that other dictionaries may omit.

Abridged ("shortened") dictionaries contain only the most commonly used words. They are convenient in size and economical to buy. These are the most practical reference books for writers and readers.

A number of specialized dictionaries focus on single areas, such as slang, word origins, synonyms, usage, or almost any other aspect of language. Whatever your interest, a specialized dictionary is probably available. Ask your reference librarian to point out what you need.

Several major dictionaries are available on CD-ROM, and others are online.

20b Choosing exact words

Careful writers pay close attention to **diction**—word choice. To choose the most appropriate and accurate word, a writer must understand the word's denotation and connotation.

When you look up a new word in the dictionary to find out exactly what it means, you are looking for its **denotation.** Words with the same general definition may have subtle differences of meaning. These differences enable you to choose precisely the right word, but they also obligate you to make sure you know what meanings your words convey. For example, describing someone as *lean* or *slender* is far different from calling that person *skinny.*

Connotation refers to the ideas implied but not directly indicated by a word. Connotations convey emotional overtones beyond a word's direct definition. What first comes to mind when you see the word *blood?* To some people *blood* represents war or injury while to others it is a symbol of family or ethnic identity; to people in the healing professions, **blood** may be interpreted as a symbol of life. Good writers understand the additional layer of meaning connotations deliver to specific audiences.

Specific words identify individual items in a group (*grape, orange, apple, plum*), whereas **general** words relate to an overall group (*fruit*). **Concrete** words identify persons and things that can be detected by senses—seen, heard, tasted, felt, smelled (the *crisp, sweet, red apple*). **Abstract** words denote qualities, concepts, relationships, acts, conditions, or ideas (*delicious*). Writers must use all these types of words. Effective writers, however, make sure to supply enough specific, concrete details to breathe life into generalizations and abstractions.

20c Increasing your vocabulary

Here are a few techniques you can use to make new words you encounter part of your vocabulary.

TECHNIQUES FOR BUILDING YOUR VOCABULARY

TO FIND WORDS

- Using a highlighter pen, mark all unfamiliar words in your textbooks and other reading material. Then define the words in the margin so you can study the meaning in context. Copy new words onto index cards or into a special notebook.
- Listen carefully to learn how speakers use the language. Jot down new words and later look them up. Write each new word and its definitions on an index card or in a special notebook.

TO STUDY WORDS

- Set aside time each day to study the new words. You can carry your cards or notebook in your pocket to study in spare moments during the day.
- Use mnemonics to memorize words (see 22a). Set a goal of learning and *using* eight to ten new words a week.
- Every few weeks go back to the words from previous weeks. Make a list of any words you do not still remember and study them again.

---

1 Knowing prefixes and suffixes

Prefixes are syllables in front of a **root** (base) word that modify its meaning. *Per* (*thoroughly*) placed before the root *form* (*to make or do*) gives *perform* ("to do thoroughly"). **Suffixes** are syllables added to the end of a root word that modify its meaning. For example, *icy* has the various forms of adjective, adverb, and noun when suffixes are added: *icy, icily, icicle, icing.*

Roots are the central parts of words to which prefixes and suffixes are added. Once you know, for example, the Latin root *bene* (*well, good*), you can decode various forms: **bene***factor*, **bene***diction.*

Knowing common prefixes and suffixes is an excellent way to learn to figure out unfamiliar words. The following charts list some of the most common prefixes and suffixes.

PREFIXES

PREFIX	MEANING	EXAMPLE
anti-	against	*antiballistic*
contra-	against	*contradict*
extra-	more	*extraordinary*
hyper-	more	*hyperactive*
super-	more	*supernatural*
ultra-	more	*ultraconservative*
dis-	not	*disagree*
il-	not	*illegal*
im-	not	*immoral*
in-	not	*inadequate*
ir-	not	*irresponsible*
mis-	not	*misunderstood*
non-	not	*noninvolvement*
un-	not	*unhappy*
semi-	half	*semicircle*
mono-	one	*monopoly*
uni-	one	*uniform*
multi-	many	*multitude*
poly-	many	*polygamy*
ante-	before	*antebellum*
pre-	before	*prehistoric*
post-	after	*postscript*
re-	back	*return*
retro-	back	*retroactive*
sub-	under	*submissive*
trans-	across	*transportation*
inter-	between	*interpersonal*
intra-	inside	*intravenous*
auto-	self	*autobiography*
mal-	poor	*malnutrition*
magni-	great	*magnificent*
omni-	all	*omnipotent*
ab-	from	*abstain*

NOUN SUFFIXES

SUFFIX	MEANING	EXAMPLE
-tion	act of	*integration*
-hood	state of	*childhood*
-ness	state of	*kindness*
-ship	state of	*friendship*
-tude	state of	*solitude*
-dom	state of	*freedom*
-eer	a doer of	*auctioneer*

VERB SUFFIXES

SUFFIX	MEANING	EXAMPLE
-ate	to make	*integrate*
-ify	to make	*unify*
-ize	to make	*computerize*
-en	to cause to be	*broaden*

ADJECTIVAL SUFFIXES

SUFFIX	MEANING	EXAMPLE
-able	able to be	*comfortable*
-ible	able to be	*compatible*
-ate	full of	*fortunate*
-ful	full of	*tactful*
-ous	full of	*pompous*
-y	full of	*gloomy*
-less	without	*penniless*
-like	characteristic of	*doglike*
-ly	characteristic of	*saintly*

2   Using context clues to figure out word meanings

The familiar words that surround an unknown word can give you hints about the new word's meaning. These **context** clues include four main types.

1. **Restatement context clue.** You can figure out an unknown word when a word you know repeats the meaning: *The dieter was **enervated**. He was even too weakened to do his exercises. Enervated* means "weakened."

2. **Contrast context clue.** You can figure out an unknown word when an opposite or contrast is presented: *We expected Uncle Roy to be **omnivorous**, but he turned out to be a picky eater. Omnivorous* means "eating any sort of food." The explanatory contrast is *but he turned out to be a picky eater.*

3. **Example context clue.** You can figure out an unfamiliar word when an example or illustration relating to the word is given: *The Board of Directors made the vice-president the **scapegoat**, saying that the pollution was a result of her policies. Scapegoat* means "one who bears the blame for mistakes of others."

4. **General sense context clue.** An entire passage can convey a general sense of a new word. For example, *After a series of victories, the tennis star came to think of herself as **invincible**.* You can figure out that *invincible* has something to do with winning consistently.

Keep in mind that a specific context will reveal only one of many possible meanings of a word. Once you have deciphered a meaning from context clues, check the exact definition of the word in a dictionary.

20-1

Name_____ Date _____

Using the Dictionary

A: Using a college-level dictionary, rewrite each word to indicate capitalization, syllabication, hyphens, and spaces between words; use a dot to represent a break between syllables.

	Spelling	**Pronunciation**
EXAMPLE bolognese	Bo • lo • gnese	*Bō lə nēz*
1. brogue		
2. broadminded		
3. cornmeal		
4. dahlia		
5. gypsy		
6. headache		
7. headstart		
8. incunabula		
9. inveigh		
10. peripatetic		

B: Give the meaning of these abbreviations and symbols. Consult your college-level dictionary if you are unsure.

EXAMPLE adj. _____*adjective*_____

1. Afr.	_____	11. cf.	_____
2. alt.	_____	12. Colloq.	_____
3. Amind.	_____	13. exc.	_____
4. art.	_____	14. ff.	_____
5. Celt.	_____	15. G.	_____
6. ger.	_____	16. L.	_____
7. Gr.	_____	17. ME.	_____
8. <	_____	18. *	_____
9. IE.	_____	19. pp.	_____
10. i.e.	_____	20. var.	_____

C: Give the past and past participle forms of these irregular verbs.

	Past	Past Participle
EXAMPLE send	_sent_	_sent_
1. have		
2. do		
3. eat		
4. choose		
5. drink		
6. go		
7. fly		
8. know		
9. pay		
10. let		

D: Give the comparative and superlative forms of these adjectives and adverbs.

	Comparative	Superlative
EXAMPLE kind	_kinder_	_kindest_
1. kindly		
2. good		
3. well		
4. bad		
5. badly		
6. intelligent		
7. intelligently		
8. happily		
9. grateful		
10. loudly		

EXERCISES

Name_____ Date _____

E: Give the plural forms of these nouns. If your dictionary gives more than one form, list them all in the order given.

EXAMPLE alligator _____*alligators, alligator*_____

1. scarf _____

2. llama _____

3. salmon _____

4. nucleus _____

5. formula _____

6. phenomenon _____

7. index _____

8. kibbutz _____

9. bandit _____

10. château _____

F: Carefully read the etymologies of these words in your dictionary. Then list (a) each word's original language and (b) its original meaning. Do not use abbreviations.

EXAMPLE house a. *Old English hus*

b. *house*

1. wife

a. _____

b. _____

2. husband

a. _____

b. _____

3. son

a. _____

b. _____

4. daughter

a. _____

b. _____

5. marry

a. _____

b. _____

6. mango

a. _____

b. _____

7. cherry

a. _____

b. _____

8. tomato

a. _____

b. _____

9. pepper

a. _____

b. _____

10. onion

a. _____

b. _____

G: Find out what you can about the origin of each of these words.

EXAMPLE sandwich

after John Montagu, fourth Earl of Sandwich (1718–1792), who was said to
have eaten these in order not to leave the gambling table for meals

1. cardigan _____

2. quixotic _____

3. pants _____

4. bedlam _____

5. saxophone _____

6. pasteurize _____

7. dunce _____

8. guillotine _____

9. hamburger _____

10. mentor _____

H: List all the parts of speech that each word below can serve as. How many meanings does
each part of speech have? Do not count the meanings of idiomatic expressions using
these words.

EXAMPLE nest *noun, 6 meanings; intransitive verb, 3 meanings, transitive verb, 3 meanings*

1. orange _____

2. period _____

3. ice _____

4. go _____

5. turn _____

I. What usage label does your dictionary assign to each of these words? If no label is
given, write *no label*.

EXAMPLE prithee   *archaic*

1. into (meaning *involved in*) _____

2. hot (meaning *stolen*) _____

3. rare (meaning *scattered*) _____

4. lift (meaning *elevator*) _____

5. ere (meaning *before*) _____

Name_____ Date _____

Understanding Differences in Denotation and Connotation

A: Underline the most appropriate word from the pair given in parentheses. If you are un-sure, consult your dictionary's synonymy. (A synonymy is a paragraph comparing and contrasting words.)

EXAMPLE   The sky was (<u>clear</u>, transparent), with not a cloud in sight.

1. The sergeant (instructed, commanded) his men to clean the barracks.

2. The plane remained (complete, intact) after passing through the severe storm.

3. The dictator was (conquered, overthrown) by his brother.

4. Astronomy calls for great (accuracy, correctness).

5. After he fell into the cesspool, his suit was so (soiled, foul) it could not be cleaned.

6. The inheritance was (divided, doled out) among her sisters.

7. The crowd (dissipated, dispersed) once the ambulance took away the accident victim.

8. The tenants (withheld, kept) their rent in protest over the long-broken boiler.

9. Most fashion models are (lofty, tall).

10. The patient was (restored, renovated) to health by physical therapy.

11. Because of his (immoderate, exorbitant) behaviour, the young man was thrown out of the restaurant.

12. The committee voted to (eliminate, suspend) voting on the budget until the missing members could be located.

13. The coach talked to the team in the (capacity, function) of a friend.

14. The family (donated, bestowed) its time to help restore the fire-damaged day-care centre.

15. The practical joker (tittered, guffawed) as his victim slipped on a banana peel.

16. The professor (praised, eulogized) the class for its good work on the midterm examination.

17. Sometimes people offer (premiums, rewards) to help capture dangerous criminals.

18. The guest wondered if it would be (impolite, boorish) to ask for a third piece of pie.

19. The man (clandestinely, secretly) took his wife's birthday present into the attic.

20. The lifeguard's (skin, hide) was dry from overexposure to the sun.

B: The following words are synonymous, but not all are equally appropriate in every situation. Check the precise meaning of each word, and then use each in a sentence. Your dictionary may have a synonymy (a paragraph comparing and contrasting all the words) listed under one of the words, so check all the definitions before writing your sentences.

EXAMPLE   laughable   *The travel book was laughable because the author had never left the tour bus.*

amusing   *We spent an amusing afternoon riding in an old, horse-drawn carriage.*

droll   *The political commentator had a droll sense of humour.*

comical   *The clowns in the circus were truly comical.*

1. danger _____

   peril _____

   hazard _____

   risk _____

2. rich _____

   wealthy _____

   affluent _____

   opulent _____

3. speak _____

   talk _____

   converse _____

   discourse _____

4. think _____

   reason _____

   reflect _____

   speculate _____

   deliberate _____

5. irritable _____

   choleric _____

   touchy _____

   cranky _____

   cross _____

EXERCISES

Name_____ Date _____

Using Concrete, Specific Language

A: Reorder the words in each list so they move from most general to most specific.

EXAMPLE   cola   *beverage*

soft drink   *soft drink*

Coca-Cola   *cola*

beverage   *Coca-Cola*

1.   sandwich   _____
food   _____
cheese sandwich   _____
Swiss cheese on rye _____

2.   A&P   _____
store   _____
business   _____
supermarket   _____

3.   bill   _____
record club charges _____
letter   _____
mail   _____

4.   clothing   _____
jeans   _____
pants   _____
stone-washed jeans _____

5.   land   _____
tropical paradise _____
islands   _____
Hawaii   _____

6.   cookbook   _____
The Joy of Cooking _____
how-to book   _____
book   _____

7.   lion   _____
hunter   _____
cat   _____
animal   _____

8.   television show   _____
entertainment   _____
dramatic series   _____
North of 60   _____

9.   *The Blue Boy*   _____
painting   _____
art   _____
portrait   _____

10. sports   _____
100-metre dash   _____
running   _____
track   _____

B: The italicized word or phrase in each sentence below is too abstract or general. Replace it with a word (or words) that is more specific or concrete. Use the lines to the right.

Example   The *beast* escaped from the zoo.   *ferocious leopard*

1. He's very proud of his new *car*.   _____

2. They planted *bushes* along the edge of the walk.   _____

3. The milk tasted *funny*.   _____

4. "I want your attention right now!" Mackenzie *said*.   _____

5. My aunt lives in the *West*.   _____

6. *Somebody* asked me to deliver these roses to you.   _____

7. She wrote a book about *history*.   _____

8. A *bird* flew into the classroom.   _____

9. To be successful, an accountant must be *good*.   _____

10. The protesters denounced *injustice*.   _____.

11. The dancer *hurt* her ankle.   _____

12. He received *jewellery* as a birthday present.   _____

13. The engine made a *strange* sound.   _____

14. He thought Economics class was a *pain*.   _____

15. The nurse was very *nice* to the patients.   _____

16. After practice, we went to a *movie*.   _____

17. Lea's new computer has *lots of* memory.   _____

18. The building is a *mess*.   _____

19. I want to get a *good* job after graduation.   _____

20. The doctor gave *everyone* a booklet about how to quit smoking.   _____

Name_____ Date _____

Using Prefixes and Suffixes

A: Add a prefix to each of these roots to form a synonym of the word or phrase in parentheses.

EXAMPLE (away)   <u>ab</u>sent

1. (use incorrectly)   _____ apply

2. (without pausing)   _____ stop

3. (coming before)   _____ ceding

4. (make over)   _____ model

5. (move something from one place to another)   _____ fer

6. (immortal)   _____ dying

7. (a person's own signature)   _____ graph

8. (make something appear greater than it is)   _____ fy

9. (knowing only one language)   _____ lingual

10. (having many parts)   _____ ple

11. (in all places at the same time)   _____ present

12. (having more than one husband or wife)   _____ gamy

B: Add a suffix to each of these roots to form a synonym of the word or phrase in paren-
    theses. Indicate any necessary changes in spelling.

EXAMPLE (state of being a child) child*hood*

1. (state of being happy)   happy _____

2. (resembling a wolf)   wolf _____

3. (act of expanding)   expan _____

4. (act of being dedicated)   dedicat _____

5. (resembling heaven)   heaven _____

6. (one who climbs mountains)   mountain _____

7. (one who flies)   aviat _____

8. (to make hard)   hard _____

9. (state of having the skill of a leader)   leader _____

10. (state of being wise)   wis _____

11. (to make larger)   magn _____

12. (able to be afforded)   afford _____

EXERCISES

Name_____ Date _____

Using Context Clues

Using context clues, write the probable meaning of each italicized word. Then check the definitions in the dictionary. Finally, revise any of your definitions that are inaccurate.

EXAMPLE   According to folklore, coffee has been popular since the ninth century. Supposedly, an Ethiopian goatherd found his flock jumping around after eating coffee beans, and when he tried some he began *gambolling* along with them.

*jumping around*_____

1. Of all the natural *commodities* in the world trade, coffee ranks second in dollar value, coming after petroleum.

_____

2. Twenty-five million people in fifty exporting countries rely on coffee for their *sustenance*.

_____

3. This is *singular*, as coffee has almost no nutritional value.

_____

4. Except for Brazil, which consumes a third of its own crop, coffee-producing nations are *loath* to encourage coffee drinking at home.

_____

5. There are greater *fiscal* benefits in exporting coffee.

_____

6. Coffee prices rose *precipitously* in 1975 and 1979, when killing frosts destroyed many of Brazil's coffee trees.

_____

7. The custom of *imbibing* coffee instead of eating it probably began in Yemen about A.D. 1000.

_____

8. Coffee had an *invigorating* effect: helping people stay awake all night when they needed to.

_____

9. For *teetotal* Muslims, coffee provided a lift they were forbidden to get from alcohol.

_____

10. Coffee was considered so *requisite* that old Turkish law allowed a wife to sue for divorce if her husband did not keep the home supplied with coffee.

   _____

11. Some doctors say that excessive coffee *consumption* presents health risks.

   _____

12. For example, too much coffee may *exacerbate* ulcers or high blood pressure.

   _____

13. However, the studies often disagree, so the results are considered *inconclusive*.

   _____

14. Meanwhile, specialty coffees *proliferate*, providing just the right accompaniment for any meal.

   _____

15. For some, coffee drinking has become an *aesthetic* experience, part of the good life.

   _____

21 Understanding the Effect of Words

To use words well, you have to make careful choices. Your awareness of your purpose in writing, your audience, and the situation in which you are writing should influence your choice of words.

21a Using appropriate language

Good writers pay special attention to **diction** (word choice), making certain that the words they use communicate their meaning as clearly and convincingly as possible.

Informal levels and highly formal levels of writing use different vocabulary and sentence structures, and the two differ clearly in **tone.** Tone reflects the attitude of the writer toward the subject and audience. It may be highly formal, informal, or in between. Different tones are appropriate for different audiences, subjects, and purposes. An **informal** tone occurs in casual conversation or letters to friends. A highly **formal** tone, in contrast, occurs in public and ceremonial documents, such as proclamations and treaties. Informal language, which creates an informal tone, may use slang, colloquialisms, and regionalisms. In addition, informal writing may include sentence fragments, contractions, and other casual forms. Medium-level language uses general English—not too casual, not too scholarly. Unlike informal language, **medium-level** or **semiformal** language is acceptable for academic writing. This level uses standard vocabulary (for example, *learn* instead of the informal *wise up*), conventional sentence structure, and few or no contractions.

The language standards you are expected to use in academic writing are those of a book like this workbook. Such language is called **standard English,** because it follows established rules of grammar, sentence structure, punctuation, and spelling as they are applied in Canada. This language is also called **edited English.** Standard English is not a fancy dialect for the elite. It is a practical set of rules about language use that most educated people observe.

Slang consists of newly created words and new meanings attached to established words. Slang words and phrases usually pass out of use quickly: *hip, cool, fresh.* **Colloquial language** is characteristic of casual conversation and informal writing: *The pileup on Highway 23 halted traffic.* **Regional (dialectal) language** is specific to some geographic areas: *They had **nary** a dime to their names.* These usages are not appropriate for academic writing.

To communicate clearly, choose words that demonstrate your fairness as a writer. When you are talking about a subject on which you hold strong opinions, do not slip into biased or emotionally loaded language—also known as **slanted language.** Suppose you were arguing against a proposed increase in tuition. If you write that the president of the university is "a blood-sucking dictator out to destroy the lives of thousands of innocent young people," a neutral audience will doubt your ability to think rationally and write fairly about the subject.

21b Avoiding sexist language

Sexist language assigns roles or characteristics to people on the basis of sex. Such practices unfairly discriminate against both sexes. Sexist language inaccurately assumes that all nurses and homemakers are female (and therefore refers to them as "she") and that all physicians and wage earners are male (and therefore refers to them as "he"). One of the most widespread occurrences of sexist language is the use of the pronoun *he* to refer to someone of unidentified sex. Although traditionally *he* has been correct in such a general situation, using only masculine pronouns to represent the human species excludes females. You can avoid this problem by using the techniques suggested in the following chart.

HOW TO AVOID SEXIST LANGUAGE

1. Avoid using only the masculine pronoun to refer to males and females together:
   a. Use a pair of pronouns, but try to avoid strings of pairs in a sentence or in several consecutive sentences.
      NO A doctor cannot read much outside **his** specialty.
      YES A doctor cannot read much outside **his or her** specialty.
   b. Revise into the plural.
      NO A successful doctor knows that **he** has to work long hours.
      YES Successful doctors know that **they** have to work long hours.
   c. Recast the sentence to omit the gender-specific pronoun.
      NO Everyone hopes that **he will** win the scholarship.
      YES Everyone hopes **to win** the scholarship.
2. Avoid using *man* when men and women are clearly intended in the meaning.
      NO **Man** is a social animal.
      YES **People** are social animals.

HOW TO AVOID SEXIST LANGUAGE *(continued)*

---

3. Avoid stereotyping jobs and roles by gender when men and women are included.

    NO   chairman; policeman; businessman; statesman

    YES chair, chairperson; police officer; businessperson, business executive; diplomat, prime minister, etc.

    NO   teacher ... she; principal ... he

    YES teachers ... they; principals ... they

4. Avoid expressions that exclude one sex.

    NO   mankind; the common man; man-sized sandwich; old wives' tale

    YES humanity; the average person; huge sandwich; superstition

5. Avoid using degrading and insulting labels.

    NO   lady lawyer; gal Friday; career girl; coed

    YES lawyer; assistant; professional woman; student

21c Using figurative language

Figurative language uses one idea or image to explain another by creating comparisons and connections. The most common figures of speech are similes and metaphors.

A **simile** states a direct comparison between two otherwise dissimilar things. It sets up the comparison by using the words *like* or *as:* A disagreeable person might be said to be *as sour as unsweetened lemonade.*

A **metaphor** implies a comparison between otherwise dissimilar things without using *like* or *as: The new tax bled lower-income families of their last hope.*

Be careful not to create an inappropriate and silly image, such as in *The rush hour traffic bled out of all the city's major arteries.* Cars are not at all like blood and their movement is not similar to the flow of blood, so the metaphor ends up confusing rather than explaining. Also be careful not to create **mixed metaphors,** illogical combinations of images: *Milking the migrant workers, the supervisor bled them dry.* Here the initial image is of taking milk from a cow, but the final image is of blood, not milk.

Irony is a figure of speech that, along with sarcasm, should be avoided in academic writing. Irony uses words to suggest the opposite of their usual sense—often, as a means of belittling a person or an idea.

21d Avoiding clichés

A **cliché** is an overused, worn-out expression that has lost its ability to communicate effectively. Some comparisons that were once clever have grown old and worn out: *dead as a doornail, gentle as a lamb.* Do not take the easiest phrase, the words that come immediately to mind. If you have heard them over and over again, so has your reader. Rephrasing clichés will improve your writing.

21e Avoiding artificial language

Always try to make what you are saying as clear as possible to your readers. Extremely complex ideas or subjects may require complex terms or phrases to explain them, but in general the simpler the language, the more likely it is to be understood.

Pretentious language is too showy and sometimes silly, calling unsuitable attention to itself with complex sentences and long words: *I had a portion of an Italian comestible for the noontime repast* [Translation: I had a slice of pizza for lunch]. Plain English that communicates clearly is far better than fancy English that makes the reader aware that you are showing off.

Jargon is specialized vocabulary of a particular group—words that an outsider would not understand. Whether or not the word is considered jargon depends on purpose and audience. For example, when a sportswriter uses words such as *gridiron* and *sacked*, a football fan understands them with no difficulty. Specialized langauge evolves in every field: professions, academic disciplines, business, even hobbies. However, using jargon unnecessarily or failing to explain it is showy and artificial.

Euphemisms attempt to avoid harsh reality by using pleasant-sounding, "tactful" words. Although they are sometimes necessary to spare someone's feelings, euphemisms drain meaning from truthful writing. People use unnecessary euphemisms to describe socially unacceptable behaviour: *Barry bends the rules* instead of *Barry cheats*. They use euphemisms to hide unpleasant facts: *She really likes her liquor* instead of *She is a drunk*. Euphemisms like these fool no one. Except in the rare cases where delicate language is needed—to soften the pain of death, for example—keep your language free of euphemisms.

Doublespeak is artificial, misleading language. For example, people who strip and sell stolen cars might call themselves "auto dismantlers and recyclers" selling "predismantled previously owned parts." Such language is distorting and dishonest. To use doublespeak is to use words that hide the truth, a highly unethical practice that tries to control people's thoughts. For example, in 1984 the U.S. State Department announced it would no longer use the word *killing* in its official reports about human rights in other countries. *Killing* was replaced with *unlawful* or *arbitrary deprivation of life*. This practice forces readers into thinking inaccurately. Such misuses of language have terrible social and political effects.

Like doublespeak, **bureaucratic language** is confusing. Unlike doublespeak, it is not intended to mislead. Rather, it is carelessly written, stuffy, overblown language, as shown in the following memo:

> You can include a page that also contains an Include instruction. The page including the Include instruction is included when you paginate the document but the included text referred to in its Include instruction is not included.

Name_____ Date _____

Recognizing Levels of Formality

Different levels of formality are appropriate in different situations. Decide which level (informal, medium or semiformal, and formal) best fits each of these situations.

Level of Formality

EXAMPLE   a letter requesting the list of winners in a sweepstakes   _medium_

1.   a note to a friend asking him or her to take a package to the   _____
     post office for you
2.   a lab report or essay abstract   _____
3.   a petition to have a candidate's name added to the   _____
     election ballot
4.   an invitation to a local community activist to speak to your   _____
     daughter's grade six class
5.   the valedictorian's speech at a college graduation ceremony   _____

Now select three of these documents, each calling for a different level of formality, and write them. Use your own paper.

Avoiding Slang, Colloquial, and Overly Formal Language

Underline the word in each sentence that best suits academic style. You may need to check your dictionary for usage labels.

EXAMPLE   That academic advisor fails to motivate students because she is (stuck-up, <u>aloof</u>).

1.   My anthropology professor is a brilliant (guy, man).
2.   The food in the main dining hall is barely (edible, comestible).
3.   (Prithee, Please) turn off the lights when leaving classrooms.
4.   The Dean of Faculty will (address, parley with) the audience at graduation.
5.   (Regardless, Irregardless) of the weather, the honours and awards ceremony will be
     held on Thursday evening.
6.   All students must wear skirts or (britches, slacks) under their graduation robes.

7. The elevator is reserved for faculty and (educands, students) with passes.

8. Remind your guests to park their (cars, wheels) in the visitors' lot.

9. Anyone parking a (motorcycle, chopper) on campus should chain it to the rack in the parking field.

10. Relatives may stay overnight in the (dormitories, dorms) provided they have written in advance and (check in, touch base) with the house parents before 10 p.m.

Revising Sentences for Appropriate Language

EXERCISE 21-3
(21a)

Revise these sentences using language appropriate for academic writing.

EXAMPLE   It stinks that I can't go skydiving more often.

It's a shame that I cannot go skydiving more often.

1. Before I tried skydiving, I thought skydivers were nuts.

2. It seemed so out there.

3. But now that I've done it, I think it's a blast.

4. The day of the jump, I was totally stoked.

5. My friends were pretty weirded out on my account, though.

6. But then, they're such wusses.

7. I thought I was going to barf just before I jumped out of the plane.

8. But it was great—it blew me away.

9. It has to be way cooler than bungee-jumping, which is, like, blink and you've missed it.

10. Yeah, skydiving definitely rocks.

Name_____ Date _____

Revising Slanted Language

| EXERCISE **21-4** |
| (21a) |

Here is the opening paragraph of a very slanted letter to the editor. Revise it, using moderate language. Try to convince the reader that you are a reasonable person with a valid argument.

The Morning Telegram
Anytown, Canada

Dear Editor:

     I just read your ridiculous article on the proposed opening of a hazardous waste storage depot just outside town. Are you crazy? Anyone who would propose such a deadly project has no soul. Those city council members who are sponsoring this monstrous facility obviously have the brains of fruit flies. If they had bothered to do a little research, they would have discovered that dreadful things can happen to any poor community that lets such a depot be forced upon it.

Revising for Appropriate Figurative Language

| EXERCISE **21-5** |
| (21c, d) |

Revise these sentences by replacing clichéd, inappropriate, or mixed metaphors with fresh, appropriate figures of speech. You may want to reduce the number of figures of speech in a sentence, or you may sometimes feel a message is best presented without any figurative language.

EXAMPLE The police set up a dragnet, certain the killer could not drop through the cracks.

    The police set up a dragnet, certain that the killer could not escape. [A net cannot have cracks.]

1. My uncle has a grip like a vise.

_____

2. He held her in an embrace as inescapable as flypaper.

_____

3. The fingers of the waves danced on the shore.

_____

4. As soon as she entered her studio, the flames of creativity swept over her like an advancing iceberg.

_____

5. They talked us into going to an expensive restaurant, so we went, reluctantly, like lambs going to the slaughter.

_____

6. Having no backbone is his Achilles' heel.

_____

7. Like a vise, he caught her eye, turned her head, and swept her off her feet.

_____

8. I burned the midnight oil studying until 6 a.m.

_____

9. The train rushed at us like a scared rabbit.

_____

10. After I painted myself in the corner, I felt like a trapped rat.

_____

11. The situation came to a head, so an investigation was set afoot.

_____

12. The mailman licked the prowler and held him for police.

_____

13. He wore his heart on his sleeve and bared his soul to her.

_____

14. This painting is pretty as a picture.

_____

15. The meteorologist's explanation of what causes mist was foggy.

_____

Name_____ Date _____

Using Figurative Language

Using new, appropriate figures of speech, write a sentence describing each of the following.

EXAMPLE   a fast train

Disappearing like the vapour trail of a jet, the train sped into the distance.

1. a graceful horse

    _____

2. a run-down shack

    _____

3. a terrible dance band

    _____

4. greasy french fries

    _____

5. being awakened by your alarm clock

    _____

6. a professor who requires too much work

    _____

7. a salesperson with a phony smile

    _____

8. a hot day in the city

    _____

9. something that is very late

    _____

10. an unpleasant singing voice

    _____

Eliminating Artificial Language

A: "Translate" these sentences into standard academic English by eliminating inappropriate jargon and euphemisms. You may need to refer to your dictionary.

EXAMPLE We received four centimetres of precipitation last night.

We got four centimetres of rain (or snow) last night.

1. After falling, the child sustained a severe hematoma of the patella.

2. Operators of automotive vehicles should be sure to utilize their seat belts before engaging engines.

3. Although she was in a family way, she continued in the fulfilment of her familial and employment responsibilities.

4. The municipal public-thoroughfare contamination controllers are on unauthorized, open-ended leave.

5. The dean has asked department heads to interface with him.

B: Find a piece of published writing that you feel uses pretentious language, unnecessary jargon, unnecessary euphemisms, doublespeak, and/or bureaucratic language. Likely sources are newsletters, business memos and reports, political mailings, solicitations for charity, and sales brochures. Be prepared to say in what ways the language is artificial and what problems that language can create for readers. Then rewrite the piece using appropriate language. Submit the original and your revision to your instructor.

22 Spelling and Hyphenation

One reason English spelling can be difficult is that our words have come from many sources. We have borrowed words from Latin, Greek, French, Spanish, and many other languages. Because of these various origins, plus differences in the ways English-speaking people pronounce words, it is unwise to rely on pronunciation in spelling a word.

Canadian spelling is influenced by both British and American spelling conventions. A special challenge for Canadians is to be consistent in the spelling style they choose.

22a Eliminating careless spelling errors

Many spelling errors are not *spelling* errors at all. They are the result of illegible handwriting, slips of the pen, or typographical errors ("typos"). While you may not be able to change your handwriting completely, you can make it legible enough so that readers know what words you are writing. Careful proofreading is required to catch typos. When you reread your papers, you are likely to read what you meant to write rather than what is actually on the page because the brain tends to "read" what it expects to see. When proofreading for typos, then, try reading the page backwards, from the last sentence to the first. Using a ruler to help you focus on one line at a time is also effective.

If you are unsure how to spell a word but you do know how it starts, look it up in the dictionary. If you do not know how to spell the beginning of a word, think of a synonym, and look that word up in a thesaurus.

When you come across unfamiliar words in a textbook, highlight or underline them as you read. Then, after you have finished reading, go back and memorize the correct spelling.

As you discover words you frequently misspell, print each carefully on a card, highlighting the problem area by using larger print, a different-coloured ink, or a highlighter.

Mnemonic devices, techniques to improve memory, can also help you to remember the spelling of difficult words:

The princi**pal** is your **pal.** A princi**ple** is a ru**le.**

The w**ea**ther is cl**ea**r. **Wh**ether is **wh**at.

22b Spelling homonyms and commonly confused words

Many words sound similar to or exactly like others (*its/it's, morning/mourning*). Words that sound alike are called **homonyms.** To avoid using the wrong word, look up unfamiliar homonyms in the dictionary, and then use mnemonic devices to help you remember their meanings.

Some expressions may be written either as one or two, depending on meaning:

An every**day** occurrence is something that happens **every day.**

The guests were there **already** by the time I was **all ready.**

When we were **all together** there were five of us **altogether.**

We were there for **a while** when the host said dinner would be **awhile** longer.

Maybe the main course will be sushi, but it **may be** tofuburgers.

When we went **in to** dinner, he walked **into** the table.

Two expressions, however, are *always* written as two words: *all right* (not *alright*) and *a lot* (not *alot*).

HOMONYMS AND NEAR SOUNDALIKES

accept / except
advice / advise
affect / effect
aisle / isle
already / all ready
altar / alter
altogether / all together
angel / angle
are / hour / our
ascent / assent
assistance / assistants
bare / bear
board / bored
brake / break
breath / breathe
buy / by
capital / capitol
choose / chose
cite / sight / site
clothes / cloths
coarse / course
complement / compliment
conscience / conscious
council / counsel
dairy / diary
dessert / desert
device / devise
dominant / dominate
die / dye
dying / dyeing
fair / fare
formally / formerly
forth / fourth
gorilla / guerrilla
hear / here
heard / herd
hole / whole

human / humane
its / it's
know / no
later / latter
lead / led
lessen / lesson
lightening / lightening
loose / lose
maybe / may be
meat / meet
miner / minor
of / off
our / hour
passed / past
patience / patients
peace / piece
personal / personnel
plain / plane
principal / principle
quiet / quite / quit
rain / reign / rein
right / rite / write
road / rode
scene / seen
sense / since
stationary / stationery
than / then
there / they're / their
through / threw / thorough
to / too / two
weak / week
weather / whether
where / were / wear
which / witch
whose / who's
your / you're / yore

Using spelling rules for plurals, suffixes, and *ie, ei* words

---

SPELLING RULES FOR PLURALS, SUFFIXES, AND *IE, EI* WORDS

PLURALS

- **Adding *-s* or *-es:*** Most plurals are formed by adding *-s*, including words that end in "hard" *-ch* (sounding like *k*): *leg, legs; shoe, shoes; stomach, stomachs.* For words ending in *-s, -sh, -x, -z,* or "soft" *-ch* (as in *beach*), add *-es* to the singular: *beach, beaches; tax, taxes; lens, lenses.*

- **Words Ending in *-o:*** Add *-s* if the *-o* is preceded by a vowel (*radio, radios; cameo, cameos*). Add *-es* if the *o* is preceded by a consonant (*potato, potatoes*). A few words can be pluralized either way, but current practice favours the *-es* form: *cargo, volcano, tornado, zero.*

- **Words Ending in *-f* or *-fe:*** Some *-f* and *-fe* words are made plural by adding *-s: belief, beliefs.* Others require changing *-f* or *-fe* to *-ves: life, lives; leaf, leaves.* Words ending in *-ff* or *-ffe* simply add *-s: staff, staffs; giraffe, giraffes.*

- **Compound Words:** For most compound words, add *-s* or *-es* at the end of the last word: *chequebooks, player-coaches.* For a few, the word to make plural is not the last one: *sister-in-law, sisters-in-law; kilometre per hour, kilometres per hour.* (For hyphenating compound words, see 22d.)

- **Internal Changes and Endings Other Than *-s:*** A few words change internally or add endings other than *-s* to become plural: *foot, feet; man, men; mouse, mice; child, children.*

- **Foreign Words:** Plurals other than *-s* or *-es* are listed in good dictionaries. In general, for many Latin words ending in *-um*, form plurals by changing *-um* to *-a: curriculum, curricula; datum, data; medium, media; stratum, strata.* For Latin words that end in *-us*, the plural is often *-i: alumnus, alumni; syllabus, syllabi* (also, *syllabuses*). For Greek *-on* words, the plural is often *-a: criterion, criteria; phenomenon, phenomena.*

- **One-Form Words:** A few spellings are the same for the singular and plural: *deer, elk, quail.* The differences are conveyed by adding words, not endings: *one deer, nine deer; rice, bowls of rice.*

SUFFIXES

- **-*y* Words:** If the letter before the final *y* is a consonant, change the *y* to *i* unless the suffix begins with an *i* (for example, *-ing*): *fry, fried, frying.* If the letter before the *-y* is a vowel, keep the final *y: employ, employed, employing.* These rules do not apply to irregular verbs (see 8d).

- **-*e* Words:** Drop a final *e* when the suffix begins with a vowel unless doing so would cause confusion (for example, *be + ing* does not become *bing*): *require, requiring; like, liking.* Keep the final *e* when the suffix begins with a consonant: *require, requirement; like, likely.* Exceptions include *argument* and *truly.*

SPELLING RULES FOR PLURALS, SUFFIXES, AND *IE, EI* WORDS *(continued)*

- **Words That Double a Final Letter:** If the final letter is a consonant, double it only if it passes these tests: (1) Its last two letters are a vowel followed by a consonant; and (2) the suffix begins with a vowel: *drop, dropped; forget, forgetful, forgettable.* (American spelling adds a third test. The word must have one syllable or be accented on the last syllable: *begin* [accent on last syllable], *beginning* **but** *travel* [accent on first syllable], *traveling.* British spelling doubles the final consonant in many words even when the accent is not on the last syllable: *travel, travelling; worship, worshipper.*)

- ***-cede, -ceed, -sede* Words:** Only one word ends in *-sede: supersede.* Three words end in *-ceed: exceed, proceed, succeed.* All other words whose endings sound like "seed" end in *-cede: concede, intercede, precede.*

- ***-ally* and *-ly* Words:** The suffixes *-ally* and *-ly* turn words into adverbs. For words ending in *-ic,* add *-ally: logically, statistically.* Otherwise, add *-ly: quickly, sharply.* (An important exception is *public, publicly.*)

- ***-ance, -ence,* and *-ible, -able:*** No consistent rules govern words with these suffixes. The best advice is "When in doubt, look it up."

THE *IE, EI* RULE: The old rhyme for *ie* and *ei* is usually true:

> "*I* before *e* [bel*ie*ve, f*ie*ld, gr*ie*f]
>
> Except after *c* [c*ei*ling, conc*ei*t],
>
> Or when sounded like *ay* [*ei*ght, v*ei*n],
>
> As in n*ei*ghbour and w*ei*gh."

You may want to memorize these major exceptions:

ie	conscience	financier	science	species
ei	either	neither	leisure	seize
	counterfeit	foreign	forfeit	sleight
	weird			

22d Using hyphens correctly

1 Hyphenating at the end of a line

Try not to divide words at the end of a line, but when you must do so, follow these guidelines.

GUIDELINES FOR END-OF-LINE HYPHENATION

- **Do not divide very short words, one-syllable words, or words pronounced as one syllable.**

No	we-alth	en-vy	scream-ed
Yes	wealth	envy	screamed

- **Do not leave or carry over only one or two letters.**

No	a-live	tax-i	he-licopter	helicopt-er
Yes	alive	taxi	heli-copter	helicop-ter

- **Divide words only between syllables.**

No	proc-ede
Yes	pro-cede

- **Always follow rules for double consonants.**

No	ful-lness	omitt-ing	asp-halt
Yes	full-ness	omit-ting	as-phalt

- **Divide hyphenated words after the hyphen, if possible, rather than at any other syllable.**

No	self-con-scious	good-look-ing report
Yes	self-conscious	good-looking report

| **2** | **Hyphenating prefixes, suffixes, compound words, and numbers** |

Prefixes and **suffixes** are syllables attached to root words. **Compound words** use two or more words together to express one concept. Some prefixes and suffixes are hyphenated; others are not. Compound words can be written as separate words (*night shift*), hyphenated words (*tractor-trailer*), or one word (*handbook*).

HYPHENATING PREFIXES, SUFFIXES, COMPOUND WORDS, AND NUMBERS

- **Use hyphens after the prefixes *all-, ex-, quasi-,* and *self-*.**

  all-inclusive   self-reliant

HYPHENATING PREFIXES, SUFFIXES, COMPOUND WORDS, AND NUMBERS
(continued)

- **Do not use a hyphen when *self* is a root word, not a prefix.**

No	self-ishness	self-less
Yes	selfishness	selfless

- **Use a hyphen to avoid a distracting string of letters.**

No	antiintellectual	belllike
Yes	anti-intellectual	bell-like

- **Use a hyphen before the suffix *-elect*.**

No	presidentelect
Yes	president-elect

- **Use a hyphen to add a prefix or suffix to a number or a word that starts with a capital letter.**

No	post1950s	proAmerican	Rembrandtlike
Yes	post-1950s	pro-American	Rembrandt-like

- **Use a hyphen to prevent confusion in meaning or pronunciation.**

Yes	re-dress ("dress again")	redress ("set right")
	un-ionize ("remove the ions")	unionize ("form a union")

- **Use a hyphen when two or more prefixes apply to one root word.**

Yes	pre- and post-war eras	two-, three-, or four-year program

COMPOUND WORDS

- **Use a hyphen between a prefix and a compound word.**

No	antigun control
Yes	anti-gun control

- **Use a hyphen for most compound modifiers that precede the noun. Do not use a hyphen for most compound modifiers after the noun.**

Yes	well-researched report	two-centimetre clearance
	report is well researched	clearance of two centimetres

- **You do not need to use a hyphen when a compound modifier starts with an *-ly* adverb.**

Yes	happily married couple	loosely tied package

→

HYPHENATING PREFIXES, SUFFIXES, COMPOUND WORDS, AND NUMBERS
(continued)

- **Do not use a hyphen when a compound modifier is in the comparative or superlative form.**

    No   better-fitting shoe   least-welcome guest
                                           most-significant factor

    Yes better fitting shoe   least welcome guest
                                           most significant factor

- **Do not use a hyphen when a compound modifier is a foreign phrase.**

    Yes *post hoc* fallacies

- **Do not use a hyphen with a possessive compound modifier.**

    No   a full-week's work   eight-hours' pay

    Yes a full week's work   eight hours' pay

SPELLED-OUT NUMBERS

- **Use a hyphen between two-word numbers from twenty-one through ninety-nine.**

    Yes thirty-five (35)   two hundred thirty-five (235)

- **Use a hyphen in a compound-word modifier formed from a number and a word.**

    Yes fifty-minute class   three-to-one odds
             [also 50-minute class]   [also 3-to-1 odds]

- **Use a hyphen between the numerator and the denominator of two-word fractions.**

    Yes one-half   two-fifths   seven-tenths

Name_____ Date _____

Recognizing Homonyms and Commonly Confused Words

Underline the word within parentheses that best fits each sentence.

Example   When (your, <u>you're</u>) in Edmonton, be sure to visit the West Edmonton Mall.

1. The winners of the Stanley Cup (road, rode) down Ste. Catherine Street in a parade.

2. After reading murder mysteries all summer, she decided to (right, write) one herself.

3. While I was cleaning, I found some (loose, lose) change under the sofa cushions.

4. Thunder and (lightning, lightening) kept the campers awake all night.

5. The young woman put a lock on her (dairy, diary) when she realized her roommate had been reading it.

6. A square has four right (angels, angles).

7. The runners stood (altogether, all together) near the starting line, waiting for the signal to take (their, there) places.

8. The trip was great, (accept, except) for the day the car broke down in the (dessert, desert).

9. The broken-hearted man wrote the (advice, advise) columnist.

10. Going to college can (altar, alter) a person's view about many things.

11. The play was an (hour, our) long.

12. The neighbourhood (counsel, council) agreed to patrol the park at night.

13. Professional bakers have special (devices, devises) that help them make (peaces, pieces) of pastry easily.

14. The amount of oxygen in the air (lessens, lessons) as climbers reach higher levels.

15. Scott Kamiel (maybe, may be) the best pitcher we have ever had.

16. Prince Charles will (reign, rein) as the next King of England.

17. Do you know (whose, who's) car is blocking the driveway.

18. The last (scene, seen) of the movie was filmed from a helicopter.

19. He hid the last chocolate bar (where, were) his brothers could not find it.

20. Everything costs more now (than, then) it used (to, too).

21. Some days the smog is Los Angeles is so thick that the people can scarcely (breath, breathe), and the paramedics have more (patients, patience) than they can handle.

22. Sundaes are popular (deserts, desserts), even though we all (no, know) they are fattening.

23. Signs in the library request (quiet, quite).

24. By the time the tourists' hot air balloon landed it was (all ready, already) too late for them to return to the hotel in time for dinner.

25. (Gorillas, Guerrillas) blew up roads in an attempt to stop the shipment of weapons to the (capital, capitol).

Writing Sentences with Homonyms and Commonly Confused Words

Use each word below in a sentence that clearly demonstrates its meaning.

EXAMPLE its   *Every plan has its disadvantages*

            it's   *It's too late to go out for pizza*

1. already _____

  all ready _____

2. its _____

  it's _____

3. than _____

  then _____

4. they're _____

  their _____

  there _____

5. to _____

  two _____

  too _____

6. your _____

  you're _____

7. passed _____

  past _____

8. quiet _____

  quite _____

EXERCISES

9. through _____

   threw _____

   thorough _____

10. whose _____

    who's _____

Writing Plural Nouns

Write the plural forms of these nouns.

EXAMPLE lamp   *lamps*

         attorney at law   *attorneys at law*

1. orange	_____	11. mother-in-law	_____
2. kiss	_____	12. datum	_____
3. stray	_____	13. ice skate	_____
4. life	_____	14. herself	_____
5. radio	_____	15. echo	_____
6. pair	_____	16. half	_____
7. speech	_____	17. child	_____
8. fly	_____	18. woman	_____
9. monkey	_____	19. phenomenon	_____
10. piano	_____	20. mouse	_____

Adding Prefixes

Combine these prefixes and roots.

EXAMPLE re + start   _____*restart*_____

1. un + able   _____

2. mis + spell   _____

3. anti + freeze   _____

4. pre + determine   _____

5. extra + ordinary   _____

6. super + human   _____

7. trans + form   _____

8. sub + marine   _____

9. re + appear   _____

10. uni + cycle   _____

What rules govern the combining of prefixes and roots?

_____

_____

_____

22-5

EXERCISE **22-5**
(22c)

Name_____ Date _____

Adding Suffixes

A: Combine these suffixes and roots. If in doubt about the spelling, look up the word in your dictionary.

EXAMPLE awake + ing _____*awaking*_____

1. motivate + ion _____
2. guide + ance _____
3. notice + able _____
4. grace + ful _____
5. true + ly _____
6. accurate + ly _____
7. mile + age _____
8. argue + ment _____
9. drive + ing _____
10. outrage + ous _____

What basic rules govern the combining of roots ending in *e* and suffixes?

_____

_____

B: Combine these suffixes and roots. If in doubt about the spelling, look up the word in your dictionary.

EXAMPLE carry + ing _____*carrying*_____

1. duty + ful _____
2. play + ing _____
3. dry + er _____
4. supply + ed _____
5. noisy + est _____
6. stray + ed _____
7. sloppy + er _____
8. gravy + s _____
9. happy + ness _____
10. buy + ing _____

What basic rules govern the combining of roots ending in *y* and suffixes?

_____

_____

C: Combine these suffixes and roots. If in doubt about the spelling, look up the word in your dictionary.

EXAMPLE trap + ed   _____trapped_____

1. grip + ing   _____
2. mend + able   _____
3. steam + ed   _____
4. begin + er   _____
5. plant + ing   _____
6. stop + er   _____
7. pour + ed   _____
8. split + ing   _____
9. occur + ence   _____
10. refer + ence   _____

What basic rules govern the doubling of final consonants when a suffix is added?

_____

_____

EXERCISE 22-6
(22c)

Distinguishing Between ei *and* ie

Fill in the blanks with *ei* or *ie*. Because there are frequent exceptions to the rule, check your dictionary whenever you are in doubt.

EXAMPLE anc___*ie*___ nt

1. bel_____ve   6. f_____ld
2. rec_____ve   7. counterf_____t
3. n_____ther   8. w_____rd
4. c_____ling   9. fr_____ght
5. for_____gn   10. n_____ce

EXERCISES

Name_____ Date _____

Correcting Common Spelling Errors

Underline the misspelled word in each sentence, and spell it correctly on the line to the right. If a sentence has no misspellings, write *correct* on the line.

EXAMPLE Some exceptions to spelling rules are <u>wierdly</u> irregular.   *weirdly*

1. The letter carrier retired after being biten by the same dog for the seventh time.   _____

2. The counterfeiter pleaded innocent, saying he had been frammed.   _____

3. In the committee's judgment, the fair succeeded because of extremely efficient management.   _____

4. The scientists received news from a reliable source about an important foriegn discovery.   _____

5. We had hoped to buy a new dinning room set with our winnings from the quiz show we competed on last month.   _____

6. It seems incredable that, after trailing in the polls for weeks, our candidate managed finally to win the election.   _____

7. Running, swimming, and jumpping rope are all ways to increase the heart's endurance.   _____

8. Many foreign-born workers have little liesure time because they often hold two or even three jobs, all paying illegally low salaries.   _____

9. Because we did not think the payments were affordable, we reluctently postponed repairing the leaky ceiling.   _____

10. The disatisfied customers tried to return the chipped benches to the manufacturer, but the factory was permanently closed.   _____

11. The young man received a commendation from the community for his incredibly couragous performance in rescuing disabled children from an overturned bus.   _____

12. When he was layed off from work, he filed a grievance with his union representative and then proceeded to the unemployment office.   _____

13. After carefully painting the attic stairs, my brother-in-law realized he had closed off his route of escape, and he was traped upstairs until the paint dried.   _____

14. When I was younger, I use to want to take drum lessons
    until I realized how tiring practising the drums could be.   _____

15. The professor stated that she would return illegable papers   _____
    without commenting on them, and she encouraged students
    to type all work carefully.

16. Although the street was usually gloomy, every New Year's Eve   _____
    it magicly transformed itself into a joyful scene for a few hours.

17. According to some philosophies, the world is constantly changing   _____
    and it is pointless to expect anything to be permanant.

18. The neighbourhood children voted to coordinate a carwash and   _____
    use the procedes to buy durable playground equipment.

19. The chef advertised in the classified section of the newspaper   _____
    for a relieable dessert-maker.

20. The school aide was payed a bonus for her invaluable   _____
    assistance during the ice storm.

21. In some cultures, it is beleived that the ghosts of ancestors   _____
    take up residence in the family home.

22. One of the most appealing aspects of watching team sports   _____
    is seeing the interraction among the players on the field.

23. The most boring part of working in a department store is   _____
    taking part in periodic inventorys of the available merchandise.

24. Each autumn, people tragically injure themselves in avoidable   _____
    falls on rain-soaked leafs.

25. *Star Wars* was a very well-received and profitible movie,   _____
    and it set the pattern for many imitations.

Name_____ Date _____

Dividing Words at the Ends of Lines

Using your dictionary, rewrite each word on the line to its right. Use a slash to indicate the best place to divide the word at the end of a line. Some words may be broken in more than one place. Pick the best place, and use dots to indicate all other syllable breaks. If the word cannot be divided, write it out as one unit.

EXAMPLES signalled   *sig/nalled*

brake   *brake*

sledgehammer *sledge/ham.mer*

1. sleepless   _____
2. slenderize   _____
3. referee   _____
4. phlegm   _____
5. palate   _____
6. muscle-bound   _____
7. indecent   _____
8. Hollywood   _____
9. expiration   _____
10. echo   _____
11. cuckoo   _____
12. cough   _____
13. butte   _____
14. avocado   _____
15. avoirdupois   _____
16. loose   _____
17. cattail   _____
18. enrol   _____
19. grouch   _____
20. progressing   _____

21. sleeve   _____
22. sapsucker   _____
23. Polynesia   _____
24. palace   _____
25. nonresident   _____
26. increase   _____
27. however   _____
28. gesticulate   _____
29. emerge   _____
30. cubic   _____
31. colourless   _____
32. caretaker   _____
33. buttermilk   _____
34. await   _____
35. antacid   _____
36. mother-in-law   _____
37. trousseau   _____
38. midget   _____
39. controlling   _____
40. farther   _____

Writing Compound Nouns and Adjectives

Using your dictionary, rewrite each of these compound words as a single word, as a hyphenated word, or as two separate words. If more than one form is correct, be prepared to explain.

EXAMPLE foot ball   *football*

1. open heart surgery _____
2. free for all   _____
3. high school   _____
4. pear shaped   _____
5. bird house   _____
6. accident prone   _____
7. pot hole   _____
8. bathing suit   _____
9. bread winner   _____
10. hand made   _____

11. head ache   _____
12. head cold   _____
13. head phone   _____
14. head to head   _____
15. head stone   _____
16. free agent   _____
17. free hand   _____
18. free form   _____
19. free spoken   _____
20. free style   _____

Using Hyphens in Numbers

Formal usage in the humanities requires that numbers, including common fractions, be written in words. Write out each of these numbers, using hyphens as needed.

EXAMPLE 2102   *twenty-one hundred and two*

1. 35 _____
2. 1/2 _____
3. 4/5 _____
4. 101 _____
5. 1st _____
6. 3457 _____
7. 495 _____

23 Periods, Question Marks, and Exclamation Points

PERIODS

23a Using a period at the end of a statement, a mild command, or an indirect question

Most sentences end with a period.

STATEMENT   Those who cannot remember the past are condemned to repeat it.

—GEORGE SANTAYANA

MILD COMMAND   Be ready at 6:00.

INDIRECT QUESTION I wondered how to select a deserving charity. [Compare with direct question (23c).]

23b Using periods with most abbreviations

Most abbreviations call for periods, but some do not. Typical abbreviations with periods that are acceptable in academic writing include *Dr.*, *Mr.*, *Mrs.*, *Ms.*, *Ph.D.*, *M.D.*, *R.N.*, and *a.m.* and *p.m.* with exact times such as *2:15 p.m.* Abbreviations not requiring periods include postal abbreviations for provinces and states, such as *SK* and *NY*; names of some organizations and government agencies, such as *CBC* and *NFB*; and acronyms (initials pronounced as words), such as *NASA* and *NAFTA*.

❖ PUNCTUATION ALERT: (1) Abbreviations of academic degrees should usually be set off with commas. When they follow city names, abbreviations of provinces and states are set off by commas. (2) When the period of an abbreviation falls at the end of a sentence, the period also serves to end the sentence. Put a sentence-ending question mark or exclamation point, however, after the period of an abbreviation. ❖

QUESTION MARKS

23c Using a question mark after a direct question

In contrast to an **indirect question**, which *reports* a question and ends with a period, a direct question *asks* a question and ends with a question mark.

What is the capital of Alberta?

How do I select a deserving charity? [Compare with indirect question (23a).]

✤ PUNCTUATION ALERT: Do not combine a question mark with a comma, a period, or an exclamation point. ✤

NO	She asked, "How are you?."
YES	She asked, "How are you?"

23d Using a question mark in parentheses

When a date or number is unknown or doubtful, you can use *(?)*.

Mary Astell, an English author who wrote pamphlets on women's rights, was born in 1666 (?) and died in 1731.

The word *about* is often a graceful substitute for *(?): Mary Astell was born about 1666.*

Do not use *(?)* to communicate that you are unsure of information or to express irony or sarcasm.

EXCLAMATION POINTS

23e Using an exclamation point for a strong command or an emphatic declaration

A strong command gives a very firm order, and an emphatic declaration makes a shocking or surprising statement.

Wait!	Sit down!	He lost the rent money!

✤ PUNCTUATION ALERT: Do not combine an exclamation point with a comma, a period, or a question mark. ✤

NO	"Halt!," shouted the guard.
YES	"Halt!" shouted the guard.

23f Avoiding the overuse of exclamation points

In academic writing your choice of words, not exclamation points, is expected to communicate the strength of your message. Overusing exclamation points can make your writing appear hysterical.

NO   Any head injury is potentially dangerous! Go to the doctor immediately in case of bleeding from the ears, eyes, or mouth! Go if the patient has been unconscious!

YES   Any head injury is potentially dangerous. Go the doctor immediately in case of bleeding from the ears, eyes, or mouth, or if the patient has been unconscious.

Supplying Appropriate End Punctuation

A: Circle all inappropriate end punctuation: periods, exclamation marks, and question marks. Then on the line to the right, copy the final word of the sentence and add the appropriate end punctuation. If the end punctuation is correct as is, write *correct* on the line.

EXAMPLE Many people wonder why nurses wear white?　　　　　　*white.*

1. Have you ever wondered why doctors wear blue or green while operating.　　　　　　_____

2. White is the traditional symbol of purity!　　　　　　_____

3. It is also easier to keep clean because it shows dirt.　　　　　　_____

4. Surgeons wore white during operations until 1914?　　　　　　_____

5. Then one surgeon decided that the sight of red blood against the white cloth was disgusting!　　　　　　_____

6. He preferred—would you believe?—a spinach green that he felt reduced the brightness of the blood?　　　　　　_____

7. After World War II, surgeons began using a different shade of green!　　　　　　_____

8. Called minty green, it looked better under the new lighting used in operating rooms.　　　　　　_____

9. The latest colour is a blue-grey!　　　　　　_____

10. Why did the doctors change again.　　　　　　_____

11. Do you believe they did it because this blue shows up better on television than green does.　　　　　　_____

12. Believe it or not.　　　　　　_____

13. The surgeons appear on in-hospital television demonstrating new techniques to medical students!　　　　　　_____

B: Add end punctuation to this paragraph as needed.

Do you know who Theodor Seuss Geisel was Sure you do He was Dr Seuss, the famous author of children's books After ten years as a successful advertising illustrator and cartoonist, Seuss managed to get his first children's book published *And to Think That I Saw It on Mulberry Street* was published in 1937 by Vanguard Press It had been rejected by 27 other publishers I wonder why They certainly were foolish What's your favourite Dr Seuss book Mine is *The Cat in the Hat*, published in 1957 Everyone has a favourite And I do mean *Everyone* His books have been translated into 17 languages, and by 1984 over a hundred million copies had been sold worldwide In fact, in 1984 Seuss received a Pulitzer Prize for his years of educating and entertaining children How fitting Sadly Dr. Seuss died in 1991 We will all miss him

Name_____ Date _____

Writing Sentences with Appropriate End Punctuation

Write a sentence to illustrate each of these uses of end punctuation.

EXAMPLE   an emphatic command

_Wipe that grin off your face!_____

1. an indirect question

_____

2. a mild command

_____

3. a direct question

_____

4. an abbreviation

_____

5. a declarative sentence containing a direct quotation

_____

6. an exclamation

_____

7. a declarative statement

_____

8. an emphatic command

_____

9. a declarative sentence containing a quoted direct question

_____

10. a declarative sentence containing an indirect quotation

_____

11. a declarative sentence containing a quoted exclamation

_____

24 Commas

24a Using a comma before a coordinating conjunction that links independent clauses

The coordinating conjunctions—*and, but, for, or, nor, yet,* and *so*—can link two or more independent clauses to create compound sentences. Use a comma before the coordinating conjunction.

❖ COMMA CAUTION: Do not put a comma *after* a coordinating conjunction that links independent clauses ❖

	and	
	but	
	for	
Independent clause,	**or**	independent clause.
	nor	
	yet	
	so	

Tea contains caffeine, **but** herbal tea does not.

Caffeine makes some people jumpy, **and** it may even keep them from sleeping.

Caffeine is found in colas, **so** heavy cola drinkers may also have trouble sleeping.

❖ COMMA CAUTION: Do not use a comma when a coordinating conjunction links words, phrases, or dependent clauses. ❖

NO	More restaurants now carry decaffeinated coffee, and fruit juice.
YES	More restaurants now carry decaffeinated coffee and fruit juice.

❖ COMMA CAUTION: To avoid creating a comma splice, do not use a comma to separate independent clauses unless they are linked by a coordinating conjunction. ❖

NO	Caffeine occurs naturally in many foods, it is even found in chocolate. [These independent clauses have no linking word. The comma cannot substitute for a linking word.]
YES	Caffeine occurs naturally in many foods, and it is even found in chocolate. [A coordinating conjunction and comma link the two independent clauses.]

When independent clauses containing other commas are linked by a coordinating conjunction, use a semicolon before the coordinating conjunction.

Some herbal teas, such as orange flavoured, have become very popular; yet some people, afraid to try anything new, refuse to taste them.

24b Using a comma after an introductory clause, phrase, or word

When a clause, phrase, or word introduces an independent clause, use a comma to signal the end of the introductory element and the beginning of the independent clause.

Introductory clause,

Introductory phrase,　　　independent clause.

Introductory word,

An **adverb clause,** one type of dependent clause, cannot stand alone as an independent unit. Although it contains a subject and verb, it begins with a subordinating conjunction (7h, 7o–2). Use a comma to set off an adverb clause that introduces an independent clause.

Whenever it rains, the lake floods local streets.

Because provincial funding is hard to get, the community will have to get private help.

When an adverb clause comes after the independent clause, do not use a comma.

The lake floods local streets whenever it rains.

The community will have to get private help because provincial funding is hard to get.

A **phrase** (7n) is a group of words that cannot stand alone as an independent unit because it lacks a subject, a verb, or both. Use a comma to set off a phrase that introduces an independent clause.

Inside even the cleanest homes, insects thrive. [prepositional phrase]

Carefully using insecticides, we can safely drive the insects out of our homes again.

Introductory transitional words (see 4d) indicate relationships between ideas in sentences and paragraphs. Use a comma to set off a transitional word or phrase that introduces an independent clause (some writers prefer to omit the comma after single-word transitions).

First, an exterminator must clear the area of open containers of food, pets, and fragile plants.

In addition, he must be careful not to transport insects to new areas when he moves these items.

24c Using commas to separate items in a series

A **series** is a group of three or more elements—words, phrases, or clauses—that match in grammatical form and have the same importance within a sentence. Use commas between items in a series and before *and* when it is used between the last items.

---

word, word, and **word**

word, word, word

phrase, phrase, and **phrase**

phrase, phrase, phrase

clause, clause, and **clause**

clause, clause, clause

Citrus fruits include **oranges, tangerines,** and **grapefruits.**

There are many varieties of oranges: **the sweet orange, the Jaffa orange, the navel orange, the mandarin.**

Lemons are good for **flavouring cakes, decorating platters,** and **removing stains.**

When the items in a series contain commas or other punctuation, or when the items are long and complex, separate them with semicolons instead of commas.

Oranges are probably native to tropical Asia, but they spread quickly centuries ago because of the Roman conquest of Asia, Europe, and North Africa; the Arab trade routes; the expansion of Islam throughout the Mediterranean, except for France and Italy; and the Crusades.

24d Using a comma to separate coordinate adjectives

Coordinate adjectives are two or more adjectives that equally modify a noun or noun group. Separate coordinate adjectives with commas or coordinating conjunctions.

---

coordinate adjective, coordinate adjective noun

The sweet orange has **broad, glossy** leaves.

Adjectives are coordinate if *and* can be inserted between them or if their order can be reversed without damaging the meaning of the sentence. Meaning does not change when the example sentence says *broad and glossy leaves or glossy, broad leaves.*

✤ COMMA CAUTIONS: (1) Don't put a comma after a final coordinate adjective and the noun it modifies—note that no comma comes between *glossy* and *leaves* in the above example. (2) Don't put a comma between adjectives that are not coordinate: *Six large oranges cost two dollars.* ✤

24e Using commas to set off nonrestrictive (nonessential) elements, but not restrictive (essential) elements

Restrictive and nonrestrictive elements are kinds of modifiers. A **nonrestrictive modifier** is also called a **nonessential modifier** because the information it provides about the modified term is "extra." If a nonrestrictive modifier is dropped, a reader can still understand the full meaning of the modified word. Nonrestrictive modifiers are set off with commas.

Nonrestrictive element, independent clause.

Beginning of independent clause, **nonrestrictive element,** end of independent clause.

Independent clause, **nonrestrictive element.**

Believe it or not, the first daily newspaper was a Roman invention. The *Acta Diurna,* **whose title means "daily events,"** was available every day. Scribes made multiple choices of each day's political and social news, **which included senate action and the results of gladiatorial games.**

When the nonrestrictive information in these examples is eliminated, the meaning of the modified terms does not change.

The first daily newspaper was a Roman invention.

The *Acta Diurna* was available every day.

Scribes made multiple copies of each day's political and social news.

In contrast, a **restrictive modifier** (also known as an **essential modifier**) cannot be omitted without creating confusion. No commas are used because the information in these passages is part of the basic message of the sentence.

✤ COMMA CAUTION: A restrictive modifier is essential. Do not use commas to set it off from the rest of the sentence. ✤

Whoever invented paper is unknown.

The Chinese printed **what are considered the first books.**

They invented a white paper **that was made of wood** and a way to transfer a carved image from stone to paper.

Compare the pairs of restrictive and nonrestrictive modifiers that follow.

NONRESTRICTIVE ELEMENT The world's oldest surviving book printed from wood blocks was published in A.D. 868 by Wang Chieh, **who followed an already long Chinese printing tradition**. [*Who followed an already long Chinese printing tradition* is a dependent clause that adds information about Wang Chieh, but it is not essential to the sentence.]

RESTRICTIVE ELEMENT Students **who wish to imitate the woodblock method** do not need many materials. [The clause clarifies which students, so it is essential.]

NONRESTRICTIVE ELEMENT **Before carving,** the student should sketch out a preliminary version of the page. [*Before carving* is a prepositional phrase that explains when to act. However, the sentence is clear without it.]

RESTRICTIVE ELEMENT Marco Polo introduced woodblock printing **to Europe.** [Prepositional phrase is essential to the message.]

An **appositive** (7m–3) is a word or group of words that renames the noun or noun group preceding it. Most appositives are nonrestrictive. Once the name of something is given, words renaming it are not usually necessary to specify or limit it even more.

Johann Gutenberg, **a German printer living in Strasbourg,** was the first European to use movable type.

Some appositives, however, are restrictive and are not set off with commas.

Mr. Jones **the rare book collector** would pay a fortune to own a Gutenberg Bible. [The appositive is essential for distinguishing this Mr. Jones from other Mr. Joneses.]

Using commas to set off transitional and parenthetical expressions, contrasts, words of direct address, and tag sentences

Words, phrases, or clauses that interrupt a sentence but—like nonrestrictive elements—do not change its basic meaning should be set off, usually with commas. (Parentheses or dashes also set material off.)

Transitional words (such as *however, for example, in addition, therefore*) sometimes express connections within sentences. When they do, they are set off with commas.

The oldest surviving document of a news event, **in fact,** is a report of a storm and earthquake in Guatemala in 1541. [Transitional expression indicating that the truth is not what one might have expected.]

❖ COMMA CAUTION: When a transitional expression links independent clauses, use a semicolon or a coordinating conjunction. A comma alone will create a comma splice: *Few old documents survive, **in fact,** the oldest surviving news report is from 1541.* ❖

Parenthetical expressions are "asides," additions to sentences that the writer thinks of as extra.

The Spanish brought the first printing press in the New World to Mexico City in 1534, but, **surprisingly,** the earliest surviving pieces of work are from 1539. [parenthetical expression]

Expressions of contrast are set off with commas.

An early printing press at Lima turned out Indian- and Spanish-language religious material, **not political or news pamphlets.** [words of contrast]

The roots of the extensive modern Spanish-language press go back to these two printing centres, **rather than to Spain itself.** [words of contrast]

Words of direct address and tag sentences should be set off with commas.

Did you know, **Rosa,** that your Spanish newspaper is part of a 400-year-old tradition? [direct address]

You are bilingual, **aren't you?** [tag sentence]

You are continuing your language study, **I hope.** [tag sentence]

24g Using commas to set off quoted words from explanatory words

Use a comma to set off quoted words from short explanations in the same sentence, such as *she said, they replied,* and *he answered.*

According to a Chinese proverb, "A book is like a garden carried in the pocket."

"When I stepped from hard manual work to writing," said Sean O'Casey, "I just stepped from one kind of hard work to another."

"I can't write five words, but that I change seven," complained Dorothy Parker.

❖ COMMA CAUTION: When quoted words end with a question mark or an exclamation point, keep that punctuation and do not add a comma even if explanatory words follow. ❖

24h

24h Using commas in dates, names, addresses, and numbers according to accepted practice

---

RULES FOR COMMAS WITH DATES

1. Use a comma between the date and the year: **November 24, 1859.**
2. Use a comma between the day and the date:; **Thursday, November 24.**
3. Within a sentence, use commas after the day and the year in a full date.
   November 24, 1859, was the date of publication of Charles Darwin's *The Origin of Species.*
4. Don't use a comma in a date that contains only the month and year or only the season and year.
   Darwin's *The Origin of Species* was published in **winter 1859.**
5. An inverted date takes no commas.
   Charles Darwin's *The Origin of Species* was first published on **24 November 1859.**

RULES FOR COMMAS WITH NAMES, PLACES, AND ADDRESSES

1. When an abbreviated title (Jr., M.D., Ph.D.) comes after a person's name, set the abbreviation off with commas.
   The company celebrated the promotion of **Susan Cohen, M.B.A.,** to senior vice president.
2. When you invert a person's name, use a comma to separate the last name from the first: **Cohen, Susan.**
3. Use a comma between a city and province: **Thompson, Manitoba.** In a sentence, use a comma after the province as well.
   Thompson, Manitoba, is not far from Flin Flon.
4. When you write a complete address as part of a sentence, use a comma to separate all the items but the postal code, which follows the province. A comma does not follow the postal code.
   The cheque from U.R. Stuk, **1313 Erewhon Lane, Naniamo, British Columbia V9S 2B2** bounced.

RULES FOR COMMAS WITH LETTERS

1. For the opening of an informal letter, use a comma: **Dear Betty,**
2. For the close of a letter, use a comma: **Sincerely yours, Love, Best regards, Very truly yours,**

RULES FOR COMMAS WITH NUMBERS

1. Counting from the right, put a comma after every three digits in numbers over four digits: **72,867 156,567,066**
   Note: the SI—the international system of metric measurements used in Canada—uses spaces in place of commas: **72 867   156 567 066**
2. In a number of four digits, a comma is optional.
   $1867 or **$1,867** or **$1 867   1867 km** or **1,867 km** or **1 867 km**
3. Don't use a comma or a space for a four-digit year—**1990** (but **25,000 B.C.** or **25 000 B.C.**); or in an address—**12161 Dean Drive**; or in a page number—**see page 1338**
4. Use a comma to separate related Imperial measurements written as words: **five feet, four inches**
5. Use a comma to separate a play's scene from an act: **act 2, scene 4**
6. Use a comma to separate a reference to a page from a reference to a line: **page 10, line 6**

24i Using commas to clarify meaning

Sometimes you will need to use a comma to clarify the meaning of a sentence, even though no other rule calls for one.

NO   In his will power to run the family business was divided among his children.

YES   In his will, power to run the family business was divided among his children.

NO   People who want to remember to vote without being reminded.

YES   People who want to, remember to vote without being reminded.

24j Avoiding misuse of the comma

Do not overuse commas by inserting them where they do not belong. Comma misuses are discussed throughout this chapter, signalled by ❖ COMMA CAUTION. ❖

Besides the misuses of commas discussed earlier, writers sometimes mistakenly use commas to separate major sentence parts.

NO	Snowfalls over the last 20 million years, have created the Antarctic ice sheet. [Do not separate a subject from its verb with a single comma.]
YES	Snowfalls over the last 20 million years have created the Antarctic ice sheet.
NO	The massive ice sheet is, 5000 metres deep. [Do not separate a verb from its complement with a single comma.]
YES	The massive ice sheet is 5000 metres deep.
NO	The weight of the ice has pushed, the continent 600 metres into the water. [Do not separate a verb from its object with a single comma.]
YES	The weight of the ice has pushed the continent 600 metres into the water
NO	Therefore, most of the continent lies below, sea level. [Do not separate a preposition from its object with a single comma.]
YES	Therefore, most of the continent lies below sea level.

Name_____ Date _____

Using Commas in Compound Sentences

A: Rewrite the following sentences, inserting commas wherever coordinating conjunctions are used to join sentences. If a sentence does not need any additional commas, write *correct* on the line.

EXAMPLE   Some people consider slime moulds protozoans but most scientists class them with the fungi.

> *Some people consider slime moulds protozoans, but most scientists class them with the fungi.*

1. Slime moulds move by creeping along and sometimes they seem to flow.

   _____

2. They have a stationary stage, however and then they are more plantlike.

   _____

3. An observer seldom sees much of the mould's body or plasmodium for it stays beneath decaying matter.

   _____

4. The main part contains several nuclei but has no cell walls.

   _____

5. Like an amoeba, its protoplasm moves in one direction and then it goes in another.

   _____

6. Not only do slime moulds come in many colours but they also come in many types.

   _____

7. Some grow on long stalks while others are stalkless.

   _____

8. Some kinds are very small and can only be seen through a microscope.

   _____

9. Most slime moulds grow on decaying wood yet some grow directly on the ground.

   _____

10. A mould depends on water so it will dry up if it lacks moisture.

   _____

11. Most mature moulds change into sporangia and the sporangia each contain many spores.

   _____

12. Scientists know that the wind carries the spores and that they eventually germinate and form new moulds.

   _____

13. The slime-mould species *Fuligo* has the largest sporangia and they dwarf others by comparison.

_____

14. Either they appear to be large sponges on the ground or they look like dark holes in the grass.

_____

B: Combine the following sentences by using the coordinating conjunctions given in parentheses. Remember to use a comma before each coordinating conjunction used to join two sentences.

EXAMPLE Most slime moulds live in the woods.
           They like soil with high humus content. (and)

           Most slime moulds live in the woods, and they like soil with high humus content.

1. Some, however, leave the forest.
    They live on cultivated plants. (and)

_____

2. They can cause clubroot of cabbage.
    They can create powdery scab of potato. (or)

_____

3. Slime moulds sound disagreeable.
    Some are quite attractive. (yet)

_____

4. One form produces unappealing stalks.
    The stalks are topped with tiny balls. (but)

_____

5. The balls appear to be woven.
    They look rather like baskets. (so)

_____

6. The woven balls are really sporangia.
    They contain spores for distribution. (and)

_____

7. Another form looks like tiny ghosts.
    Its white moulds could be small sheeted figures. (for)

_____

8. Serpent slime mould is yellow.
    It can look like a miniature snake on top of a decaying log. (and)

_____

9. One would have to work hard to find it on the Prairies.
    It is most common in the tropics. (for)

_____

10. After one learns about slime moulds, they no longer seem disgusting.
    They do not even seem disagreeable. (nor)

_____

Using Commas after
Introductory Elements

A: Applying the rules regarding commas and introductory elements, rewrite these sentences, inserting commas as needed. If any sentence does not need an additional comma, write *correct* on the line.

EXAMPLE   Known as the Empty Quarter the Rub al-Khali is the largest of the deserts in Saudi Arabia.

Known as the Empty Quarter, the Rub al-Khali is the largest of the deserts in Saudi Arabia.

1. In fact it is the largest continuous body of sand in the world.

_____

2. Extending over 650 000 square kilometres the Rub al-Khali comprises more than one-third of Saudi Arabia.

_____

3. As a point of comparison Saskatchewan is just slightly larger.

_____

4. Because it is almost completely devoid of rain the Rub al-Khali is one of the driest places on the planet.

_____

5. Despite the existence of a few scattered shrubs the desert is largely a sand sea.

_____

6. However its eastern side develops massive dunes with salt basins.

_____

7. Except for the hardy Bedouins the Rub al-Khali is uninhabited.

_____

8. Indeed it is considered one of the most forbidding places on earth.

_____

9. Until Bertram Thomas crossed it in 1931 it was unexplored by outsiders.

_____

10. Even after oil was discovered in Arabia exploration in the Empty Quarter was limited.

_____

11. Losing heavy equipment in the deep sand made such exploration expensive.

_____

12. To facilitate exploration huge sand tires were developed in the 1950s.

_____

13. Shortly thereafter drilling rigs began operating in the Rub al-Khali.

_____

14. We now know that the Empty Quarter sits on huge reserves of oil.

_____

15. As it turns out the Empty Quarter is not so empty after all.

_____

B: Applying the rules governing commas and introductory elements, insert commas as needed in this paragraph.

[1]As might be expected the Rub al-Khali is hot all year round. [2]In contrast the Gobi Desert is hot in the summer but extremely cold in the winter. [3]Located in China and Mongolia the Gobi is twice the size of Saskatchewan. [4]Unlike the Rub al-Khali the Gobi has some permanent settlers. [5]Nevertheless most of its inhabitants are nomadic. [6]To avoid the subzero winters the nomads move their herds at the end of summer. [7]When the harsh winters subside they return to the sparse desert vegetation.

Using Commas in Series and with Coordinate Adjectives

EXERCISE **24-3**
(24c–d)

A: In each sentence, first underline all items in series and all coordinate adjectives. Then rewrite each sentence, adding any necessary commas. If no commas are needed, explain why.

EXAMPLE   Vicunas guanacos llamas and alpacas are all South American members of the camel family.

Vicunas, guanacos, llamas, and alpacas are all South American members of the camel family.

1. The vicuna, the smallest member of the camel family, lives in the mountains of Ecuador Bolivia and Peru.

_____

2. The guanaco is the wild humpless ancestor of the llama and the alpaca.

_____

3. The llama stands four feet tall is about four feet long and is the largest of the South American camels.

_____

4. A llama's coat may be white brown black or shades in between.

_____

5. Indians of the Andes use llamas to carry loads to bear wool and to produce meat.

_____

EXERCISES

6. Llamas are foraging animals that live on lichens shrubs and other available plants.

   _____

7. Because they can go without water for weeks, llamas are economical practical pack animals.

   _____

8. The alpaca has a longer lower body than the llama.

   _____

9. It has wool of greater length of higher quality and of superior softness.

   _____

10. Alpaca wool is straighter finer and warmer than sheep's wool.

   _____

B: Write complete sentences as described below. Take special care to follow the rules governing the use of commas in lists and between coordinate adjectives.

EXAMPLE Mention three favourite holidays.
   My favourite holidays are Christmas, New Year's Day, and Easter.

1. Give at least three reasons to spend those holidays with relatives.

   _____
   _____

2. List your three favourite fast foods.

   _____
   _____

3. Mention your four preferred vacation activities.

   _____
   _____

4. Using two or three coordinate adjectives, describe a pet.

   _____
   _____

5. Use a series of adjectives to describe a favourite movie.

   _____
   _____

6. Use a series of prepositional phrases to tell where the groom found rice after the wedding.

   _____
   _____

7. Using a series of verbs or verb phrases, tell what John does at his fitness centre.

   _____
   _____

8. Use coordinate adjectives to describe John's improved appearance as a result of working out.

   _____
   _____

Name_____ Date _____

Using Commas with Nonrestrictive, Parenthetical, and Transitional Elements

Rewrite these sentences to punctuate nonrestrictive clauses, phrases, appositives, and transitional expressions. If a sentence needs no commas, write *correct* on the line.

EXAMPLE   Ballet a sophisticated form of dance is a theatrical art.

Ballet, a sophisticated form of dance, is a theatrical art.

1. A ballet contains a sequence of dances that are performed to music.

    _____

    _____

2. The dances both solos and ensembles express emotion or tell a story.

    _____

    _____

3. The person who composes the actual dance steps is the choreographer.

    _____

    _____

4. A ballet's steps called its choreography become standardized over many years of performance.

    _____

    _____

5. The choreographer Marius Petipa created the blend of steps still used in most productions of *Swan Lake*.

    _____

    _____

6. The steps all with French names combine solos and groups.

    _____

    _____

7. The *corps de ballet* the ballet company excluding its star soloists may dance together or in small ensembles.

    _____

    _____

8. One soloist may join another for a *pas de deux* a dance for two.

    _____

    _____

EXERCISES

9. Ensemble members not just soloists must be proficient at pliés and arabesques.

_____

_____

10. Children wanting to become professionals must practise for years.

_____

_____

11. It is important therefore to start lessons early.

_____

_____

12. In Russia which has some of the most stringent ballet training students begin at age three.

_____

_____

Expanding Sentences with Restrictive and Nonrestrictive Elements

EXERCISE 24-5
(24e)

Expand each sentence twice: first with a restrictive word, phrase, or clause, and then with a nonrestrictive word, phrase, or clause. Place commas as needed.

EXAMPLE   Comics are usually funny.

> *1. (restrictive) Comics in the newspaper are usually funny.*
>
> *2. (nonrestrictive) Comics, for all their absurdity, are usually funny.*

1. The dahlias did not bloom this year.

_____

_____

2. I dislike gossip.

_____

_____

3. The computer does not work.

_____

_____

4. The man would not go home.

_____

_____

5. The child can walk now.

_____

_____

6. The creek overflowed its banks.

_____

_____

7. I need to lose two kilograms.

_____

_____

8. My cousin adores opera.

_____

_____

9. The teacher read the _Iliad_ aloud.

_____

_____

10. He finally turned down the sound system.

_____

_____

Using Commas with Quotations

> **EXERCISE 24-6**
> **(24g)**

Using the rules governing the use of commas to attach quotations to their speaker tags, place commas in these sentences.

EXAMPLE   According to Herbert Samuel, "It takes two to make a marriage a success and only one to make it a failure."

1. "Marriage" said Joseph Barth "is our last, best chance to grow up."
2. Peter De Vries was right when he said "The difficulty with marriage is that we fall in love with a personality, but must live with a character."
3. According to André Maurois "A successful marriage is an edifice that must be rebuilt every day."
4. "Heaven" said Andrew Jackson "will be no heaven to me if I do not meet my wife there."
5. "Marriage resembles a pair of shears, so joined that they cannot be separated; often moving in opposite directions, yet always punishing any one who comes between them" observed Sydney Smith.
6. "Chains do not hold a marriage together" said Simone Signoret. "It is threads, hundreds of tiny threads which sew people together through the years."
7. An anonymous wise person said "If there is anything better than to be loved it is loving."
8. "The way to love anything is to realize that it might be lost" advised Gilbert K. Chesterton.
9. "Love gives itself; it is not bought" observed Longfellow.
10. "Love does not consist in gazing at each other" said Antoine de Saint-Exupéry "but in looking outward together in the same direction."

EXERCISES

Name_____ Date _____

Using Commas and Spaces in Dates, Names, Addresses, and Numbers

EXERCISE **24-7**
(24h)

Rewrite the following sentences, inserting commas (or spaces, where appropriate) to punctuate dates, names, addresses, and numbers. If a sentence is correct as written, write *correct* on the line.

EXAMPLE   January 1 1975 was the beginning of a momentous year.

January 1, 1975, was the beginning of a momentous year.

1. In the northwest part of China, 6000 pottery figures were found.

   _____

2. Construction workers uncovered a terra cotta army in July 1975.

   _____

3. The life-sized warriors and horses had been buried for 2200 years.

   _____

4. The figures were in a huge tomb near the city of Xi'an China.

   _____

5. Archaeologists also unearthed almost 10000 artifacts from the excavation site.

   _____

6. It did not take John Doe Ph.D. to realize that this was an extraordinary find.

   _____

7. Some of the figures were displayed in Memphis Tennessee twenty years later.

   _____

8. Running from 18 April 1995 to 18 September 1995, the exhibit featured 250 objects from the imperial tombs of China.

   _____

9. The exhibit was open from 9 a.m. to 10 p.m. daily.

   _____

10. To get tickets, one could write to the Memphis Cook Convention Center 255 North Main Memphis TN 38103.

   _____

Adding Commas

A: Rewrite the following sentences, inserting commas as needed. If a sentence is correct as written, write *correct* on the line.

EXAMPLE Ancient writers both Greek and Roman wrote about the seven wonders of the world.

Ancient writers, both Greek and Roman, wrote about the seven wonders of the world.

1. One was the statue of Olympian Zeus which was covered with precious stones.

   _____

2. Unfortunately it was taken to Constantinople in A.D. 475 and there destroyed by fire.

   _____

3. The Hanging Gardens of Babylon built for Nebuchadnezzar were considered a wonder.

   _____

4. They were probably irrigated terraces connected by marble stairways.

   _____

5. To lift water from the Euphrates slaves had to work in shifts.

   _____

6. The Colossus of Rhodes was a huge impressive statue built to honour the sun god Helios.

   _____

7. Constructed near the harbour it was intended to astonish all who saw it.

   _____

8. Another wonder was the Lighthouse at Alexandria Egypt.

   _____

9. Because it stood on the island of Pharos the word *pharos* has come to mean lighthouse.

   _____

10. After the death of Mausolus king of Caria his widow erected a richly adorned monument to honour him.

    _____

11. With sculptures by famous artists the Mausoleum at Halicarnassus amazed the ancient world.

    _____

EXERCISES

12. The Temple of Artemis at Ephesus an important Ionian city was also considered a wonder.

_____

13. It was burned rebuilt and burned again.

_____

14. Some wonders such as the Colossus and the Mausoleum were destroyed by earth-quakes.

_____

15. Of the seven works that astounded the ancients only the pyramids of Egypt survive.

_____

B: Add commas as needed. You will not need to add any words or other marks of punctuation.

[1]St. Andrews Scotland is an old city. [2]Named for a Christian saint the city was once an object of devout pilgrimage. [3]Its cathedral the largest in Scotland is now a ruin. [4]It was destroyed in 1559 by followers of the reformer John Knox. [5]All the revered carefully preserved relics of St. Andrew disappeared. [6]Although the castle of St. Andrews also lies in ruins it preserves two fascinating remnants of medieval history. [7]One is a bottle-shaped dungeon and the other is a countermine. [8]When attackers tried to mine under castle walls defenders tried to intercept the tunnel with a countermine. [9]Interestingly one can actually enter both mine and countermine. [10]The University of St. Andrews which is the oldest university in Scotland was established in 1412. [11]From all parts of the globe students come to study there. [12]Nevertheless most people who think of St. Andrews associate it with golf. [13]Even golf at St. Andrews is old the first reference dating to January 25 1552. [14]The famous Old Course is only one of four courses from which the avid golfer may choose. [15]St. Andrews is still an object of pilgrimage but today's pilgrims come with drivers wedges and putters.

Name_____ Date _____

Eliminating Unnecessary Commas

Rewrite this paragraph, omitting any unnecessary commas. You will not need to add any words or marks of punctuation.

[1]The Victoria Falls, were discovered by Dr. David Livingstone in 1855. [2]The waterfall is part of, the Zambezi River in Africa. [3]The falls are 108 metres high, and 1370 metres wide. [4]Depending upon the time of year, up to 4.7 million cubic metres of water may pass over the falls each day. [5]The falls are, the result of an unusual geological condition. [6]The river bed abruptly funnels, into a deep crack. [7]The trapped water can escape, under great pressure, only through a narrow, crevice. [8]The rapidly moving water is divided by a number of small islands, and, each of the falls is named separately: the Devil's Cataract, the main falls, the Rainbow Falls, and the Eastern Cataract. [9]Once water has passed over the falls, it continues through narrow, savage, Batoka Gorge, and flows under the railroad bridge that joins Zimbabwe and Zambia. [10]The area has changed very little since, Livingstone's day. [11]Herds of wild animals live protected in the nearby, national parks, and the area is largely, undeveloped.

Adding and Deleting Commas

Rewrite this paragraph, adding or deleting commas as needed. You will not have to change any words or other marks of punctuation. Number each change you make, and on the lines below indicate the reason for each addition or omission.

      Money, in terms of its value is really a matter, of trust and confidence in the government. By definition money is anything that society, accepts as having value. With such a broad definition it is not surprising, that money has, throughout history taken on some forms that were both creative and unique. Precious stones, fish hooks,
5 nails livestock, throwing knives, and axe-heads, are just a few examples of money that is equivalent to ours today. In a successful, society, money must serve three, basic functions: It must serve as a store of wealth a medium of exchange and a unit against which items are valued. Forms of money, must be portable, easy to store durable, and relatively hard to acquire. Successful forms of money, like gold and silver have all these
10 qualities. However, trust is also, necessary in a society such as ours that uses paper money. Although the paper itself is of little value we trust that a bill is, worth the number printed on the front of it.

Commas Added   *Commas Deleted*

_____	_____
_____	_____
_____	_____
_____	_____
_____	_____
_____	_____
_____	_____
_____	_____
_____	_____
_____	_____
_____	_____
_____	_____

25 | Semicolons

25a Using a semicolon between closely related independent clauses

When independent clauses are related in meaning, you can separate them with a semicolon instead of a period.

❖ COMMA CAUTION: Do not use only a comma between independent clauses, or you will create a comma splice (see Chapter 14) ❖

> **SEMICOLON PATTERN I**
>
> Independent clause; independent clause.

All changes are not growth; all movement is not forward.

—Ellen Glasgow

25b Using a semicolon before a coordinating conjunction joining independent clauses containing commas

You will usually use a comma to separate independent clauses linked by a coordinating conjunction (see 7h). When the independent clauses already contain commas, however, use a semicolon instead to separate the clauses.

> **SEMICOLON PATTERN II**
>
> • Independent clause, one that contains commas; coordinating conjunction independent clause.
>
> • Independent clause; coordinating conjunction independent clause, one that contains commas.
>
> • Independent clause, one that contains commas; coordinating conjunction independent clause, one that contains commas.

Aim at the sun, and you may not reach it; but your arrow will fly far higher than if aimed at an object on a level with yourself.

—JOEL HAWES

25c Using a semicolon when conjunctive adverbs or other transitional expressions connect independent clauses

Use a semicolon between two independent clauses when the second clause begins with a conjunctive adverb or other transitional word (4d).

✤ COMMA CAUTION: Do not use only a comma between independent clauses connected by a conjunctive adverb or other words of transition, or you will create a comma splice (see Chapter 14) ✤

SEMICOLON PATTERN III

Independent clause; conjunctive adverb or other transition, independent clause.

A coelacanth, a supposedly extinct fish, was caught by an African fisherman in 1938; as a result, some scientists believe other "extinct" animals may still live in remote parts of the world.

✤ COMMA ALERT: When you place a conjunctive adverb or a transition after the subject of an independent clause, set if off with commas: *This theory may be true; some people, however, even suggest the Loch Ness Monster may be a dinosaur.* ✤

25d Using a semicolon between items in a series

When a sentence contains a series of words, phrases, or clauses, commas usually separate one item from the next. When the items are long and contain commas for other purposes, you can make your message clearer by separating the items with semicolons instead of commas.

SEMICOLON PATTERN IV

Independent clause that includes a series of items, any of which contain a comma; another item in the series; another item in the series.

Many are always praising the by-gone time, for it is natural that the old should extol the days of their youth; the weak, the time of their strength; the sick, the season of their vigor; and the disappointed, the spring-tide of their hopes.

—CALEB BINGHAM

25e Avoiding misuse of the semicolon

Don't use a semicolon after an introductory phrase or between a dependent clause and an independent clause; use a comma: *Because the price of new cars continues to rise, people are keeping their old cars.*

Don't use a semicolon to introduce a list; use a colon: *Keeping these old cars running can be expensive too: rebuilt engines, new transmissions, and replacement tires.*

Name_____ Date _____

Using the Semicolon

A: Insert semicolons where needed. They may be placed where there is now no punctu-ation or they may replace commas. Some sentences may require more than one semi-colon. If an item is correct, write *correct* in the left margin.

EXAMPLE   Vision is our most important sense; we get most of our information about the world by seeing.

1. The sclera is the outer cover of the eye, it helps the eye keep its shape because the sclera is fairly hard.
2. The choroid is just inside the sclera it keeps out unneeded light.
3. The pupil is the opening in the eye this is where the light enters.
4. The cornea is the clear cover of the pupil, therefore, light can enter the eye.
5. The pupil is opened or closed by muscles in the iris, in fact, in bright light the iris closes to decrease the amount of light entering, in low light, it opens to increase the light.
6. After passing through the pupil, light shines on the retina, which sends messages to the brain.
7. The retina contains cells, cones and rods, which are outgrowths of the brain when light strikes them, nerve impulses travel to the brain.
8. The optic nerve connects the eye to the brain, thus any damage to the nerve can cause blindness.
9. Cone cells give us colour vision, they are most effective in the day.
10. Rods are sensitive to low light they are involved in night vision.

B: This paragraph is missing seven semicolons. Insert them where needed.

     Hearing is based on sound waves these are pressure changes spreading out from a vibrating source. If we could see sound waves, they might remind us of ripples on water like ripples, sound waves vary in number, size, and speed. When these waves reach us, our ears and brain translate them into pitch, loudness, and timbre. Pitch is the number
5 of wave vibrations per second it determines whether a tone is high or low, whether a singer is a soprano or an alto. Loudness is a measure of the intensity of the waves this is called their amplitude. When we turn up the volume on the stereo, we are raising the amplitude. Sound intensity is measured in decibels. Any sound registering over 130 decibels is painful however, people still listen to loud music or live near railroad tracks.
10 Timbre is hard to describe in everyday language in physics terms, however, timbre is the main wavelength plus any other wavelengths that may come from a particular source. Timbre explains why a note played on a violin sounds different from the same note played on an electric guitar or why two people singing the same note sound different.
15 Physics defines *noise* as too many unrelated frequencies vibrating together neverthe-less, people still disagree over whether some sounds are noise or exciting music.

Using the Semicolon

and the Comma

Add commas or semicolons as needed to fill in the blanks appropriately.

EXAMPLE   One out of every twenty-five people is colourblind ___,___ unable to tell certain
colours apart.

1. Colourblindness is inherited _____ it appears more often in men than in women.

2. The most common colourblindness is the inability to tell red from green _____ but more
than green and red are involved.

3. Different colours, the result of differences in light wavelengths, create a spectrum
_____ the spectrum of colours is red, orange, yellow, green, blue, indigo, and violet.

4. People who are severely red-green colourblind cannot "see" any colours at that end
of the spectrum _____ that is _____ they cannot tell the difference between blue-greens,
reds, or yellow-greens.

5. Colourblindness varies from person to person _____ people who can distinguish red
from green a little are called colour-weak.

6. Some people have no cone cells (the cells that send signals about colour to the brain)
_____ so they are completely colourblind.

7. They have achromatism _____ a rare condition.

8. Such people can see only black, white, and greys _____ what a boring view of the world.

9. However, their problem is much more serious than this _____ they also have trouble
focusing on objects.

10. The part of the eye that usually receives images is the fovea, which contains the cone
cells _____ achromatics' foveas are blank and cannot receive images.

11. To compensate, they look at objects off centre _____ to pick up images with their rod
(black and white) cells.

12. It is possible to be colourblind and not know it _____ how can people miss what they have
never known?

13. There are several tests for colourblindness _____ most involve seeing (or not seeing) a
number or word written on a background of a complementary colour _____ for example,
a red *48* on a green background.

26 Colons

In sentence punctuation, the colon introduces what comes after it: a quotation, a summary or restatement, or a list. The colon also has a few separating functions.

26a Using a colon after an independent clause to introduce a list, an appositive, or a quotation

Use a colon to introduce a list or series of items announced by an independent clause.

In selecting a major, consider these factors: your talent for the subject, the number of years needed to qualify professionally, and the availability of jobs.

When you use phrases such as *the following* or *as follows*, a colon is usually required. A colon is *not* called for with the words *such as* or *including* (see 26d).

Woods commonly used in fine furniture include the following: black walnut, mahogany, oak, and pecan.

You can use a colon to lead into a final appositive—a word or group of words that renames a noun or pronoun.

A hot plate can enable any student to become a dormitory chef, preparing simple and satisfying meals: omelets, stir-fired vegetables, even stews.

Use a colon at the end of a grammatically complete statement that introduces a formal quotation.

Francis Bacon was referring to men and women when he wrote of the destructiveness of seeking vengeance: "A man that studieth revenge keeps his own wounds green."

COLON PATTERN I
• Independent clause: list.
• Independent clause: appositive.
• Independent clause: "Quoted words."

26b Using a colon between two independent clauses

You can use a colon at the end of an independent clause to introduce statements that summarize, restate, or explain what is said in that clause.

The makers of some movies aimed at teenagers think that their audience is interested in little more than car chases, violence, and nudity: they sadly underestimate young people.

COLON PATTERN II

Independent clause: Independent clause.

26c Using a colon in standard formats

TITLE AND SUBTITLE
Broca's Brain: Reflections on the Romance of Science

HOURS, MINUTES, AND SECONDS
The lecture began at 9:15 a.m.

CHAPTERS AND VERSES OF THE BIBLE
Ecclesiastes 3:1

LETTER SALUTATION
Dear Ms. Winters:

MEMO FORM
> TO: Dean Elliot Gordon
> FROM: Professor Steven Wang
> RE: Honours and Awards Ceremony

26d Avoiding misuse of the colon

A colon must follow a complete independent clause when it separates standard material (26c). Lead-in words must make a grammatically complete statement. When they do not, do not use a colon. Also do not use a colon after the words *such as, like,* and *including,* or forms of the verb *be.*

NO The shop sold: T-shirts, bumper stickers, posters, and greeting cards.

YES The shop sold T-shirts, bumper stickers, posters, and greeting cards.

NO	Students work in many of the town's businesses, such as: the diner, the grocery, the laundromat, and the gas station.
YES	Students work in many of the town's businesses, such as the diner, the grocery, the laundromat, and the gas station.
YES	Students work in many of the town's businesses: the diner, the grocery, the laundromat, and the gas station.

Do not use a colon to separate a phrase or dependent clause from an independent clause.

NO	When summer comes: the town is almost deserted.
YES	When summer comes, the town is almost deserted.

26-1

Using the Colon

Rewrite the following sentences, adding colons as needed. If no colon is needed, write *correct* in the left margin.

EXAMPLE   A survey identified Canadian parents' favourite names for their babies Michael and Jessica.

> *A survey identified Canadian parents' favourite names for their babies: Michael and Jessica.*

1. People believe that Napoleon was short, but he was average height 5′6″.

2. According to an ABC News-Harris Survey, U.S. males' three favourite freetime activities are as follows eating, watching TV, and fixing things around the house.

3. According to the same survey, females' favourite activities include eating, reading books, and listening to music.

4. If you want my opinion, these are the most common street names in Canada Queen, King, Elm, and Maple.

5. I plan to call my autobiography *Burrowing The Adventures of a Bookworm.*

6. The train, 20 minutes late, was due at 640.

7. She said just what we were fearing "I forgot to tell you—classroom participation also counts."

8. When walking alone at night, remember one thing Be alert!

9. The nineteenth century was a bad time for Turkey it lost three wars to Russia and three to Egypt, and it lost control over Greece.

10. Few animals eat humans, but those that do include the following bears, crocodiles, giant squid, leopards, lions, piranhas, sharks, and tigers.

Name_____ Date _____

| EXERCISE **26-2** |
| (26a–d) |

Writing Sentences with the Colon

Write complete sentences in answer to these questions. Use a colon in each sentence.

EXAMPLE   What time do you wake up?

*I wake up at 5:45*_____

1.   What is the full title and subtitle of one of your textbooks?

_____

2.   What are your favourite classes? (Use the expression *as follows*.)

_____

3.   What is your advice to someone going to a job interview?

_____

4.   Who are the star players on your favourite team?

_____

5.   What streets or geographical features mark the borders of your campus?

_____

_____

27 Apostrophes

The apostrophe plays four major roles: it creates the possessive case of nouns; it creates the possessive case of indefinite pronouns; it stands for omitted letters; and it can help to form the plurals of letters and numerals. It *does* not belong with plurals of nouns or the possessive case of personal pronouns.

27a Using an apostrophe to form the possessive case of nouns and indefinite pronouns

The possessive case shows ownership (*the scientist's invention*) or close relationship (*the premier's policy, the movie's ending*). It indicates the same meaning as phrases beginning *of the* (*the invention of the scientist*).

When nouns and indefinite pronouns do not end in -*s*, add *'s* to show possession.

The **doctor's** diplomas are on her office wall. [singular noun not ending in -s]

The class studied the **women's** rights movement. [plural noun not ending in -s]

Good health is **everyone's** wish. [indefinite pronoun not ending in -s]

When singular nouns end in -*s*, add *'s* to show possession.

The **waitress's** tip was less than she expected.

Les's phone bill was enormous.

When a plural noun ends in -*s*, use only an apostrophe to show possession.

The **workers'** tools were all over the room.

Their **supervisors'** reports were critical of their sloppiness.

In compound words, add *'s* to the last word.

The **police chief's** retirement party was held in the hotel ballroom.

They held their wedding in her **sister-in-law's** backyard.

In individual possession, add *'s* to each noun.

Pat's and Lee's songs are hits. [Pat and Lee each wrote some of the songs; they did not write the songs together.]

Dali's and Turner's paintings were sold for record prices. [Dali and Turner painted different canvasses.]

In joint or group possession, add *'s* to only the last noun.

Pat and Lee's songs are hits. [Pat and Lee wrote the songs together.]

Dali and Turner's show at the art museum was a hit. [Dali and Turner are featured in the same show.]

Not using an apostrophe with the possessive forms of personal pronouns

Some pronouns have their own possessive forms. Do not use an apostrophe with these forms: *his, her, hers, its, our, ours, your, yours, their, theirs, whose.* Be especially careful in using *its/it's* and *whose/who's*, which are often confused. *It's* stands for *it is; its* is a personal pronoun showing possession. *Who's* stands for *who is; whose* is a personal pronoun showing possession.

NO   The province will elect **it's** legislature next week.

YES   The province will elect **its** legislature next week.

NO   The leader **who's** ads appear on television daily expects to win.

YES   The leader **whose** ads appear on television daily expects to win.

27c Using an apostrophe to stand for omitted letters, numbers, or words in contractions

In informal English, some words may be combined by omitting one or more letters and inserting apostrophes to signal the omission: *I'm* (*I am*), *aren't* (*are not*), *he'll* (*he will*), and others. These words are called **contractions.**

Apostrophes also indicate the omission of the first two numerals in years: *The professor spoke of the sit-ins of '68.* (Avoid this contraction in academic writing.) No apostrophe is used when you indicate a span of years: *1948–52.*

27d Using an apostrophe to form plurals of letters, numerals, symbols, and words used as terms

The child practised writing her Q's.

The computer went berserk and printed out pages of 4's.

In writing the plural form of years, two styles are acceptable: with an apostrophe (1990's) or without (1990s). Whichever form you prefer, use it consistently.

27e Avoiding misuse of the apostrophe

Do not use an apostrophe with the present-tense verb form.

NO   Cholesterol **plays'** an important role in how long we live.

YES   Cholesterol **plays** an important role in how long we live.

Do not add an apostrophe at the end of a nonpossessive noun ending in *s*.

NO   Medical **studies'** reveal that cholesterol is the primary cause of coronary heart disease.

YES   Medical **studies** reveal that cholesterol is the primary cause of coronary heart disease.

Use an apostrophe after the *s* in the possessive plural of a noun.

NO   The medical community is seeking more information from **doctor's** investigations into heart disease.

YES   The medical community is seeking more information from **doctors'** investigations into heart disease.

Do not use an apostrophe to form a nonpossessive plural.

NO   **Team's** of doctors are trying to predict who might be most harmed by cholesterol.

YES   **Teams** of doctors are trying to predict who might be most harmed by cholesterol.

Name_____ Date _____

Using the Apostrophe in Possessive Nouns

EXERCISE **27-1**
(27a–b)

Write the possessive forms, singular and plural, for each of the following words. If you are unsure how to form the plural of any word, see your dictionary or section 22c.

	Singular Possessive	**Plural Possessive**
EXAMPLE cow	cow's	cows'
1. sheep	_____	_____
2. pony	_____	_____
3. turkey	_____	_____
4. lion	_____	_____
5. mouse	_____	_____
6. she	_____	_____
7. gorilla	_____	_____
8. goose	_____	_____
9. gnu	_____	_____
10. ox	_____	_____
11. you	_____	_____
12. buffalo	_____	_____
13. zebra	_____	_____
14. ibex	_____	_____
15. fly	_____	_____
16. I	_____	_____
17. giraffe	_____	_____
18. dodo	_____	_____
19. zoo	_____	_____
20. zoo keeper	_____	_____
21. he	_____	_____
22. farm	_____	_____
23. farmer	_____	_____
24. ranch	_____	_____
25. it	_____	_____

Using the Apostrophe
in Possessive Expressions

Rewrite each of these noun phrases as a possessive noun followed by another noun.

EXAMPLE   the schedule of the student

the student's schedule

1. the menu of the restaurant

2. the daughter of the boss

3. the waiting room of the doctor

4. the waiting room of the doctors

5. the guess of anyone

6. the scripts of the actor

7. the scripts of the actors

8. the crew of the ship

9. the reputation of someone

10. the tools of my father-in-law

27-3

Using Apostrophes in Contractions

| EXERCISE **27-3** |
| (27c) |

Write contractions of the following expressions.

EXAMPLE   he + is =   *he's* _____

1. are + not = _____

2. will + not = _____

3. let + us = _____

4. he + had = _____

5. was + not = _____

6. you + would = _____

7. did + not = _____

8. I + will = _____

9. what + is = _____

10. I + am = _____

11. is + not = _____

12. would + not = _____

13. can + not = _____

14. does + not = _____

15. I + have = _____

16. you + are = _____

17. there + is = _____

18. we + would = _____

19. were + not = _____

20. they + are = _____

21. it + is = _____

22. we + have = _____

23. she + will = _____

24. we + are = _____

25. do + not = _____

Using Apostrophes

Insert apostrophes as needed. If no apostrophes are called for in a sentence, write *correct* in the left margin.

EXAMPLE   The detective storys roots go back to at least 1841.

The detective story's roots go back to at least 1841.

1. The modern detective story began with Edgar Allan Poes "The Murders in the Rue Morgue."
2. Its detective reappeared in "The Mystery of Marie Rogêt" in 1842–43.
3. The authors last pure detective story was "The Purloined Letter."
4. The three stories featured amateur detective C. August Dupins ability to solve crimes by using logic.
5. Poe didnt use the word *detective* in the stories.
6. The publics response was not enthusiastic, perhaps because the heros personality was unpleasant.
7. This may explain why there werent any more detective stories by Poe.
8. Twenty years later, in 66, a Frenchman revived the detective story, and this time it was a great success.
9. Soon after, Englishman Wilkie Collins published *The Moonstone*.
10. Collins book was the first full-length detective novel in English.
11. The books hero was a professional detective who grew roses when he wasnt working.
12. *The Moonstones* hero had a better personality than Dupin, so the publics acceptance of him is understandable.
13. Charles Dickens, Collins friend, was writing a mystery novel when he died.
14. The fragment of *The Mystery of Edwin Drood* has been studied for years, but no ones been able to figure out how Dickens planned to explain the mystery.
15. Its been one of my favourite literary puzzles for years.
16. Arthur Conan Doyles Sherlock Holmes made his debut in "A Study in Scarlet" in 1887.
17. Holmes popularity really dates from July 1891, when "A Scandal in Bohemia" was published.
18. Peoples attention was finally captured, and they demanded more and more stories featuring Holmes.
19. Conan Doyle became so tired of the character that he wrote about Holmes death, killing him in a fall over a waterfall.
20. The readers outcry was so great that Holmes was brought back for more stories in 1902.
21. Then in 1905, Holmes earlier absence was explained.
22. The explanation was weak, but the fans couldnt have been happier.

28 Quotation Marks

Quotation marks most frequently enclose direct quotations—the exact words of a speaker or writer. Quotation marks also set off some titles, and they can call attention to words used in special senses. Always use quotation marks in pairs. Be especially careful not to forget the second (closing) quotation mark.

28a Using quotation marks to enclose short direct quotations

Direct quotations present exact words copied from an original source. Use double quotation marks to enclose short quotations (no more than four lines).

SHORT QUOTATION

According to Marvin Harris in *Cows, Pigs, Wars, and Witches*, "We seem to be more interested in working in order to get people to admire us for our wealth than in the actual wealth itself."

Longer quotations are not enclosed in quotation marks. They are displayed, starting on a new line, and all lines of the quotation are indented ten spaces.

When the words of a short quotation already contain quotation marks, use double quotation marks at the start and end of the directly quoted words. Then substitute single quotation marks (' ') wherever there are double quotation marks in your original source.

Carl Sagan begins his essay called "In Defense of Robots" by telling us, "The word 'Robot,' first introduced by the Czech writer Karl Čapek, is derived from the Slavic root for 'worker.'"

When the words of a longer quotation already contain quotation marks, display the quotation without enclosing it in quotation marks. Then use quotation marks exactly as they were used in your original source.

Use double quotation marks to enclose a short quotation of poetry (no more than three lines of the poem). If you quote more than one line of poetry, use slashes to show the line divisions (see 29e).

Not everyone would agree with Emily Dickinson's statement: "Success is counted sweetest/By those who ne'er succeed."

Quotation marks are also used to enclose speakers' words in **direct discourse.** Whether you are reporting the exact words of a real speaker or making up dialogue in, for example, a short story, quotation marks let your readers know which words belong to the speaker and which words do not. Use double quotation marks at the beginning and end of a speaker's words, and start a new paragraph each time the speaker changes.

> "The marks were some twenty yards from the body and no one gave them a thought. I don't suppose I should have done so had I not known the legend."
> "There are many sheep dogs on the moor?"
> "No doubt, but this was no sheep dog."
> "You say it was large?"
> "Enormous."
>
> —Sir Arthur Conan Doyle, *The Hound of the Baskervilles*

In contrast to direct discourse, **indirect discourse** reports only the spirit of what a speaker said. Do not enclose indirect discourse in quotation marks.

DIRECT DISCOURSE The professor said, "Your midterm is a week from Tuesday."

INDIRECT DISCOURSE The professor said that our midterm would be a week from Tuesday.

28b Using quotation marks with titles of short works

Use quotation marks around the titles of short published works, such as pamphlets and brochures. Also use them around song titles, episodes of television series, and titles of works that are parts of longer works or parts of collected works: poems, short stories, essays, and articles from periodicals.

Stephen Jay Gould examines what we know about dinosaur intelligence in the essay "Were Dinosaurs Dumb?"

Modern readers still enjoy Edgar Allan Poe's story "The Tell-Tale Heart."

28c Using quotation marks for words used in special senses or for special purposes

Writers sometimes use quotation marks to indicate words or phrases that are not meant to be taken at face value.

The "free" CDs came with a bill for ten dollars—for postage and handling.

Writers sometimes put technical terms in quotation marks and define them the first time they are used. No quotation marks are used after such terms have been introduced and defined.

"Plagiarism"—the unacknowledged use of another person's words or ideas—can result in expulsion. Plagiarism is a serious offence.

Words being referred to as words can be either enclosed in quotation marks or italicized (or underlined).

YES   Do not confuse "then" and "than."

YES   Do not confuse *then* and *than.*

28d Avoiding the misuse of quotation marks

Writers sometimes place quotation marks around words they are uncomfortable about using. Instead of resorting to this practice, find appropriate words.

NO   Einstein's theory of relativity is very "heavy stuff."

YES   Einstein's theory of relativity is very sophisticated.

Do not enclose a word in quotation marks merely to call attention to it.

NO   The report is due on Friday, "or else."

YES   The report is due on Friday, or else.

Do not put quotation marks around the title of your own papers (on a title page or at the top of the first page). The only exception is if your paper's title includes words that require quotation marks for one of the reasons discussed in 28a–c.

28e Following accepted practices for quotation marks with other punctuation

Place commas and periods inside closing quotation marks.

Besides writing such stories as "The Premature Burial," Edgar Allan Poe was also a respected literary critic and poet.

The bill read, "Registration fees must be paid in full one week before the start of classes."

Place colons and semicolons outside closing quotation marks.

The label on the ketchup said "low salt": it was also low taste.

Some people prefer the bilingual version of "O Canada"; it allows the singer to omit the awkward parts in both official languages.

Place question marks, exclamation points, and dashes inside or outside closing quotation marks, according to the situation. If a question mark, exclamation point, or dash belongs with the words enclosed in quotation marks, put that punctuation mark *inside* the closing quotation mark.

"Where is Andorra?" asked the quiz show host.

Before she was dragged off, the demonstrator managed to shout, "Long live free Pa—"

If a question mark, exclamation point, or dash belongs with words that are *not* included in quotation marks, put the punctuation mark *outside* the closing quotation mark.

Do you know Adrienne Rich's poem "Aunt Jennifer's Tigers"?

Grieving for a dead friend, Tennyson spent seventeen years writing "In Memoriam A.H.H."!

Name_____ Date _____

Using Quotation Marks

Insert additional quotation marks as needed. Use double quotation marks unless single quotation marks are specifically needed. Remember to place quotation marks carefully in relation to other marks of punctuation. If a sentence needs no additional quotation marks, write *correct* in the left margin.

EXAMPLE   Speaking of an old friend, Winston Churchill said, In those days he was wiser than he is now; he used frequently to take my advice.

> *Speaking of an old friend, Winston Churchill said, "In those days he was wiser than he is now; he used frequently to take my advice."*

1. According to Chesterfield, Advice is seldom welcome.

2. "If you are looking for trouble, offer some good advice, says Herbert V. Prochnow.

3. Marie Dressler was right: No vice is so bad as advice.

4. Someone once remarked, How we do admire the wisdom of those who come to us for advice!

5. "Free advice, it has been noted, is the kind that costs you nothing unless you act upon it."

6. "The only thing to do with good advice is to pass it on; it is never of any use to oneself." believed Oscar Wilde.

7. I sometimes give myself admirable advice, said Lady Mary Wortley Mantague, but I am incapable of taking it.

8. Says Tom Masson, "'Be yourself! is the worst advice you can give to some people.

9. The Beatles' song With a Little Help from My Friends contains some good advice.

10. Do you seriously advise me to marry that man?

11. My uncle advised me. The next time you are depressed, read Lewis Carroll's poem Jabberwocky.

12. Do you recall the Beach Boys' words: Be true to your school?

13. Many marriage counsellors advise us never to go to sleep angry with our mate.

14. However, comedienne Phyllis Diller suggests, Never go to bed mad. Stay up and fight.

15. Rachel Carson advised, The discipline of the writer is to learn to be still and listen to what his subject has to tell him.

16. If I had to give students advice in choosing a career, I would tell them to select a field that interests them passionately.

Writing Direct Quotations

Rewrite these indirect quotations as direct quotations. You will need to add commas, colons, capitals, and quotation marks. You may need to change the final punctuation mark. If necessary, change pronouns and verbs to suitable forms.

EXAMPLE   The student representative said that she had a question for the chair.

The student representative said, "I have a question for the chair."

1. She said that rumours had reached her about cuts to the Fine Arts Department.

   _____

2. She told the committee that nothing like that was forecast in the budget.

   _____

3. She asked if it was true, then, that two sessional instructors would not have their contracts renewed. [Make this a split quotation.]

   _____

4. The Dean of Arts and Science suggested that the matter should be studied at the next month's meeting.

   _____

5. Two students in the audience shouted that they wanted answers now.

   _____

6. The chair replied to them by reciting the text of rule 48.2(a), that audience members may be excluded from a meeting at the discretion of the chair.

   _____

Writing Properly Punctuated Dialogue

Write an original dialogue using proper punctuation and appropriate pronouns and verb tenses. Select one of the following situations, letting each person speak at least three times. Remember to start a new paragraph each time the speaker changes. Use your own paper.

1. You are asking your boss for a raise.
2. You are asking one of your parents for advice.
3. You are trying to talk a traffic officer out of giving you a ticket.
4. You and your boyfriend/girlfriend are trying to decide what movie to see.
5. You are trying to convince your younger brother/sister not to drop out of high school.

29 Other Punctuation Marks

THE DASH

29a Using the dash

The dash, or a pair of dashes, lets you interrupt a sentence to add information. Dashes are like parentheses (see 29b) in that they set off extra material at the beginning, in the middle, or at the end of a sentence. Unlike parentheses, dashes emphasize the interruptions. Use dashes sparingly—so that their dramatic impact is not blunted.

Use a dash or dashes to emphasize explanations, including appositives, examples, and definitions, and to point out contrasts.

EXAMPLE

In general, only mute things are eaten alive—plants and invertebrates. If oysters shrieked as they were pried open, or squealed when jabbed with a fork, I doubt whether they would be eaten alive.

—MARSTON BATES

DEFINITION

Personal space—"elbow room"—is a vital commodity for the human animal, and one that cannot be ignored without risking serious trouble.

—DESMOND MORRIS, "Territorial Behavior"

APPOSITIVE

Many's the long night I've dreamed of cheese—toasted, mostly.

—Robert Louis Stevenson

CONTRAST

I know a lot of people didn't expect our relationship to last—but we've just celebrated our two months' anniversary.

—BRITT EKLAND

Use a dash or dashes to emphasize an "aside." Asides are writers' comments within the structure of a sentence or paragraph.

343

These five passages have not been picked out because they are especially bad—I could have quoted far worse if I had chosen—but because they illustrate various of the mental vices from which we now suffer.

—GEORGE ORWELL, "Politics and the English Language"

Commas, semicolons, colons, and periods are not used next to dashes, but if the words you put between a pair of dashes would take a question mark or an exclamation point written as a separate sentence, use that punctuation before the second dash.

The tour guide—do you remember her name?—recommended an excellent restaurant.

Use a dash to show hesitating or broken-off speech.

"Yes," he said. "That is why I am here, you see. They thought we might be interested in that footprint."
"That footprint?" cried Dorothy. "You mean—?"
"No, no; not your footprint, Miss Brant. Another one."

—CARTER DICKSON, "The Footprint in the Sky"

PARENTHESES

29b Using parentheses

Parentheses let you interrupt a sentence's structure to add information of many kinds. Parentheses are like dashes in that they set off extra or interrupting words. However, unlike dashes, which make interruptions stand out, parentheses de-emphasize what they enclose.

Use parentheses to enclose interrupting words, including explanations, examples, and asides.

EXPLANATION

On the second night of his visit, our distinguished guest (Sir Charles Dilke) met Laura in the passage on her way to bed; he said to her: "If you will kiss me, I will give you a signed photograph of myself." To which she answered: "It's awfully good of you, Sir Charles, but I would rather not, for what on earth should I do with the photograph?"

—MARGOT ASQUITH

EXAMPLE

Many books we read to children (*Alice in Wonderland*, for example) may be even more enjoyable when we reread them as adults.

ASIDE

I have heard of novelists who say that, while they are creating a novel, the people in it are ever with them, accompanying them on walks, for all I know on drives (though this must be distracting in traffic), to the bath, to bed itself.

—ROSE MACAULAY

Use parentheses for certain numbers and letters of listed items. When you number listed items within a sentence, enclose the numbers (or letters) in parentheses.

I plan to do four things during summer vacation: (1) sleep, (2) work to save money for next semester's tuition, (3) catch up on my reading, and (4) have fun.

In business and legal writing, use parentheses to enclose a numeral repeating a spelled-out number.

The monthly fee to lease a colour television is forty dollars ($40).

Never put a comma before an opening parenthesis even if what comes before the parenthetical material requires a comma. Put the parenthetical material in, and then use the comma immediately after the closing parenthesis.

Even though I grew up in a big city (Calgary), I prefer small-town life.

You can use a question mark or an exclamation point with parenthetical words that occur within the structure of a sentence.

We entered the old attic (what a mess!) and began the dirty job of organizing the junk of three generations.

Use a period, however, only when you enclose a complete statement in parentheses outside the structure of another sentence. In this case, use a capital letter as well.

We entered the old attic and began the dirty job of organizing the junk of three generations. (The place was a mess.)

BRACKETS

29c Using brackets

When you work quoted words into your own sentences, you may have to change a word or two to make the quoted words fit into your structure. You may also want to add explanations to quoted material. Enclose your own words within brackets.

According to John Ackerman, "He [Dylan Thomas] was aware of the extent to which his temperament and his imagination were the products of his Welsh environment."

When you find a mistake in something you want to quote—for example, a wrong date or a misspelled word—you cannot change another writer's words. So that readers do not think you made the error, insert the Latin word *sic* (meaning "so" or "thus") in brackets next to the error. Doing this indicates that this is exactly what you found in the original.

The student wrote that "the Vikings came to North America long before Columbus's arrival in 1942 [*sic*]."

You can also use brackets to enclose very brief parenthetical material inside parentheses.

From that point on, Thomas Parker simply disappears. (His death [c. 1441] is unrecorded officially, but a gravestone marker is mentioned in a 1640 parish report.)

THE ELLIPSIS

29d Using the ellipsis

An ellipsis is a series of three spaced dots. In quotations, it is used to show that you have left out some of the writer's original words. Ellipses can also show hesitant or broken-off speech.

Ellipses can show that you have omitted words from material you are quoting. In Modern Languages Association (MLA) style, discussed in Chapter 34 of the *Simon & Schuster Handbook for Writers*, Third Canadian Edition, brackets are used to enclose an ellipsis that you insert into material you quote. The example in this section demonstrates MLA style. Section 29d of the *Simon & Schuster Handbook* gives further examples.

ORIGINAL

My aunt has survived the deaths of her husband and my parents in typical, if I may say so, West Indian fashion. Now in her 70s, and no longer principal of a New York City public school, she rises at 5 a.m. every day to prepare for another day of complicated duties as the volunteer principal of a small black private academy.

—JUNE JORDAN, "Thank You, America"

SOME MATERIAL USED IN A QUOTATION

My aunt has survived the deaths of her husband and my parents. [...] Now in her 70s, and no longer principal of a New York City public school, she rises at 5 a.m. every day to prepare for another day [...] as the volunteer principal of a small black private academy.

If an omission occurs at the beginning of your quoted words, you do not need to use an ellipsis. Also, you do not need to use an ellipsis at the end as long as you end with a complete sentence. If an ellipsis occurs after a complete sentence, use a fourth dot to represent the period of that sentence (for an example of this, see the first ellipsis in the above quotation).

Also, you can use ellipses to show broken-off speech.

"And, anyway, what do you know of him?"
"Nothing, That is why I ask you ..."
"I would prefer never to speak of him."

—UMBERTO ECO, *The Name of the Rose*

If you omit a line or more from a poetry quotation, use a full line of spaced dots, enclosed in square brackets.

THE SLASH

29e Using the slash

If you quote more than three lines of a poem in writing, set the poetry off with space and indentations as you would a prose quotation of more than four lines. For three lines or less, quote poetry—enclosed in quotation marks—in sentence format, with a slash to divide one line from the next. Leave a space on each side of the slash.

> Robert Frost makes an important point when he writes, "Before I built a wall I'd want to know / What I was walling in or walling out / And to whom I was like to give offense."

Capitalize and punctuate each line as it is in the original, with this exception: end your sentence with a period, even if the quoted line of poetry does not have one.

If you have to type numerical fractions, use the slash to separate numerator and denominator and a hyphen to separate a whole number from its fraction: *1/16, 1–2/3, 2/5, 3–7/8.*

You will not use word combinations such as *and/or* often, but where use is acceptable, separate the words with a slash. Leave no space before or after the slash. *He/she* is one option available to you in avoiding sexist language (see 11q and 21b).

Using Dashes, Parentheses, Brackets, Ellipses, and Slashes

Add dashes, parentheses, brackets, ellipses, or slashes as needed. If more than one kind of punctuation is possible, choose the one you think best. Be prepared to explain your decision.

EXAMPLE   "I'll pay by Do you accept cheques?"

"I'll pay by—Do you accept cheques?"

1. Niagara Falls is not the tallest waterfall in Canada Della Falls, British Columbia, is.
2. The next tallest waterfalls are 2 Takakkaw Falls, British Columbia, 3 Hunlen Falls, British Columbia, and 4 Panther Falls, Alberta.
3. Niagara Falls is relatively low it stands about one-seventh the height of Della Falls.
4. Greenland the largest island in the world was given its name by Eric the Red in 985.
5. The name was a masterstroke of publicity convincing settlers to come to what was actually an ice-covered wasteland.
6. Let's go to New Orleans for Mardi Oops! I have exams that week.
7. The most expensive part of a trip the airfare can be reduced by careful planning.
8. Contest rules say "The winner must appear to claim his her prize in person."
9. "Broadway my favourite street is a main artery of New York—the hardened artery," claimed Walter Winchell. [Note: my favourite street is not part of the quotation.]
10. Punctuate the shortened version of the following quotation: "Too often travel, instead of broadening the mind, merely lengthens the conversation," said Elizabeth Drew. "Too often travel merely lengthens the conversation," said Elizabeth Drew.
11. Northern Ontraio sic has some spectacular parks for camping.
12. Once a camper has been there, he she will always want to return.
13. I can say only one thing about camping I hate it.
14. We leave as soon as Have you seen the bug spray? we finish packing.
15. "Let's take Highway 69 across" "Are you crazy?"
16. Finding an inexpensive hotel motel isn't always easy.
17. Motels named from a combination of *motorist* and *hotel* are usually cheaper than regular hotels.
18. When travelling, always remember to a leave a schedule with friends, b carry as little cash as possible, and c use the hotel safe for valuables.

Name_____ Date _____

Using Assorted Punctuation

A: Add missing punctuation or change mistaken punctuation as needed. There may be more than one choice possible. If so, use the punctuation mark you think best. Be prepared to explain your answers.

The cheetah, is the fastest animal on earth, it can accelerate from 1.6 kilometres an hour to 65 kilometres an hour in under two seconds. Briefly reaching speeds of up to 110 kilometres an hour. Its stride, may during these bursts of speed, be as much as (7 metres). To help it run at these speeds: the cheetah is built unlike any of the other large cats—powerful heart, oversized liver, long, thin leg bones, relatively small teeth, and a muscular tail (used for balance. Unlike other cats; it cannot pull in its claws. They are blunted by constant contact (with the earth), and so are of little use, in the hunt. The cheetah—instead, makes use of a strong dewclaw on the inside of its front, legs to grab and hold down prey.

B.   Add whatever punctuation is needed to this completely unpunctuated paragraph. Be sure to add capital letters as needed, too. If more than one kind of punctuation is suitable, select the best one. Be prepared to explain your choices.

Have you ever wondered how instant coffee is made first the coffee beans are prepared as they would be for regular coffee they are roasted blended and ground at the factory workers brew great batches of coffee 800 to 900 kilograms at a time the coffee is then passed through tubes under great pressure at a high temperature this causes much of the water to boil away creating coffee liquor with a high percentage of solids at this point a decision must be made about what the final product will be powdered instant coffee or freeze dried coffee powdered instant coffee is made by heating the coffee liquor to 500°F 200°C in a large drier this boils away the remaining water and the powdered coffee is simply gathered from the bottom of the drier and packed if freeze dried coffee is being made the coffee liquor is frozen into pieces which are then broken into small granules the granules are placed in a vacuum box a box containing no air which turns the frozen water into steam which is removed all that is left are coffee solids some people say they prefer freeze dried coffee because the high temperature used to make regular instant coffee destroys some of the flavour either way the coffee is more convenient than home-brewed coffee

30 Capitals, Italics, Abbreviations, and Numbers

CAPITALS

30a Capitalizing the first word of a sentence

Always capitalize the first letter of the first word in a sentence, a question, or a command.

Pain is useful because it warns us of danger.

Does pain serve any purpose?

Never ignore severe pain.

Whether to capitalize the first letter of a complete sentence enclosed in parentheses depends upon whether that sentence stands alone or falls within the structure of another sentence. Those that stand alone start with a capital letter; those that fall within the structure of another sentence do not start with a capital letter.

I didn't know till years later that they called it the Cuban Missile Crisis. But I remember Castro. (We called him Castor Oil and were awed by his beard—beards were rare in those days.) We might not have worried so much (what would the Communists want with our small New Hampshire town?) except that we lived 10 miles from an air base.

—Joyce Maynard, "An 18-Year-Old Looks Back on Life"

30b Capitalizing listed items

A **run-in list** works its items into the structure of a sentence. When the items in a run-in list are complete sentences, capitalize the first letter of each item.

Three groups attended the town meeting on rent control: (1) Landlords brought proof of their expenses. (2) Tenants came to complain about poor maintenance. (3) Real estate agents came to see how the new rules would affect them.

When the items in a run-in list are not complete sentences, do not begin them with capital letters.

Three groups attended the town meeting on rent control: (1) landlords, (2) tenants, and (3) real estate agents.

30c Capitalizing the first letter of an introduced quotation

When you quote another person's words, do not capitalize the first quoted word if you have made the quoted words part of the structure of your own sentence.

Thomas Henry Huxley called science "trained and organized common sense."

However, if your own words in your sentence serve only to introduce quoted words or if you are directly quoting speech, capitalize the first letter of the quoted words.

According to Thomas Henry Huxley, "Science is nothing but trained and organized common sense."

Do not capitalize a partial quotation or a quotation you resume within a sentence.

"We," said Queen Victoria, "are not amused."

30d Capitalizing short words

Once upon a midnight dreary, while **I** pondered, weak and weary,...

—EDGAR ALLAN POE, "The Raven"

Temper, **O** fair Love, Love's impetuous rage.

—JOHN DONNE, "On His Mistress"

30e Capitalizing nouns and adjectives according to standard practice

Capitalize proper nouns (7a) and adjectives made from them.

PROPER NOUNS	PROPER ADJECTIVES
Korea	the Korean language
Hollywood	a Hollywood studio

Notice that the articles (*the, a, an*) are not capitalized.

Do not capitalize common nouns (nouns that name general classes of people, places, or things) unless they start a sentence: *a country, the movies, friends, planes.* Many common nouns are capitalized when names or titles are added to them. For example, *lake* is not ordinarily capitalized, but when a specific name is added, it is: *Lake Erie.* Without the specific name, however, even if the specific name is implied, the common noun is not capitalized.

I would like to visit the Welland Canal, because the canal is an important part of the St. Lawrence Seaway.

On the next page is a list to help you with capitalization questions. Although it cannot cover all possibilities, you can apply what you find in the list to similar items.

CAPITALIZATION GUIDE

	CAPITALS	LOWER-CASE LETTERS
Names	Bob Ojeda	
	Mother (name)	my mother (relationship)
Titles	the Prime Minister (usually reserved for the prime minister in office)	a prime minister
	Professor Edgar Day	the professor
Groups of Humankind	Caucasian (race)	white (or White)
	Negro (race)	black (or Black)
	Oriental (race)	
Organizations	Parliament	parliamentary
	the Rotary Club	the club
Places	St. John	
	India	
	the East (a region)	turn east (a direction)
	Main Street	the street
Buildings	Carr High School	the high school
	the China Lights	the restaurant
Scientific Terms	Mars, Martian	the moon, the sun
	the Milky Way galaxy	the galaxy
Languages	Portuguese	
School Courses	Chemistry 342	the chemistry course
Names of Things	the *Times-Transcript*	the newspaper
	Memorial University	the university
	the Toyota Sienna	
Time Names	Friday	spring, summer,
	August	fall, autumn, winter
Historical Periods	World War II	the war
	the Great Depression	the depression (any other depression)
Religious Terms	God	a god, a goddess
	Buddhism	
	the Torah	
Letter Parts	Dear Ms. Tauber:	
	Sincerely yours,	
Titles of Works	"The Lottery"	
	Catcher in the Rye	
Acronyms	CRTC	
	NATO	
	CUPE	

ITALICS (UNDERLINING)

In printed material, **roman type** is the standard. Type that slants to the right is called **italic.** Words in italics contrast with standard roman type, so italics create an emphasis readers can see. Most word-processing programs give you the option of italics; in handwritten manuscripts, underline to indicate italics.

30f **Using standard practice for italicizing titles and other words, letters, or numbers**

Some titles require italics (or underlining): long written works, names of ships, trains, and some aircraft, film titles, titles of television series. Italics also call readers' attention to words in languages other than English and to letters, numbers, and words used in ways other than for their meaning. The list below shows these uses. It also shows (and explains) some titles that call for quotation marks and some names and titles neither italicized nor in quotation marks.

GUIDE TO USE OF ITALICS (OR UNDERLINING)

TITLES

ITALICIZE OR UNDERLINE	DO NOT ITALICIZE OR UNDERLINE
Jane of Lantern Hill [a novel]	your own paper's title
Farther West [a play]	
Who Do You Think You Are? [a collection of short stories]	"Royal Beatings" [one story in the collection]
Simon & Schuster Handbook for Writers [a book]	"Writing Research" [one chapter in the book]
Active Voice: An Anthology of Canadian, American and Commonwealth Prose [a collection of essays]	"The Calgary Stampede" [one essay in the collection]
The Iliad [a long poem]	"Ark Anatomical" [a short poem]
The Lotus Eaters [a film]	
Equinox [a magazine]	"Nanook Passage" [an article in the magazine]
The Barber of Seville [title of an opera]	Concerto in B-flat Minor [identification of a musical work by form, number, and key. Use neither quotation marks nor italics (underlining).]
Symphonie Fantastique [title of a long musical work]	
The Road to Avonlea [a television series]	"After the Honeymoon" [an episode of a television series]
The Visit [a CD or tape]	"Greensleeves" [a song or a single selection on a CD or tape] ➜

GUIDE TO UNDERLINING *(continued)*

TITLES

the *Brandon Sun* [a newspaper. Note: Even if *The* is part of the title printed on a newspaper, do not use a capital letter and do not italicize (or underline) it in your writing. In MLA and CM documentation, omit the word *The*. In APA and CBE documentation, keep *The*.]

DO NOT ITALICIZE OR UNDERLINE

Lotus 1-2-3 [software program names are neither italicized nor enclosed in quotation marks]

OTHER WORDS

the *Intrepid* [a ship; don't italicize preceding initials like U.S.S. or H.M.S.]

Voyager 2 [names of specific aircraft, spacecraft, and satellites]

summa cum laude [term in a language other than English]

What does *our* imply? [a word referred to as such]

the *abc's;* confusing *3*'s and *8*'s [letters and numbers referred to as themselves]

aircraft carrier [a general class of ship]

Boeing 747 [general names shared by classes of aircraft, spacecraft, and satellites]

burrito, chutzpah [widely used and commonly understood words from languages other than English]

Use italics sparingly for special emphasis

Instead of counting on italics (or underlining) to deliver impact, try to make word choices and sentence structures convey emphasis.

ABBREVIATIONS

Using abbreviations with time and symbols

What you are writing and who will read that writing should help you to determine whether to use an abbreviation or a spelled-out word. A few abbreviations are standard in any writing circumstance.

A.M. AND P.M. WITH SPECIFIC TIMES

8:20 a.m. or 8:20 A.M.   9:35 p.m. or 9:35 P.M.

A.D. AND B.C. WITH SPECIFIC YEARS

A.D. 576 [A.D. precedes the year.]   33 B.C. [B.C. follows the year.]

Symbols are seldom used in the body of papers written for courses in the humanities. You can use a percent symbol (%) or a cent sign (¢), for example, in a table, graph, or other illustration, but in the body of the paper spell out *percent* and *cent*. You can, however, use a dollar sign with specific dollar amounts: *$1.29, $10 million.*

Technical and scientific styles require writers to abbreviate many terms and measurements. Many writers abbreviate SI (metric) units in almost any context.

Let common sense and your readers' needs guide you. If you mention temperatures once or twice in a paper, spell them out: *thirty degrees, minus twenty-six degrees.* If you mention temperatures throughout a paper, use figures (see 30l) and symbols: *30°, −26°.*

30i Using abbreviations with titles, names and terms, and addresses

TITLES OF ADDRESS BEFORE NAMES

Dr. P. C. Smith   Mr. Scott Kamiel

Ms. Rachel Wang   Mrs. Ann Wenter

ACADEMIC DEGREES AFTER NAMES

Jean Loft, Ph.D.   Peter Kim, J.D.

Asha Rohra, M.D.   Verna Johnson, D.D.

❖ ABBREVIATION CAUTION: Do not use a title of address before a name *and* academic degree after a name. Use one or the other. ❖

If you use a long name or term often in a paper, you can abbreviate it. The first time you use it, give the full term, with the abbreviation in parentheses right after the spelled-out form. After that you can use the abbreviation alone.

Canadian University Services Overseas (CUSO) is often compared to the U.S. Peace Corps, but CUSO has never been an arm of the government.

You can abbreviate *U.S.* or *U.K.* as modifiers (*the U.S. economy*), but spell out *United States* and *United Kingdom* when you use them as nouns.

If you include a full address—street, city, and province—in the body of a paper, you can use the postal abbreviation for the province's name, but spell out any other combination of a city and a province.

| NO | Toronto, ON, appears to have the largest Aboriginal community in Canada. |

| YES | Toronto, Ontario, appears to have the largest Aboriginal community in Canada. |

30j Using abbreviations in documentation according to standard practice

Documentation means giving the source of any material that you quote (see 31c), paraphrase (see 31d), or summarize (see 31e). Styles of documentation are discussed in Chapter 34 of the *Simon & Schuster Handbook;* useful scholarly abbreviations, as well as abbreviations that commonly appear in documentation, are listed in Chapter 30 of the *Handbook.*

30k Using *etc.*

Etc. is the abbreviation for the Latin *et cetera,* meaning *and the rest.* Do not use it in academic writing; acceptable substitutes are *and the like, and so on,* or *and so forth.*

> The Greenlawn Resort offers water sports such as snorkelling, scuba diving, windsurfing, **and the like** [not *etc.*].

NUMBERS

30l Using spelled-out numbers

Depending on how often numbers appear in a paper and what they refer to, you will sometimes express numbers in words and sometimes in figures. The guidelines here are those used in the humanities. For the guidelines that other disciplines follow, ask your instructor or consult style manuals written for specific fields.

If numerical exactness is not a prime purpose in your paper and you mention numbers only a few times, spell out numbers that can be expressed in one or two words.

> Most people need to take the road test for their driver's licence **two or three** times.

> Eating one extra slice of bread a day can lead to a weight gain of about **three** kilograms per year.

❖ HYPHENATION ALERT: Use a hyphen between spelled-out two-word numbers from *twenty-one* through *ninety-nine.* ❖

If you use numbers frequently in a paper, spell out numbers from *one* to *nine* and use figures for numbers *10* and above.

two shirts	12 blocks
third base	21st year

Never start a sentence with a figure. If a sentence starts with a number, spell it out or revise so that the number does not come first.

Thirteen is known as a baker's dozen because bakers used to give an extra roll or pastry to customers who placed large orders.

Two thousand was the year celebrated as the start of the new millennium.

The world celebrated the start of the new millennium in 2000.

30m Using numbers according to standard practice

Give specific numbers—dates, addresses, measurements, identification numbers—in figures.

GUIDE FOR USING SPECIFIC NUMBERS	
Dates	August 6, 1941 1732–1845 34 B.C. to A.D. 230
Addresses	10 Downing Street 237 North 8th Street (*or* 237 North Eighth Street) Calgary, AB T2E 1A1
Times	8:09 a.m.; 3:30 (*but* half past three, quarter to seven, six o'clock)
Decimals and Fractions	5.55; 98.6; 3.1415; 7/8; 12-1/4 (*but* one-quarter, one-half, two-thirds)
Chapters and Pages	Chapter 27; page 245; p. 475; pp. 660–62
Scores and Statistics	a 6–0 score; a 5 to 3 ratio; 29 percent
Identification Numbers	94.4 on the FM dial; call 1–212–555–0000
Measurements	2 metres or two metres—or 2 m (*not* two m); 80.6 kilometres per hour; 2 level teaspoons; 3 litres; 8½" x 11" paper or 8½ x 11-inch paper
Act, Scene, and Line Numbers	act 4, scene 2, lines 75–79
Temperatures	43°F; –4°C
Money	$1.2 billion; $3.41; 25 cents *or* 25¢

30-1

Using Capital Letters

A: Select the passage in each pair that needs capital letters. Then rewrite the passage correctly on the line provided.

EXAMPLE (a) going to the city next summer

          (b) going to winnipeg in june

          (b) going to Winnipeg in June

1. (a) prime minister laurier
   (b) the seventh prime minister

2. (a) the ancient gods
   (b) god's love

3. (a) the board of broadcast governors
   (b) a government board

4. (a) a meeting in the afternoon
   (b) a meeting on friday

5. (a) my favourite aunt
   (b) my aunt clara

6. (a) when i graduate
   (b) when we graduate

7. (a) the musical ride
   (b) ceremonial ride to music

8. (a) mother teresa
   (b) my mother

9. (a) dinner at a fine restaurant
   (b) dinner at the steak palace

10. (a) english 202
    (b) a literature course

11. (a) across the main street
    (b) across main street

12. (a) the edmonton oilers
    (b) a hockey team

13. (a) a group of seven artists
    (b) the group of seven

14. (a) west of town
    (b) a town in the west

15. (a) a college in british columbia
    (b) a college on the coast

16. (a) "the gift of the maji"
    (b) a story about sacrifice

17. (a) learning a second language
    (b) learning french

18. (a) victoria township medical centre
    (b) the local hospital

Name_____ Date _____

19. (a) stars shining in the sky
    (b) the moon and venus shining in the sky

    _____

20. (a) the st. lawrence river
    (b) the polluted river

    _____

B: Rewrite these sentences on the lines provided, adding or deleting capital letters as needed. If no capitals are needed, write *correct* on the line.

EXAMPLE My uncle Peter and my Aunt are visiting.

      My uncle Peter and my aunt are visiting.

1. The Spring semester starts in february.

_____

2. They live ten kilometres North of Elm street.

_____

3. The Hotel has 450 rooms.

_____

4. Green, the Ambassador, had a meeting with Foreign Minister Ramirez.

_____

5. I want to visit lake Louise to go Skiing.

_____

6. The bible is full of great adventures.

_____

7. They plan to open an italian restaurant Downtown.

_____

8. The new democratic party believes in the democratic system.

_____

9. The teachers' union campaigned for better textbooks.

_____

10. Springfield high school has a large pta.

_____

11. Texans will always Remember the Alamo.

_____

12. Travelling around the cape of Good Hope is dangerous.

_____

13. Rembrandt's "Aristotle contemplating the bust of Homer" is one of his best known paintings.

_____

14. The Manitoba Theatre centre is in Winnipeg.

_____

15. Tickets to the grey cup were not available at the Stadium.

_____

EXERCISE 30-2
(30g)

Using Italics

A: Select the passage in each of these pairs that needs italics added. Then rewrite the passage correctly on the line provided, using underlining to indicate italics.

EXAMPLE   (a) My favourite movie is a mystery.

(b) My favourite movie is Citizen Kane.

(b) My favourite movie is <u>Citizen Kane</u>.

1. (a) a book about war and peace
   (b) War and Peace

_____

2. (a) the humour of Bill Cosby
   (b) The Bill Cosby Show

_____

3. (a) London Free Press
   (b) a London, Ontario, newspaper

_____

4. (a) a cruise ship
   (b) The Queen Elizabeth II

_____

5. (a) a space ship
   (b) the U.S.S. Enterprise

_____

Name_____ Date _____

6. (a) We are Homo sapiens.
   (b) We are human beings.

   _____

7. (a) pay particular attention
   (b) nota bene

   _____

8. (a) Many words have the common root, cycle.
   (b) Many words come from the same source.

   _____

9. (a) Don't tease your pets.
   (b) Never tease a hungry crocodile.

   _____

10. (a) The Orient Express was the setting of a famous mystery novel.
    (b) VIA Rail carries passengers across Canada.

    _____

B: Rewrite these sentences on the lines provided, adding italics (underlining) as needed.
   If no italics are needed, write *correct* on the line.

EXAMPLE   How do you pronounce chamois?

   How do you pronounce <u>chamois</u>? [sham'ē]

1. The word cool has many meanings.

   _____

2. The new hospital is shaped like the letter H.

   _____

3. Scientifically the chimpanzee is called Pan troglodytes and the gorilla is Gorilla gorilla.

   _____

4. You bought us tickets to see Les Misérables? Merci beaucoup.

   _____

5. The H.M.S. Bounty was a real ship.

   _____

6. The troubles of its crew are told in the book Mutiny on the Bounty.

   _____

7. I subscribe to a Regina newspaper.

   _____

8. Clifford Sifton, a key member of Prime Minister Laurier's cabinet, was the owner of an important newspaper, the Manitoba Free Press.

_____

9. Sifton encouraged immigration to the Canadian Prairies, which he publicized with the expression "the last, best West."

_____

10. Years later, the Hollywood movie Rose Marie (1936), with its singing Mounties and maidens, also publicized the Canadian Prairies.

_____

Using Abbreviations

EXERCISE **30-3**
(30h–i)

A. Rewrite each of these sentences, replacing inappropriate abbreviations with their full forms. If a sentence is correct as given, write *correct* on the line.

EXAMPLE   It takes years to become a dr.

    *It takes years to become a doctor.*_____

1. The Chang bros. are opening a fishing charter co.

_____

2. It will be off pier no. 17, not far from L.A., Calif.

_____

3. At the aquarium we saw giant tortoises that were more than 100 yrs. old.

_____

4. Easter always falls on the Sun. following the 1st full moon in spring—either in Mar. or in Apr.

_____

5. What did you get for Xmas?

_____

6. Everyone ought to know the story of Wm. Lyon Mackenzie King, 10th PM of Canada.

_____

7. He is mentioned in my textbook on the hist. of poli. sci. and econ.

_____

8. The prof. says the midterm will cover chaps. 1-5.

_____

9. The midterm & final each count 40%.

_____

Name_____ Date _____

10. The quarterback picked up 160 yds. in passing in the first ½.

_____

11. Some people will do anything for a few $'s.

_____

12. A kilo. equals 2.2 lbs.

_____

13. The counsellor had an MSW degree from UBC.

_____

14. She had put herself through school working as an assist. mgr. in a fast-food rest.

_____

15. Mr. and Mrs. McDonald live on Maple Ave. in Corner Brook, Nfld.

_____

B. Rewrite each of these sentences, replacing inappropriate full forms with standard abbreviations. It may be necessary to slightly rearrange some sentences.

EXAMPLE   Canadians celebrate their national day on the first day of July.

Canadians celebrate their national day on July 1st.
_____

1. The bank's loan officer awoke at 2:00 *ante meridiem.*

_____

2. He was thinking about the family that had applied for a loan of thirty thousand dollars.

_____

3. Doctor Jones had given them a letter of reference.

_____

4. Bill Smith, Chartered Accountant, had also sent a letter.

_____

5. For collateral, they offered a Spanish doubloon dated *Anno Domini* 1642 .

_____

6. The doubloon had been in the family since nineteen nineteen.

_____

7. Mister and Missus Grossman wanted to use the money to set up a company to make precision measuring devices.

_____

8. They already had a contract with the National Aeronautics and Space Administration.

_____

9. The banker wanted to give his okay, but loans this big had to be co-authorized by the bank president.

_____

10. However, the president had taken her Self-Contained-Underwater-Breathing-Apparatus and gone on a vacation.

_____

> **EXERCISE 30-4**
> **(30k, l)**

Using Figures

Rewrite each of these sentences, replacing inappropriate figures with words or inappropriate words with figures. If a sentence is correct as given, write *correct* on the line.

EXAMPLE   He is six feet four and a half inches.

> *He is 6'4½"*

1. There are a hundred and seven women in the first-year class at the law school this year.

_____

2. Ten years ago there were only 47.

_____

3. 1/3 the faculty is female now compared with 1/10 then.

_____

4. Many students share apartments in a building that charges nine hundred dollars for two rooms, $1400 for three rooms, and $1850 for 4 rooms.

_____

5. The semester begins on September fourteenth.

_____

6. The entering class will graduate on June first, nineteen ninety-nine.

_____

7. Entrance requirements are on pages thirty to thirty-five.

_____

8. The average law student is expected to drink two point five litres of coffee a day over the next 3 years.

_____

9. The drop-out rate is about twenty-nine percent.

_____

10. The law school is located at Fifteen Clark Street.

_____

31 Using Sources and Avoiding Plagiarism

For many writing assignments, you are expected to draw upon outside sources—books, articles, videos, interviews, and online databases—to explain and support your ideas. **Paraphrasing, summarizing,** and **quoting** are three techniques that writers use (1) to take notes from sources and (2) to incorporate into their own writing the ideas and sometimes the words of sources.

GUIDELINES FOR USING OUTSIDE SOURCES IN YOUR WRITING

1. Apply the concepts and skills of critical thinking, reading, and writing.

2. Avoid plagiarism by always giving credit for ideas and words not originally yours.

3. Document sources accurately and completely.

4. Know how and when to use the techniques of paraphrase, summary, and quotation.

31a Avoiding plagiarism

To plagiarize is to present another person's words or ideas as if they were your own. Plagiarism is stealing. It is a serious offence that can be grounds for failure of a course or expulsion from a college or university. Plagiarism can be intentional, as when you deliberately copy or borrow from the work of other people in your writing without mentioning and documenting the source. Plagiarism can be unintentional—but no less serious an offence—if you are unaware of what must be acknowledged and how to go about documenting. All postsecondary students are expected to know what plagiarism is and how to avoid it. If you are not absolutely clear about what is involved, take time *now* to learn the rules so that you never expose yourself to charges of plagiarism.

You are not expected to document (give the source of) *common knowledge—* for example, that Columbus's ships landed in the Americas in 1492. You might have to look up the date on which Neil Armstrong walked on the moon, but such material is common knowledge nevertheless. Similarly, you should not document *personal knowledge*—for example, that your grandmother was born June 6, 1916—or your own original thinking.

What should you document? You must acknowledge the source of any words you quote, paraphrase, or summarize. Along with your documentation of quotations, you must always use quotation marks or, if the material is more than three lines, an indented format. In addition, you must give your source when you present someone else's ideas in your own words.

To prevent plagiarism when taking notes, follow these three steps: (1) Become familiar with the documentation style you will need and write a bibliographic card for each source. (Web pages need the same level of documentation as other sources.) (2) Record complete documentation information as you go along. (3) Use a consistent notetaking system that distinguishes between material paraphrased or summarized from a source, quotations from a source, and your own thoughts.

31b Understanding the concept of documentation

Basic to paraphrasing, summarizing, and quoting is documentation—acknowledging your sources by giving full and accurate information about the author, title, and date of publication, and related facts. For information about how to document properly in a particular discipline, ask your instructor or refer to the *Simon & Schuster Handbook for Writers.*

31c Using quotations effectively

Quotations have special impact in your writing. While paraphrase and summary put one step between your source and your readers, quotations give your readers the chance to encounter directly the words of your source. A carefully chosen, brief quotation from an expert can establish the validity of what you say.

GUIDELINES FOR USING QUOTATIONS

1. Use quotations from authorities in your subject to *support* what you say, not for your thesis statement or main points.
2. Select quotations that fit your message.
3. Choose a quotation only if
   a. its language is particularly appropriate or distinctive;
   b. its idea is particularly hard to paraphrase accurately;
   c. the authority of the source is especially important to support your material;
   d. the source's words are open to more than one interpretation, so your reader needs to see the original.
4. Do not use quotations for more than a quarter of the text of your paper; rely mostly on paraphrase and summary.
5. Quote accurately.
6. Integrate quotations smoothly into your prose, paying special attention to the verbs that help you to do so effectively (see 31f).
7. Avoid plagiarism. Always document your source. Enclose quotations of four lines or fewer in quotation marks. Even if you do not use the entire quotation in your paper, the quotation marks signal that all words they enclose are words quoted directly from a source.

31d Paraphrasing accurately

When you **paraphrase**, you restate in your own words a passage written by another author. Your paraphrasings offer an account of what various authorities have to say, not in their words but in yours. These ideas give substance and believability to your message. Also, paraphrasing forces you to read closely and to get the words' precise meaning into your notes. To do so, use words that come naturally to you, even if it means using more words than the author does. Use synonyms for the author's words wherever you can, but make sure that the sentences in your paraphrase make sense.

GUIDELINES FOR WRITING A PARAPHRASE

---

1. Say what the source says, but no more.
2. Reproduce the source's order of ideas and emphases.
3. Use your own words and phrasing to restate the message. If certain synonyms are awkward, quote the material—but do this very sparingly.
4. Read over your sentences to make sure that they make sense and do not distort the source's meaning.
5. Expect your material to be as long as, and possibly longer than, the original.
6. Use verbs that help you integrate paragraphs smoothly into your prose (see 31f).
7. **Avoid plagiarism.**
8. As you take notes, write down all documentation facts so that you can document your source when you use it in your writing.

31e Summarizing accurately

Summary reviews the main points of a passage. A summary gives you a written overview of what you have read. It is probably the most frequently used device in notetaking for papers.

To summarize a paragraph, a passage, or a chapter, you isolate its main points and write a general statement about each topic. A formal summary is composed of these sentences tied together with appropriate transitions. In an informal summary for your notes, you can worry less about transitions because the notes are meant only to give you the essence of the source.

GUIDELINES FOR WRITING A SUMMARY

---

1. Identify the main points, and condense them without losing the essence of the material.
2. Use your own words to condense the message.
3. Keep your summary short.
4. Use verbs effectively to integrate summaries into your prose (see 31f).
5. **Avoid plagiarism.**
6. As you take notes, write down all documentation facts so that you can document your source accurately and avoid plagiarism.

Using verbs effectively to integrate source material into your prose

Many verbs can help you work quotations, paraphrases, and summaries smoothly into your writing. Be aware that some of these verbs imply your position toward the source material (for example, *argue, complain, concede, deny, grant, insist,* and *reveal*); others are general or neutral in meaning (*comment, describe, explain, note, say,* and *write*). Choose them according to the meaning that you want your sentences to deliver.

VERBS USEFUL FOR INTEGRATING QUOTATIONS, PARAPHRASES, AND SUMMARIES				
agree	complain	emphasize	note	see
analyze	concede	explain	observe	show
argue	conclude	find	offer	speculate
ask	consider	grant	point out	state
assert	contend	illustrate	refute	suggest
believe	declare	imply	report	suppose
claim	deny	insist	reveal	think
comment	describe	maintain	say	write

31-1

Quoting

A. Select the portion of this passage that could be usefully quoted in a report. Carefully and accurately copy that portion of the passage. Be prepared to explain why quoting, rather than summarizing or paraphrasing, is called for.

The problem with cosmetics exists only when women feel invisible or inadequate without them. The problem with working out exists only if women hate ourselves when we don't. When a woman is forced to adorn herself to buy a hearing, when she needs her grooming in order to protect her identity, when she goes hungry in order to keep her job, when she must attract a lover so that she can take care of her children, that is exactly what makes "beauty" hurt. Because what hurts women about the beauty myth is not adornment, or expressed sexuality, or time spent grooming, or the desire to attract a lover. Many mammals groom, and every culture uses adornment. "Natural" and "unnatural" are not the terms in question. The actual struggle is between pain and pleasure, freedom and compulsion.

—Naomi Wolf, *The Beauty Myth*

B. Select any sample paragraph in Chapter 4 and write a paraphrase that includes the most important passages as quotations.

C. Select a paragraph from one of your textbooks or any other nonfiction work, and take notes that combine paraphrase with careful, selective quotation.

Paraphrasing

A. Paraphrase the following paragraph.

Though the words are often used interchangeably, branding and advertising are not the same process. Advertising any given product is only one part of branding's grand plan, as are sponsorship and logo licensing. Think of the brand as the core meaning of the modern corporation, and of the advertisement as one vehicle used to convey that meaning to the world. The first mass-marketing companies, starting in the second half of the nineteenth century, had more to do with advertising than with branding as we understand it today. Faced with a range of recently invented products—the radio, phonograph, car, light bulb and so on—advertisers had more pressing tasks than creating a brand identity for any given corporation; first, they had to change the way people lived their lives. Ads had to inform consumers about the existence of some new invention, then convince them that their lives would be better if they used, for example, cars instead of wagons, telephones instead of mail and electric light instead of oil lamps. Many of these new products bore brand names—some of which are still around today—but these were almost incidental.

—Naomi Klein, *No Logo*

Name_____ Date _____

B.   Select any sample paragraph in Chapter 4 and paraphrase it.

C.   Select a paragraph from one of your textbooks or any other nonfiction work and paraphrase it.

Summarizing

A.   Summarize the following paragraph.

During the past decade, women breached the power structure; meanwhile, eating disorders rose exponentially and cosmetic surgery became the fastest-growing medical specialty. During the past five years, consumer spending doubled, pornography became the main media category, ahead of legitimate films and records combined, and thirty-three thousand American women told researchers that they would rather lose ten to fifteen pounds than achieve any other goal. More women have more money and power and scope and legal recognition than we have ever had before; but in terms of how we feel about ourselves *physically*, we may actually be worse off than our unliberated grandmothers. Recent research consistently shows that inside the majority of the West's controlled, attractive, successful working women, there is a secret "underlife" poisoning our freedom; infused with notions of beauty, is a dark vein of self-hatred, physical obsessions, terror of aging, and dread of lost control.

—NAOMI WOLF, *The Beauty Myth*

B.   Select any sample paragraph in Chapter 4 and summarize it.

C.   Select a paragraph from one of your textbooks or any other nonfiction work and summarize it.

37 Comparing the Different Disciplines

37a Recognizing similarities and differences among the disciplines

Each field of study has its own way of looking at the world. The humanities—philosophy, arts, and languages—are concerned with human individuality. The social sciences, on the other hand, focus on group behaviour, while the natural sciences report observations of natural phenomena. As you study and write in each of the academic disciplines, you can learn their specialized vocabularies and experience the power of these different ways of thinking.

In writing across the disciplines, you will employ many transferable skills and principles. For example, regardless of the field of study, you will need to consider purpose, audience, and tone. You will also need to develop paragraphs thoroughly, reason well, and use correct spelling and grammar. However, each discipline also has its unique requirements, and you should be aware of these:

1. Conduct primary and secondary research as appropriate to the discipline.
2. Select a style of documentation appropriate to the discipline.
3. Follow the manuscript format requirements of the discipline.
4. Use specialized language as needed for the discipline.

1 Conducting research and selecting sources according to each discipline

Research methods differ among the disciplines where sources are concerned. This is true of both **primary sources** (those that offer firsthand exposure to information) and **secondary sources** (articles and books that draw on primary sources.

In the humanities, existing documents are the primary sources, and it is the task of the researcher to analyze and interpret them directly. Secondary sources represent other writers' efforts to do this.

> **Please note:** There are no *Workbook* exercises that correspond to Chapters 32–36 of the *Simon & Schuster Handbook for Writers*, Third Canadian Edition.

In the social and natural sciences, primary research means designing and carrying out experiments involving direct observation. Researchers must either conduct the experiments themselves or read firsthand reports by those who have conducted them. Secondary sources in these disciplines summarize and synthesize findings and draw parallels that offer new insights.

2 Selecting a style of documentation appropriate to each discipline

Styles of **documentation**—the way in which writers give credit to the sources they have used—also differ among the disciplines.

In the humanities, most fields of study use the documentation style of the Modern Languages Association (MLA) as explained and illustrated in section 34c of the *Simon & Schuster Handbook for Writers*, Third Canadian Edition. CM (Chicago Manual) style is sometimes used as an alternative (see section 34e).

In the social sciences, most fields use APA (American Psychological Association) style (see section 34d) in the *Simon & Schuster Handbook for Writers*, Third Canadian Edition. In the natural sciences, documentation styles vary widely (see section 34f).

In quoting online sources, Columbia online style (COS) is gaining popularity (see section 34g in the *Simon & Schuster Handbook for Writers*, Third Canadian Edition).

Name_____ Date _____

Sources and Documentation

A. Look at the Works Cited list for one of the secondary sources you are using. Underline those you feel might help you understand the secondary source—and hence the primary source—better. Locate and read at least one additional secondary source.

B. Find out the correct method of documentation for the types of secondary sources used most often in your discipline.

38 Writing About Literature

Literature is the result of people's impulses to discover and communicate meaning by telling stories, acting out events, and singing or chanting. It encompasses fiction, drama, and poetry.

38a Understanding methods of inquiry into literature

All questions about literature assume close reading of a literary work. However, you should read a question carefully for the approach it asks you to take. You may be asked to explain the literal meaning of a piece or to describe its historical context. Usually, however, you will be asked to read between and beyond the lines of a story, play, or poem. You may be asked to discuss poetic techniques or to compare and contrast dramatic characters. You may even be asked for your personal response to a work. At all times, keep in mind the difference between summary (merely restating what is in the material) and synthesis (reflecting on what you have summarized, making connections, and discovering what you have to say).

38b Understanding purposes and practices in writing about literature

Rules concerning when to use the first person (*I, we, our*) and when to use the third person (*he, she, it, they*) are becoming less rigid. Be sure to ask about your instructor's requirements.

You should use the present tense when discussing what occurs within a literary work. Reserve the past tense for historical events or biographical information about the author.

38c Using documentation style for writing about literature

In writing about literature, you should always document your sources. The most commonly used documentation style is that of the Modern Language Association (MLA). The styles of the American Psychological Association (APA) and the University of Chicago Press (CM) are also sometimes used. These styles are covered in detail in Chapter 34 in the *Simon & Schuster Handbook for Writers,* Third Canadian Edition.

38d Writing different types of papers about literature

Just as there are different types of literary inquiry, there are different types of papers about literature.

1 Writing reaction papers

In a **reaction paper**, you may write about why you did or did not enjoy a piece of writing, how it does or does not relate to your personal experience, or what it made you think about. As evidence for your reactions, you should use quotations from the work.

2 Writing book reports

A **report** will use summary techniques to inform readers about the content of a book, play, or poem. This should be followed by your discussion of the work's purpose, significance, structure, and audience.

3 Writing interpretations

An **interpretation** will discus either what you think the author means by the work or what the work means personally to you.

Questions to ask when writing an interpretation paper:

1. What is the overall theme of the work?
2. How are the particular parts of the work related to this theme?
3. If patterns exist in parts of the work, what do they mean?
4. What is the author's message?
5. Why does the work end as it does?

4 **Writing analyses**

In a **literary analysis**, you will discuss the ideas and insights you have after close reading of an entire work. These will emerge from the patterns and connections you see as you read the work thoroughly, again and again. Make notes as you go along so that you have a record of both the patterns you see and your reflections on them.

Major aspects of literary works to analyze:

1.	Plot	The events and their sequence
2.	Theme	Central idea or message
3.	Structure	Organization and relationship of parts to the whole
4.	Characterization	Traits, thoughts, and actions of the people involved
5.	Setting	Time and place of the action
6.	Point of View	The perspective from which the material is presented
7.	Style	How words and sentence structures are used
8.	Imagery	Pictures created by the words
9.	Tone	Attitude of the author toward the subject
10.	Figures of Speech	Nonliteral use of words for enhanced vividness
11.	Symbolism	Underlying meaning of words and images
12.	Rhythm	Beat or metre of the words
13.	Rhyme	Repetition of similar sounds for effect

Name_____ Date _____

Verb Tenses and Analysis

A. Look at a draft paper you are writing. Check that present and past tenses have been used correctly and consistently.

B. Consider a literary work you have been asked to analyze. What aspects of the work seem most accessible to you as you try to interpret it?

39 Writing in the Social Sciences and Natural Sciences

SOCIAL SCIENCES

The social sciences focus on the behaviour of people as individuals and in groups. They include disciplines such as economics, education, geography, political sciences, psychology, and sociology. History is sometimes considered a social science; otherwise, it is treated as part of the humanities.

39a Understanding methods of inquiry in the social sciences

Observation is a common method of inquiry in the social sciences. Tools such as tape recorders or cameras may be used as part of observation. In a report of your observations, be sure to say what tools or equipment you used, as they may have affected the outcome.

Interviewing is another common method of inquiry used by social scientists. If you interview, remember that it is not a completely reliable way to gather information. Interviewees may recall things inaccurately or try to present themselves in a favourable light. Interviewing as many people as possible and cross-checking your information can help to rectify this.

Note: During observation or an interview, you may wish to use abbreviations to speed your notetaking. Be sure to write out the meanings of these abbreviations so that you can understand your notes later on. Also, before any interview, master your equipment so that mechanical problems do not hold you up.

Questionnaires are another useful method of inquiry in the social sciences. Be sure to circulate them to enough people, however. You do not want to reach conclusions based on too small a sample of responses.

Guidelines for writing questions for a questionnaire:

1. Define what you want to find out and formulate appropriate questions.
2. Phrase questions so that they are easy to understand.
3. Use appropriate, straightforward language.
4. Ensure that your choice of words does not imply what you want to hear.

5. Avoid questions that invite one-word answers about complex matters.

6. Test a draft of the questionnaire on a small group of people and revise as necessary.

39b Understanding writing purposes and practices in the social sciences

Summary and **synthesis** (see 5f) are fundamental strategies for analytical writing in the social sciences. **Analysis** (see 4f-6 and 5a) is useful for breaking problems down into their constituent parts. Social scientists may also use **analogy** (likening an unfamiliar idea to a familiar one—see 4f-8—for clarity's sake. **Definition of terms** is particularly important. Social scientists must be very clear about the boundaries of what they mean by a particular word.

In social science courses, it is acceptable to use the first person when writing about your own reactions and experiences. However, your goal is usually to be a neutral observer, so most of the time writers use the third person.

Note: Style manuals for the social sciences recommend using the active voice whenever possible.

39c Using documentation style in the social sciences

The most commonly used documentation style for writing in the social sciences is that of the American Psychological Association (APA). APA style uses parenthetical references in the body of a paper and a reference list at the end (see section 34d in the *Simon & Schuster Handbook for Writers*, Third Canadian Edition). Chicago Manual style (CM) is also sometimes used (see section 34e).

39d Writing different types of papers in the social sciences

Case studies and research papers are the two major types of papers written in the social sciences.

1 Writing case studies in the social sciences

A case study is an intensive study of one group or individual. You should describe situations as a neutral observer, refraining from interpreting them unless your assignment states that you can add an interpretation at the end. Be careful not to present something as fact when it is really your interpretation or opinion of something you have seen.

Most case studies about an individual or a group will present the following:

1. Basic identifying information
2. History
3. Observations of behaviour
4. Conclusions (and perhaps recomendations)

2 Writing research papers in the social sciences

Research papers in the social sciences can be based on primary field research or on secondary sources (articles and books that present the findings of other people's research).

NATURAL SCIENCES

39e Understanding ways of gathering information in the sciences

The natural sciences include disciplines such as astronomy, biology, chemistry, geology, and physics. Scientists form and test hypotheses in order to explain cause and effect as systematically and objectively as possible.

The **scientific method** is a procedure for gathering information related to a specific hypothesis.

Guidelines for using the scientific method:

1. Formulate a hypothesis—a tentative, specific explanation for a scientific phenomenon.
2. Read and summarize previously published information related to your hypothesis.
3. Plan and outline a method of investigation to test your hypothesis.
4. Experiment, exactly following the investigative procedures you have outlined.
5. Observe closely the results of the experiment, making careful notes.
6. Analyze the results. If they prove the hypothesis to be false, rework the investigation. If they confirm the hypothesis, say so.
7. Write a report of your research. At the end, you may suggest additional hypotheses for investigation.

39f Understanding writing purposes and practices in the natural sciences

The techniques of **summary** and **synthesis** are fundamental to writing in the natural sciences. Exactness is also important. Scientific readers expect descriptions of procedures so precise that they could, if they wished, replicate the experiment and come up with the same findings. Completeness matters, too. Without complete information, a reader can misunderstand the writer's message and reach a wrong conclusion.

Because science writing depends on objective observation—and because it is the experiment, not the experimenter, that is important—scientists generally avoid using the first person in their writing.

Science writers often follow fixed formats in summarizing a project and presenting its results. They may also use charts, graphs, tables, diagrams, and other illustrations to present material.

39g Using documentation style in the natural sciences

If you use secondary sources in writing about the sciences, consult your instructor about which documentation style to use. The Council of Biology Editors (CBE) has compiled style and documentation guidelines for the life sciences, the physical sciences, and mathematics (see section 34f in the *Simon & Schuster Handbook for Writers*, Third Canadian Edition).

39h Writing different types of papers in the natural sciences

Two major types of papers in the sciences are reports and reviews.

1 Writing science reports

Science reports tell about observations and experiments. They feature eight elements.

Parts of a science report:

1.	Title	A precise description of what your report is about.
2.	Abstract	A short overview of your report.
3.	Introduction	A statement of your purpose and hypothesis. Background information and a review of any relevant literature.
4.	Methods and Materials	A description of your equipment, material, and procedures.

5. Results   The information obtained from your efforts. Charts, graphs, and photographs to help present the data.

6. Discussion   Your interpretation and evaluation of the results.

7. Conclusion   Your conclusions about the hypothesis and the outcomes of your efforts. Theoretical implications that can be drawn from your work. Specific suggestions for further research.

8. References Cited   A properly formatted list of references cited in any review of the literature.

2   Writing science reviews

A **science review** is a paper discussing published information on a scientific topic or issue. Its usual purpose is to summarize for readers all the current knowledge about the topic or issue.

Some science reviews will synthesize information, i.e., put forward a new interpretation of existing material in the light of more recent evidence.

If you are required to write a science review, use the following guidelines:

1. Choose a very limited issue that is currently being researched.
2. Use the most current sources you can.
3. Accurately summarize and paraphrase source material (see 31d and 31e).
4. Document your sources (see section 34f of the *Simon & Schuster Handbook for Writers*, Third Canadian Edition).

Name_____ Date _____

Interviewing and Citation

A. Consider any research you have carried out involving interviews. Did you learn anything new about the interviewing process? What is most important for you to remember next time?

B. Identify a *type* of secondary source that you have not used before in writing a science report. Locate an example of this type of source and cite it, using the documentation style your instructor requires.

Business Writing

As with all writing, business and public writing starts with thinking about purpose and audience (see 1c and 1d).

Guidelines for business and public writing:

1. Consider your audience's needs and expectations.
2. Have a clear purpose. Understand the context of your communication.
3. Put essential information first.
4. Make your points clearly and directly.
5. Use conventional formats.

 Writing and formatting a business letter

Business letters are written to inform, to build goodwill, or to establish a foundation for discussions or transactions. Letters that are likely to get good results are short, simple, direct, and human.

Basic advice for writing business letters:

1. Address the recipient by name.
2. State what your letter is about in the first paragraph.
3. Be honest.
4. Be clear and specific.
5. Use correct English.
6. Be positive and natural.
7. Edit ruthlessly.

GUIDELINES FOR BUSINESS LETTERS:

Format	Select block style (all lines begin at left margin) or modified block style (lines for inside address and body begin at left margin; heading, closing, and signature begin about halfway across the page).
Paper	Use only $8 \frac{1}{2}$ x 11 inch paper (white or very light beige).
Letterhead	Use the official letterhead of the company you are writing from. If you are writing on your own behalf, create letterhead by centring your full name, address, and telephone number at the top of the page, using a larger font size than usual. Avoid fancy fonts.
Name of recipient	Be as specific as possible (exact names will impress). If using department names, put the key word first (e.g., Billing Department). Avoid using "To Whom It May Concern."
Spacing	Use single spacing except between paragraphs.
Content	Write clearly and concisely. Explain your purpose at the beginning, and ensure all information is relevant and accurate. Use reasonable language even when expressing disappointment.
Tone	Use a semiformal level of language unless you are sure informal language will be acceptable.
Final copy	Proofread carefully so that your letter reflects well on you and your organization.

WRITING A GENDER-NEUTRAL SALUTATION:

1. Telephone the company to which you are writing. State your reason for sending the letter and ask for the name of the person who should receive it.
2. Do not address the person by first name. For a man, use *Mr.* or another appropriate title. For a woman, use *Ms.* or another appropriate title unless instructed to use *Miss* or *Mrs.*
3. If you use a title alone, keep it generic and gender-neutral (e.g., Dear Human Resources Officer).

40b Writing and formatting a job application letter

You should always send a cover letter with your résumé. Do not repeat what is on the résumé, but make relevant connections between your experience and the company's expectation. In other words, highlight how your background has prepared you for this position.

Guidelines for a job application letter:

- Use one page only.
- Use the same name, context, and format guidelines as for a business letter (40a).
- Open by identifying the position you are applying for.
- Address the recipient by name and job title or (if you have to) by job title only.
- Consider your letter a polite sales pitch on your own behalf. Don't be shy—but don't exaggerate either.
- Explain how your background fits you for this particular job.
- Stress relevant qualifications.
- If the job will be your first, mention key attributes about yourself (if they are relevant and true).
- State when you are available for an interview and how you can be reached.
- Edit and proofread carefully.

40c Writing and formatting a résumé

A résumé details your employment experience and other accomplishments for a potential employer. Take time to create one that will stand out. Use an easy-to-read format, and include only information that is relevant to the position for which are you are applying.

Guidelines for writing a résumé:

- Emphasize *relevant* facts about yourself.
- Try not to exceed one page. (If you do, put the most important information on the first page.)
- Use clear headings to separate blocks of information.
- Use headings, write telegraphically (omitting words like *I, a, an, the*).
- Put most recent information first.
- Don't "pad."
- Never lie.
- Include references or state that you can supply them (and have them ready to go).

- Use high-quality paper (white or very light beige).
- Do not include personal information such as age, marital status, or religion.

40d Writing e-mail

A great deal of business and local communication is conducted by electronic mail. E-mail is less formal than a letter, but certain conventions still apply:

- Include a subject.
- Single-space within paragraphs; double-space between paragraphs.
- Do not use ALL CAPITALS. This is considered shouting.
- Use bulleted or numbered lists when itemizing.
- Keep your message brief.
- Be cautious (e-mails can easily be forwarded without your permission). Do not give out personal information to strangers or give credit information on a nonsecure site.
- Ask the sender's permission before you forward an e-mail message.
- Check your document for clarity, tone, and accuracy before sending it out.
- Use "emoticons" only if you are sure the reader appreciates them.
- Never "flame" (use e-mail to make personal attacks on others).
- Never "spam" (use e-mail to send junk mail).

If you need to e-mail a longer document, compose it in a word-processing program and attach it to an e-mail, making sure that your recipient is able to open attachments.

40e Writing a memo

Memos can be sent on paper or via e-mail. Their audience is usually "local"—co-workers, management, customers, or people who share your interests or beliefs. Be as specific as possible in naming your memo's audience, and write a clear heading so they can determine the importance of your message.

Memos are short documents (1–2 pages) written for a variety of purposes. Memos can make announcements, requests, or suggestions; recap known information; make things official; and record recent happenings. Most word-processing software provides formats for memos. (In Microsoft™ Word, for example, go to FILE/NEW/MEMO. The style named "professional" is a good choice for workplace use.)

Memo headings:

TO: [Specific audience]

FROM: [Your name]

DATE: [Month, day, year of writing]

SUBJECT: [Concise statement of topic]

Contents:

Introductory paragraph   [Purpose for writing and background information]

Body paragraph   [Point you are making or data required]

Conclusion   [One-to-one sentence summary or specific recommendation; final instructions or "thank you"]

Name_____ Date _____

Business Writing

A. Find examples of business letters you have received (e.g., unsolicited mail, letters from the government, replies from companies or colleges). Have the senders followed all the guidelines given in 40a? If not, has this affected the impact of the letters?

B. Locate advertisements for two different jobs that interest you. Adapt your résumé to each one and draft suitable covering letters.

C. Compare the e-mails you write to friends with those you write to strangers. Which conventions do you ignore when you are writing to friends? Which conventions are you particularly careful to observe when writing to strangers?

41 Writing Under Pressure

Writing under pressure need not be overwhelming. If you break the challenge into a sequence of small steps, you can succeed. If you tend to freeze under pressure, use relaxation techniques such as deep breathing or counting backward from ten. When you turn to the task, remember to break the whole into parts so that the process is easier to work through.

41a Understanding cue words and key terms

Most essay questions contain a word of direction, often called a **cue word**, that tells you what to emphasize in your answer. Familiarity with the major cue words and their meanings can help you plan efficiently and write effectively.

CUE WORDS FOUND IN QUESTIONS FOR ESSAY TESTS:	
Analyze	Separate something into parts and then discuss those parts and their meanings.
Clarify	Make something clear, often by defining a key term and illustrating it with examples.
Classify	Arrange things into groups on the basis of shared characteristics.
Compare and contrast	Show similarities and differences.
Criticize	Give your opinion concerning the good and bad points of something.
Define	State precisely what something is and thereby differentiate it from similar things.
Describe	Explain the features of an object, procedure, or event.
Discuss	Consider as many elements as possible concerning an issue or event.
Evaluate	Give your opinion concerning the importance of something.
Explain	Make clear something that needs to be understood or interpreted.
Illustrate	Give examples of something.

CUE WORDS FOUND IN QUESTIONS FOR ESSAY TESTS: *(continued)*	
Interpret	Explain the meaning of something.
Justify	Show or prove that something is valid or correct.
Prove	Present evidence that cannot be refuted logically or with other evidence.
Relate	Show the connections between two or more things.
Review	Evaluate or summarize something critically.
Show	Point out or demonstrate something.
Summarize	Identify the major points of something.
Support	Argue in favour of something.

Essay questions also contain one or more **key terms** that tell you what to cover in your answer, i.e., what information, topics, and ideas you should write about. For example, in the question "Criticize the architectural function of the modern football stadium," the key terms are *architectural function* and *football stadium*.

41b Writing effective responses to essay-test questions

An effective response to an essay question is tightly organized, easy to follow, and to the point. It shows discernment regarding what readers need to know. An ineffective response shows no such discernment. It may define terms unnecessarily, include throwaway sentences, and leave out important information. Its organization will appear illogical or even nonexistent.

41c Using strategies when writing under pressure

Strategies can be very helpful when writing under pressure. They represent ways of staying comfortable and focused as you attempt to show what you know in a clear, direct, and well-organized way. Practise these strategies by anticipating questions that might come up and then timing yourself as you write the answers.

Strategies for writing essay tests:

1. Do not start writing immediately.
2. Read all the set questions and determine how many of them you are supposed to answer. If you have a choice, select questions about which you know the most and which you can cover most completely in the time available. Allocate appropriate amounts of time for each question.

3. Underline each question's cue words and key terms to help you determine exactly what is required.

4. Allot time for planning and revision as well as actual writing. For a one-hour test on one question, take about ten minutes at the beginning to plan and ten minutes at the end to reread, revise, and edit. If you feel blocked, freewrite (see 2f) to get your thoughts moving. If you are suddenly pressed for time, consider skipping a question that you know you cannot answer well or one that counts less toward your total score.

5. Support any generalizations with specifics (see 4c).

6. Stay on topic. Do not try to reshape the question to one you would prefer to write about. Be guided by the cue words and key terms you have been given.

Name_____ Date _____

Cue Words and Key Terms

A. Draft two questions that you think might come up in your next exam, paying particular attention to cue words. Then write a rough plan showing how you would organize your answers.

B. Look at a sample exam paper and underline the key terms in each question.

ESL 1 Singulars and Plurals

HOW TO USE CHAPTER ESL-1 EFFECTIVELY

This chapter corresponds to Chapter 42 ESL in the *Handbook*.
1. Use this chapter together with these workbook sections:
    *   7a nouns
    *   8c -*s* forms of verbs
    *   11a-11l subject–verb agreement
    *   12f nouns as modifiers
2. Use any cross-references (usually given in parentheses) to find full explanations.

 ESL 1a

Understanding the concept of count and noncount nouns

Count nouns name items that can be counted; *hand, ball, ring, interpretation.* Count nouns can be singular or plural (*hands, balls*).

Noncount nouns name things that are thought of as a whole and not separated into individual parts: *flour, heritage.* (Noncount nouns are used in the singular form only.) The following chart lists eleven categories of uncountable items, and it gives examples of noncount nouns in each category.

UNCOUNTABLE ITEMS

- **Groups of similar items making up "wholes":** baggage, fruit, garbage, hardware, makeup, and others
- **Abstractions:** education, evidence, patience, luck, and others
- **Liquids:** tea, milk, oil, ginger ale, wine, and others
- **Gases:** air, hydrogen, nitrogen, oxygen, pollution, and others
- **Materials:** gold, iron, paper, silver, wood, and others
- **Food:** cheese, chicken, lamb, pasta, venison, and others
- **Particles or grains:** corn, grass, pepper, rye, sand, and others
- **Sports, games, activities:** baseball, bridge, checkers, football, tennis, and others
- **Language:** French, German, Japanese, Latin, Thai, and others
- **Fields of study:** architecture, chemistry, engineering, geology, nursing, and others
- **Events in nature:** darkness, dew, fog, snow, lightning, and others

---

If you want to check whether a noun is count or noncount, look it up in a dictionary such as the *Longman Dictionary of Contemporary English* or the *Oxford Advanced Learner's Dictionary*. These two dictionaries use the terms *countable* and *uncountable*. Noncount nouns are indicated by the letter *U*. Nouns without a *U* are always count.

Some nouns, including some listed in the previous chart, can be countable or uncountable. Most such nouns name things that can be meant individually or as "wholes" made up of individual parts depending on the meaning you want to deliver in each sentence.

COUNT	Our instructor expects ten **papers** this semester. [In this sentence, *papers* is meant as individual, countable items.]
NONCOUNT	I ran out of **paper** before I finished. [In this sentence, *paper* is meant as a whole.]
COUNT	The **chickens** escaped from the coup. [In this sentence, *chickens* is meant as individual, countable items.]
NONCOUNT	Fried **chicken** is John's favourite food. [In this sentence *chicken* is meant as a whole.]

When you are editing your writing (see section 3d), be sure that you have not added a plural -*s* to any noncount nouns, for they are always singular in form.

♣ VERB ALERT: Be sure to use a singular verb with any noncount noun that functions as a subject in your sentences. ♣

ESL
1b

Using determiners with singular and plural nouns

Determiners, also called *expressions of quantity*, are a group of words that traditionally are called adjectives but that are used to tell "how much" or "how many" about nouns. Additional names for determiners include *limiting adjectives, noun markers*, and *articles*. (For information about articles—the words *a, an, the*—which occur in English more often than any other determiners, see Chapter ESL-2).

Choosing the correct determiner with a noun depends first on whether the noun is count or noncount (see ESL-1a). For count nouns, you must also decide whether the noun is singular or plural. The following chart lists many determiners and singular count nouns, noncount nouns, plural (count) nouns that they can accompany.

♣ USAGE ALERT: the phrases *a few* and *a little* convey the meaning "some": *I have a few worries* means "I have some worries." *The Joneses spend a little time with their children* means "The Joneses spend some time with their children."

Without the word *a, few* and *little* convey the meaning "almost none" or "not enough": *I have few [or very few] worries* means "I have almost no worries." *The Joneses spend little time with their children* means "The Joneses spend almost no time with their children." ♣

DETERMINERS TO USE WITH COUNT AND NONCOUNT NOUNS

• With every **singular count noun**, always use one of the determiners listed in Group 1.

  NO   We live in **apartment** in large, white **house**.

  YES   We live in **an apartment** in **that** large white **house**.

GROUP 1: Determiners for singular count nouns

  a, an, the
  | **a chair** | **an apple** | **the room** |

  one, any, some, every, each, either, neither, another, the other
  | **any chair** | **each apple** | **another room** |

  my, our, your, his, her, its, their, nouns with 's or s'
  | **your chair** | **its apple** | **Connie's room** |

  this, that
  | **this chair** | **that apple** | **this car** |

  one, no, the first, the second, and so on
  | **one chair** | **no apple** | **the fifth room** |

DETERMINERS TO USE WITH COUNT AND NONCOUNT NOUNS (*continued*)

- With every **plural count noun**, use one of the determiners listed in Group 2. Count nouns are sometimes used without determiners, as discussed fully in Chapter ESL-2.

  YES   Be sure that the tomatoes you select are ripe.

  YES   Tomatoes are tasty in salad.

GROUP 2: Determiners for plural count nouns

the

| **the signs** | **the rugs** | **the headaches** |

some, any, both, many, more, most, few, fewer, the fewest, a number of, other, several, all, all the, a lot of

| **some signs** | **many rugs** | **all headaches** |

my, our, your, his, her, its, their, nouns with 's or s'

| **our signs** | **her rugs** | **students' headaches** |

these, those

| **these signs** | **those rugs** | **these headaches** |

no, two, three, four, and so on, the first, the second, the third, and so on

| **no signs** | **four rugs** | **the first headache** |

- With every **noncount noun** (always singular), use one of the determiners listed in Group 3. Noncount nouns can also be used without determiners, as discussed in Chapter ELS-2.

  YES   I bought **the fish** we ate for supper.

  YES   I bought **fish** for supper.

GROUP 3: Determiners for noncount nouns

the

| **the cream** | **the light** | **the progress** |

some, any, much, more, most, other, the other, little, less, the least, enough, all, all the, a lot of

| **enough cream** | **a lot of light** | **more progress** |

my, our, your, his, her, its, their, nouns with 's or s'

| **their cream** | **its light** | **your progress** |

this, that

| **this cream** | **that light** | **this progress** |

no, the first, the second, the third, and so on

| **no cream** | **the first light** | **no progress** |

ESL
1c

Using correct forms in *one of* constructions, for nouns used as adjectives, and with *States* in names or titles

One of *constructions*

One of constructions include *one of the* and *one of* followed by a pronoun in the possessive case (*one of my, one of your, one of his, one of her, one of its, one of their*). Always use a plural noun as the object when you begin a phrase with *one of.*

NO	One of our **goal** is progress.
YES	One of our **goals** is progress.

NO	One of his **pet** has died.
YES	One of his **pets** has died.

The verb in *one of* constructions is always singular. The verb agrees with *one*, not with a plural noun: *One of the most important inventions of the twentieth century* **is** [not are] *television.*

Nouns used as adjectives

Some words that function as nouns can also function as adjectives.

The bird's wingspan is 25 **centimetres.** [*Centimetres* functions here as a noun.]

The bird has a 25-**centimetre** wingspan. [*Centimetre* functions here as an adjective.]

Adjectives in English do not have plural forms. When you use a noun as an adjective, therefore, do not add -*s* or -*es* to the adjective even when the noun or pronoun it modifies is plural.

NO	Many **Canadians** students are basketball fans.
YES	Many **Canadian** students are basketball fans.

Names and titles that include the word **States**

The word *states* is always plural. However, names such as the *United States* or the *Organization of American States* refer to singular things—a country and an organization—so they are singular nouns and therefore require singular verbs.

NO	The United **State** has a large entertainment industry.
NO	The United **States** have a large entertainment industry.
YES	The United **States has** a large entertainment industry.

**ESL
1d** Using nouns with irregular plurals

Some English nouns have irregular spellings. Here are some that often cause difficulties.

Plurals of foreign nouns and other irregular nouns

Whenever you are unsure whether a noun is plural, look it up in a dictionary. If no plural is given for a singular noun, add an -s.

Many nouns from other languages that are used unchanged in English have only one plural. If two plurals are listed in the dictionary, look carefully for differences in meaning. Some words, for example, keep the plural form from the original language for scientific usage and have another English-form plural that is used in non-science contexts. Examples include *antenna, antennae, antennas; formula, formulae, formulas; appendix, appendices, appendixes; index, indices, indexes; medium, media, mediums; cactus, cacti, cactuses;* and *fungus, fungi, funguses.*

Words of Latin origin that end in -*is* in their singular form become plural by substituting -*es: parenthesis, parentheses; thesis, theses; oasis, oases,* for example.

Other words

Medical terms for diseases involving an inflammation end in -*itis: tonsillitis, appendicitis.* They are always singular.

The word *news,* although it ends in *s,* is always singular: *The news is encouraging.* The words *people, police,* and *clergy* are always plural even though they do not end in *s: The police are prepared.*

Name_____ Date _____

Identifying Nouns

Divide the following list of words into count and noncount nouns. Give the plural forms of the count nouns. List in all columns any words that can be both count and noncount.

advice	fern	jewellery	paragraph
book	flour	library	physics
calculator	gold	lightning	pollution
chocolate	hair	man	rain
desk	happiness	news	report
earring	homework	novel	storm
essay	honesty	occupation	time
experiment	information	paper	weather

	Noncount	Count	Plural
1.	_____	_____	_____
2.	_____	_____	_____
3.	_____	_____	_____
4.	_____	_____	_____
5.	_____	_____	_____
6.	_____	_____	_____
7.	_____	_____	_____
8.	_____	_____	_____
9.	_____	_____	_____
10.	_____	_____	_____
11.	_____	_____	_____
12.	_____	_____	_____
13.	_____	_____	_____
14.	_____	_____	_____
15.	_____	_____	_____
16.	_____	_____	_____

17. _____ _____ _____

18. _____ _____ _____

19. _____ _____ _____

20. _____ _____ _____

21. _____ _____ _____

22. _____ _____ _____

23. _____ _____ _____

24. _____ _____ _____

25. _____ _____ _____

26. _____ _____ _____

27. _____ _____ _____

28. _____ _____ _____

29. _____ _____ _____

30. _____ _____ _____

31. _____ _____ _____

32. _____ _____ _____

Name_____ Date _____

Correct Forms

Choose the correct forms of the nouns in parentheses and write them on the lines at the right.

EXAMPLE Some _____ (hiker) return to

    _____ (nature) by walking the

    Bruce Trail.

          hikers

          nature

1. Hikers with little _____ (money) but much

  _____ (fortitude) can begin the hike in Niagara Falls

  and continue to the Bruce Peninsula in Lake Huron.

      _____

      _____

2. The 720- _____ (kilometre) trail goes through

  many picturesque _____ (town) along the Niagara Escarpment.

      _____

      _____

3. The trail passes cultivated _____ (farm) and

  untamed _____ (wilderness).

      _____

      _____

4. The caves and cliffs of the Niagara Escarpment make the Bruce

  Trail one of the most interesting _____ (trail) in Canada or

  the United _____ (State).

      _____

      _____

5. Few _____ (hiker) have anything but praise

  for their _____ (experience) on the trail.

      _____

      _____

6. Many _____ (youngster) would gladly give up _____ (piano)

  lessons or _____ (homework) to be

  climbing wooded _____ (path).

      _____

      _____

      _____

7. The Bruce Trail is one of the nation's _____ (treasure).

      _____

Articles

ESL 2

HOW TO USE CHAPTER ESL-2 EFFECTIVELY

This chapter corresponds to Chapter 43 ESL in the *Handbook*. Use this chapter together with these workbook sections:

- 7a articles and nouns
- ESL-1a singulars and plurals with count and noncount nouns
- ESL-1b determiners with count and noncount nouns

ESL 2a Using *a*, *an*, or *the* with singular count nouns

The words *a* and *an* are called **indefinite articles.** The word *the* is called a **definite article.** Articles are one type of determiner. (For other types of determiners, see the chart in ESL-1b.) Articles signal that a noun will follow and that any modifiers between the article and the noun refer to that noun.

a sandwich

a fresh tuna sandwich

the guest

the welcome guest

Every time you use a singular count noun, the noun requires some kind of determiner. To choose between *a* or *an* and *the*, you need to determine whether the noun is **specific** or **nonspecific.** A noun is considered specific when anyone who reads your writing can understand from the context of your message exactly and specifically to what the noun is referring.

For nonspecific singular count nouns, use *a* (or *an*). When a singular noun is specific, use *the* or some other determiner. Use the following chart to help you determine when a noun is specific and therefore requires the article *the*.

One common exception affects Rule 4 in the chart. Even when a noun has been used in an earlier sentence, it my require *a* (or *an*) if one or more descriptive adjectives come between the article and the noun: *I bought a computer today. It was a* [not *the*] *used computer.* Other information may make the noun specific so that *the* is correct. For example, *It was the used computer that I saw advertised on the bulletin board* uses *the* because the *that* clause lets a reader know which specific used computer is meant.

♣ USAGE ALERT: Use *an* before words that begin with a vowel sound. Use *a* before words that begin with a consonant sound. Words that begin with *h* or *u* can have either a vowel or a consonant sound. Make the choice based on the sound of the first word after the article even if that word is not the noun.

a cat	**an** axiom	**a** fine day
a unicorn	**an** underpass	**a** united front
a heretic	**an** herb	**a** happy smile ♣

FOUR RULES: WHEN A SINGULAR COUNT NOUN IS SPECIFIC AND REQUIRES *THE*

- **Rule 1: A noun is specific and requires *the* when it names something unique or generally known.**
  The stars lit his way. [Because *stars* is a generally known noun, it is a specific noun in the context of this sentence.]

- **Rule 2: A noun is specific and requires *the* when it names something used in a representative or abstract sense.**
  The termite is actually a fascinating insect. [Because *termite* is a representative reference rather than a reference to a particular termite, it is a specific noun in the context of this sentence.]

- **Rule 3: A noun is specific and requires *the* when it names something defined elsewhere in the same sentence or in an earlier sentence.**
  The disease bilharzia is a serious threat in some parts of the world. [The word *bilharzia* names a specific disease.]
  The face in the painting startled me. [*In the painting* defines exactly which face is meant, so *face* is a specific noun in this context.]
  I know **a good place** to eat. **The place** is near my home. [*Place* is not specific in the first sentence, so it uses *a*. In the second sentence *place* has been made specific by the first sentence, so it uses *the*.]

- **Rule 4: A noun is specific and requires *the* when it names something that can be inferred from the context.**
  The chef is excellent. [If this sentence follows the two sentences about a place in Rule 3 above, *chef* is specific in this context.]

One common exception affects Rule 3 in the Four Rules Chart. A noun may still require *a* (or *an*) after the first use if one or more descriptive adjectives comes between the article and the noun: *I bought* **a sweater** today. *It was* **a** [not *the*] **red sweater.**

Other information may make the noun specific so that *the* is correct. For example, It was **the red sweater that I saw in the store yesterday** uses *the* because the *that* clause makes specific which red sweater is meant.

Using articles with plural nouns and with noncount nouns

With plural nouns and noncount nouns, you must decide about articles whether to use *the* or to use no article at all.

What you learned in section ESL-2a about nonspecific and specific nouns can help you make the choice between using *the* or using no article. The Four Rules Chart in section ESL-2a explains when a singular count noun's meaning is specific and calls for *the.* Plural nouns and noncount nouns with specific meanings usually use *the* in the same circumstances. However, a plural noun or a noncount noun with a general or nonspecific meaning usually does not use *the.*

I need **nuts** and **chocolate chips** for this recipe. I also need **flour.**

Plural nouns

A plural noun's meaning may be specific because it is widely known.

The crops may not survive the drought. [Because the meaning of *crops* is widely understood, *the* is correct to use. This example is related to Rule 1 in the Four Rules Chart.]

A plural noun's meaning may also be made specific by a word, phrase, or clause in the same sentence.

I don't know *the students* in my apartment building. [Because the phrase *in my apartment building* makes *students* specific, *the* is correct to use. This example is related to Rule 3 in the Four Rules Chart.]

A plural noun's meaning usually becomes specific by being used in an earlier sentence.

We have begun doing **exercises.** We hope **the exercises** will develop our stamina. [*Exercises* is used in a general sense in the first sentence, without *the.* Because the first sentence makes *exercises* specific, *the exercises* is correct in the second sentence. This example is related to Rule 4 in the Four Rules Chart.]

A plural noun's meaning may be made specific by the context.

The aerobics should be particularly beneficial. [In the context of the sentences about exercises, *aerobics* is specific and calls for *the.* This example is related to Rule 4 in the Four Rules Chart.]

Noncount nouns

Noncount nouns are always singular in form (see ESL-1a). Like plural nouns, noncount nouns use either *the* or no article. When a noncount noun's meaning is specific, use *the* before it. If its meaning is general or nonspecific, do not use *the.*

Li served us **tea.** He had brought **the tea** from China. [*Tea* is a noncount noun. This example is related to Rule 4 in the Four Rules Chart. By the second sentence, *tea* has become specific, so *the* is used.]

Li served us **the tea that he had brought from China.** [*Tea* is a noncount noun. This example is related to Rule 3 in the Four Rules Chart: *Tea* is made specific by the clause *that he had brought from China,* so *the* is used.]

Generalizations with plural or noncount nouns

Rule 2 in the Four Rules Chart tells you to use *the* with singular count nouns used in a general sense. With generalizations using plural or noncount nouns, omit *the.*

NO	**The elephants** live longer than **the zebras.**
YES	**Elephants** live longer than **zebras.**

Using *the* with proper nouns and with gerunds

Proper nouns

Proper nouns name specific people, places, or things (see 7a). Most proper nouns do not require articles: *I spent my holidays with Asda at Crystal Beach.* As shown in the following chart, however, certain types of proper nouns do require *the.*

PROPER NOUNS THAT USE *THE*

- **Nouns with the pattern** *the . . . of . . .*
  the Dominion **of** Canada
  the Isle **of** Wight
  the Fourth **of** July
  the University **of** British Columbia

- **Plural proper nouns**
  the Randalls
  the Trossachs
  the Rocky Mountains   [but Mount Everest]
  the Virgin Islands   [but Vancouver Island]
  the Great Lakes   [but Lake Titicaca]
  the Montreal Canadiens

- **Collective proper nouns (nouns that name a group)**
  the Lions Club
  the Children's Aid Society

- **Some (but not all) geographical features**
  the Amazon River
  the Indian Ocean
  the Gobi Desert

- **A few countries and cities**
  the Congo
  the Hague [capital of the Netherlands]
  the Czech Republic
  the Pas

Gerunds

Gerunds are present participles (the *-ing* form of verbs) used as nouns: ***Skating is invigorating.*** Gerunds usually are not preceded by *the*.

NO   The **painting** wood fences is necessary to make them last.

YES   **Painting** wood fences is necessary to make them last.

Use *the* before a gerund when two conditions are met: (1) the gerund is used in a specific sense and (2) the gerund does not have a direct object.

NO   **The designing** fabric is a fine art. [*Fabric* is a direct object of *designing*, so *the* should not be used.]

YES   **Designing** fabric is a fine art. [*Designing* is a gerund, so *the* is not used.]

YES   **The designing of fabric** is a fine art. [*The* is used because *fabric* is the object of the preposition *of* and *designing* is meant in a specific sense.]

EXERCISES

Name_____ Date _____

Articles

In the following blanks write *a*, *an*, or *the* as needed. If no article is necessary, put a *0* in the blank.

In 1872 _____ U.S. Congress passed _____ Yellowstone Act, establishing _____ Yellowstone as _____ first national park in _____ United States and indeed in _____ world. For centuries _____ wealthy set aside _____ private preserves for their own recreational use, but except for _____ few public parks in _____ major cities, setting aside _____ vast area for _____ national enjoyment was _____ novel idea. It became _____ popular one. Since _____ founding of _____ Yellowstone, forty-nine other national parks have been established in _____ United States and its territories.

_____ Yellowstone is _____ largest national park in _____ United States. It occupies 9000 square kilometres at _____ juncture of _____ states of _____ Wyoming, _____ Montana, and _____ Idaho. Although _____ Native American habitation goes back 800 years, _____ park's remoteness from _____ centres of _____ population left it undiscovered by _____ white settlers until _____ nineteenth century.

_____ John Colter is thought to be _____ first explorer to venture into _____ area. Colter was _____ member of _____ Lewis and Clark Expedition. When _____ expedition returned to _____ St. Louis, he remained in _____ region of _____ upper Missouri River to become _____ mountain man. In 1807 he explored _____ Yellowstone Basin. When he later wrote about _____ thermal wonders of _____ area, many people did not believe such natural phenomena existed. They continue to amaze _____ tourists today.

Yellowstone is truly _____ natural fantasy land. Its features include _____ geysers, _____ hot springs, and _____ mud volcanoes along with _____ forests, _____ lakes, _____ mountains, and _____ waterfalls. _____ most famous of _____ park's attractions is _____ "Old Faithful," _____ geyser which erupts on _____ average of every 65 minutes. It shoots _____ steaming water from 37 to 52 metres into _____ air. Each eruption lasts approximately four minutes and spews out 37 850 _____ litres of _____ water.

Other active geysers in _____ six geyser basins may be less predictable but are no less spectacular. Some of _____ more than 200 just emit _____ steam and _____ spooky underground noises. _____ silica in _____ geyser water builds up around _____ walls of _____ geyser craters, making _____ craters very colourful and beautiful to view even when _____ geysers are not spouting.

_____ hot springs are another Yellowstone attraction. There are more than 3000 of them ranged throughout _____ park. Some, such as _____ Emerald Spring, are remarkable because of their colour. _____ Morning Glory Spring looks like its flower namesake.

_____ Yellowstone Lake, _____ Golden Gate Canyon, and _____ Tower Falls are just some of _____ features that combine with _____ geysers and _____ hot springs to make _____ Yellowstone National Park _____ extraordinary place to visit.

ESL 3 Word Order

Understanding standard and inverted word order in sentences

In **standard word order**, the most common pattern for declarative sentences in English, the subject comes before the verb. (To better understand these concepts, review sections 7k-7o.)

SUBJECT   VERB
↓   ↓
My schedule   is full.

With **inverted word order,** the main verb or an auxiliary verb comes before the subject. The most common use of inverted word order in English is forming direct questions. Questions that can be answered with "yes" or "no" begin with a form of *be* used as a main verb, or with an auxiliary verb (*be, do,* or *have*), or with a modal auxiliary (*can, should, will,* and others—see Chapter ESL-6).

Questions that can be answered with "yes" or "no"

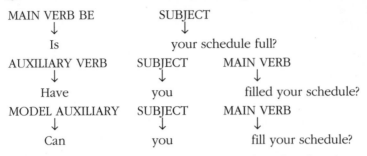

MAIN VERB BE	SUBJECT	
↓	↓	
Is	your schedule full?	

AUXILIARY VERB	SUBJECT	MAIN VERB
↓	↓	↓
Have	you	filled your schedule?

MODEL AUXILIARY	SUBJECT	MAIN VERB
↓	↓	↓
Can	you	fill your schedule?

To form a **yes/no question** with a verb order other than *be* as the main verb and when there is no auxiliary or modal as part of a verb phrase, use the appropriate form of the auxiliary verb *do*.

AUXILIARY VERB	SUBJECT	MAIN VERB
↓	↓	↓
Does	Mako	wear only black?

You may sometimes see a question formed with the main verb at the beginning.

MAIN VERB	SUBJECT	
↓	↓	
Has	she	no other option?

It is equally correct and more common to see the question formed with *do* as an auxiliary and *have* as a main verb, following the pattern of auxiliary verb-subject-main verb: *Does she have no other option?*

A question that begins with a question-forming word like *why, when, where,* or *how* cannot be answered with "yes" or "no": *Why did the doorbell ring?* Such a question communicates that information must be provided to answer it; the answer cannot be "yes" or "no." Information is needed: for example, *Suki rang it.*

Most information questions follow the same rules of inverted word order as yes/no questions.

Information questions: Inverted order

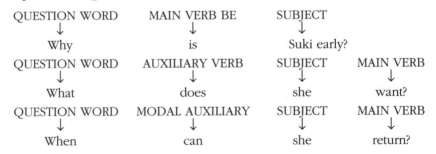

QUESTION WORD	MAIN VERB BE	SUBJECT	
↓	↓	↓	
Why	is	Suki early?	

QUESTION WORD	AUXILIARY VERB	SUBJECT	MAIN VERB
↓	↓	↓	↓
What	does	she	want?

QUESTION WORD	MODAL AUXILIARY	SUBJECT	MAIN VERB
↓	↓	↓	↓
When	can	she	return?

When **who** or **what** functions as the subject in a question, however, use standard word order.

**ESL
3b**

Information questions: Standard order

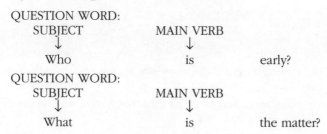

QUESTION WORD:
    SUBJECT   MAIN VERB
       ↓   ↓

     Who   is   early?

QUESTION WORD:
    SUBJECT   MAIN VERB
       ↓   ↓

     What   is   the matter?

❖ **ALERT:** When a question has more than one auxiliary verb, put the subject after the first auxiliary verb.

FIRST AUXILIARY   SUBJECT   SECOND AUXILIARY   MAIN VERB
     ↓   ↓   ↓   ↓

   Could   she   have   returned later? ❖

The same rules apply to emphatic exclamations: *Was that soup delicious! Did it hit the spot!*

Also, when you use negatives such as *never, hardly ever, seldom, rarely, not only* or *nor* to start a clause, use **inverted order.** These sentence pairs show the differences.

> I have never been so embarrassed. [standard order]
>
> Never have I been so embarrassed! [inverted order]

> Ho is not only a chemist but also a writer. [standard order]
>
> Not only is Ho a chemist, but he is also a writer. [inverted order]

> Paul did not study, and his brother didn't either. [standard order]
>
> Paul did not study, and neither did his brother. [inverted order]

❖ **USAGE ALERT:** With indirect questions, use standard word order: *She asked when Suki could return* (not *She asked when could Suki return.*) ❖

❖ **STYLE ALERT:** Word order deliberately inverted can be effective, when used sparingly, to create emphasis in a sentence that is neither a question nor an exclamation (also see 19f). ❖

**ESL
3b**   **Understanding the placement of adjectives**

Adjectives modify—that is, they describe or limit—nouns, pronouns, and word groups that function as nouns (see section 7e). In English, an adjective comes directly before the noun it describes. However, when more than one adjective describes the same noun, several sequences may be possible. The following chart shows the most common order for positioning several adjectives.

| | WORD ORDER FOR MORE THAN ONE ADJECTIVE |

1. **Determiners, if any:** *a, an, the, my, your, Jan's, this, that, these, those,* and so on
2. **Expressions of order, including ordinal numbers, if any:** *first, second, third, next, last, final,* and so on
3. **Expressions of quantity, including cardinal (counting) numbers, if any:** *one, two, three, few, each, every, some,* and so on
4. **Adjectives of judgment or opinion, if any:** *pretty, happy, ugly, sad, interesting, boring,* and so on
5. **Adjectives of size and/or shape, if any:** *big, small, short, round, square,* and so on
6. **Adjectives of age and/or condition, if any:** *new, young, broken, dirty, shiny,* and so on
7. **Adjectives of colour, if any:** *red, green, blue,* and so on
8. **Adjectives that can also be used as nouns, if any:** *French, Protestant, metal, cotton,* and so on
9. **The noun**

1	2	3	4	5	6	7	8	9
A		few		tiny		red		ants
The	last	six					Thai	carvings
My			fine		old		oak	table

ESL 3c Understanding the placement of adverbs

Adverbs modify—that is, describe or limit—verbs, adjectives, other adverbs, or entire sentences (see section 7f). Adverbs are usually positioned first, in the middle, or last in a clause. The following chart summarizes adverb types, what they tell about the words they modify, and where each type can be placed.

TYPES OF ADVERBS AND WHERE TO POSITION THEM

- **Adverbs of manner**
  - describe *how* something is done
  - usually are in middle or last position

    Boris **thoroughly** cleaned his car.
    Boris cleaned his car **thoroughly.**

- **Adverbs of time**
  - describe *when* or *how long* about an event
  - usually are in the first or last position

    First, he scrubbed the wheels.
    He scrubbed the wheels **first.**

  - include *just*, *still*, and *already*, and similar adverbs, which usually are in the middle position

    He had **already** vacuumed the interior.

- **Adverbs of place**
  - describe *where* an event takes place
  - usually are in the last position

    He cleaned the car **outdoors.**

- **Adverbs of frequency**
  - describe *how often* an event takes place
  - usually are in the middle position

    Boris **rarely** takes the car to a car wash.

  - are in the first position when they modify an entire sentence (see Sentence adverbs below)

    Occasionally, he waxes the car.

- **Adverbs of degree or emphasis**
  - describe *how much* or *to what extent* about other modifiers
  - are directly before the word they modify

    Boris is **extremely** proud of his car. [*Extremely* modifies *proud*.]

  - include *only*, which is easy to misplace (see 15b)

- **Sentence adverbs**
  - modify the entire sentence rather than just one word or few words
  - include transitional words and expressions (see 4d) as well as *maybe*, *probably*, *possibly*, *fortunately*, *unfortunately*, *incredibly*, and others
  - are in first position

    Surprisingly, he doesn't mind loaning it.

✣ **PUNCTUATION ALERT:** Unless they are very short (fewer than five letters), adverbs in the first position are usually followed by a comma. ✣

✣ **USAGE ALERT:** Do not let an adverb in a middle position separate a verb from its direct object or indirect object (see section 15b). ✣

ESL
3-1

Name_____ Date _____

Question Form

Convert the following sentences into questions.

EXAMPLE We should have called first

Should we have called first?

1. That pizza is enough for all of us.

   _____

2. Henri understood the lesson.

   _____

3. You have my lab manual. (two ways)

   _____

   _____

4. Juanita will have finished by the time we return.

   _____

5. Everyone in the room can see the screen.

   _____

Order in Adjectives and Adverbs

ESL EXERCISE **3-2**
(ESL–3b–c)

Rewrite the following sentences using correct word order.

EXAMPLE   Our English class took a field final trip to an auction large house.

Our English class took a final field trip to a large auction house.

1. Katrina purchased two Limoges lovely boxes.

   _____

2. A black leather comfortable chair appealed to Nils.

   _____

3. He waited to bid on it patiently.

   _____

4. We left unfortunately before it was auctioned.

   _____

5. Mario wanted a wooden old table but bought a silver worn spoon.

   _____

6. Suchen outbid someone for a green round interesting hatbox.

   _____

7. She was delighted extremely to get it.

   _____

8. She has admired often such hatboxes.

   _____

9. The English entire class bought something except Ingrid.

   _____

10. Because she brought an empty small purse, she bought nothing at all.

   _____

Prepositions

HOW TO USE CHAPTER ESL-4 EFFECTIVELY

This chapter corresponds to Chapter 45 ESL in the *Handbook*. Use this chapter together with these workbook sections:

- 7g prepositions
- 21a using appropriate language

Prepositions function with other words in prepositional phrases. Prepositional phrases usually indicate **where** (direction or location), how (by what means or in what way), or **when** (at what time or how long), about the words they modify.

This chapter can help you with several uses of prepositions, which function in combination with other words in ways that are often idiomatic. An idiom's meaning differs from the literal meaning of each individual word (see 20a). For example, *Yao-Ming broke into a smile* means that a smile appeared on Yao-Ming's face. However, the dictionary definitions of *break* and *into* imply that *broke into a smile* means "shattered the form of" a smile. Knowing which preposition to use in a specific context takes much experience reading, listening to, and speaking the language. A dictionary like the *Longman Dictionary of Contemporary English* or the *Oxford Advanced Learner's Dictionary* can be especially helpful when you need to find the correct preposition to use in cases not covered by this chapter.

ESL 4a Recognizing prepositions

The following chart shows many common prepositions.

COMMON PREPOSITIONS

about	despite	out
above	down	out of
according to	during	outside
across	except	over
after	except for	past
against	excepting	regarding
along	for	round
along with	from	since
among	in	through
apart from	in addition to	throughout
around	in back of	till
as	in case of	to
as for	in front of	toward
at	in place of	under
because of	inside	underneath
before	in spite of	unlike
behind	instead of	until
below	into	up
beneath	like	upon
beside	near	up to
between	next	with
beyond	of	within
but	off	without
by	on	
by means of	onto	
concerning	on top of	

Using prepositions with expressions of time and place

The following chart shows how to use the prepositions *in*, *at*, and *on* to deliver some common kinds of information about time and place. The chart, however, does not convey every preposition that indicates time or place, nor does it cover all uses of *in*, *at*, and *to*. For example, it does not explain the subtle difference in meaning delivered by the prepositions *at* and *in* in these two correct sentences: *I have a chequing account **at** that bank and I have a safe-deposit box **in** that bank*. Also, the chart does not include expressions that operate outside the general rules. (Both these sentences are correct: *You ride in the car* and *You ride on the bus*.)

420

USING *IN*, *AT*, AND *ON* TO SHOW TIME AND PLACE

TIME

- ***in* a year or a month** (*during* is also correct but less common)
  - **in** 1995   **in** May

- ***in* a period of time**
  - **in** a few months (seconds, days, years)

- ***in* a period of the day**
  - **in** the morning (afternoon, evening)
  - **in** the daytime (morning, evening), *but* **at** night

- ***on* a specific day**
  - **on** Friday
  - **on** my birthday

- ***at* a specific time or period of time**
  - **at** noon   **at** 2:00
  - **at** dawn   **at** nightfall
  - **at** takeoff (the time a plane leaves)
  - **at** breakfast (the time a specific meal takes place)

PLACE

- ***in* a location surrounded by something else**
  - **in** Alberta
  - **in** Utah   **in** downtown Bombay
  - **in** the kitchen   **in** my apartment
  - **in** the bathtub

- ***at* a specific location**
  - **at** your house   **at** the bank
  - **at** the corner of Third Avenue and Main Street

- ***on* the top of the surface of something**
  - **on** page 20   **on** the mezzanine
  - **on** Queen Street   **on** street level
  - **on** the second floor, *but* **in** the attic *or* **in** the basement

---

Using prepositions in phrasal verbs

Phrasal verbs, also called *two-word verbs* and *three-word verbs,* are verbs that combine with prepositions to deliver their meaning.

In some phrasal verbs, the verb and the preposition should not be separated by other words.

Look at the moon [not **Look** the moon **at**]

In **separable phrasal verbs,** other words in the sentence can separate the verb and the preposition without interfering with meaning: *I **threw away** my homework* is as correct as *I **threw** my homework **away**.*

Here is a list of some common phrasal verbs. The ones that cannot be separated are marked with an asterisk (*).

LIST OF SELECTED PHRASAL VERBS

ask out	get along with*	look into
break down	get back	look out for*
bring about	get off*	look over
call back	go over*	make up
drop off	hand in	run across*
figure out	keep up with*	speak to*
fill out	leave out	speak with*
fill up	look after*	throw away
find out	look around	throw out

Position a pronoun object between the words of a separable phrasal verb: *I threw it away*. Also, you can position an object phrase of several words between the parts of a separable phrasal verb: *I threw **my research paper** away*. However, when the object is a clause, do not let it separate the parts of the phrasal verb: *I threw away **all the papers that I wrote last year.***

Many phrasal verbs are informal and are used more in speaking than in writing. For academic writing, a more formal verb may be more appropriate than a phrasal verb. In a research paper, for example, *propose* or *suggest* might be better choices than *come up with*. For academic writing acceptable phrasal verbs include *believe in, benefit from, concentrate on, consist of, depend on, dream of* (or *dream about*), *insist on, participate in, prepare for,* and *stare at*. None of these phrasal verbs can be separated.

 ## Using prepositions in common expressions

In many common expressions, different prepositions convey great differences in meaning. For example, four prepositions can be used with the verb *agree* to create five different meanings.

agree to = to give consent (*I cannot **agree to** buy you a new car.*)

agree about = to arrive at a satisfactory understanding (*We **agree about** your needing a car.*)

agree on = to arrive at a satisfactory understanding (*You and the seller must **agree on** a price for the car.*)

agree with = to have the same opinion (*I **agree with** you that you need a car.*)

agree with = be suitable or healthful (*The idea of such a major expense does not **agree with** me.*)

You can find entire books filled with English expressions that include prepositions. This list shows a few that you are likely to use often.

LIST OF SELECTED EXPRESSIONS WITH PREPOSITIONS

ability in	different from	involved with [*someone*]
access to	faith in	knowledge of
accustomed to	familiar with	made of
afraid of	famous for	married to
angry with *or* at	frightened by	opposed to
authority on	happy with	patience with
aware of	in charge of	proud of
based on	independent of	reason for
capable of	in favour of	related to
certain of	influence on *or* over	suspicious of
confidence in	interested in	time for
dependent on	involved in [*something*]	tired of

**ESL
4-1**

In, At, On

In the following blanks, use *in*, *at*, or *on* to show time or place.

EXAMPLE   The University of Virginia, located _____ Charlottesville, was founded by Thomas Jefferson.

The University of Virginia, located __*in*__ Charlottesville, was founded by Thomas Jefferson.

1. Others wanted to put the new university _____ Staunton or Lexington.

2. _____ 1818, Dalhousie University opened _____ Halifax, Nova Scotia, the same year as Jefferson's.

3. Jefferson designed his university so that students and faculty lived together _____ an "academical village."

4. A rotunda building for classes sits _____ one end of a lawn.

5. _____ both sides of the lawn are sets of student rooms.

6. Faculty members lived _____ pavilions between the sets of student rooms.

7. A similar scheme inspired the design of Ontario's Trent University, whose main campus opened _____ 1966.

8. _____ your next visit to the University of Toronto, you can stand _____ a window _____ the University College Quadrangle and see how that nineteenth-century college was designed with the same idea in mind.

9. _____ his deathbed, Jefferson included founding the university as one of the three accomplishments for which he hoped to be remembered.

10. Today students at the University of Virginia consider it an honour to live _____ the rooms that Jefferson designed.

Name_____ Date _____

Phrasal Verbs

ESL EXERCISE 4-2
(ESL–4c)

A: Fill in each blank with a phrasal verb from the list in section ESL 4c. Use each phrasal verb only once. More than one phrasal verb may be appropriate for some blanks.

EXAMPLE Walid cannot _____ why it takes so long to register.

Walid cannot _figure out_ why it takes so long to register.

1. Ravi will _____ Walid and explain.

2. First he must _____ all the forms.

3. He must _____ all his records to make sure he does not _____ anything.

4. He must then _____ the forms at the registrar's office.

5. Should he _____ the forms without some vital information, the registrar will _____ him _____ to get it.

6. Walid will have to _____ the forms and _____ what is missing.

7. He must not _____ any records until he has finished the procedure.

B: Now rewrite the sentences using as many formal verbs as possible.

ESL Gerunds, Infinitives,
5 and Participles

HOW TO USE CHAPTER ESL-5 EFFECTIVELY

This chapter corresponds to Chapter 46 ESL in the *Handbook*. Use this chapter together with these workbook sections:

- 7d verbals
- 11a subject–verb agreement
- 7k-7l subjects and objects
- 18a-18c parallelism
- 8b principal parts of verbs

Participles are verb forms (see 8b). A verb's *-ing* form is its present participle. The *-ed* form of a *regular verb* is its past participle; irregular verbs form their past participles in various ways (for example, *bend, bent; eat, eaten; think, thought*—for a complete list, see the chart in section 8d). Participles can function as adjectives (*a **smiling** face, a **closed** book*).

A verb's *-ing* form can also function as a noun (***sneezing** spreads colds*), which is called a **gerund.** Another verb form, the **infinitive,** also functions as a noun. An infinitive is a verb's simple or base form usually preceded by the word *to* (*Tell everyone **to smile***). Verb forms—participles, gerunds, and infinitives—functioning as nouns or modifiers are called **verbals,** as explained in section 7d.

ESL 5a Using gerunds and infinitives as subjects

Gerunds are used more commonly than infinitives as subjects. Sometimes, however, either is acceptable.

Choosing the best instructor is difficult.
To choose the best instructor is difficult.

❖ VERB ALERT: When a gerund or an infinitive is used alone as a subject, it is singular and requires a singular verb. When two or more gerunds or infinitives create a compound subject, they require a plural verb. (See sections 7k and 11d.) ❖

ESL 5b Using a gerund, not an infinitive, as an object after certain verbs

Some verbs must be followed by gerunds used as direct objects. Other verbs must be followed by infinitives. Still other verbs can be followed by either a gerund or an infinitive. (A few verbs can change meaning depending on whether they are followed by a gerund or an infinitive; see ESL-5d.) The following chart lists common verbs that must be followed by gerunds, not infinitives.

Sasha **considered** *dropping* [not *to drop*] her accounting class.

She **was having trouble** *understanding* [not *to understand*] the teacher.

Her advisor **recommended** *hiring* [not *to hire*] a tutor.

VERBS AND EXPRESSIONS THAT USE GERUNDS AFTER THEM

acknowledge	detest	mind
admit	discuss	object to
advise	dislike	postpone
anticipate	dream about	practise
appreciate	enjoy	put off
avoid	escape	quit
cannot bear	evade	recall
cannot help	favour	recommend
cannot resist	finish	regret
complain about	give up	resent
consider	have trouble	resist
consist of	imagine	risk
contemplate	include	suggest
delay	insist on	talk about
deny	keep (on)	tolerate
deter from	mention	understand

Gerund after go

Go is usually followed by an infinitive: *We can* **go to hear** [not *go hearing*] *a band after the show.* Sometimes, however, *go* is followed by a gerund in phrases such as *go swimming, go fishing, go shopping,* and *go driving.*

I will **go swimming** [not go to swim] after class.

427

Gerund after **be** + *complement* + *preposition*

Many common expressions use a form of the verb *be* plus a complement plus a preposition. In such expressions, use a gerund, not an infinitive, after the preposition. Here is a list of some of the most frequently used expressions in this pattern.

LIST OF SELECTED *BE* + COMPLEMENT + PREPOSITION EXPRESSIONS

be (get) accustomed to	be interested in
be angry about	be prepared for
be bored with	be responsible for
be capable of	be tired of
be committed to	be (get) used to
be excited about	be worried about

Hari **is tired of** *waiting* [not *to wait*] for his grades.

Katrina **is bored with** *learning* [not *to learn*] to ski.

❖ USAGE ALERT: Always use a gerund, not an infinitive, as the object of a preposition. Be especially careful when the word *to* is functioning as a preposition in a phrasal verb (see ESL-4c): *We are* **committed to changing** [not *to change*] *the rules.* ❖

 Using an infinitive, not a gerund, as an object after certain verbs

The following chart lists selected common verbs and expressions that must be followed by infinitives, not gerunds, as objects.

Niki **hoped** *to go* [not *hoped going*] home for the holidays.

Astrid **decided** *to remain* [not *remaining*] in the dormitory.

VERBS AND EXPRESSIONS THAT USE INFINITIVES AFTER THEM

afford	claim	hope	promise
agree	consent	intend	refuse
aim	decide	know how	seem
appear	decline	learn	struggle
arrange	demand	like	tend
ask	deserve	manage	threaten
attempt	do not care	mean	volunteer
be left	expect	offer	vote
beg	fail	plan	wait
cannot afford	give permission	prepare	want
care	hesitate	pretend	would like

**ESL
5c**

Infinitives after **be + complement**

Gerunds are common in constructions that use forms of the verb **be**, a complement, and a preposition (see ESL-5b). However, use an infinitive, not a gerund, when *be* plus a complement is not followed by a preposition.

We **are glad** *to see* [not *seeing*] you so happy.

Maria **is ready** *to learn* [not *learning*] to cook.

Infinitives to indicate purpose

Use an infinitive in expressions that indicate purpose.

I wore an old shirt ***to gather*** berries.

This sentence means "I wore an old shirt for the purpose of gathering berries." *To gather* delivers the idea of purpose more concisely (see Chapter 16) than expressions such as "so that I can" or "in order to."

Infinitives with **the first, the last, the one**

Use an infinitive after the expressions *the first, the last, the one*.

Colin is the first ***to start*** [not *starting*] *and the last* ***to quit*** [not *quitting*] *on this project.*

Unmarked infinitives

Infinitives used without the word *to* are called **unmarked infinitives** or **bare infinitives**. An unmarked infinitive may be hard to recognize because it is not preceded by *to*. Some common verbs followed by unmarked infinitives are *feel, have, hear, let, listen to, look at, make,* (meaning "compel"), *notice, see,* and *watch*.

Please make your son **behave** [not *to behave*]. [unmarked infinitive]

I asked your son **to behave**. [marked infinitive]

The verb *help* can be followed by either a marked or an unmarked infinitive. Either is correct.

Help me **count** [or **to count**] the receipts.

❖ USAGE ALERT: Be careful to use parallel structure (see Chapter 18) correctly when you use two or more gerunds or infinitives after verbs. If two or more verbal objects follow one verb, put the verbals into the same form.

NO	We like **skating** and to **ski**.
YES	We like **skating** and **skiing**.
YES	We like **to skate** and **to ski**.

Conversely, if you are using verbal objects with compound predicates, be sure to use the kind of verbal that each verb requires.

NO	We enjoyed **scuba diving** but do not plan **sailing** again.
	[*Enjoyed* requires a gerund object and *plan* requires an infinitive object; see the Charts in ESL-4b and ESL-5b.)
YES	We enjoyed **scuba diving** but do not plan **to sail** again. ❖

ESL 5d **Knowing how meaning changes when certain verbs are followed by a gerund or an infinitive as an object**

With stop

The verb *stop* followed by a gerund means "finish, quit." *Stop* followed by an infinitive means "stop or interrupt one activity to begin another."

We **stopped eating.** [We finished our meal.]

We **stopped to eat.** [We stopped another activity, such as driving, in order to eat.]

With remember *and* forget

The verb *remember* followed by an infinitive means "not to forget to do something."

I must **remember to talk** with Isa.

Remember followed by a gerund means "recall a memory."

I **remember talking** in my sleep last night.

The verb *forget* followed by an infinitive means "to not do something."

If you **forget to put** a stamp on that letter, it will be returned.

Forget followed by a gerund means "to do something and not recall it."

I **forget having put** the stamps in the refrigerator.

With try

The verb *try* followed by an infinitive means "made an effort."

I **tried to find** your jacket.

Followed by a gerund, *try* means "experimented with."

I **tried jogging** but found it too difficult.

ESL 5e **Understanding that meaning does not change whether a gerund or an infinitive follows certain sense verbs**

Sense verbs include words such as *see, notice, hear, observe, watch, feel, listen to,* and *look at.* The meaning of these verbs is usually not affected whether the verb is followed by a gerund or an infinitive as an object. *I **saw** the water **rise** and I **saw** the water **rising*** both have the same meaning.

Choosing between -*ing* forms and -*ed* forms for adjectives

Deciding whether to use the -*ing* form (*present participle*) or the -*ed* form (*past participle of a regular verb*) as an adjective in a specific sentence can be difficult. For example, *I am amused* and *I am amusing* are both correct in English, but their meanings are very different. To make the right choice, decide whether the modified noun or pronoun is causing or experiencing what the participle describes.

Use a present participle (-*ing*) to modify a noun or pronoun that is the agent or the cause of the action.

> Mica described your **interesting** plan. [The noun *plan* causes what its modifier describes—*interest;* so *interesting* is correct.]

> I find your plan **exciting.** [The noun *plan* causes what its modifier describes—*excitement;* so *exciting* is correct.]

Use a past participle (-*ed* in regular verbs) to modify a noun or pronoun that experiences or receives whatever the modifier describes.

> An **interested** committee wants to hear your plan. [The noun *committee* experiences what its modifier describes—*interest;* so *interested* is correct.]

> **Excited** by your plan, I called a board meeting. [The pronoun *I* experiences what its modifier describes—*excitement;* so *excited* is correct.]

Here is a list of some frequently used participles that require your close attention when you use them as adjectives. To choose the right form, decide whether the noun or pronoun experiences or causes what the participle describes.

amused, amusing	frightened, frightening
annoyed, annoying	insulted, insulting
appalled, appalling	offended, offending
bored, boring	overwhelmed, overwhelming
confused, confusing	pleased, pleasing
depressed, depressing	reassured, reassuring
disgusted, disgusting	satisfied, satisfying
fascinated, fascinating	shocked, shocking

Use of Verbals

Complete each sentence with the appropriate gerund, infinitive, or participle form of the verb in parentheses.

EXAMPLE   Most students at a university hope _____ (prepare) themselves for a career.

Most students at a university hope _to prepare_ (prepare) themselves for a career.

1. They are worried about _____ (get) jobs after graduation.

2. They may want _____ (study) for the pure enjoyment of learning.

3. They may even dream about _____ (be) philosophers or writers.

4. However, many parents refuse _____ (support) students who lack a definite career goal.

5. They are happy _____ (help) their children reach their goals.

6. They resist _____ (aid) children who lack direction.

7. Yet _____ (read) widely in the liberal arts is one way for students _____ (know) themselves.

8. Students of the humanities are the first _____ (see) the value of a liberal education.

9. When they hear their parents _____ (complain) about wasting money, students try _____ (explain) their positions.

10. They recommend _____ (learn) about life before _____ (train) for a specific job.

Modal Auxiliary Verbs

HOW TO USE CHAPTER ESL-6 EFFECTIVELY

This chapter corresponds to Chapter 47 ESL in the *Handbook*. Use this chapter together with these workbook sections:
- 7c recognizing verbs
- 8j progressive tenses
- 8e auxiliary verbs
- 8g verb tense
- 8l-m subjunctive mood

Auxiliary verbs are known as *helping verbs* because adding an auxiliary verb to a main verb helps the main verb convey additional information (see 8e). For example, the auxiliary verb *do* is important in turning sentences into questions. *You have to sleep* becomes a question when *do* is added: *Do you have to sleep?* The most common auxiliary verbs are forms of *be*, *have*, and *do*.

Modal auxiliary verbs are one type of auxiliary verb. They include *can, could, may, might, should, had better, must, will, would,* and others discussed in this chapter. They have only two forms: the present-future and the past. Modals differ from *be, have,* and *do* used as auxiliary verbs in the ways discussed in the following chart.

SUMMARY OF MODALS AND THEIR DIFFERENCES FROM OTHER AUXILIARY VERBS

- Modals in the present or future are always followed by the simple form of a main verb: *I might **go** tomorrow.*
- One-word modals have no *s* ending in the third-person singular: *She **could** go with me, you **could** go with me, they **could** go with me.* (The two-word modal *have to* changes form to agree with its subject: *I **have to** leave, she **has to** leave.*) Auxiliary verbs other than modals usually change form for third-person singular: *I **have** talked with her, he **has** talked with her.*

→

433

- Some modals change form in the past. Others (*should, would, must* when it conveys probability, and *ought to*) use have + a past participle. *I* **can** *do it* becomes *I* **could** *do it* in past-tense clauses about ability. *I* **could** *do it* becomes "*I* **could have** done it" in clauses about possibility.
- Modals convey meaning about ability, advisability, necessity, possibility, and other conditions: for example, *I can go* means "I am able to go." Modals do not indicate actual occurrences.

ESL
6a

Conveying ability, necessity, advisability, possibility, and probability with modals

Conveying ability

The modal *can* conveys ability now (in the present) and *could* conveys ability before (in the past). These words deliver the meaning of "able to." For the future, use *will be able to.*

> Luis **can** beat Pepe at tennis. [*Can* conveys present ability.]
>
> He **could** beat him last month too. [*Could* conveys past ability.]
>
> If he practises, he **will be able to** beat him next month. [*Will be able to* conveys future ability.]

> Adding *not* between a modal and the main verb makes the clause negative.

> Mondana **can not** (or **cannot**) attend the study session; she **could not** attend last night; she **will not be able to** attend next Monday.

❖ USAGE ALERT: You will often see negative forms of modals turned into contractions: *can't, couldn't, won't, wouldn't,* and others. Because contractions are considered informal usage by some instructors, you will never be wrong if you avoid them in academic writing except for reproducing spoken words. ❖

Conveying necessity

The modals *must* and *have to* convey the message of a need to do something. Both *must* and *have to* are followed by the simple form of the main verb. In the present tense, *have to* changes form to agree with its subject.

> You **must** turn your paper in on time.
>
> You **have** to meet the minimum requirements.

In the past tense, *must* is never used to express necessity. Instead, use *had to*.

PRESENT TENSE   We **must** submit our papers today.

                       We **have to** abide by the rules.

PAST TENSE   We **had to** [not *We must*] write our first paper yesterday.

The negative forms of *must* and *have to* also have different meanings. *Must not* conveys that something is forbidden; *do not have to* conveys that something is not necessary.

You **must not** miss the lecture. [Missing the lecture is forbidden.]

You **do not have to** miss the lecture. [Missing the lecture is not necessary (if you cannot be there on time, for example). You can watch it on television.]

Conveying advisability or the notion of a good idea

The modals *should* and *ought to* express the idea that doing the action of the main verb is advisable or is a good idea.

You **should** write in your journal daily.

In the past tense, *should* and *ought to* convey regret or knowing something through hindsight. They mean that good advice was not taken.

You **should have** written in it yesterday.

I **ought to have** written in mine too.

The modal *had better* delivers the meaning of good advice or warning or threat. It does not change form for tense.

You **had better** start writing before you get behind.

Need to is often used to express strong advice, too. Its past-tense form is *needed to*.

You **need to** be a more conscientious student.

Conveying possibility

The modals *may, might*, and *could* can be used to convey an idea of possibility or likelihood.

We **may** travel during our fall break.

We **could** leave Friday after classes end.

The past-tense forms for *may, might*, and *could* use these words followed by *have* and the past participle of the main verb.

We **could have** travelled during the summer, but we both attended summer school.

Conveying probability

The modal *must* can convey probability or likelihood in addition to its conveying necessity (see Conveying Necessity). It means that a well-informed guess is being made.

Shakir **must** be a gregarious person. Everyone on campus seems to know him.

When *must* conveys probability, the past tense is *must have* plus the past participle of the main verb.

We hoped Marisa would come to the party; she **must have** had to study.

Conveying preferences, plans, and past habits with modals

Conveying preferences

The modals *would rather* and *would rather have* express a preference. *Would rather* (present tense) is used with the simple form of the main verb and *would rather have* (past participle) is used with the past participle of the main verb.

Carlos **would rather** work on the computer than sleep.

He **would rather have** had an earlier class.

Conveying plan or obligation

A form of *be* followed by *supposed to* and the simple form of a main verb delivers a meaning of something planned or of an obligation.

Lucia **was supposed to be** here an hour ago.

Conveying past habit

The modals *used to* and *would* express the idea that something happened repeatedly in the past.

Inger **used to** dream of studying in the States.

She **would** imagine what it would be like.

❖ USAGE ALERT: Both *used to* and *would* can be used to express repeated actions in the past, but *would* cannot be used for a situation that has lasted for a duration of time in the past.

NO	I **would** be a physics major.
YES	I **used to** be a physics major. ❖

ESL 6c Recognizing modals in the passive voice

Modals use the active voice, as shown in sections ESL-6a and ESL-6b. In the active voice, the subject does the action expressed in the main verb (see 8m-8o).

Modals can also use the passive voice. In the passive voice, the doer of the main verb's action is either unexpressed or is expressed as an object in a prepositional phrase starting with the word *by*.

PASSIVE	The rooftop **can be reached** from a door in the east tower.
ACTIVE	I **can reach** the rooftop from a door in the east tower.
PASSIVE	The assignment **must be completed** by Friday.
ACTIVE	Everyone **must complete** the assignment by Friday.

ESL 6-1

Modal Auxiliaries

Fill in the blanks with the correct modal auxiliary forms.

EXAMPLE _____ (present ability) you name a stranger political system than Canada's?

      Can (present ability) you name a stranger political system than Canada's?

1. You _____ (present possibility, negative) be aware that Canada's head of state does not live in Canada.

2. We _____ (present advisability, negative) forget, though, that in law, the British monarch is Canada's highest political authority.

3. You _____ (past possibility) heard the prime minister mistakenly being called the head of state.

4. Laws passed in Parliament _____ (present passive necessity) signed, however, by the Queen or her representative, the Governor General.

5. Fortunately, the days when the Governor General _____ (past habit) interfere in government are long past.

6. But as late as 1926, Prime Minister Mackenzie King _____ (past necessity) leave office when instructed by the Governor General.

7. Do you think we _____ (past advisability) changed the Constitution to have the prime minister elected by all voters and not just by voters in one riding?

8. There is no evidence that most Canadians _____ (preference) live under a different political system, however.

9. Still, you _____ (present necessity) admit that it is a strange system.

10. But it is the system that we use, so somebody _____ (past probability) guessed that it would work.

Answer Key

Chapter 1: **Thinking About Purposes and Audiences**
Chapter 2: **Planning and Shaping**
Chapter 3: **Drafting and Revising**

Exercise 1-1: Answers will vary.
1. This statement should emphasize the human catastrophe and urgency of the situation, while detailing specific ways in which your organization can help and how donors can reach you. The tone should be medium level and the vocabulary simple.
2. This letter should seek to minimize the danger, explaining the steps that you would take if an earthquake were to hit. The tone should be informal.
3. This piece should provide colourful description and personal reflections, and, if possible, some analysis. The tone should be between medium and formal.
4. This letter should detail the damages systematically and point out the contrast with surrounding buildings. Your writing should be calm and factual, and the tone between medium and formal.

Exercise 2-2: Answers will vary.
1. talent: whether talent is innate
2. someone I can count on: the ways in which my sister has helped me
3. travelling alone: safety tips for the young solo traveller
4. fitness: how to design a personal fitness regimen
5. graduation: thoughts on moving out into the "real" world
6. restaurants: the growing popularity of exotic restaurants
7. the beach: the effect of pollution on the local beaches
8. my grandparents: the obstacles faced by the author's grandparents in raising their families
9. a personal loss: reaction to the death of a loved one
10. choosing a computer: what is essential and what is an expensive option

Exercise 2-3: Answers will vary.

Exercise 2-4A: Answers will vary.
1. Unacceptable. Planned budget cuts will affect university services, housing, and scholarships.
2. Unacceptable. A regular study schedule can improve student grades.
3. Unacceptable. Recent theories suggest three principal causes of contemporary violence.

4. Unacceptable. The Canadian style of hockey is still capable of encouraging skill and artistry.
5. Unacceptable. My first adolescent crush was a painful experience.
6. Unacceptable. Giving brief but complete answers on a job application will make the best impression.
7. Acceptable.
8. Acceptable.
9. Unacceptable. My May visit to Turkey provided an opportunity to learn about history and archaeology.
10. Unacceptable. The Norman Conquest brought dramatic changes to Britain.

Exercise 2-4B: Answers will vary.
1. success: Definitions of success vary from person to person, but I will consider myself successful if I have a well-paying job that I enjoy doing and a happy, healthy family.
2. being a good friend: The hardest thing a good friend has to do is tell the truth even when it might hurt.
3. summer in the city: The heat of summer brings people together because it is too hot to stay inside.
4. laughter: Recent scientific studies indicate that laughter, as well as the positive mental attitude it represents, speeds up recovery from illness.
5. travel safety tips: Young people preparing to travel alone should make an inventory of what they can do without and of what they would need if left in a difficult situation.
6. graduation: Surveys show that a graduate's success in confronting the "real" world correlates with attitudes he or she developed well before starting post-secondary education.
7. exotic restaurants: Despite what some people think, the popularity of exotic restaurants has little to do with Canadians' attitudes toward multiculturalism.
8. a personal loss: The death of my youngest uncle made me confront issues of life and its purpose that I had never really considered.
9. sacrifice: My grandparents gave up everything they had to come Canada.
10. shopping: Buying by mail is an easy way to beat the Christmas crowds at the malls.

Exercise 2-5:
Thesis Statement: Leaving a roommate for a single apartment can have definite drawbacks.
I. Unsatisfactory furnishings
    A. Appliances
        1. Major
           a. Stove
           b. Refrigerator
           c. Washer
           d. Dryer
        2. Minor
           a. Microwave
           b. Blender
           c. Toaster
           d. Mixer

        B. Furniture
            1. Bedroom
                a. Futon
                b. Dresser
            2. Living room
                a. Sofa
                b. Chairs
                c. Tables
            3. Kitchen
                a. Table
                b. Chairs
        C. Equipment
            1. For entertainment
            2. For exercise
II. Insufficient finances
        A. Rent
        B. Utilities
            1. Gas
            2. Electricity
            3. Phone
        C. Food
        D. Entertainment
III. Inadequate companionship
        A. Frequent loneliness
        B. Occasional fear

Exercise 2-6: Answers will vary.

Exercise 3-7: Answers will vary.

A: A Brief History of Utensils

Forks, knives, and spoons seem so natural to most of us that it is hard to imagine eating dinner without them. Yet, many people, such as the Chinese, use chopsticks instead, and others use their hands to eat.

Knives are the oldest Western utensils. The first ones were made of stone 1.5 million years ago. They were originally used to cut up animals after a hunt. The same knife was used to butcher game, slice cooked food, and kill enemies. Even later in history, nobles were the only ones who could afford separate knives for different uses. People used all-purpose knives, pointed like today's steak knives. The round-tipped dinner knife is a modern invention. It became popular in seventeenth-century France because hostesses wanted to stop guests from picking their teeth with the points of their dinner knives.

The spoon is also an ancient tool. Wooden spoons twenty thousand years old have been found in Asia; spoons of stone, wood, ivory, and even gold have been found in Egyptian tombs. Spoons were originally used to scoop up food that were too thick to sip from a bowl.

The fork is a newcomer. Forks did not become widely accepted until the eighteenth century, when the French nobility adopted the fork as a status symbol and eating with one's hands became unfashionable. At about the same time, individual settings became the rule too. Previously, even rich people had shared plates and glasses at meals, but now the rich demanded individual plates, glasses, forks, spoons, and knives. Today in North America, a full set of utensils is considered a necessity. We forget that as recently as the American Revolution some people considered anyone who used a fork to be a fussy showoff.

B: Thoughts on a Solo Canoe Trip

Last year I had an adventure of the sort that many people never experience in their lives. In a way, however, it was a typical Canadian experience, or at least a part of Canadian folklore. I went on a solo canoe trip to Northern Ontario's Temagami region. It was a journey that had benefits for both body and spirit.

I have been a good canoeist since I was young. Nevertheless, when I told my friends of my intention to do a solo trip, they replied, "Isn't that a dangerous thing you're planning to do?" Admittedly, a solo trip may be dangerous. Still, many other sports and activities—including rock climbing, which has become hugely popular—are dangerous as well. A solo canoe trip need not be a cause for concern, as long as the canoeist is experienced and takes the proper precautions. It is essential to be in good physical condition, of course, and to wear a life jacket in the canoe at all times. The canoeist should come prepared with extra food and warm clothing, and should have learned and be able to apply the techniques of woodcraft and other skills. Once I had met all these conditions, the final preparation was to inform my friends and local people of my route and the expected day of my return.

I chose a route that I knew I could do; a solo trip is no time to show foolish bravado. Then off I went. For six days I was alone beneath the vast sky, paddling hard against the waves and winds of Temagami. All the while, my senses were heightened, for my safety was in my own hands. My eyes, ears, and nose were alert to smells, signs of wild animals, and changes in the weather. I listened to the wind roaring at night. One day I sat out a powerful storm in my tent, perched on the shore of a tiny island. Later that afternoon, I watched with mounting excitement as a strong west wind gradually drove off the clouds and freed me from the storm: I could continue my travels. Every night I crawled into my tent exhausted but pleased with what I had accomplished.

On the last day, I rode the high waves of Ferguson Bay to my final destination, pitching up on the sandy shore with a breath of relief. For my body, the trip had the benefit of giving me exercise in the outdoors. For my spirit, the trip let me feel the deep, meditative calm of being alone with myself and my thoughts. I was reminded how small and vulnerable one single person is, faced with the might of nature. At the same time, I had the satisfaction of depending only on myself and overcoming the challenges that confronted me.

Chapter 4:   Writing Paragraphs

Exercise 4-1: Topic Sentence; Irrelevant Sentence
1.   2; 3
2.   1; 4
3.   1; 3; 7
4.   1; 7
5.   1; 7; 9

Exercise 4-2:
1. but; similarly; and
2. however; in the United States; but; in fact
3. unlike; nor; in fact; and; since its beginnings; in addition to; finally
4. finally; because; or; certainly; unfortunately; actually; so
5. although; in most places; during the French Revolution; within a year

Exercise 4-3:
1. so; before; them; while; of course; instead; so; for other reasons as well; and; in fact
2. painted/painting; lines; straight; machine/machines; marks; road; truck; one-person/four-person; hot plastic; paint; crew
3. sentence 6: same structure on either side of semicolon highlights contrast; sentence 9: two items in list in same form
4. road or street: it; truck: it; crewmembers: they

Exercise 4-4:
1. b, d, a, e, c
2. c, a, e, b, d
3. d, c, e, b, f, a
4. c, d, e, a, b, f

Exercise 4-5: Answers will vary. Here are some likely details:
1. broadening cultural horizons; approach to foreign literatures; insight into structures and peculiarities of English; discipline of memorization
2. credit doesn't feel like real money; easy to forget how much one has already spent; high interest rates; adverse credit ratings
3. music; food; vocabulary; art
4. the thrill of the crowd; long-standing rivalries; close scores; skilful playing
5. based on an old, outdated view; too harsh; discriminatory; don't affect behaviour
6. size; academic ranking; location; sports

Exercise 4-6: Answers will vary.
1. preparing for vacation
   Topic Sentence: A few simple steps can reduce the tension sometimes connected with a major vacation.
   Details: 1. Begin planning early.
   2. Arrange for time off from work.
   3. Use a travel agent to get the best details.
   4. Get maps and/or booklets about local attractions.
   5. Make a packing list early enough to purchase needed items in advance.
   6. Take enough cash or travellers' cheques.
2. the floor plan of the local video rental store
   Topic Sentence: The floor plan at Jim's Video makes finding the tapes I want easy.
   Details: 1. movie classics on the left wall
   2. comedies on the right wall
   3. science fiction and horror in the front centre
   4. kids' movies in the rear centre
   5. the counter across the back wall

3. the disadvantages of working while attending school full time
   Topic Sentence: The difficulty with working while attending school full time is that I never have any time for myself.
   Details: 1. heavy classload
   2. homework and studying for tests
   3. hours at work
   4. required overtime at holidays
   5. family responsibilities
4. why I've chosen my career
   Topic Sentence: I think I would enjoy being a college professor.
   Details: 1. summers off
   2. opportunity to work with young people
   3. high status
   4. chance to study what interests me

Exercise 4-7: Answers will vary.
1. Topic Sentence: Walking alone at night on campus can be risky.
   Examples: a. It's easy to trip on cracked pavement in the dark.
   b. Drunks bother women in front of the Rathskeller.
   c. Two purses were snatched last week.
   d. Someone was robbed at the bus stop a few days ago.
2. Topic Sentence: Peer pressure can be hard to resist.
   Example: My first semester grades were low because I could not say no to all the invitations to go out and party after classes.

Exercise 4-8: Answers will vary.
1. a success story
   Topic Sentence: Sometimes the hardest part about succeeding is just deciding to try.
   Events: 1. invited to a gathering in Calgary
   2. fearful of driving that far alone
   3. trying to get someone else to go — and drive
   4. studying the map
   5. the ease of the trip itself
2. an odd person in my neighbourhood
   Topic Sentence: The people on my block are worried about Crazy John.
   Details: 1. dresses shabbily
   2. talks to himself
   3. lives with his elderly parents
   4. can't keep a job
   5. refuses to accept medical help
3. how to study for a test
   Topic Sentence: Studying for a test does not begin the night before the examination.
   Steps: 1. Read assignments as they are given.
   2. Highlight or take notes.
   3. Answer review questions or work sample problems.
   4. Ask questions in class.
   5. Review in short study sessions.

4. my ideal job
   Topic Sentence: My ideal job would enable me to help other people
   at the same time that it would allow me to be
   creative and earn a living wage.
   Qualities: 1. importance of contributing to my community
                2. helping others take care of themselves
                3. not routine
                4. challenging
                5. money
5. bosses
   Topic Sentence: In my experience, bad bosses fall into a few distinct
   categories.
   Subgroups: 1. bullies
               2. socializers
               3. the disorganized
               4. control freaks
6. my sister and I
   Topic sentence: No one believes my sister and I are related.
   Points: 1. looks
                2. choice of friends
                3. career choices
                4. political choices
                5. treatment of others
7. a lie and a forest fire
   Topic Sentence: Sometimes even a small lie can be like a match
   tossed carelessly into a forest.
   Similarities: 1. a thoughtless act
                 2. may land where it can't be controlled
                 3. destructive
                 4. can hurt the person who began it all
8. why I chose the school I am now attending
   Topic Sentence: Picking a college was not easy, but I finally chose X
   for several reasons.
   Causes or Effects: a. far away enough to live on campus, close
                          enough to visit home on weekends
                       b. good Art Department
                       c. reasonable tuition
                       d. friends going too
                       e. near sports arena and theatres

Exercise 4-9: Revised paragraphs will vary. Students should, however,
note the following weaknesses.
1. introduction: apologizes; lists topics that will not be discussed
   conclusion: announces what has been done; gives a key definition
                    too late to be of use
2. introduction: lacks thesis or main idea sentence; all specifics, no
                    generalization; has no apparent connection to topic
   conclusion: too abrupt
3. introduction: refers to the title instead of stating thesis; doesn't
                    show connection between capital punishment and
                    getting criminals off streets (a logical fallacy)

	conclusion:	contains several absolute claims
4.	introduction:	an unadorned thesis statement, not a complete introduction
	conclusion:	has no conclusion; this is a body paragraph
5.	introduction:	announces what will be done
	conclusion:	introduces new material

Exercise 4-10: Answers will vary.

Chapter 5:   Critical Thinking, Reading, and Writing

Exercise 5-1A:

1. fact
2. fact
3. opinion
4. fact
5. fact
6. opinion
7. fact
8. fact
9. opinion
10. opinion
11. fact
12. opinion
13. fact
14. opinion
15. opinion

Exercise 5-1B:

1. fact
2. opinion
3. opinion
4. fact
5. opinion
6. fact
7. fact
8. fact
9. opinion
10. fact
11. opinion
12. opinion
13. fact
14. opinion

Chapter 6:   Writing Argument

No exercises

Chapter 7:   Parts of Speech and Sentence Structures

Exercise 7-1:

1. observers, e-books, books, paper
2. books, appliances
3. book, version, work
4. file
5. appliance, device, laptop
6. dollars, appliances, screens, keyboards
7. time, batteries, books
8. appliances, library, books
9. appliance, books, computer
10. devices, modems, works, libraries, lines, telephones, faxes
11. companies, software, books, computer
12. books, counterparts
13. screens, environment, texts
14. highlighting, annotating, book
15. types, books, form
16. dictionaries, encyclopedias, directories, catalogues, manuals
17. readers, type, book, amount, information
18. reading, people, text
19. paper, technology, interface

Exercise 7-2:

1. their
2. they, her, she
3. they, her, she
4. she
5. that
6. this, their
7. their, themselves
8. none
9. she, her
10. she, anyone, who
11. what, they
12. whose, them
13. us
14. everyone, this
15. some, one another
16. what, you
17. you, your

Exercise 7-3:

1. can lead
2. recognize
3. has
4. should think
5. may cause
6. discuss
7. might ask
8. is, is
9. take
10. may require
11. might lead
12. tolerate
13. accept
14. do dwell
15. are
16. might learn
17. look
18. be, to assist
19. would do
20. find, enjoy

Exercise 7-4:

1. verb
2. gerund
3. infinitive
4. verb
5. verb
6. past participle
7. verb
8. past participle
9. verb
10. verb
11. infinitive
12. verb
13. present participle
14. present participle
15. verb
16. infinitive
17. verb
18. present participle
19. verb
20. infinitive

Exercise 7-5:

1. arithmetical
2. familiar, Chinese
3. small, parallel
4. rectangular
5. first, straight, shallow
6. later, firm, entire
7. portable, parallel
8. each, exact, unique
9. fundamental, place-value
10. ingenious, few, large
11. numerical, one
12. each, previous
13. first, new
14. other

15. memory, mental
16. Asian
17. Japanese, *soroban*
18. Russian, *tschoty*
19. one, calculating, complex
20. these, physical, mental

Exercise 7-6:
1. adverb: only
2. adverb: most
3. adverb: most; adverb: easily
4. adverb: typically; conjunctive adverb: however; adverb: mostly
5. adverb: more
6. adverb: extremely; conjunctive adverb: indeed; adverb: often
7. conjunctive adverb: however; adverb: when humans enter their territory; adverb: usually
8. adverb: while living in the forest; adverb: just; adverb: to get around
9. adverb: quite; adverb: on the ground
10. adverb: generally; adverb: on all fours; conjunctive adverb: still; adverb: sometimes; adverb: in an upright position; adverb: much like a human
11. conjunctive adverb: in fact; adverb: when standing erect

Exercise 7-7:

prepositions	objects
1. in	China
over	300 million bicycles
on	the road
2. after	the creation
of	a French model, the *célérifère*
3. of	foot-powered scooter
unlike	those that followed
4. until	the invention
of	a German baron
of	the stationary front wheel
5. for	his new bicycle
6. in	a Scottish workshop
with	pedals
7. to	the rear wheels
by means of	cranks
8. during	the 1860s
to	the front wheels
9. in	England
in	1876
with	a chain and sprocket
10. for	today's bicycle
11. instead of	a larger front wheel
in	size
12. during	the 1880s
with	compressed air

13. along with   the derailleur gear
     in   the 1890s
14. of   the bicycle
     to   attempts to motorize it

Exercise 7-8:

1. and: CC
2. when: SC
3. if: SC
4. before: SC
5. because: SC
6. where: SC
7. but: CC
8. for: CC; whenever: SC
9. when: SC
10. unless: SC

Exercise 7-9:

1. adjective
2. verb
3. preposition
4. noun
5. noun
6. conjunction
7. adverb
8. preposition
9. verb
10. pronoun
11. adjective
12. conjunction
13. adjective
14. preposition
15. verb
16. verb
17. preposition
18. verb
19. verb
20. preposition
21. noun
22. adverb
23. adjective
24. adverb
25. adjective

Exercise 7-10A:

1. Warm air/cannot...
2. The temperature beneath the ice/is...
3. This/keeps...
4. The ice at a figure-skating rink/is...
5. Ice hockey rinks/have...
6. The ice/is...
7. The concrete/contains...
8. An Olympic-sized rink/has...
9. A very cold liquid, like the antifreeze in cars/circulates...
10. The liquid/absorbs...
11. Machinery/keeps...
12. More and more people/are...

Exercise 7-10B:

subject	verb
1. toothbrushes	were
2. people	rubbed
3. toothbrushes	originated
4. bristles	came
5. hogs	grew
6. Europeans	brushed
7. toothbrushes sponges	were used
8. men women	picked
9. stems toothpicks	were employed

10.	toothpicks	were
11.	germs	developed
12.	solution	was
13.	discovery	led
		made
14.	nylon	was
		resisted
15.	brushes	were sold
16.	they	were
17.	tissue	scratched
		bled
18.	version	was developed
19.	it	cost
20.	care	improved
21.	dentists	have made
	surgeons	
22.	toothbrushes	should be used
		should be replaced
23.	bristles	are
		can cut

Exercise 7-11:

	direct object	indirect object
1.	popcorn	children
2.	necklaces	Columbus
3.	strings	—
4.	machines	friends
5.	popcorn	themselves
6.	dollar	customers
7.	poppers	—
8.	popcorn	customers
9.	origin	—
10.	hot dogs	people
11.	hot dogs	New Yorkers
12.	buns	customers
13.	gloves	customers
14.	fortune	vendors

Exercise 7-12:

1.	SC/N	9.	SC/N	17.	SC/N
2.	SC/N	10.	SC/N	18.	SC/N
3.	SC/Adj.	11.	SC/Adj.	19.	SC/N
4.	SC/N	12.	SC/Adj.	20.	SC/N
5.	OC/Adj.	13.	SC/Adj.	21.	OC/Adj.
6.	OC/Adj.	14.	SC/N	22.	SC/Adj.
7.	OC/Adj.	15.	OC/N	23.	OC/Adj.
8.	OC/Adj.	16.	SC/N		

Exercise 7-13A:

1. d. adjective
   e. adjective
2. f. adverb
   g. adjective
3. h. adverb
   i. adjective
4. j. adjective
   k. adjective
5. l. adjective
   m. adjective

6. n. adverb
   o. adjective
7. p. adverb
   q. adverb
8. r. adverb
   s. adjective
9. t. adverb
   u. adjective
10. v. adjective
    w. adjective

Exercise 7-13B:

1. early: adverb
2. empty: adjective
3. already: adverb
4. new: adjective
5. much: adverb
6. easily: adverb; convenient: adjective
7. luckily: adverb; small: adjective
8. really: adverb; excellent: adjective
9. expensive: adjective; fortunately: adverb
10. finally: adverb; completely: adverb

Exercise 7-14:

1. hockey game
2. match
3. telephone
4. radio transmitter
5. broadcasting studio
6. Maple Leaf Gardens
7. broadcasts
8. shout
9. phrase
10. names
11. the 1950s
12. Hewitt's son
13. Foster Hewitt
14. series

Exercise 7-15A:

1. NP
2. VP
3. NP
4. PP
5. AP

6. NP
7. VP
8. AP
9. VP
10. NP

11. PP
12. PP
13. AP
14. VP

Exercise 7-15B:

1.	part	6.	inf	11.	part
2.	inf	7.	part	12.	ger
3.	part	8.	part	13.	inf
4.	ger	9.	ger	14.	ger
5.	ger	10.	inf		

Exercise 7-16:

1.	who. . . gold	7.	than. . . does
2.	Because. . . food	8.	wherever. . . can
3.	which. . . time	9.	where. . . potato
4.	If. . . butter	10.	When. . . gallon
5.	Since. . . grain	11.	that. . . year
6.	although. . . animals	12.	while. . . percent

Exercise 7-17:

1. <u>Since</u> potatoes grown from seed may not inherit the parent plant's characteristics, potatoes are usually grown from the eye of a planted piece of potato.
2. <u>Because</u> potato blossoms look like those of the poisonous nightshade plant, centuries ago Europeans were afraid to eat potatoes.
3. <u>Although</u> tomatoes, tobacco, and eggplant are all relatives of the potato, they do not look alike.
4. The sweet potato is not related to the potato <u>even though</u> its Indian name, <u>batata</u>, was mistakenly taken to mean "potato" by its European "discoverers."
5. Most people throw away the potato skin, <u>which</u> is a good source of dietary fiber.
6. <u>While</u> about 25 percent of Canada's potato-farming land is located in Prince Edward Island, this island province has only 0.1 percent of Canada's total land area.
7. Would you believe <u>that</u> twelve percent of the U.S. crop is made into potato chips?
8. There are misinformed people <u>who</u> believe that the potato is only a poor person's food.
9. They overlook <u>that</u> potatoes have nourished the people of Europe since the eighteenth century.
10. Nutritious potatoes allowed the population to expand, <u>until</u> 1845, <u>when</u> Europe—especially Ireland—was almost destroyed by a disease that killed the potato crop.
11. Potato chips were created in New England <u>because</u> a hotel chef became angry with a fussy customer.
12. <u>Although</u> no one else had ever complained, the customer sent back his french fries twice, saying they were not crisp enough.
13. The chef, <u>who</u> apparently had a bad temper, decided to teach the man a lesson.
14. He cut the potatoes paper-thin and fried them <u>until</u> they were too crisp to pick up with a fork.
15. <u>Once</u> the customer tasted these potatoes, he was delighted.
16. These "chips" became very popular, <u>so that</u> the chef never got his revenge, but he did get his own restaurant.

Exercise 7-18:

1. <u>Forgetting</u> <u>is</u> not always permanent. Simple

2. <u>Interference</u> sometimes <u>keeps</u> us from remembering. Simple

3. *SC*
   (When) this <u>happens</u>, <u>we</u> <u>may</u> not <u>be able</u> to stop thinking about something else (even though) <u>we</u> <u>know</u> it is wrong. Complex

4. *SC* *CC*
   For example, <u>we</u> <u>may</u> not <u>recall</u> a friend's name, (and) <u>we</u> <u>may</u> even <u>want</u> to call her by someone else's name. Compound

5. *CC*
   Other times, <u>we</u> <u>try</u> hard to remember, (but) our <u>memories</u> <u>may</u> not <u>work</u> at all. Compound

6. *SC* *RP*
   The <u>information</u> <u>seems</u> lost (until) <u>we</u> <u>receive</u> a clue (that) <u>helps</u> us remember. Complex

7. *RP* *CC*
   Some <u>scientists</u> <u>believe</u> (that) <u>memories</u> <u>may</u> completely <u>fade</u> away, (and) then <u>we</u> <u>can</u> never <u>get</u> them back. Compound

8. *RP*
   Recent <u>studies</u> <u>show</u> (that) <u>storing</u> memory <u>changes</u> the brain tissue. Complex

9. *OR* *RP* *CC*
   (However,) no one <u>has shown</u> (that) these <u>changes</u> <u>can be erased,</u> (so) the "fading-away" <u>theory</u> of forgetting <u>remains</u> unproven. Compound-Complex

10. *RP*
    <u>Scientists</u> (who) <u>believe</u> in the interference theory of forgetting <u>identify</u> different kinds of interference. Complex

11. Sometimes <u>learning</u> new material <u>is made</u> difficult by conflicting old material. Simple

12. <u>Confusion</u> between the old material and the new <u>makes</u> it hard to remember either one. Simple

13. <u>Coming</u> upon similar material soon after learning something <u>can</u> also <u>interfere</u>. Simple

14. *CC*
    <u>Scientists</u> <u>have shown</u> this in experiments, (but) everyday <u>experience</u> <u>can convince</u> us too. Compound

15. <u>Anyone</u> trying to learn two similar languages, such as French and Spanish, at the same time <u>knows</u> the feeling of confusion. Simple

Exercise 7-19A: Answers will vary.
1. Psychoanalysis helps people deal with these forgotten memories, for it works at exploring them consciously.
2. Repression, which is the burying in the unconscious of fearful experiences, can make life difficult.
3. People repress frightening thoughts and experiences, and then they try to go on living normally.
4. When people repress experiences, they avoid having to relive them, so they feel better for a time.
5. Experiments show that people forget bad experiences more quickly (than they forget) good experiences.
6. Repression occurs in the mentally ill, but it also occurs in healthy people.
7. A learning atmosphere where people can relax leads to better memory.
8. Any student knows this, and so does any teacher.
9. Because people are often distracted in stressful situations, they simply do not see everything; therefore, they cannot remember everything.
10. This may explain why accident victims often do not recall details of their experiences.
11. Many people do not remember much from their childhoods, but this does not mean that they are repressing bad memories.
12. They may have been too interested in some events to notice others that were happening at the same time, or maybe their childhoods were simply too boring to remember.

Exercise 7-19B: Answers will vary.
1. Compound: Fast food is not cheap, and it is not especially healthful.
   Complex: Although it is less expensive than other options, fast food is not cheap.
   Compound-Complex: Although it is very popular, fast food is not cheap, nor is it appetizing.
2. Compound: The movie theatre was crowded, so the manager turned up the air conditioner.
   Complex: Because too many tickets were sold, the movie theatre was crowded.
   Compound-Complex: After the announcement that the star would make a personal appearance, the movie theatre was crowded, and the line stretched around the block.
3. Compound: Read contracts before you sign them, or you could end up in financial trouble.
   Complex: Whenever you purchase goods or services, read contracts before you sign them.
   Compound-Complex: When you rent an apartment, always ask for a written lease, but read contracts before you sign them.
4. Compound: Ice cream is a popular dessert, and sales increase every year.
   Complex: Although it is fattening, ice cream is a popular dessert.
   Compound-Complex: Since the opening of the new diner, more people are eating out, and ice cream is a popular dessert.
5. Compound: Grocery stores should be open twenty-four hours a day, and so should banks.

Complex: If staff can be hired, grocery stores should be open
twenty-four hours a day.
Compound-Complex: Because more and more people are working off
schedules, grocery stores should be open twenty-four hours a
day, and bus service should be frequent.

Exercise 7-19C: Answers will vary.
1. Because she speaks Cantonese, she has begun to research West Coast immigrant experiences.
2. Whoever found my keys left them with the security guard.
3. Consult the speaker's guidelines before you rule on the motion from the floor.
4. Even though he had a valid ticket, he waited for an hour to get into the Picasso exhibit.
5. Who knows where my cat has gone?
6. The so-called Rolex that she bought from a sidewalk vendor stopped working after three months.
7. I would like to know who has the floppy disk with my essay.
8. Since she took an Internet tutorial, she has emerged from her room only to order the occasional pizza.
9. I have forgotten whether this boa constrictor is the friendly one.
10. If the sky looks threatening, take an umbrella.

Chapter 8:   Verbs

Exercise 8-1:

1. rushes
2. ties
3. weighs
4. needs
5. attempts
6. fails
7. starts
8. opens
9. waits
10. occurs
11. reports
12. affects
13. recommends
14. warns
15. posts
16. stops
17. requires
18. knows
19. hears
20. allows
21. remains
22. brakes
23. causes
24. faces
25. practises

Exercise 8-2:

1. started
2. recorded
3. developed
4. used
5. inserted
6. issued, startled
7. perceived
8. jerked, headed
9. employed
10. pulled
11. experimented
12. imagined

Exercise 8-3:

1.	ran	7.	set	13.	became
2.	arose	8.	made	14.	oversaw
3.	built	9.	began	15.	meant
4.	fell, brought	10.	cost	16.	grew
5.	had	11.	gave	17.	led
6.	found	12.	chose		

Exercise 8-4:

person	present tense	past tense
first	am	was
second	are	were
third	is	was
first	are	were
second	are	were
third	are	were

present participle: being   past participle: been

Exercise 8-5:

For some people a garden <u>is</u> a hobby. For others it <u>is</u> a necessity. In either case, <u>being</u> a gardener is hard work.

The first thing you must do each spring <u>is</u> prepare the garden plot with spade, plow, or rototiller. Your muscles <u>are</u> sure to ache after a day of turning the soil. Planting and mulching <u>are</u> next. I <u>am</u> always excited to see new plants coming up. You will <u>be</u> too. However, weeds <u>are</u> apt to grow faster than the seeds you planted.

Unless your idea of an aerobic workout <u>is</u> thirty minutes with a hoe, you should <u>be</u> enthusiastic about mulch. Mulch can <u>be</u> straw mounded around plants or plastic sheets covering the ground between rows. If you <u>are</u> using plastic, <u>be</u> sure you have the kind that can breathe. Otherwise, there will <u>be</u> inadequate moisture for your plants.

A garden <u>is</u> guaranteed to cultivate your patience while you <u>are</u> cultivating it. It cannot <u>be</u> rushed. If you hope <u>to be</u> a successful gardener, you must <u>be</u> willing to work at it.

Exercise 8-6: Answers will vary.

1. are
2. was
3. may
4. do
5. does
6. seem
7. can
8. should
9. will
10. is
11. can
12. would
13. could
14. were
15. can
16. be
17. has
18. have

Exercise 8-7:

1. transitive
2. linking
3. intransitive
4. transitive
5. transitive
6. transitive
7. linking
8. intransitive
9. transitive
10. intransitive
11. transitive
12. linking
13. transitive
14. intransitive
15. transitive
16. linking

Exercise 8-8:

1. intransitive: The doctor operated with confidence.
   transitive: Jane operated the backhoe skillfully.
2. intransitive: Rabbits multiply rapidly.
   transitive: The store owner multiplied the profit per sweater by the number of sweaters sold.
3. intransitive: We met unexpectedly.
   transitive: I met my best friend in math class.
4. intransitive: The hot air balloon lifted over the mountains.
   transitive: Ants can lift several times their own weight.
5. intransitive: The dew evaporated in the morning sun.
   transitive: Food dehydrators evaporate the moisture in meats and vegetables.

Exercise 8-9A:

	-s form	past tense	past participle	present participle
lie	lies	lay	lain	lying
lay	lays	laid	laid	laying
sit	sits	sat	sat	sitting
set	sets	set	set	setting
rise	rises	rose	risen	rising
raise	raises	raised	raised	raising

Exercise 8-9B:

1. sitting
2. lay, lies
3. raised
4. laying
5. lain
6. sat
7. rose, laid
8. raised
9. set
10. raise

457

Exercise 8-10:

1. have discovered
2. have been kissing
3. are beginning
4. has been studying
5. has found
6. had been getting
7. are earning
8. had said
9. are living
10. have been having
11. has suggested
12. are starting
13. have known
14. have understood
15. have been studying

Exercise 8-11:

1. The Louvre in Paris <u>was</u> not <u>built</u> as an art museum.   passive
2. The original Louvre <u>was constructed</u> in the twelfth century as a fortress.   passive
3. Francis I <u>erected</u> the present building as a residence.   active
4. A gallery connecting it with the Tuileries Palace <u>was started</u> by Henry IV and <u>completed</u> by Louis XIV.   passive
5. A second gallery, begun by Napoleon, <u>would have enclosed</u> a great square.   active
6. However, it <u>was not finished</u> until after his abdication.   passive
7. Revolutionaries <u>overthrew</u> the Bastille on July 14, 1789.   active
8. Just four years later the art collection of the Louvre <u>was opened</u> to the public.   passive
9. The collection <u>can be traced</u> back to Francis I.   passive
10. Francis, an ardent collector, <u>invited</u> Leonardo da Vinci to France in 1515.   active
11. Leonardo <u>brought</u> the *Mona Lisa* with him from Italy.   active
12. Nevertheless, the royal art collection <u>may have been expanded</u> more by ministers than by kings.   passive
13. Cardinals Richelieu and Mazarin <u>can take credit</u> for many important acquisitions.   active
14. Today the Louvre <u>has</u> a new entrance.   active
15. The entrance, a glass pyramid in the courtyard, <u>was designed</u> by I. M. Pei.   passive
16. Pei's name <u>can be added</u> to a distinguished list of Louvre architects.   passive

Exercise 8-12:

1. passive People outside Africa did not know about the ruins until 1868.
2. active
3. passive Acceptable. The building is more important than who built it.
4. passive Acceptable. The unknown builders are less important than the way it was built.
5. passive A nine-metre wall encircles a lower, elliptical building.
6. active
7. passive Acceptable. Emphasis on the sculptures, not the discoverers.
8. active
9. active
10. passive Acceptable. Tools are stressed, not the scavengers who found them.
11. active

Chapter 9:   Case of Nouns and Pronouns

Exercise 9-1:

	person	subject	object	possessive
singular	first	I	me	my/mine
	second	you	you	you/yours
	third	he	him	his
		she	her	her/hers
		it	it	its
plural	first	we	us	our/ours
	second	you	you	your/yours
	third	they	them	their/theirs

Exercise 9-2:

pronoun	case
1. me	objective
2. they	subjective
you	objective
3. his	possessive
4. he	subjective
5. him	objective
6. their	possessive
they	subjective
7. they	subjective
8. them	objective
9. it	subjective
10. they	subjective
11. its	possessive
12. she	subjective
their	possessive
13. they	subjective
their	possessive
14. them	objective
15. it	objective
its	possessive
16. us	objective
they	subjective
17. our	possessive
them	objective
18. we	subjective
them	objective

Exercise 9-3:

1. we, we
2. It
3. us
4. he
5. He, I
6. our
7. he, I, themselves
8. him, himself
9. them, itself
10. their
11. us
12. my

13. himself
15. her
17. you, you
19. themselves

14. me, us
16. her
18. them
20. yours

Exercise 9-4A:

1. <u>he</u> and <u>she</u>: appositives of <u>the partners</u>
2. <u>he</u>: complement of <u>a legend</u>
3. <u>ours</u>: appositive of <u>the best cheesecake</u>
4. <u>they</u>: complement of <u>the first ones</u>
5. <u>me</u>: appositive of <u>the addressee</u>

Exercise 9-4B:

1. she
2. me
3. he
4. him
5. I

Exercise 9-5:

1. who
2. who
3. whoever
4. whom
5. whoever
6. who
7. who
8. who

9. whom
10. who
11. whom
12. whomever
13. who
14. who
15. whom
16. whom

Exercise 9-6:

1. himself
2. him
3. His
4. he
5. he
6. them
7. its

8. itself
9. it
10. him
11. itself
12. their
13. themselves

Chapter 10: Pronoun Reference

Exercise 10-1:

1. them
   Unlike most recent Canadian prime ministers, three out of the first five Canadian prime ministers were born in Scotland or England. Most <u>recent Canadian prime ministers</u> were born in Canada.
2. he
   The first Canadian-born prime minister, Sir John Abbott, held office in 1891 and 1892; the last British-born prime minister was John Turner. <u>Turner</u> led the government for a few weeks in 1984.

3. he

   For religious reasons, Zachary Taylor refused to take the presidential oath of office on a Sunday, so David Rice Atchison (president of the Senate) as president for a day. <u>Atchison</u> spent the day appointing his temporary cabinet.

4. his

   Correct

5. he

   An American Indian, Charles Curtis, became vice-president when Herbert Hoover was elected president in 1928. <u>Curtis</u> was one-half Kaw.

6. he

   William DeVance King, vice-president under Franklin Pierce, was in Cuba during the election and had to be sworn in by an act of Congress, never bothering to return to Washington. A month later, never having carried out any official duties, <u>King</u> died.

7. their, their

   Correct

8. their, theirs

   Correct

9. she

   The first woman presidential candidate was Victoria Woodhull. Years before Geraldine Ferraro ran for vice president, <u>Woodhull</u> was on the Equal Rights Party ticket — in 1872.

10. She

   The first woman to lead a major party in the Canadian House of Commons was Audrey McLaughlin, and the second was Kim Campbell. <u>Campbell</u> became the first woman prime minister.

11. He, he

   As a child, president-to-be Andrew Johnson was sold as an indentured servant to a tailor. <u>Johnson</u> was supposed to work for seven years, but <u>he</u> ran away.

Exercise 10-2: Answers will vary.

1. A California company called the Space Island Group is planning to recycle one of the shortest-lived components of the space shuttle. <u>The company's plan</u> is ingenious.

2. Engineers at SIG plan to construct dozens of wheel-shaped space stations using empty shuttle fuel tanks. <u>The tanks</u> are eminently suited to the task.

3. A shuttle's fuel tanks are huge. Each one is 8.5 metres in diameter and nearly 50 metres long—approximately the size of a jumbo jet. <u>The shuttle</u> jettisons <u>the tanks</u> just before it reaches orbit, leaving them to burn up and crash into the ocean.

4. Over a hundred of these tanks, known as ETs, have been used and destroyed since the first shuttle launch in 1981. So <u>it is obvious</u> how much hardware has gone to waste.

5. Using ETs to form manned space stations—and developing passenger shuttles to take people to them—was originally NASA's idea. At first, <u>NASA was</u> enthusiastic about this possibility.

6. However, it would have taken too long for NASA to develop and test passenger shuttles, so <u>the idea</u> was dropped.

7. SIG's plan is to build the passenger shuttles and lease them to commercial airlines. <u>SIG believes</u> that this is the fastest way to get ordinary people into space.

8. The space stations will also be leased—at a rate of US $10 to $20 per cubic foot per day—to anyone wishing to run a business in space. <u>Businesspeople will</u> simply take the shuttle, transfer to the space station, and set up <u>their offices</u>.
9. While the space stations have a projected life of 30 years, <u>SIG claims</u> that tenants would fully pay for them within 2 to 3 years. This means that the passenger shuttle program could actually operate at a profit.

Exercise 10-3: Answers may vary by using <u>she</u> or <u>he or she</u> in place of <u>he</u>.

Everyone has to be careful when buying on credit. Otherwise, a person may wind up so heavily in debt that it may take years to straighten out his life. Credit cards are easy for a person to get if he is working, and many finance companies are eager to give anyone instalment loans at high interest rates. Once someone is hooked, he may find himself taking out loans to pay his loans. When this happens, he is doomed to being forever in debt.

There are, of course, times when using credit makes sense. If a person has the money (or will have it when the bill comes), a credit card can enable him to shop without carrying cash. Someone may also want to keep a few gasoline credit cards with him in case his car breaks down on the road. Using credit will allow a person to deal with other emergencies (tuition, a broken water heater) when he lacks the cash. He can also use credit to take advantage of sales. However, he needs to recognize the difference between a sale item he needs and one he wants. If he can't do this, he may find himself dealing with collection agents, car repossessors, or even bankruptcy lawyers.

Chapter 11: Agreement

Exercise 11-1A:

1. occupy
2. associates
3. wear
4. refers
5. work
6. consists
7. use
8. bastes
9. cuts
10. reveal

Exercise 11-1B:

1. needs
2. makes
3. are
4. deserve
5. seems
6. are
7. means
8. is
9. becomes
10. are

Exercise 11-1C:

subject	verb	correction
1. Ken, Sara	has visited	have visited
2. places	is	are
they	should see	correct
3. cities	is	correct
that	transmit	correct
4. history	seems	correct
5. more	is	are
6. castles, residences	are	correct

7.	gardens	is	are
8.	art, architecture	reveals	reveal
9.	city	is	correct
10.	visitors	comes	come

Exercise 11-1D:

1.	is	6.	share
2.	are	7.	is
3.	is	8.	is
4.	have	9.	prefers
5.	are	10.	are

Exercise 11-1E:

1.	mystery/continues	6.	decoration/appears
2.	anyone/sees	7.	pictures/stem
3.	book/is	8.	birds/wear
4.	no one/studies	9.	humour/pervades
5.	paintings/are	10.	text/is

Exercise 11-1F:

1.	seems	6.	makes
2.	is	7.	remains
3.	shows	8.	deals
4.	is	9.	get
5.	belong	10.	rates

Exercise 11-1G:

1.	knows, dream	8.	believe	15.	have
2.	occur	9.	spend	16.	claim
3.	stands	10.	receive	17.	protect
4.	gets	11.	devote	18.	exists, proposes
5.	are, means	12.	form	19.	learn
6.	suggest	13.	think	20.	combines, are
7.	represent	14.	lacks		

Exercise 11-2:

1.	his; her; his or her	7.	his; her; his or her	13.	they; you
2.	they	8.	one/oneself; he/himself; she/herself	14.	its
3.	himself; herself			15.	their
4.	his; her; his or her	9.	they	16.	his
5.	its	10.	their	17.	their
6.	their	11.	their	18.	their
		12.	his	19.	its
				20.	they

Exercise 11-3: Answers will vary.
1. The number of people that needs to be absorbed into Canada each month is 48 000. <u>It is</u> made up of 33 000 births and 15 000 immigrants.
2. All need to have basic services. <u>They need</u> food, clothing, and shelter.

3. A higher birth rate and a greater survival rate are modern trends. Together, <u>they</u> <u>make</u> the world population double in 35 years.
4. Either disease or war may be the result, some people say. <u>It will be a way</u> of reducing the population.
5. There are theories about how many people the earth can support, but <u>they vary</u> from 500 000 000 (less than 10 percent of the current population) to 15 billion (between two and three times the current population).
6. Anyone in a world of 15 billion people would not have many luxuries in <u>his or her life</u>.
7. Life in the poorest tropical countries is horrible <u>It is</u> often very short and miserable.
8. The food supply in these countries is already too small, but rapidly growing populations means <u>it</u> will become even less adequate.
9. <u>None of us</u> can be sure of the outcome if we do not make some changes. <u>We</u> can be sure, however, that more people will go hungry.
10. Neither the dependence on only a few grain crops nor the beef-eating habit is likely to last much into the future. <u>It is</u> too wasteful of food resources.
11. China and India have a combined population of over two billion. <u>That is</u> about one-third of the world's people.
12. To make room for more towns, some tropical countries are cutting down <u>their</u> rain forests.
13. Third World governments must take steps to use the forest wisely, or <u>it</u> will disappear.

Chapter 12: Using Adjectives and Adverbs

Exercise 12-1:

1. adjective	8. adjective	15. adverb
2. adverb	9. adverb	16. adverb
3. adverb	10. adjective	17. adjective
4. adjective	11. adjective	18. adverb
5. adverb	12. adjective	19. adjective
6. adjective	13. adjective	20. adverb
7. adjective	14. adverb	

Exercise 12-2:

1. annually	8. dangerous	15. quickly
2. available	9. slowly	16. popular
3. well	10. high	17. lately
4. serious	11. lengthy	18. regularly
5. commonly	12. ancient	19. quick
6. bad	13. chemically	20. carefully
7. delicate	14. recently	

Exercise 12-3A:

	comparative	superlative
1.	worse	worst
2.	worse	worst
3.	more forgiving	most forgiving

4. freer	freest
5. better	best
6. more gracefully	most gracefully
7. handsomer	handsomest
8. hotter	hottest
9. littler	littlest
10. more loudly	most loudly
11. more	most
12. more	most
13. more powerfully	most powerfully
14. prettier	prettiest
15. more quickly	most quickly
16. more	most
17. more sweetly	most sweetly
18. more sympathetically	most sympathetically
19. more talented	most talented
20. better	best

Exercise 12-3B: Answers will vary.

Exercise 12-4: Answers will vary.

Chapter 13: Sentence Fragments

Exercise 13-1A: Answers will vary.
1. This is a prepositional phrase.
   Ling left his glasses beside the rice cooker.
2. There is no subject.
   Every Saturday Yuri tutors his roommate in Russian.
3. This is a noun clause.
   The prize goes to whoever breaks the piñata.
4. This is a past participial phrase.
   Considered the best in her class, Janice strives to excel.
5. This is part of a compound predicate.
   Next month my brother begins school and plans to study Swahili.
6. This is a noun phrase.
   Remedial English is my least favourite course this term.
7. This is either a gerund or a participial phrase.
   Studying constantly is causing severe eyestrain. (gerund phrase)
   Studying constantly, Gretta gradually gave up her social life. (participial   phrase)
8. This is a dependent adverb clause.
   When Ahmed entered the university, he was only seventeen.
9. This is a dependent adjective clause.
   Here is a Web site where you can locate ten dialogues by Plato.
10. This lacks a helping verb.
    Kofi is hoping for understanding.

Exercise 13-1B:
1. No one knows when Natasha arrived on campus. (noun clause)
    When Natasha arrived on campus, no one was there to meet her. (adverb clause)
2. Someone who looks for affordable child care in this city will have difficulty. (part of a dependent adjective clause)
    Shannon seldom looks for affordable child care. (predicate)
3. The neighbour who borrowed my vacuum cleaner didn't return it. (dependent adjective clause)
    Who borrowed my vacuum cleaner? (question)
4. I must learn to use HTML or another markup language. (infinitive phrase as direct object)
    In this job it is imperative to use HTML or another markup language. (infinitive phrase as adverb)
5. There lay my sandals, buried under last week's laundry. (past participial phrase)
    Buford's homework was buried under last week's laundry. (part of the predicate)
6. At the embassy I saw Irving trying to get a visa. (present participial phrase)
    Trying to get a visa requires infinite patience. (gerund phrase)
7. Historians and anthropologists deal with human history in different ways. (compound subject)
    Two kinds of professors, historians and anthropologists, learn about the present by looking at the past. (appositives)
8. Dr. Carlucci is the instructor who helped me the most. (noun as subject complement plus adjective clause)
    The instructor who helped me the most is no longer here. (noun as subject plus adjective clause)
9. Maria works ten hours a week in the computer lab. (prepositional phrase as adverb)
    Her job in the computer lab is not very demanding. (prepositional phrase as adjective)
10. We witnessed a man shaking hands with his enemy. (participial phrase)
    A man was shaking hands with his enemy. (part of the predicate)

Exercise 13-2:
1. The oldest shoe ever found was a sandal, which dated from 2000 B.C. It was found in an Egyptian tomb. Sandals were the usual footwear in tropical areas.
2. Archaeologists are interested in the clothing of our ancestors. They have discovered hundreds of sandal designs, each usually representative of a particular culture at a particular time. However, other types of shoes were also worn.
3. The oldest nonsandal shoe found has been a leather wrap-around shaped like a moccasin. Rawhide lacing could be pulled tight to keep the shoe snugly on the foot. This shoe came from Babylonia.
4. Upper-class Greek women favoured a similar shoe. The preferred colours were red and white. Roman women also wore red and white closed shoes, and green or yellow ones for special occasions.
5. Lower-ranking Roman women wore undyed open sandals. Senators wore brown shoes, with tied black leather straps wound around the lower leg. Consuls, who were high-ranking officials, wore white shoes.
6. Boots were first used by soldiers. The Assyrians created a calf-high laced leather boot. The sole was reinforced with metal, enabling the Assyrians to walk and fight in relative comfort.

7. Greek and Roman soldiers resisted wearing Assyrian-style boots. They preferred sandals with hobnail soles, to provide better grip and extended wear. They did wear boots for long journeys.
8. Horse-riding cultures adopted boots quickly. They appreciated the boot's sturdiness and the ability of the boot heel to help their foot stay in the stirrup. Boots became standard combat gear.
9. The heeled boot was the ancestor of modern high-heeled shoes. The original high heels were worn by men in sixteenth-century France. Women's shoe fashions at the time were less dramatic because women's feet were covered by floor-length dresses.
10. During this time, the overcrowded cities were filthy. The streets were filled with human and animal waste. The elevation provided by high heels and thick soles kept men out of the muck and enabled them to stay a bit cleaner.
11. The clogs of Northern Europe served a similar purpose. Worn over good leather shoes in the winter, these wooden shoes protected the wearer from snow and mud. They could also be worn alone in warm weather.
12. King Louis XIV of France was short. During his seventy-two-year reign, the longest in the history of Europe, France was a centre of culture and refinement. France was also at its peak of military power.
13. Louis hated being short. To compensate, he wore high-heeled boots. He was imitated by his courtiers, the males as well as the females.
14. Louis's response was to wear even higher heels. His people tried to keep up with him. Once the competition was over, the men returned to their regular height.
15. The female members of Louis's court kept their high heels, thus beginning the pattern we have today. With rare exceptions, such as in the mid-1970s, men have been expected to keep their feet on the ground. Women still have the choice to wear or not wear high heels.
16. Athletic shoes earned the name "sneakers" because of their rubber bottoms, which enabled wearers to walk silently, to "sneak" around. The invention of the sneaker depended upon another invention. Charles Goodyear mixed rubber with sulphur to make it more useful.
17. Before this important discovery in the 1860s, using rubber was impractical because it became sticky when warm and brittle when cold. People immediately realized the value of Goodyear's discovery. Rubber-soled shoes became popular.
18. The first athletic shoes appeared shortly after this, rubber soles on canvas tops, called Keds. The name came from a blend of *ped*, the root form of the Latin word for "foot," and "kid." The brand is still around.
19. The kirst Keds were not very stylish by modern standards. The soles were black and the canvas was brown, in imitation of men's leather shoes.
20. Flat soles were standard on sneakers until 1972. In that year, new shoes with a number of startling changes were introduced. Featuring lightweight nylon tops, waffle soles for traction, a wedged heel, and a cushioned mid-sole to reduce impact shock, these shoes began to drive the old ones off the market.

Exercise 13-3: Answers will vary. The following passages are fragments.
A: 1, 2, 5, 7, 9, 10, 12, 13, 14
B: 2, 3, 5, 7, 8, 10, 11, 14, 16, 17, 20, 22, 23, 27

Chapter 14: Comma Splices and Run-Together Sentences

Exercise 14-1A: Answers will vary. Possible answers are shown below.
1. . . . meaning "horse." Thus a knight. . .
2. . . . lived; it became. . .
3. . . . class. Only knighthood. . .
4. . . . not a right; it had. . .
5. . . . he considered worthy, but he took. . .
6. . . . horse and armour. Unless. . .
7. Although many knights pledged fealty to one noble, some became. . .

Exercise 14-1B:
1. Even princes considered knighthood an honour; it made them part of a universal fraternity.
2. The honour was conferred by tapping the knight on the shoulders with the flat of a sword. After three taps the knight was given a belt and spurs to signify his new rank.
3. For his part, the knight vowed to uphold the code of chivalry, which established certain rules of behaviour.
4. The knight promised loyalty to his faith and to his feudal lord; moreover, he pledged to die willingly for either should death be necessary.
5. Although he was expected to fight to uphold his ideals, he was also expected to show mercy.
6. Knighthood is still granted in England; it is given for outstanding achievement.
7. Today recipients include both men and women, and their achievements are often related to statesmanship or the arts.

Exercise 14-1C:
1. . . . branch. They bury. . .
   . . . branch; they bury. . .
   . . . branch, and they bury. . .
   . . . branch, which they bury. . .
2. . . . branch. The Aborigines. . .
   . . . branch; the Aborigines. . .
   . . . branch, and the Aborigines. . .
   After termites eat out the middle of the branch, the Aborigines dig it up.
3. . . . instrument. They decorate. . .
   . . . instrument; they decorate. . .
   . . . instrument, and they decorate. . .
   As they carve the instrument, they decorate it with pigments.
4. . . . into one end. It makes. . .
   . . . into one end; it makes. . .
   . . . into one end, and it makes. . .
   When they play it by blowing into one end, it makes. . .
5. The pitch is low. The sound carries well.
   The pitch is low; the sound carries well.
   The pitch is low, and the sound carries well.
   Because the pitch is low, the sound carries well.

Exercise 14-2: Answers will vary. Possible answers are shown below.

1. The king Jayavarman II introduced into the empire an Indian royal cult. The cult held that the king was related spiritually to one of the Hindu gods; consequently, the king was thought to fill on earth the role the gods had in the universe.

2. Each king was expected to build a stone temple. The temple, or *wat*, was dedicated to a god, usually Shiva or Vishnu. When the king died, the temple became a monument to him as well.

3. Over the centuries the kings erected more than seventy temples within 200 km^2. They added towers and gates, and they created canals and reservoirs for an irrigation system.

4. The irrigation system made it possible for farmers to produce several rice crops a year. Although such abundant harvests supported a highly evolved culture, the irrigation system and the rice production were what we would call labour-intensive.

5. The greatest of the temples is Angkor Wat, which was built by Suryavarman II in the 12th century. Like the other temples, it represents Mount Meru, the home of the Hindu gods. The towers represent Mount Meru's peaks while the walls represent the mountains beyond.

6. The gallery walls are covered with bas-reliefs that depict historical events. They show the king at his court, and they show him engaging in activities that brought glory to his empire.

7. The walls also portray divine images. There are sculptures of *apsarases*, who are attractive women thought to inhabit heaven. There are mythical scenes on the walls as well.

8. One scene shows the Hindu myth of the churning of the Sea of Milk. On one side of the god Vishnu are demons who tug on the end of a long serpent; on the other are heavenly beings who tug on the other end. All the tugging churns the water.

9. Vishnu is the god to whom Angkor Wat is dedicated. In Hindu myth he oversees the churning of the waters. That churning is ultimately a source of immortality.

10. Another temple is the Bayon, which was built by Jayavarman VII around 1200 A. D. Jayavarman VII was the last of the great kings of Angkor. He built the Bayon in the exact centre of the city.

11. The Bayon resembles a step pyramid. It has steep stairs which lead to terraces near the top. Around its base are many galleries. Its towers are carved with faces which look out in all directions.

12. Because Jayavarman VII was a Buddhist, the representations on Bayon are different from those on earlier temples. Some scholars think they depict a Buddhist deity with whom the king felt closely aligned.

13. To build each temple required thousands of labourers who worked for years. After cutting the stone in far-off quarries, they had to transport it by canal or cart. Some stone may have been brought in on elephants.

14. Once cut, the stones had to be carved and fitted together into lasting edifices. Thus, in addition to requiring labourers, each project needed artisans, architects, and engineers. Each temple was a massive project.

15. After Angkor was conquered by the Thais in the 1400s, it was almost completely abandoned. The local inhabitants did continue to use the temples for worship, however, and a few late Khmer kings tried to restore the city.

16. The Western world did not learn about Angkor until the nineteenth century, when a French explorer published an account of the site. French archaeologists and conservators later worked in the area and restored some of the temples. More recent archaeologists have come from India.

17. Today the Angkor Conservancy has removed many of the temple statues. Some of the statues need repair; all of them need protection from thieves. Unfortunately, traffic in Angkor art has become big business among people with no scruples. There is even a booming business in Angkor fakes.
18. Theft is just one of the problems Angkor faces today. Political upheaval has taken its toll. Although Angkor mostly escaped Cambodia's civil war, some war damage has occurred.
19. More damage has been done by nature, however. Trees choke some of the archways, vines strangle the statues, and monsoons undermine the basic structures.
20. Today many Cambodians do what they can to maintain the temples of Angkor. They clean stones or sweep courtyards or pull weeds. No one pays them; they do it for themselves and their heritage.

Chapter 15: Awkward Sentences

Exercise 15-1A: Answers will vary.

    The next time you watch a western movie, notice whether it contains any sign language. Some people consider sign language the first universal language. Although few people use it today, it is a Native American language with a lengthy history. One can find some tribal differences, but basic root signs were clear to everyone who tried to interpret them.

    Sign language differs from the signage used by hearing-impaired people. For instance, they indicate the forehead to mean *think* while a Sioux pointed to the heart. One also uses extensive facial expression in speaking to someone with a hearing loss while Native Americans maintained a stoic countenance. They believed the signs could speak for themselves. Ideally they made the signs in round, sweeping motions. They tried to make conversation beautiful.

Exercise 15-1B: Answers will vary.

    No one knows why sailors wear bell-bottom pants. However, three theories are popular. First, bell-bottom pants fit over boots and keep sea spray and rain from getting in. Second, bell-bottoms can be rolled up over the knees, so they stay dry when a sailor must wade ashore and stay clean when he scrubs the ship's deck. Third, because bell-bottoms are loose, they are easy to take off in the water if a sailor falls overboard. In their training course, sailors are taught another advantage to bell-bottoms. By taking them off and tying the legs at the ends, a sailor who has fallen into the ocean can change his bell-bottom pants into a life preserver.

Exercise 15-1C: Answers will vary.
1. 2. The Aran Isles are situated off the coast of Ireland. <u>They are not far from Galway</u>.
2. 1. <u>Islanders have difficult lives</u>. They must make their living by fishing in a treacherous sea.
3. 2. They use a simple boat called a *curragh* for fishing. <u>They also use it</u> to ferry their market animals to barges.
4. 3. Island houses <u>stand</u> out against the empty landscape. Their walls provide scant protection from a hostile environment.
5. 2. In 1898 John Millington Synge first visited the Aran Isles. <u>He used them</u> as the setting for *Riders to the Sea* and other of his works.

6. 1. Whether people see the Synge play or Ralph Vaughan Williams' operatic version of *Riders to the Sea*, <u>they</u> will feel the harshness of Aran life.
7. 3. The mother Maurya has lost her husband and several sons. They <u>have</u> all drowned at sea.
8. 2. When the body of another son is washed onto the shore, <u>it is identified</u> from the pattern knitted into his sweater.
9. 3. Each Aran knitter develops her own combination of patterns. The patterns not only produce a beautiful sweater, but <u>they have</u> a very practical purpose.
10. 3. The oiled wool <u>protects</u> the fisherman from the sea spray while the intricate patterns offer symbolic protection as well as identification when necessary.
11. 4. When you knit your first Aran Isle sweater, you should learn what the stitches mean. <u>You should not</u> choose a pattern just because it is easy.
12. 2. A cable stitch represents a fisherman's rope; <u>a zigzag stitch depicts winding cliff paths</u>.
13. 3. Bobbles symbolize men in a curragh while the basket stitch <u>represents</u> a fisherman's creel and the hope that it will come home full.
14. 3. The tree of life signifies strong sons and family unity. It <u>is</u> also a fertility symbol.
15. 5. When someone asks you <u>whether</u> you knitted your Aran Isle yourself, you can proudly say that you did and you also chose the patterns.

Exercise 15-2A:
1. To paint one's house, one must <u>frequently</u> do it oneself.
2. <u>Almost</u> all homeowners try to paint at one time or another.
3. They <u>usually</u> try to begin on a bedroom.
4. <u>By doing so</u>, they think no one will see it if they botch the job.
5. <u>In no time</u>, most people can learn to paint.
6. <u>Only</u> the uncoordinated should not try it.
7. People <u>that have strong arm muscles</u> have a distinct advantage.
8. <u>Lacking strength</u>, prospective painters can always exercise.
9. Novices need to purchase all supplies, such as brushes, rollers, and drop cloths, <u>carefully</u>.
10. They must bring home paint chips to match <u>exactly</u> the shade desired.
11. It takes <u>nearly</u> as much time to prepare to paint as it does to do the actual job.
12. Painters <u>who think they are done with the last paint stroke</u> are in for a surprise.
13. Painters need to clean their own brushes <u>immediately</u> and put away all equipment.
14. <u>In the long run</u>, they can be proud of their accomplishment.
15. <u>Only</u> then can they enjoy the results of their labour.
16. <u>When all is said and done</u>, painting one's own home can be extremely satisfying.

Exercise 15-2B:
1. Playing the role of a caring and wise father, <u>Richardson told the girls</u> how to handle various situations.
2. To help the girls, <u>Richardson sometimes wrote</u> letters to their suitors.

3. After writing a number of successful letters, <u>Richardson had the idea</u> <u>to write a book of model letters</u>.
4. To prepare the books, <u>Richardson wrote letters</u> as if from adults to sons, daughters, nieces, and nephews.
5. When ready to send advice, <u>a parent copied out a letter and just</u> <u>changed the names</u>.
6. Bought by many, <u>Richardson's book was a success</u>.
7. While working on one letter (. . .), Richardson thought of enough <u>ideas for a whole book</u>.
8. By writing a series of letters between a girl and her faraway parents, <u>Richardson hoped to entertain and instruct young readers</u>.
9. Upon finishing *Pamela*, or *Virtue Rewarded* in 1740, <u>Richardson knew he had invented a new form of literature</u>.
10. After years of development, <u>this form became the novel</u>.
11. Being a nasty person, <u>Horace Walpole wrote an only novel</u> that wasn't very attractive.
12. Correct.
13. Although badly written, <u>it contained</u> the themes, atmosphere, mood, and plots that have filled gothic novels ever since.
14. Featuring gloomy castles filled with dark secrets, <u>gothic movies also entertain people</u>.

Exercise 15-2C: Answers will vary.

[1]Sailors developed scrimshaw, the art of carving or engraving marine articles, while sailing on long voyages. [2]Because scrimshaw was practised primarily by whalermen, sperm whale teeth were the most popular articles. [3]Baleen, which was also called whalebone, was another popular choice. [4]With whaling voyages taking several years, a sailor needed something to occupy his time. [5]Only imagination or available material limited scrimshaw. [6]All kinds of objects—canes, corset busks, cribbage boards—were produced by the scrimshander. [7]The sailor used everything from whaling scenes to mermaids to decorate his work. [8]Often a sailor doing scrimshaw drew his own ship. [9]The most frequently depicted ship, the *Charles W. Morgan*, is presently a museum ship at Mystic Seaport. [10]It is easily possible to see it on a visit to Connecticut.

Exercise 15-3A: Answers will vary.
1. Carl Fabergé created Easter eggs for the tsars.
2. Because Fabergé was a talented goldsmith, he was able to make exquisite objects.
3. Working for the court of Imperial Russia enabled him to combine craftsmanship and ingenuity.
4. Fabergé pleased his clients by creating unique works of art.
5. He included gems in his creations, but they did not overshadow his workmanship.
6. In adapting enamelling techniques, he achieved a level seldom matched by other artisans.
7. Buyers in Europe expanded his clientele beyond the Russian royal family.
8. Because he had no money worries, he had few restrictions on imagination.
9. Although Fabergé created other examples of the jeweler's art, it is the Imperial Easter eggs for which he is most remembered.
10. The most famous eggs contained surprises inside—a hen, a ship, a coach.
11. One egg opened to reveal a model of a palace.
12. The most ambitious creation represented an egg surrounded by parts of a cathedral.
13. An artist is one who practises an imaginative art.
14. One reason Fabergé is so admired is that he was a true artist.

Exercise 15-3B: Answers will vary. These are possible answers only.

1. The use of cuneiform began <u>in</u> and spread throughout ancient Sumer.
2. This picture language of the Sumerians is thought to be older than <u>that of</u> the Egyptians.
3. Like hieroglyphics, early cuneiform used easily recognizable pictures <u>to</u> represent objects.
4. When scribes began using a wedge-shaped stylus, <u>great</u> changes occurred.
5. The new marks were different <u>from the early pictographs</u>.
6. They had become so stylized <u>that the origin was often</u> <u>unrecognizable</u>.
7. Early Sumerian tablets recorded practical things such <u>as</u> lists of grain in storage.
8. Some tablets were put <u>into</u> clay envelopes that were themselves inscribed.
9. Gradually ordinary people used cuneiform as much as official scribes <u>did</u>.
10. *The Epic of Gilgamesh*, written in Akkadian cuneiform, is older than any <u>other</u> epic.
11. The Code of Hammurabi recorded in cuneiform a more comprehensive set of laws <u>than any previously set down</u>.
12. Correct.
13. Because it was written in three languages, it served the same purpose <u>as the Rosetta Stone</u>.
14. Today we understand cuneiform as much <u>as</u>, if not more than, we understand hieroglyphics.

Exercise 15-3C: Answers will vary.

¹Wild rice may be the caviar of grains, but it is not really rice. ²It is, however, truly wild. ³One reason is that it needs marshy places in order to thrive. ⁴Planting it in man-made paddies can produce abundant crops. ⁵Nevertheless, most wild rice grows naturally along rivers and lake shores in northern states and Canada. ⁶In certain areas only Native Americans are allowed to harvest the rice. ⁷Connoisseurs think wild rice tastes better than any other grain. ⁸It is surely the most expensive of all grains. ⁹Some hostesses serve it with Cornish hens exclusively, but the creative cook serves it with many dishes. ¹⁰Try it in quiche or pancakes; your guests will be so pleased that they will ask for more.

Chapter 16: Conciseness

Exercise 16-1:

1. Art Deco took its name from a 1925 Paris exposition.
2. Art Deco used bold and streamlined shapes and experimented with new materials.
3. In the 1920s public fascination with futuristic technology influenced Art Deco.
4. In addition to dominating architecture, the style pervaded glassware, appliances, furniture, and even advertising art.
5. The Marine Building in Vancouver and the Chrysler Building in New York exemplified Art Deco's dynamic style.
6. After the 1929 stock market crash, Art Deco expressed modern ideas and themes less extravagantly.
7. The Art Deco of the Great Depression had restraint and austerity.
8. Architects used rounded corners, glass blocks, and porthole windows.
9. They liked flat roofs.
10. Buildings with plain exteriors often had lavish interiors and furniture to match.

Exercise 16-2:
1. The Romans gave sacrifices to the goddess Maia on the first day of the month named for her.
2. The Celts also celebrated May Day as the midpoint of their year.
3. One of the most important of the May Day celebrations is the Maypole.
4. The Maypole represented rebirth.
5. In Germany a Maypole tree was often stripped of all but the top branches to represent new life.
6. In Sweden floral wreaths were suspended from a crossbar on the pole.
7. The English had a different tradition.
8. Holding streamers attached to the top of the Maypole, villagers danced around it enthusiastically.
9. Because May Day had pagan beginnings, the Puritans disapproved of it.
10. Thus Oliver Cromwell suppressed it after the overthrow of Charles I.

Exercise 16-3:
1. Many new collectors express amazement at the number of stamps to be collected.
2. They get excited about each new stamp they acquire.
3. They hope to make their collection complete.
4. Soon it becomes clear that a complete collection is impossible.
5. Then they may take the pragmatic approach.
6. They confine their collections to one country, continent, or decade.
7. At that point, their collections will again provide great satisfaction.
8. It is a consensus that collecting stamps can be educational.
9. It can teach about history or geography.
10. Nevertheless, a new collector should not become discouraged by trying to collect too much.

Exercise 16-4A: Answers will vary.

The bubonic plague, which originated in Asia, killed one-third of Europe's population in the fourteenth century. It began when a group of merchants from Genoa was attacked at a Crimean trading post by infected bandits. The Genoese became ill when the bandits threw diseased corpses over the outpost walls. Many of the merchants got the plague, and most of them died. The survivors went home, bringing the infection with them. The first European city to have an outbreak was Constantinople in 1334. The horrible disease then spread throughout Europe.

Exercise 16-4B: Answers will vary.

Auguste Escoffier was the most famous chef between 1880 and World War I. He was the leader of the culinary world of his day. Until then the best chefs were found in private homes. With Escoffier came an era of fine dining at restaurants to which the nobility and wealthy flocked. After Escoffier joined César Ritz, the luxury hotel owner, they worked together to attract such patrons as the Prince of Wales. Ritz made each guest feel personally welcome. Escoffier added the crowning touch by preparing dishes especially for guests. He created dishes for the prince and for celebrities in the entertainment world. He concocted *consommé favori de Sarah Bernhardt* for the actress. For an opera singer he created *poularde Adelina Patti*. Another singer was fortunate to have more than one dish named for her. When the Australian Nellie Melba sang in *Lohengrin,* Escoffier served *pêches melba*, a combination of poached peaches and vanilla ice cream. To commemorate the swans of *Lohengrin*, he served the dessert in an ice swan. Melba toast was created by Escoffier during one of Melba's periodic diets. Today although many people have not heard of Nellie Melba, they are familiar with melba toast. As a young army chef, Escoffier had to prepare horse meat and even rat meat to feed the troops. Obviously he left those days far behind him when he became the most renowned chef of his day.

Chapter 17: Coordination and Subordination

Exercise 17-1: Answers will vary.
1. Many Canadians made their fortunes as newspaper owners, and others bought newspapers after making their mark in other fields.
2. Reformer George Brown wanted to promote his political ideals, so he founded the *Globe* in 1844.
3. K. C. Irving of New Brunswick founded a huge industrial empire based on oil refining, transportation, and pulp and paper; later he added local newspapers to his holdings.
4. Conrad Black likes to tell how he started his newspaper empire with a small loan, but his wealthy family already had major business investments in other fields.
5. We should not forget other Canadian newspaper tycoons such as the Thomsons and the Beaverbrooks, nor should we ignore lesser-known mavericks like Margaret "Ma" Murray, owner of the *Bridge River-Lillooet News*.
6. The Trudeau government was concerned that newspaper ownership was becoming concentrated in too few hands, so in 1980 it set up a royal commission to study the problem.
7. Tom Kent was named head of the commission, for he had been a newspaper editor and adviser to prime ministers.
8. Kent recommended that the government limit the size of newspaper empires, or soon Canadians would all be reading the same opinions written by employees of a small number of wealthy men.
9. Little was done about the Kent Commission recommendations, and the newspaper empires continued to grow.
10. Kent did not know that his report would be ignored by the Trudeau government, nor could he have guessed that by the 1990s, Conrad Black would own the majority of Canada's daily newspapers.
11. Defenders of big newspaper chains say that size is a good thing, for only wealthy owners can afford the staff and resources to produce the best newspapers.
12. Some people also look back with nostalgia to the legendary days of the strong-willed newspaper boss, and they argue that we can find their counterparts today only among opinionated media tycoons.

Exercise 17-2:
1. A company in Toronto was one of the first ones to install a fragrancing unit in its office ventilation system, in order to control employee behaviour.
2. The company was careful about which fragrances it introduced into the workplace, because some fragrances rev people up, and some calm them down.
3. The scents were designed by Toronto-based Aromasphere, Inc., which created a time-release mechanism to send the scents directly into the work area.

4. Once Bodywise Ltd. in Great Britain received a patent for a fragrance, it began to market its scent, which contains androstenone, an ingredient of male sweat.
5. The scent was adopted by a U.S. debt-collection agency after another agency in Australia reported that chronic debtors who receive scented letters were 17 percent more likely to pay than were those who received unscented letters.
6. Although researchers have recently discovered how much odour can influence behaviour, smell is still the least understood of the five senses.
7. Aromasphere's employees have been asked to keep logs of their moods while they are in the workplace.
8. Researchers have raised many concerns about trying to change human behaviour, for they feel that this kind of tampering may lead to too much control over employees.
9. Smells can have an effect on people, although they may be completely unaware of what is happening.
10. Employees are forewarned that they will be exposed to mood-altering fragrances, even though such employees may protest against the introduction of the scents in the workplace.
11. Even psychiatric wards emit a scent that makes the patients calm.
12. International Flavors and Fragrances of New York, which is the world's largest manufacturer of artificial flavours and aromas, has developed many of the scents commonly used today.
13. It has even created a bagel scent, since bagels lose their aroma when they are kept in plexiglass.
14. There wasn't a true commercial interest in these products until researchers began to understand the anatomy of smell.
15. It turns out that olfactory signals travel to the limbic region of the brain, which regulates hormones of the autonomic nervous system.

Exercise 17-3: Answers will vary.
1. Public transportation in the city is inadequate, and the streets are too crowded to ride a bicycle safely.
   Because of the recent increase in the population, public transportation in the city is inadequate.
2. Teaching a nervous partner to dance can be frustrating, but it is a real thrill to see a person gain confidence.
   Teaching a nervous partner to dance can be frustrating because fear makes the beginner still and prone to clumsiness.
3. The park looked especially beautiful at sunset, yet few people took advantage of the view.
   When the cherry trees were in bloom, the park looked especially beautiful at sunset.
4. Never buy a stereo without listening to it first, and resist the urge to buy more advanced equipment than you need.
   Although the description in the sales brochure may be enticing, never buy a stereo without listening to it first.
5. Exercise can be fun, and it can be a way to meet new people.
   Exercise can be fun if you don't push yourself too hard too soon.
6. Mexican food is tasty, but some people find it too spicy.
   Although it may be different from the food you eat every day, Mexican food is tasty.

7. Watching a tape at home with friends is better than going to the movies, so I try to do it at least once a week.

Watching a tape at home with friends is better than going to the movies because we are free to talk back to the screen.

8. The cost of food keeps going up, yet farmers and ranchers are not seeing larger profits.

The cost of food keeps going up because of shipping and storage expenses.

9. A small car may be difficult to handle in rough weather, so consider getting a larger vehicle if you do a lot of winter driving.

Although there are many advantages to owning a subcompact, a small car may be difficult to handle in rough weather.

10. Keeping a pet in an apartment requires compromises, and even then not all landlords will allow it.

Although many people want dogs for safety and companionship, keeping a pet in an apartment requires compromises.

Exercise 17-4: Answers will vary.

Senet is a game that was played by ancient Egyptians. Because it was very popular, Egyptians began putting senet boards into tombs as early as 3100 B. C. Tomb objects were intended for use in the afterlife, yet they give us a good idea of daily life.

Many senet boards and playing pieces have been found in tombs, where the hot, dry air preserved them well. Tomb paintings frequently show people playing the game while hieroglyphic texts describe it. Because numerous descriptions of the game survive, Egyptologists think it was a national pastime.

Senet was a game for two people who played it on a board marked with thirty squares. Each player had several playing pieces. They probably each had seven, but the number did not matter as long as it was the same for both. Opponents moved by throwing flat sticks that were an early form of dice although sometimes they threw pairs of lamb knuckles instead. Players sat across from each other, and they moved their pieces in a backward S line. The squares represented houses through which they moved.

By the New Kingdom the game began to take on religious overtones. The thirty squares were given individual names, and they were seen as stages on the journey of the soul through the netherworld. When New Kingdom tomb paintings showed the deceased playing senet with an unseen opponent, the object was to win eternal life. The living still played the game, but they played it in anticipation of the supernatural match to come.

Chapter 18: Parallelism

Exercise 18-1:
1. exploration, travel
2. proud, evil
3. he had made plans for a helicopter, he made plans for an underwater ship
4. designed by a British mathematician, built by a Dutch inventor
5. designed in 1578, built in 1620, tested from 1620–24
6. on the surface, below the surface
7. boarded the submarine, took a short ride
8. the talk of the town, the focus of scientific investigation

9. When the vessel was to submerge, the bags would fill with water and pull the ship downward; when the vessel was to rise, a twisting rod would force water from the bags and the lightened ship would surface
10. designed, built
11. sneak up on British warships, attach explosives to their hulls
12. launching, steering
13. small four-person ships called "Davids," a full-sized submarine called the "Hunley"
14. providing dependable power, steering to navigate
15. the development of the gasoline engine, the invention of the periscope

Exercise 18-2: Answers will vary.
1. She rides her bicycle ten kilometres a day because she loves <u>exercise</u> but hates <u>gyms</u>.
2. <u>Fixing</u> a broken cell phone is much more difficult than <u>buying</u> a new one.
3. After work tonight, I'd like to pick up my favourite movie, <u>hurry home</u>, <u>phone some friends</u>, and <u>order a pizza</u>.
4. Librarians must be <u>well organized</u> and <u>computer literate</u>.
5. When I misplaced my new sunglasses, I checked for them <u>in my jacket</u> and <u>under my desk</u>.
6. We took the children to a park <u>to play Frisbee</u>, <u>to look at the geese</u>, and <u>to stuff themselves on hot dogs</u>.
7. In my spare time, I listen to music that is <u>noisy</u> and <u>raucous</u>.
8. My professor is always on the move: constantly <u>rushing around</u>, and <u>never sitting still</u>.
9. The player who is the most <u>respected</u> and <u>least penalized</u> will receive the award.
10. The best place to buy concert tickets at a reduced rate is located at <u>Elm Street</u> and <u>Howard Drive</u>.
11. A successful attorney is <u>quick thinking</u> and <u>hard working</u>.
12. For the recital, Sarah wants to <u>play guitar</u> and <u>sing folk music</u>.
13. After it began to <u>rain</u> and <u>pour</u>, he shut the windows so that the rain wouldn't get inside the house.
14. I'll call my sister either <u>this afternoon</u> or <u>tomorrow evening</u>.
15. The students <u>whined</u> and <u>moaned</u> until the professor granted them a larger curve on the exam.

Chapter 19: Variety and Emphasis

Exercise 19-1: Answers will vary.
1. The dances teenagers like always appear strange to their parents.
2. In the early 1900s, the management of one magazine fired fifteen women.
3. Their offence was dancing the Turkey Trot during their lunch hour, according to management.
4. The Grizzly Bear, the Kangaroo Dip, and the Bunny Hug were other popular dances of the period.
5. Flagpole sitting was invented by Alvin "Shipwreck" Kelly.
6. The source of his nickname is unknown.
7. The first Frisbees were pie plates from the Frisbee Baking Company.
8. The goldfish swallowing fad was begun by a Harvard student in 1939.
9. He swallowed a live three-inch fish in front of reporters.
10. The Hula Hoop was invented in Australia for use in gym classes.

Exercise 19-2A: Answers will vary. These are suggestions only.
1. The comfortable sofa is wearing out.
    Although we try to protect it, the sofa is wearing out.
    Mended too many times, the sofa is wearing out.
2. My father swam in the ocean daily.
    My dauntless father swam daily.
    When we were at the seashore, my father swam daily.
3. The performance was truly splendid.
    The performance that he gave without rehearsal was splendid.
    The costumes having arrived on time, the performance was splendid.
4. Descending in huge flakes, the snow fell silently.
    The snow fell silently but quickly.
    The snow that we had longed for fell silently.
5. His excitement growing as he worked, Lewis finished writing the concerto.
    In the wee hours of the morning, Lewis finished writing the concerto.
    Lewis finished writing the lengthy concerto.

Exercise 19-2B: Answers will vary.
1. The <u>big</u> celebration included <u>a loud</u> parade <u>up Main Street</u>.
2. <u>The day being very hot</u>, the crowd was dressed in shorts and <u>thin</u> shirts.
3. The mayor, <u>who was the only one with the power</u>, stopped traffic <u>because he wanted to let the parade go on without interruption</u>.
4. The <u>young</u> astronaut rode <u>comfortably</u> in an open car.
5. <u>Because there was such a fuss</u>, youngsters <u>who had no interest in the space program</u> tried to get autographs.
6. <u>The parade reaching city hall</u>, the mayor gave a <u>long, boring</u> speech.
7. <u>When it was over</u>, everyone cheered <u>because a street fair was about</u> to start.
8. The celebration ended <u>with a fireworks display over the harbour</u>.
9. <u>Walking tiredly</u>, everyone headed home.
10. <u>Once the streets were empty</u>, the street cleaners came out <u>in two garbage trucks</u>.

Exercise 19-3: Answers will vary.
1. With a new emphasis on teamwork and on trust in the workplace, managers hope that the shift in attitude will benefit their businesses.
2. Companies that are trying to make a difference are experimenting with group talks among employees, who discuss issues dealing with workers as individuals and as team members.
3. These talks are very helpful for managers and for the workers who are still with the company and have survived the massive cutbacks, and need a boost in morale.
4. These experimental groups also break down barriers in the workplace that tend to separate one department from another, taking away any feelings of teamwork and cooperation.
5. Teamwork is critical for companies that want to regain competitiveness, and these groups strive to remove obstacles that prevent communication and respect among workers, for teamwork is a necessary step in the right direction.

Chapter 20: Understanding the Meaning of Words

Exercise 20-1A:

spelling	pronunciation
1. brogue	brög
2. broad-mind/ed	brôd mïn´ did
3. corn•meal	kôrn´ mel´
4. dah/lia	däl´ y
5. gyp/sy	jip´ së
6. head ache	hed äk´
7. head start	hed stärt
8. in•cu•nab/u•la	in´ kyöö nab´ yöö lə
9. in•veigh	in vä´
10. per/i•pa•tet/ic	per´ i p tet´ ik

Exercise 20-1B:

1. African	11. compare
2. alternative	12. colloquial
3. American Indian	13. except
4. article	14. following
5. Celtic	15. German
6. gerund	16. Latin
7. Greek	17. Middle English
8. derived form	18. hypothetical
9. Indo-European	19. past participle
10. that is	20. variant; variety

Exercise 20-1C:

past	past participle
1. had	had
2. did	done
3. ate	eaten
4. chose	chosen
5. drank	drunk
6. went	gone
7. flew	flown
8. knew	known
9. paid	paid
10. let	let

Exercise 20-1D:

comparative	superlative
1. kindlier	kindliest
2. better	best
3. better	best
4. worse	worst
5. worse	worst
6. more intelligent	most intelligent
7. more intelligently	most intelligently

8. more happily	most happily
9. more grateful	most grateful
10. more loudly	most loudly

Exercise 20-1E:

1. scarfs, scarves
2. llamas, llama
3. salmon, salmons
4. nuclei, nucleuses
5. formulas, formulae
6. phenomena, phenomenons
7. indexes, indices
8. kibbutzim
9. bandits, banditti
10. châteaux, châteaus

Exercise 20-1F:

1. Old English <u>wif</u>; a woman
2. Old English <u>husbondi</u>; householder
3. Old English <u>sunu</u>; son
4. Old English <u>dohtor</u>; daughter
5. Latin <u>maritus</u>; a husband, married
6. Tamil <u>man-kay</u>; mango tree fruit
7. Greek <u>kerasion</u>; cherry
8. Nahuatl <u>tomatl</u>; tomato
9. Sanskrit <u>pippali</u>; peppercorn
10. Latin <u>unio</u>; oneness, unity

Exercise 20-1G:

1. after 7th Early of Cardigan (1797–1868), English general
2. of or like Don Quixote, the hero of a seventeenth-century Spanish satirical romance novel
3. from <u>pantaloons</u> < French < Italian <u>Pantalone</u>, a character in Italian comedy; also the garment he wore
4. an old insane asylum (St. Mary of Bethlehem)
5. named after A. J. Sax (1814–1894), Belgian inventor
6. after Louis Pasteur, French scientist
7. after John Duns Scotus, who with his followers (Dunsmen, Dunses, Dunces), was considered a foe of Renaissance humanism
8. after J. Guillotin (1738–1814), French physician who advocated its use during the French Revolution
9. after Hamburg in northwest Germany
10. after Mentor, the loyal friend and advisor of Odysseus

Exercise 20-1H:

1. noun - 4; adjective - 3
2. noun - 13; adjective - 1; interjection - 1
3. transitive verb - 4; intransitive verb - 3; noun - 6
4. intransitive verb - 40; transitive verb - 6; noun - 8; adjective - 2
5. transitive verb - 31; intransitive verb - 23; noun - 22

Exercise 20-1I:
1. colloquial
2. slang
3. obsolete
4. Briticism
5. archaic or poetic

Exercise 20-2A:

1. commanded	11. immoderate
2. intact	12. suspend
3. overthrown	13. capacity
4. accuracy	14. donated
5. foul	15. guffawed
6. divided	16. praised
7. dispersed	17. rewards
8. withheld	18. impolite
9. tall	19. secretly
10. restored	20. skin

Exercise 20-2B: Answers will vary.
1. There was <u>danger</u> wherever the private investigator went.
   The skiers were in <u>peril</u> of being buried by the avalanche.
   White-water canoeing can be <u>hazardous</u>.
   The game-show contestant decided to <u>risk</u> everything for a chance to win a car.
2. His <u>rich</u> uncle left him $10,000.
   <u>Wealthy</u> people often travel to Europe to shop.
   The <u>affluent</u> sometimes own several homes around the world.
   The <u>opulent</u> mansion contained a private movie theatre and a large indoor pool.
3. The meeting ended after the president <u>spoke</u> to us.
   Let's <u>talk</u> about where to go on vacation.
   The priest and the rabbi <u>conversed</u> about how to get better attendance at services.
   The professor <u>discoursed</u> on igneous rock.
4. The philosophy course required students to <u>think</u> about their most deeply held convictions.
   Sherlock Holmes <u>reasoned</u> his way to the solution.
   The bridegroom-to-be <u>reflected</u> on his future.
   Doctors <u>speculated</u> on the source of the infection.
   The committee <u>deliberated</u> about when to hold an open meeting.
5. Having a cold made him <u>irritable</u>.
   Don't disagree with her; she's <u>choleric</u>.
   He's very <u>touchy</u> about his height.
   She always gets <u>cranky</u> if people don't do as she says.
   Ask the boss for an increase later; she's <u>cross</u> about the shipping delay.

Exercise 20-3A:

1. food
   sandwich
   cheese sandwich
   Swiss cheese on rye
2. business
   store
   supermarket
   A&P
3. mail
   letter
   bill
   record club charges
4. clothing
   pants
   jeans
   stone-washed jeans
5. land
   islands
   tropical paradise
   Hawaii
6. book
   how-to book
   cookbook
   The Joy of Cooking
7. animal
   hunter
   cat
   lion
8. entertainment
   television show
   dramatic series
   North of 60
9. art
   painting
   portrait
   The Blue Boy
10. sports
    track
    running
    100-metre dash

Exercise 20-3B:

1. Mustang
2. azaleas
3. sour
4. shouted
5. Calgary, Alberta
6. your boyfriend
7. the unification of Italy
8. pigeon
9. accurate
10. discrimination against the poor
11. sprained
12. a gold chain
13. grinding
14. difficult
15. considerate of
16. Tom Hanks' latest movie
17. 256 megabytes of
18. in need of new plumbing
    and wiring
19. steady, well-paying
20. all her patients who smoke

Exercise 20-4A:

1. misapply
2. nonstop
3. preceding
4. remodel
5. transfer
6. undying
7. autograph
8. magnify
9. monolingual
10. multiple
11. omnipresent
12. polygamy

Exercise 20-4B:

1. happiness
2. wolflike
3. expansion
4. dedication
5. heavenly
6. mountaineer
7. aviator
8. harden
9. leadership
10. wisdom
11. magnify
12. affordable

Exercise 20-5:

1. anything bought or sold
2. means of livelihood; support
3. extraordinary
4. unwilling
5. financial
6. steeply
7. drinking
8. energizing
9. people who never drink alcohol
10. essential
11. a consuming or being consumed
12. to make more intense or sharp
13. not conclusive or final
14. to multiply rapidly
15. of beauty

Chapter 21: Understanding the Effect of Words

Exercise 21-1:

1. informal
2. medium or semiformal
3. formal
4. medium
5. medium or semiformal

Exercise 21-2:

1.	man	6.	slacks
2.	edible	7.	students
3.	please	8.	cars
4.	address	9.	motorcycle
5.	regardless	10.	dormitories, check in

Exercise 21-3: Answers may vary.

1. Before I tried skydiving, I thought skydivers were out of their minds.
2. It seemed so bizarre.
3. But now that I've done it, I think it is a great experience.
4. The day of the jump, I was extremely excited.
5. My friends were very concerned on my account, though.
6. But then, they are less adventurous than I am.
7. I was feeling nauseated just before I jumped out of the airplane.
8. But it was phenomenal—I felt exhilarated.
9. It is much more fun than bungee-jumping, which happens far too quickly.
10. Skydiving is an extraordinary activity.

Exercise 21-4: Answers will vary.

Exercise 21-5: Answers will vary.

1. My uncle has a grip like a car crusher.
2. He held her in an embrace as inescapable as his love for her.
3. The fingers of the waves strummed the shore.
4. As soon as she entered her studio, creativity warmed her like a fire in the hearth.
5. They talked us into going to an expensive restaurant, so we went, reluctantly, like crooked businessmen to an IRS audit.
6. Having no determination is his great weakness.
7. Once he caught her attention, she quickly fell in love with him.
8. I studied until 6 A.M.
9. The train rushed at us like a charging elephant.
10. After I painted myself in the corner, I felt like a prisoner in a cell with invisible bars.
11. The situation became intolerable, so an investigation was begun.
12. The mailman subdued the prowler and held him for the police.
13. He declared his love and bared his deepest feelings to her.
14. This is a beautiful painting.
15. The meteorologist's explanation of what causes mist was confusing.

Exercise 21-6: Answers will vary.

1. The horse seemed to float past us, like a silken banner in a gentle wind.
2. The shack stood off alone in the woods, looking like a moldy gingerbread house.
3. XYZ sound like a dozen monkeys trapped in a garbage can.
4. Grease oozed off the fries onto the paper plate, creating an oil slick that no EPA regulation could control.
5. At 5 A.M. I was awoken by my alarm clock, sounding like the finale at the demolition derby.
6. Professor ABC must think he is an Egyptian pharaoh; he treats his students like slaves.
7. The salesman had a grin like the Cheshire cat's — and like the cat itself, the grin faded away when I said, "I'm not interested."
8. It was so hot that the pigeons were fanning themselves with tattered sheets from last week's newspapers.
9. The library books were so overdue that the records showing they had been charged out were written on parchment.
10. Her voice is so shrill it could shatter plexiglass.

Exercise 21-7: Answers will vary.

1. After falling off her bicycle, the child bruised her knee.
2. Drivers should fasten their seat belts before starting their cars.
3. Although she was pregnant, she continued to fulfill her responsibilities at home and at work.
4. The city street cleaners are on strike.
5. The dean has asked department heads to meet/cooperate with him.

Chapter 22: Spelling and Hyphenation

Exercise 22-1:

1. rode
2. write
3. loose
4. lightning
5. diary
6. angles
7. all together, their
8. except, desert
9. advice
10. alter
11. hour
12. council
13. devices, pieces
14. lessens
15. may be
16. reign
17. whose
18. scene
19. where
20. than, to
21. breathe, patients
22. desserts, know
23. quiet
24. already
25. Guerillas, capital

Exercise 22-2: Answers will vary.

1. The show doesn't start for an hour, but the theatre is <u>already</u> crowded.
   I am <u>all ready</u> to begin my vacation.
2. The city is about to celebrate <u>its</u> 300th anniversary.
   <u>It's</u> too late to enroll in any new classes this semester.
3. Overnight delivery costs more <u>than</u> regular mail.
   He finished dinner, <u>then</u> he read the paper.
4. <u>They're</u> my cousins.
   <u>Their</u> flight came in two hours late.
   <u>There</u> is a new shopping centre just down the road.
5. My parents are going <u>to</u> Mexico for their anniversary.
   I have <u>two</u> tickets for the symphony.
   The bridegroom was <u>too</u> nervous to eat breakfast.
6. How many rooms does <u>your</u> apartment have?
   <u>You're</u> going to fail the exam if you don't study.
7. All the students <u>passed</u> the test.
   One should learn from the <u>past</u> but not dwell on it.
8. The library is a <u>quiet</u> place to work.
   My brother is <u>quite</u> a ladies man.
9. Blood flows <u>through</u> our veins and arteries.
   The pitcher <u>threw</u> the ball past the catcher.
   The police were very <u>thorough</u> in their search for clues.
10. <u>Whose</u> car keys are these?
    I don't know <u>who's</u> going, do you?

Exercise 22-3:

1. oranges
2. kisses
3. strays
4. lives
5. radios
6. pairs
7. speeches
8. flies
9. monkeys
10. pianos
11. mothers-in-law
12. data

13. ice skates
14. themselves
15. echoes
16. halves

17. children
18. women
19. phenomena
20. mice

Exercise 22-4:

1. unable
2. misspell
3. antifreeze
4. predetermine
5. extraordinary

6. superhuman
7. transform
8. submarine
9. reappear
10. unicycle

Prefixes do not affect the spelling of roots. Simply add the prefix to the beginning of the word.

Exercise 22-5A:

1. motivation
2. guidance
3. noticeable
4. graceful
5. truly

6. accurately
7. mileage
8. argument
9. driving
10. outrageous

Drop the final *e* before a suffix beginning with a vowel, but keep it if the suffix begins with a consonant. (Note that numbers 3, 5, 7, 9, 10 are exceptions.)

Exercise 22-5B:

1. dutiful
2. playing
3. drier
4. supplied
5. noisiest

6. strayed
7. sloppier
8. gravies
9. happiness
10. buying

If the final *y* is preceded by a consonant, change the *y* to *i* before adding a suffix, unless the suffix begins with *i*. If the final *y* is preceded by a vowel, retain the *y*.

Exercise 22-5C:

1. gripping
2. mendable
3. steamed
4. beginner
5. planting

6. stopper
7. poured
8. splitting
9. occurrence
10. reference

If a one-syllable word ends in a consonant preceded by a single vowel, double the final consonant before adding a suffix. With two-syllable words, double the final consonant only if the last syllable of the stem is accented.

Exercise 22-6:

1. believe
2. receive
3. neither
4. ceiling
5. foreign

6. field
7. counterfeit
8. weird
9. freight
10. niece

Exercise 22-7:

1. bitten
2. framed
3. management
4. foreign
5. dining
6. incredible
7. jumping
8. leisure
9. reluctantly
10. dissatisfied
11. courageous
12. laid
13. trapped
14. used
15. illegible
16. magically
17. permanent
18. proceeds
19. reliable
20. paid
21. believed
22. interaction
23. inventories
24. leaves
25. profitable

Exercise 22-8:

1. sleep/less
2. slend•der/ize
3. ref•er/ee
4. phlegm
5. pal/ate
6. mus•cle-/bound
7. in•de/cent (rule #3)
8. Hol•ly/wood
9. ex•pi•ra/tion
10. echo (rule #3)
11. cuck•oo (rule #3)
12. cough
13. butte
14. av•o/ca•do
15. av•oir/du•pois or
    av•oir•du/pois
16. loose
17. cat/tail
18. en•rol (rule #3)
19. grouch
20. pro/gress•ing
21. sleeve
22. sap/suck•er
23. Pol•y/ne•sia
24. pal/ace
25. non/res•i•dent
26. increase (rule #3)
27. how/ev•er
28. ges/tic•u•late, ges•tic/u•late,
    or ges•tic•u/late
29. e•merge (rule #3)
30. cu•bic (rule #3)
31. col•our/less
32. care/tak•er
33. but•ter/milk
34. a•wait (rule #3)
35. ant/ac•id
36. moth•er-/in-•law or moth•er-•in/law
37. trous/seau
38. midg•et (rule #3)
39. con•trol/ling
40. far/ther

Exercise 22-9:

1. open-heart surgery
2. free-for-all
3. high school
4. pear-shaped
5. birdhouse
6. accident-prone
7. pothole
8. bathing suit
9. breadwinner
10. handmade
11. headache
12. head cold
13. headphone
14. head-to-head
15. headstone
16. free agent
17. freehand
18. free-form
19. free-spoken
20. freestyle

Exercise 22-10:
1. thirty-five
2. one-half
3. four-fifths
4. one hundred and one
5. first
6. three thousand four hundred and fifty-seven
7. four hundred and ninety-five

Chapter 23: Periods, Question Marks, and Exclamation Points

Exercise 23-1A:
1. operating?
2. purity.
3. correct
4. 1914.
5. disgusting.
6. blood.
7. green.
8. correct
9. blue-grey.
10. again?
11. does?
12. not!
13. students.

Exercise 23-1B:

Do you know who Theodor Seuss Geisel was? Sure you do. He was Dr. Seuss, the famous author of children's books. After ten years as a successful advertising illustrator and cartoonist, Seuss managed to get his first children's book published. And to Think That I Saw It on Mulberry Street was published in 1937 by Vanguard Press. It had been rejected by 27 other publishers. I wonder why. They certainly were foolish! What is your favourite Dr. Seuss book? Mine is The Cat in the Hat, published in 1957. Everyone has a favourite. And I do mean Everyone! His books have been translated into 17 languages, and by 1984 over a hundred million copies had been sold worldwide. In fact, in 1984 Seuss received a Pulitzer Prize for his years of educating and entertaining children. How fitting! Sadly Dr. Seuss died in 1991. We will all miss him.

Exercise 23-2: Answers will vary.
1. The doctor asked me what was wrong.
2. Please close the door.
3. How much does the piano weigh?
4. Dr. Jones specialized in delivering twins.
5. Oscar Wilde said, "To love oneself is the beginning of a lifelong romance."
6. Wow!
7. Eggs are a good source of protein.
8. Sit down!
9. He asked, "What time does the train reach Montreal?"
10. The shoemaker said that my boots would be ready tomorrow.
11. When I saw my birthday present, all I could say was "Great!"

Chapter 24: Commas

Exercise 24-1A:
1. . . . along, and . . .
2. . . . however, and. . .
3. . . . plasmodium, for. . .
4. correct
5. . . . direction, and. . .
6. . . . colours, but. . .
7. correct
8. correct
9. . . . wood, yet. . .
10. . . . water, so. . .
11. . . . sporangia, and. . .
12. correct
13. . . . sporangia, and. . .
14. . . . ground, or. . .

Exercise 24-1B:
1. Some, however, leave the forest, <u>and </u>they live on cultivated plants.
2. They can cause clubroot of cabbage, <u>or</u> they can create powdery scab of potato.
3. Slime moulds sound disagreeable, <u>yet</u> some are quite attractive.
4. One form produces unappealing stalks, <u>but</u> the stalks are topped with tiny balls.
5. The balls appear to be woven, <u>so</u> they look rather like baskets.
6. The woven balls are really sporangia, <u>and</u> they contain spores for distribution.
7. Another form looks like tiny ghosts, <u>for</u> its white moulds could be small sheeted figures.
8. Serpent slime mould is yellow, <u>and</u> it can look like a miniature snake on top of a decaying log.
9. One would have to work hard to find it in on the Prairies, <u>for</u> it is most common in the tropics.
10. After one learns about slime moulds, they no longer seem disgusting, <u>nor</u> do they even seem disagreeable.

Exercise 24-2A:
1. In fact, it is the largest continuous body of sand in the world.
2. Extending over 250,000 square miles, the Rub al-Khali. . .
3. As a point of comparison, Texas is just slightly larger.
4. Because it is almost completely devoid of rain, the Rub al-Khali. . .
5. Despite the existence of a few scattered shrubs, the desert is largely a sand sea.
6. However, its eastern side develops massive dunes with salt basins.
7. Except for the hardy Bedouins, the Rub al-Khali is uninhabited.
8. Indeed, it is considered one of the most forbidding places on earth.
9. Until Bertram Thomas crossed it in 1931, it was unexplored by outsiders.
10. Even after oil was discovered in Arabia, exploration. . .
11. correct
12. To facilitate exploration, huge sand tires were developed in the 1950s.
13. Shortly thereafter, drilling rigs began operating in the Rub al-Khali.
14. correct
15. As it turns out, the Empty Quarter is not so empty after all.

Exercise 24-2B:
[1]As might be expected, the Rub al-Khali is hot all year round. [2]In contrast, the Gobi Desert is hot in the summer but extremely cold in the winter. [3]Located in China and Mongolia, the Gobi Desert is twice the size of Saskatchewan. [4]Unlike the Rub al-Khali, the Gobi has some permanent settlers. [5]Nevertheless, most of its inhabitants are nomadic. [6]To avoid the subzero winters, the nomads move their herds at the end of summer. [7]When the harsh winters subside, they return to the sparse desert vegetation.

Exercise 24-3A:
1. The vicuna, the smallest member of the camel family, lives in the mountains of <u>Ecuador</u>, <u>Bolivia</u>, and <u>Peru</u>.
2. The guanaco is the <u>wild</u>, <u>humpless</u> ancestor of the llama and the alpaca.
3. The llama <u>stands four feet tall</u>, <u>is about four feet long</u>, and <u>is the largest of the South American camels</u>.
4. A llama's coat may be <u>white</u>, <u>brown</u>, <u>black</u>, or <u>shades</u> in between.
5. Indians of the Andes use llamas <u>to carry loads</u>, <u>to bear wool</u>, and <u>to produce meat</u>.
6. Llamas are foraging animals that live on <u>lichens</u>, <u>shrubs</u>, and <u>other</u> <u>available plants</u>.
7. Because they can go without water for weeks, llamas are <u>economical</u>, <u>practical</u> pack animals.
8. The alpaca has a <u>longer</u>, <u>lower</u> body than the llama.
9. It has wool <u>of greater length</u>, <u>of higher quality</u>, and <u>of superior</u> softness.
10. Alpaca wool is <u>straighter</u>, <u>finer</u>, and <u>warmer</u> than sheep's wool.

Exercise 24-3B:
1. I like to spend those holidays with relatives because I like my relatives, I rarely get other chances to see them, and I enjoy their company.
2. My favourite fast foods are hot dogs, hamburgers, and pizza.
3. Swimming, hiking, reading, and sleeping are my preferred vacation activities.
4. My new puppy is a soft, silky cocker spaniel.
5. I found *The Sweet Hereafter* moody, mysterious, and mesmerizing.
6. The groom found rice in his hair, in his ears, and in his shoes.
7. John lifts weights, does pushups, and uses a treadmill.
8. John is developing a sleek, streamlined physique as a result of working out.

Exercise 24-4:
1. correct
2. The dances, both solos and ensembles, express emotion or tell a story.
3. correct
4. A ballet's steps, called its choreography, become standardized over many years of performance.
5. correct
6. The steps, all with French names, combine solos and groups.
7. The *corps de ballet*, the ballet company excluding its star soloists, may dance together or in small ensembles.
8. One soloist may join another for a *pas de deux*, a dance for two.
9. Ensemble members, not just soloists, must be proficient at pliés and arabesques.
10. correct
11. It is important, therefore, to start lessons early.
12. In Russia, which has some of the most stringent ballet training, students begin at age three.

Exercise 24-5:
1. The dahlias along the garden did not bloom this year.
   The dahlias, which I planted just to please Elizabeth, did not bloom this year.
2. I dislike gossip of any kind.
   I dislike gossip, which is always hurtful.
3. The computer that I bought last month does not work.
   The computer, which drives me crazy anyway, does not work.

4. The man who came to visit would not go home.
   The man, who sorely tried my patience, would not go home.
5. The child approaching us can walk now.
   The child, crawling though he may be, can walk now.
6. The creek in the meadow overflowed its banks.
   The creek, rushing and full, overflowed its banks.
7. I need to lose five pounds around my waist.
   I need to lose five pounds, which seems like a lot of weight.
8. My cousin Phyllis adores opera.
   John Thatcher, my cousin, adores opera.
9. The teacher trying out for the role of Achilles read the *Iliad* aloud.
   The teacher, wanting to impress his students, read the *Iliad* aloud.
10. He finally turned down the sound system in his apartment.
    He finally turned down the sound system, which was annoying his neighbours.

Exercise 24-6:
1. "Marriage," said Joseph Barth, "is. . .
2. Peter DeVries was right when he said, "The difficulty. . .
3. According to André Maurois, "A successful marriage. . .
4. "Heaven," said Andrew Jackson, "will be no heaven. . .
5. . . . anyone who comes between them," observed Sydney Smith.
6. "Chains do not hold a marriage together," said Simone Signoret. "It is threads. . .
7. An anonymous wise person said, "If there is anything. . .
8. "The way to love anything is to realize that it might be lost," advised Gilbert K. Chesterton.
9. "Love gives itself; it is not bought," observed Longfellow.
10. "Love does not consist in gazing at each other," said Antoine de Saint-Exupery, "but in looking. . .

Exercise 24-7:
1. In the northwest part of China, 6000 pottery figures were found.
2. correct
3. The life-sized warriors and horses had been buried for 2200 years.
4. The figures were in a huge tomb near the city of Xi'an, China.
5. Archaeologists also unearthed almost 10 000 artifacts from the excavation site.
6. It did not take John Doe, Ph.D., to realize that this was an extraordinary find.
7. Some of the figures were displayed in Memphis, Tennessee, twenty years later.
8. correct
9. correct
10. To get tickets, one could write to the Memphis Cook Convention Center, 255 North Main, Memphis, TN 38103.

Exercise 24-8A:
1. One was the statue of Olympian Zeus, which was covered with precious stones.
2. Unfortunately, it was taken to Constantinople in A.D. 475 and there destroyed by fire.
3. The Hanging Gardens of Babylon, built for Nebuchadnezzar, were considered a wonder.
4. correct
5. To lift water from the Euphrates, slaves had to work in shifts.

6. The Colossus of Rhodes was a huge, impressive statue built to honour the sun god Helios.
7. Constructed near the harbour, it was intended to astonish all who saw it.
8. Another wonder was the Lighthouse at Alexandria, Egypt.
9. Because it stood on the island of Pharos, the word *pharos* has come to mean light-house.
10. After the death of Mausolus, king of Caria, his widow erected a richly adorned monument to honour him.
11. With sculptures by famous artists, the Mausoleum at Halicarnassus amazed the ancient world.
12. The Temple of Artemis at Ephesus, an important Ionian city, was also considered a wonder.
13. It was burned, rebuilt, and burned again.
14. Some wonders, such as the Colossus and the Mausoleum, were destroyed by earthquakes.
15. Of the seven works that astounded the ancients, only the pyramids of Egypt survive.

Exercise 24-8B:

[1]St. Andrews, Scotland, is an old city. [2]Named for a Christian saint, the city was once an object of devout pilgrimage. [3]Its cathedral, the largest in Scotland, is now a ruin. [4]It was destroyed in 1559 by followers of the reformer John Knox. [5]All the revered, carefully preserved relics of St. Andrew disappeared. [6]Although the castle of St. Andrews also lies in ruins, it preserves two fascinating remnants of medieval history. [7]One is a bottle-shaped dungeon, and the other is a counter-mine. [8]When attackers tried to mine under castle walls, defenders tried to intercept the tunnel with a countermine. [9]Interestingly, one can actually enter both mine and countermine. [10]The University of St. Andrews, which is the oldest university in Scotland, was established in 1412. [11]From all parts of the globe, students come to study there. [12]Nevertheless, most people who think of St. Andrews associate it with golf. [13]Even golf at St. Andrews is old, the first reference dating to January 25, 1552. [14]The famous Old Course is only one of four courses from which the avid golfer may choose. [15]St. Andrews is still an object of pilgrimage, but today's pilgrims come with drivers, wedges, and putters.

Exercise 24-9:
1. The Victoria Falls were discovered. . .
2. The waterfall is part of the . . .
3. The falls are 108 metres high and. . .
4. correct
5. The falls are the result. . .
6. The river bed abruptly funnels into a deep crack.
7. . . . through a narrow crevice.
8. . . . a number of small islands and each of. . .
9. . . . through narrow, savage Batoka Gorge and flows. . .
10. . . . little since Livingstone's day.
11. . . . in the nearby national parks, and the area is largely undeveloped.

Exercise 24-10:

Money, in terms of its value, is really a matter of trust and confidence in the government. By definition, money is anything that a society accepts as having value. With such a broad definition, it is not surprising that money has, throughout history, taken on some forms that were both creative and unique. Precious stones, fish hooks, nails, livestock, throwing knives, and axe-heads are just a few examples of money that is equivalent to ours today. In a successful society, money must serve three basic functions: It must serve as a store of wealth, a medium of exchange, and a unit against which items are valued. Forms of money must be portable, easy to store, durable, and relatively hard to acquire. Successful forms of money, like gold and silver, have all these properties. However, trust is also necessary in a society, such as ours, that uses paper money. Although the paper itself is of little value, we trust that a bill is worth the number printed on the front of it.

Chapter 25: Semicolons

Exercise 25-1A:
1. The sclera is the outer cover of the eye; it helps. . .
2. The choroid is just inside the sclera; it keeps. . .
3. The pupil is the opening in the eye; this is where. . .
4. The cornea is the clear cover of the pupil; therefore. .
5. The pupil is opened or closed by muscles in the iris; in fact, in bright light the iris closes to decrease the amount of light entering; in low light. . .
6. correct
7. The retina contains cells, cones, and rods, which are outgrowths of the brain; when light. . .
8. The optic nerve connects the eye to the brain; thus. . .
9. Cone cells give us colour vision; they. . .
10. Rods are sensitive to low light; they. . .

Exercise 25-1B: Semicolons appear in the following lines.
line 1   Hearing is based on sound waves; these are. . .
line 2   ripples on water; like ripples. . .
line 5   Pitch is the number of wave vibrations per second; it. . .
line 6   waves; this is called. . .
line 9   130 decibels is painful; however, people. . .
line 10   Timbre is hard to describe in everyday language; in physics terms. . .
line 14   as too many unrelated frequencies vibrating together; nevertheless. . .

Exercise 25-2:
1. Colourblindness is inherited; it appears. . .
2. The most common colourblindness is the inability to tell red from green; but more. . .
3. Different colours, the result of differences in light wavelengths, create a spectrum; the spectrum. . .
4. People who are severely red-green colourblind cannot "see" any colours at that end of the spectrum; that is, they cannot. . .
5. Colourblindness varies from person to person; people. . .
6. Some people have no cone cells (the cells that send signals about colour to the brain), so they. . .
7. They have achromatism, a rare condition.

8. Such people can see only black, white, and grays; what. . .
9. However, their problem is much more serious than this; they also have. . .
10. The part of the eye that usually receives images is the fovea, which contains the cone cells; achromatics'. . .
11. To compensate, they look at objects off centre, to pick. . .
12. It is possible to be colourblind and not know it; how. . .
13. There are several tests for colourblindness; most involve seeing (or not seeing) a number or word written on a background of a complementary colour, for example. . .

Chapter 26: Colons

Exercise 26-1:
1. People believe that Napoleon was short, but he was average height: 5'6".
2. . . . U.S. males; three favourite freetime activities are as follows: eating. . .
3. correct
4. . . . these are the most common street names in Canada: Queen. . .
5. . . . *Burrowing: The Adventures of a Bookworm.*
6. The train, 20 minutes late, was due at 6:40.
7. . . . what we were fearing: "I forgot . . ."
8. . . . remember one thing: Be alert!
9. The nineteenth century was a bad time for Turkey: it lost. . .
10. . . . those that do include the following: bears. . .

Exercise 26-2: Answers will vary.
1. Parallel Lives: Five Victorian Marriages
2. My favourite classes are as follows: English, Drama, and History.
3. Here is some advice about what to do when you go on a job interview: Don't be afraid to tell what you can do, but don't brag needlessly.
4. The star players on the X are these: a, b, c, and d.
5. The University of British Columbia has a large campus bordered by public streets, and most notably by a nature preserve and an arm of the Pacific Ocean: the University Endowment Lands and the Strait of Georgia.

Chapter 27: Apostrophes

Exercise 27-1:

	singular possessive	plural possessive
1.	sheep's	sheep's
2.	pony's	ponies'
3.	turkey's	turkeys'
4.	lion's	lions'
5.	mouse's	mice's
6.	her	their
7.	gorilla's	gorillas'
8.	goose's	geese's
9.	gnu's	gnus'
10.	ox's	oxen's
11.	your	your

singular possessive	plural possessive
12. buffalo's	buffalos'
13. zebra's	zebras'
14. ibex's	ibexes'
15. fly's	flies'
16. my	our
17. giraffe's	giraffes'
18. dodo's	dodos'
19. zoo's	zoos'
20. zoo keeper's	zoo keepers'
21. his	their
22. farm's	farms'
23. farmer's	farmers'
24. ranch's	ranches'
25. its	their

Exercise 27-2:
1. the restaurant's menu
2. the boss's daughter (the boss' daughter is also acceptable)
3. the doctor's waiting room
4. the doctors' waiting room
5. anyone's guess
6. the actor's scripts
7. the actors' scripts
8. the ship's crew
9. someone's reputation
10. my father-in-law's tools

Exercise 27-3:

1. aren't
2. won't
3. let's
4. he'd
5. wasn't
6. you'd
7. didn't
8. I'll
9. what's
10. I'm
11. isn't
12. wouldn't
13. can't
14. doesn't
15. I've
16. you're
17. there's
18. we'd
19. weren't
20. they're
21. it's
22. we've
23. she'll
24. we're
25. don't

Exercise 27-4:

1. Poe's
2. correct
3. author's
4. Dupin's
5. didn't
6. public's, hero's
7. weren't
8. '66
9. correct
10. Collins's
11. book's, wasn't
12. *The Moonstone's*, public's
13. Collins's
14. one's
15. It's
16. Doyle's
17. Holmes's
18. People's
19. Holmes's
20. readers'
21. Holmes's
22. couldn't

Chapter 28: Quotation Marks

Exercise 28-1:
1. According to Chesterfield, "Advice is seldom welcome."
2. "If you are looking for trouble, offer some good advice," says Herbert V. Prochnow.
3. Marie Dressler was right: "No vice is so bad as advice."
4. Someone once remarked, "How we do admire the wisdom of those who come to us for advice!"
5. "Free advice," it has been noted, "is the kind that costs you nothing unless you act upon it."
6. correct
7. "I sometimes give myself admirable advice," said Lady Mary Wortley Montagu, "but I am incapable of taking it."
8. Says Tom Masson, "'Be yourself!' is the worst advice you can give to some people."
9. The Beatles' song "With a Little Help from My Friends" contains some good advice.
10. correct
11. My uncle advised me, "The next time you are depressed, read Lewis Carroll's poem 'Jabberwocky.'"
12. Do you recall the Beach Boys' words: "Be true to your school"?
13. correct
14. However, comedienne Phyllis Diller suggests, "Never go to bed mad. Stay up and fight."
15. Rachel Carson advised, "The discipline of the writer is to learn to be still and listen to what his subject has to tell him."
16. correct

Exercise 28-2: Answers may vary slightly.
1. She said, "Rumours have reached me about cuts to the Fine Arts Department."
2. "Nothing like that was forecast in the budget," she told the committee.
3. "Is it true, then," she asked, "that two sessional instructors will not have their contracts renewed?"
4. The Dean of Arts and Science suggested, "Let's study the matter at next month's meeting."
5. Two students in the audience shouted, "We want answers now!"
6. The chair replied to them by reciting the text of rule 48.2(a): "Audience members may be excluded from a meeting at the discretion of the chair."

Exercise 28-3: Answers will vary.

Chapter 29: Other Punctuation Marks

Exercise 29-1: Answers may vary slightly.
1. Niagara Falls is not the tallest waterfall in Canada — Della Falls, British Columbia, is.
2. The next tallest waterfalls are (2) Takakkaw Falls, British Columbia, (3) Hunley Falls, British Columbia, and (4) Panther Falls, Alberta.
3. Niagara Falls is relatively low — it stands about one-seventh the height of Della Falls.
4. Greenland (the largest island in the world) was given . . .
5. The name was a masterstroke of publicity — convincing . . .
6. Let's go to New Orleans for Mardi — Oops! . . .

7. The most expensive part of a trip — the airfare — can be reduced. . .
8. . . . "the winner must appear to claim his/her prize in person."
9. "Broadway [my favourite street] is a . . .
10. "Too often travel ... merely lengthens the conversation,". . . (Note that you have the option of enclosing the ellipsis in brackets, according to MLA style.)
11. Northern Ontraio [sic] has . . .
12. . . . he/she will always want to return.
13. I can only say one thing about camping — I hate it.
14. We leave as soon as — Have you seen the bug spray? — we finish packing.
15. "Let's take Highway 69 across —" "Are you crazy?"
16. Finding an inexpensive hotel/motel isn't always easy.
17. Motels (named for a combination of *motorist* and *hotel*). . .
18. When travelling, always remember to (a) leave a schedule with friends, (b) carry as little cash as possible, and (c) use the hotel safe for valuables.

Exercise 29-2A: Answers will vary.

The cheetah is the fastest animal on earth. It can accelerate from 1.6 kilometres an hour to 65 kilometres an hour in under two seconds, briefly reaching speeds of up to 110 kilometres an hour. Its stride may, during these bursts of speed, be as much as 7 metres. To help it run at these speeds, the cheetah is built unlike any of the other large cats: powerful heart; oversized liver; long, thin leg bones; relatively small teeth; and a muscular tail used for balance. Unlike other cats, it cannot pull in its claws. They are blunted by constant contact with the earth, and so are of little use in the hunt. The cheetah, instead, makes use of a strong dewclaw on the inside of its front legs to grab and hold down prey.

Exercise 29-2B: Answers will vary.

Have you ever wondered how instant coffee is made? First the coffee beans are prepared as they would be for regular coffee. They are roasted, blended, and ground. At the factory, workers brew great batches of coffee — 800 to 900 kilograms at a time. The coffee is then passed through tubes under great pressure at a high temperature. This causes much of the water to boil away, creating coffee liquor (coffee with a high percentage of solids). At this point a decision must be made about what the final product will be: powdered coffee or freeze-dried coffee. Powdered instant coffee is made by heating the coffee liquor to 500°F (200°C) in a large drier. This boils away the remaining water, and the powdered coffee is simply gathered from the bottom of the drier and packed. If freeze-dried coffee is being made, the coffee liquor is frozen into pieces which are then broken into small granules. The granules are placed in a vacuum box (a box containing no air), which turns the frozen water into steam which is removed. All that is left are coffee solids. Some people say they prefer freeze-dried coffee because the high temperature used to make regular instant coffee destroys some of the flavour. Either way, the coffee is more convenient than home-brewed coffee.

Chapter 30: Capitals, Italics, Abbreviations, and Numbers

Exercise 30-1A:
1. Prime Minister Laurier
2. God's love
3. the Board of Broadcast Governors

4. a meeting on Friday
5. my Aunt Clara
6. when I graduate
7. The Musical Ride
8. Mother Teresa.
9. dinner at the Steak Palace
10. English 202
11. across Main Street
12. the Edmonton Oilers
13. the Group of Seven
14. a town in the West
15. a college in British Columbia
16. "The Gift of the Magi"
17. learning French
18. Victoria Township Medical Centre
19. the moon and Venus shining in the sky
20. the St. Lawrence River

Exercise 30-1B:
1. The spring semester starts in February.
2. They live ten kilometres north of Elm Street.
3. The hotel has 450 rooms.
4. Green, the ambassador, had a meeting with Foreign Minister Ramirez.
5. I want to visit Lake Louise to go skiing.
6. The Bible is full of great adventures.
7. They plan to open an Italian restaurant downtown.
8. The New Democratic Party believes in the democratic system.
9. correct.
10. Springfield High School has a large PTA.
11. Texans will always remember the Alamo.
12. Travelling around the cape of Good Hope is dangerous.
13. Rembrandt's "Aristotle Contemplating the Bust of Homer" is one of his best known paintings.
14. The Manitoba Theatre Centre is in Winnipeg.
15. Tickets to the Grey Cup were not available at the stadium.

Exercise 30-2A:
1. b. <u>War and Peace</u>
2. b. <u>The Bill Cosby Show</u>
3. a. The <u>London Free Press</u>
4. b. <u>The Queen Elizabeth II</u>
5. b. The U.S.S. <u>Enterprise</u>
6. a. We are <u>homo sapiens</u>.
7. b. <u>nota bene</u>
8. a. Many words have the common root, <u>cycle</u>.
9. b. <u>Never</u> tease a hungry crocodile.
10. a. <u>The Orient Express</u> was the setting of a famous mystery novel.

Exercise 30-2B:
1. The word <u>cool</u> has many meanings.
2. The new hospital is shaped like the letter <u>H</u>.
3. Scientifically, the chimpanzee is called <u>Pan troglodytes</u> and the gorilla is <u>Gorilla gorilla</u>.
4. You bought us tickets to see <u>Les Misérables</u>? <u>Merci beaucoup</u>.
5. The H.M.S. <u>Bounty</u> was a real ship.
6. The troubles of its crew are told in the book <u>Mutiny on the Bounty</u>.
7. correct
8. Clifford Sifton, a key member of Prime Minister Laurier's cabinet, was the owner of an important newspaper, the <u>Manitoba Free Press</u>.
9. correct
10. Years later, the Hollywood movie <u>Rose Marie</u> (1936), with its singing Mounties and maidens, also publicized the Canadian Prairies.

Exercise 30-3A:
1. The Chang brothers are opening a fishing charter company.
2. It will be off pier number 17, not far from Los Angeles, California.
3. At the aquarium we saw giant tortoises that were more than 100 years old.
4. Easter always falls on the Sunday following the first full moon in spring—either in March or in April.
5. What did you get for Christmas?
6. Everyone ought to know the story of William Lyon MacKenzie King, tenth prime minister of Canada.
7. He is mentioned in my textbook on the history of political science and philosophy.
8. The professor says the midterm will cover chapters 1 through 5.
9. The midterm and the final each count 40 percent.
10. The quarterback picked up 160 yards in passing in the first half.
11. Some people will do anything for a few dollars.
12. A kilogram equals 2.2 pounds.
13. The counsellor had an MSW (or Master of Social Work) degree from University of British Columbia.
14. She had put herself through school working as an assistant manager in a fast food restaurant.
15. Mr. and Mrs. McDonald live on Maple Avenue in Corner Brook, Newfoundland.

Exercise 30-3B:
1. 2:00 A.M.
2. $30 000
3. Dr. Jones
4. Bill Smith, a CPA
5. A.D. 1642
6. 1919
7. Mr. and Mrs. Grossman
8. NASA
9. OK
10. SCUBA gear

Exercise 30-4:
1. There are 107 women. . .
2. Ten years ago there were only forty-seven. (Note: A case could be made for "47," as this is a precise discussion involving numerous figures.)
3. One-third of the faculty is female now compared with one-tenth then.
4. . . . $900 for two rooms, $1400 for three rooms, and $1850 for four rooms.
5. correct or . . . September 14.

6. . . . June 1, 1999.
7. correct
8. . . . to drink two-and-a-half litres of coffee a day over the next three years. (Note: "2.5 litres" is also correct.)
9. correct or . . . 29 percent.
10. correct or . . . 15 Clark Street.

Chapter 31:   Using Sources and Avoiding Plagiarism

Exercise 31-1A: Answers will vary.
"When a woman is forced to adorn herself to buy a hearing, when she needs her grooming in order to protect her identity, when she goes hungry in order to keep her job, when she must attract a lover so that she can take care of her children, that is exactly what makes "beauty" hurt."

The parallel structure creates a cumulative effect that would be lost in a paraphrase or summary. If the researcher/writer wishes to convey the power of Wolf's style, this is a good passage to quote.

Exercise 31-1B: Answers will vary.

Exercise 31-1C: Answers will vary.

Exercise 31-2A: Answers will vary.
Branding is different from advertising. Sponsorship, logo licensing, and advertising are tools of branding; the brand, however, is the "core meaning of the modern corporation." Mass-marketing, developed late in the nineteenth century, was not very concerned with brand identities. Rather, it advertised newly invented products—informing people of the products' existence and persuading people that the new products would improve their lives.

Exercise 31-2B: Answers will vary.

Exercise 31-2C: Answers will vary.

Exercise 31-3A: Answers will vary.
The increase in women's power in the work world has been accompanied by a decrease in women's self-confidence, rooted in insecurity about our bodies.

Exercise 31-3B: Answers will vary.

Exercise 31-3C: Answers will vary.

Chapter 37:   Comparing the Different Disciplines

Exercise 37-1A: Answers will vary.

Exercise 37-1B: Answers will vary.

Chapter 38: Writing About Literature

Exercise 38-1: Answers will vary.

Chapter 39: Writing in the Social Sciences and Natural Sciences

Exercise 39-1: Answers will vary.

Chapter 40: Business Writing

Exercise 40-1A: Answers will vary.

Exercise 40-1B: Answers will vary.

Exercise 40-1C: Answers will vary.

Chapter 41: Writing Under Pressure

Exercise 41-1A: Answers will vary.

Exercise 41-1B: Answers will vary.

ESL Chapter 1: Singulars and Plurals

ESL Exercise 1-1:

	Noncount	Count	Plural
1.	advice	——	——
2.	——	book	books
3.	——	calculator	calculators
4.	chocolate	chocolate	chocolates
5.	——	desk	desks
6.	——	earring	earrings
7.	——	essay	essays
8.	——	experiment	experiments
9.	——	fern	ferns
10.	flour	——	——
11.	gold	——	——
12.	hair	hair	hair
13.	happiness	——	——
14.	homework	——	——
15.	honesty	——	——
16.	information	——	——
17.	jewellry	——	——
18.	——	library	libraries
19.	lightning	——	——
20.	——	man	men
21.	news	——	——
22.	——	novel	novels
23.	——	occupation	occupations

24. paper	paper	papers
25. ——	paragraph	paragraphs
26. physics		——
27. ——	pollution	pollutions
28. rain	rain	rains
29. ——	report	reports
30. ——	storm	storms
31. time	time	times
32. weather	——	——

ESL Exercise 1-2:

1. Hikers with little <u>money</u> but much <u>fortitude</u> can begin the hike in Niagara Falls and continue to the Bruce Peninsula in Lake Huron.
2. The 720-<u>kilometre</u> trail goes through many picturesque <u>towns</u> along the Niagara Escarpment.
3. The trail passes cultivated <u>farms</u> and untamed <u>wilderness</u>.
4. The caves and cliffs of the Niagara Escarpment make the Bruce Trail one of the most interesting <u>trails</u> in Canada or the United <u>States</u>.
5. Few <u>hikers</u> have anything but praise for their <u>experiences</u> on the trail.
6. Many <u>youngsters</u> would gladly give up <u>piano</u> lessons or <u>homework</u> to be climbing wooded <u>paths</u>.
7. The Bruce Trail is one of the nation's <u>treasures</u>.

ESL Chapter 2: Articles

ESL Exercise 2-1:

In 1872 <u>the</u> U.S. Congress passed <u>the</u> Yellowstone Act, establishing Ø Yellowstone as <u>the</u> first national park in <u>the</u> United States and indeed in <u>the</u> world. For centuries <u>the</u> wealthy set aside Ø private preserves for their own recreational use, but except for <u>a</u> few public parks in Ø major cities, setting aside <u>a</u> vast area for Ø national enjoyment was <u>a</u> novel idea. It became <u>a</u> popular one. Since <u>the</u> founding of Ø Yellowstone, forty-nine other national parks have been established in <u>the</u> United States and its territories.

Ø Yellowstone is <u>the</u> largest national park in <u>the</u> United States. It occupies 9000 square kilometres at <u>the</u> juncture of <u>the</u> states of Ø Wyoming, Ø Montana, and Ø Idaho. Although Ø Native American habitation goes back 800 years, <u>the</u> park's remoteness from <u>the</u> centres of Ø population left it undiscovered by Ø white settlers until <u>the</u> nineteenth century.

Ø John Colter is thought to be <u>the</u> first explorer to venture into <u>the</u> area. Colter was <u>a</u> member of <u>the</u> Lewis and Clark Expedition. When <u>the</u> expedition returned to $\emptyset$ St. Louis, he remained in the region of the upper Missouri River to become a mountain man. In 1807 he explored the Yellowstone Basin. When he later wrote about the thermal wonders of the area, many people did not believe such natural phenomena existed. They continue to amaze $\emptyset$ tourists today.

Yellowstone is truly a natural fantasy land. Its features include $\emptyset$ geysers, $\emptyset$ hot springs, and $\emptyset$ mud volcanoes along with $\emptyset$ forests, $\emptyset$ lakes, $\emptyset$ mountains, and $\emptyset$ waterfalls. The most famous of the park's attractions is $\emptyset$ "Old Faithful," a geyser which erupts on the average of every 65 minutes. It shoots $\emptyset$ steaming water from 37 to 52 metres into the air. Each eruption lasts approximately four minutes and spews out 37 850 $\emptyset$ litres of $\emptyset$ water.

Other active geysers in the six geyser basins may be less predictable but are no less spectacular. Some of the more than 200 just emit $\emptyset$ steam and $\emptyset$ spooky underground noises. $\emptyset$ Silica in the geyser water builds up around the walls of the geyser craters, making the craters very colourful and beautiful to view even when the geysers are not spouting.

$\emptyset$ Hot springs are another Yellowstone attraction. There are more than 3000 of them ranged throughout the park. Some, such as $\emptyset$ Emerald Spring, are remarkable because of their colour. $\emptyset$ Morning Glory Spring looks like its flower namesake.

$\emptyset$ Yellowstone Lake, $\emptyset$ Golden Gate Canyon, and $\emptyset$ Tower Falls are just some of the features that combine with the geysers and $\emptyset$ hot springs to make $\emptyset$ Yellowstone National Park an extraordinary place to visit.

ESL Chapter 3: Word Order

ESL Exercise 3-1:
1. Is that pizza enough for all of us?
2. Did Henri understand the lesson?
3. Do you have my lab manual?; Have you my lab manual?
4. Will Juanita have finished by the time we return?
5. Can everyone in the room see the screen?

ESL Exercise 3-2:

1. Katrina purchased two lovely Limoges boxes.
2. A comfortable black leather chair appealed to Nils.
3. He patiently waited to bid on it.
4. Unfortunately, we left before it was auctioned.
5. Mario wanted an old wooden table but bought a worn silver spoon.
6. Suchen outbid someone for an interesting round green hatbox.
7. She was extremely delighted to get it.
8. She has often admired such hatboxes.
9. The entire English class bought something except Ingrid.
10. Because she brought a small empty purse, she bought nothing at all.

ESL Chapter 4: Prepositions

ESL Exercise 4-1:

1. Others wanted to put the new university <u>in</u> Staunton or Lexington.
2. <u>In</u> 1818, Dalhousie University opened <u>in</u> Halifax, Nova Scotia, the same year as Jefferson's.
3. Jefferson designed his university so that students and faculty lived together <u>in</u> an "academical village."
4. A rotunda building for classes sits <u>at</u> one end of a lawn.
5. <u>On</u> both sides of the lawn are sets of student rooms.
6. Faculty members lived <u>in</u> pavilions between the sets of student rooms.
7. A similar scheme inspired the design of Ontario's Trent University, whose main campus opened <u>in</u> 1966.
8. <u>On</u> your next visit to the University of Toronto, you can stand <u>at</u> a window <u>in</u> the University College Quadrangle and see how that nineteenth-century college was designed with the same idea in mind.
9. <u>On</u> his deathbed, Jefferson included founding the university as one of the three accomplishments for which he hoped to be remembered.
10. Today students at the University of Virginia consider it an honour to live <u>in</u> the rooms that Jefferson designed.

ESL Exercise 4-2A: Answers will vary.

1. Ravi will <u>speak to</u> Walid and explain.
2. First he must <u>fill out</u> all the forms.
3. He must <u>go over</u> all his records to make sure he does not <u>leave out</u> anything.
4. He must then <u>drop off</u> the forms at the registrar's office.
5. Should he <u>hand in</u> the forms without some vital information, the registrar will <u>call him back</u> to get it.
6. Walid will have to <u>look over</u> the forms and <u>find out</u> what is missing.
7. He must not <u>throw away</u> any records until he has finished the procedure.

ESL Exercise 4-2B: Answers will vary.

1. Ravi will <u>speak to</u> Walid and explain.
2. First he must <u>complete</u> all the forms.
3. He must <u>review</u> all his records to make sure he does not <u>omit</u> anything.
4. He must then <u>leave</u> the forms at the registrar's office.
5. Should he <u>submit</u> the forms without some vital information, the registrar will <u>call him back</u> to get it.

6. Walid will have to <u>examine</u> the forms and <u>discover</u> what is missing.
7. He must not <u>discard</u> any records until he has finished the procedure.

ESL Chapter 5: Gerunds, Infinitives, and Participles

ESL Exercise 5-1:
1. They are worried about <u>getting</u> jobs after graduation.
2. They may want <u>to study</u> for the pure enjoyment of learning.
3. They may even dream about <u>being</u> philosophers or writers.
4. However, many parents refuse <u>to support</u> students who lack a definite career goal.
5. They are happy <u>to help</u> their children reach their goals.
6. They resist <u>aiding</u> children who lack direction.
7. Yet <u>reading</u> widely in the liberal arts is one way for students <u>to know</u> themselves.
8. Students of the humanities are the first <u>to see</u> the value of a liberal education.
9. When they hear their parents <u>complain</u> about wasting money, students try <u>to explain</u> their position.
10. They recommend <u>learning</u> about life before <u>training</u> for a specific job.

ESL Chapter 6: Modal Auxiliary Verbs

ESL Exercise 6-1:
1. You <u>may not</u> (present possibility, negative) be aware that Canada's head of state does not live in Canada.
2. We <u>should not</u> (present advisability, negative) forget, though, that in law, the British monarch is Canada's highest political authority.
3. You <u>might have</u> (past possibility) heard the prime minister mistakenly being called the head of state.
4. Laws passed in Parliament <u>must be</u> (present passive necessity) signed, however, by the Queen or her representative, the Governor General.
5. Fortunately, the days when the Governor General <u>used to</u> [or <u>would</u>] (past habit) interfere in government are long past.
6. But as late as 1926, Prime Minister Mackenzie King <u>had to</u> (necessity) leave office when instructed by the Governor General.
7. Do you think we <u>should have</u> (past advisability) changed the Constitution to have the prime minister elected by all voters and not just by voters in one riding?
8. There is no evidence that most Canadians <u>would rather</u> (preference) live under a different political system, however.
9. Still, you <u>have to</u> [or <u>must</u>] (present necessity) admit that it is a strange system.
10. But it is the system that we use, so somebody <u>must have</u> (past probability) guessed that it would work.